Disinterested Pleasure and Beauty

Disinterested Pleasure and Beauty

Perspectives from Kantian and Contemporary Aesthetics

Edited by
Larissa Berger

DE GRUYTER

ISBN 978-3-11-221378-0
e-ISBN (PDF) 978-3-11-072768-5
e-ISBN (EPUB) 978-3-11-072775-3

Library of Congress Control Number: 2023934586

Bibliographic information published by the Deutsche Nationalbibliothek
The Deutsche Nationalbibliothek lists this publication in the Deutsche Nationalbibliografie; detailed bibliographic data are available on the internet at http://dnb.dnb.de.

© 2025 Walter de Gruyter GmbH, Berlin/Boston
This volume is text- and page-identical with the hardback published in 2023.
 Cover image: © tolgart / iStock / Getty Images Plus
Printing and binding: CPI books GmbH, Leck

www.degruyter.com

Acknowledgments

The idea for this volume was born at the conference "Disinterested Pleasure in Kantian and Contemporary Philosophy" held at the University of Siegen in 2018. During this conference, one could feel a strong enthusiasm to discuss the topic of disinterestedness and to bridge the two realms of Kant scholarship and contemporary aesthetics. I am optimistic that some of this enthusiasm has found its way into this volume and will be passed on to further discussions on disinterestedness.

I would like to thank all authors for their contributions, many helpful and insightful discussions in Siegen, and their enthusiasm regarding this volume. I am grateful to the Philosophy Department at the University of Siegen for hosting the conference, and to *Fritz Thyssen-Stiftung* for funding it. I would also like to thank an anonymous reviewer for De Gruyter for extremely helpful feedback on this volume. Finally, I would like to express my deepest gratitude to Dieter Schönecker who not only co-organized the conference in Siegen with me and encouraged me to edit this volume, but also helped me with its realization in very many ways.

Table of Contents

Larissa Berger
Introduction —— 1

Part I **Disinterestedness in Kant**

Paul Guyer
Disinterestedness by Any Other Name: Kant and Mendelssohn —— 11

Larissa Berger
What Is It Like to Feel Beauty? The Complex Meaning of Kant's Thesis of Disinterestedness —— 31

Nick Zangwill
Disinterestedness: Analysis and Partial Defense —— 59

Christian Helmut Wenzel
Disinterestedness and Its Role in Kant's Aesthetics —— 87

Stefano Velotti
Making Sense: Disinterestedness and Control —— 105

Part II **Disinterestedness With and Beyond Kant**

(a) **Disinterest Advocates**

Keren Gorodeisky
The Myth of the Absent Self: Disinterest, the Self, and Evaluative Self-Consciousness —— 135

Thomas Hilgers
Aesthetic Disinterestedness Revisited —— 167

(b) Something in Between

Fiona Hughes
The Playful Negotiation of Interests: Kant in Conversation with Fried and Winnicott —— 183

Lisa Schmalzried
Human Beauty, Attraction, and Disinterested Pleasure —— 211

(c) Disinterest Critics

Dominic McIver Lopes
Pleasure, Desire, and Beauty —— 233

James Shelley
Beyond Hedonism about Aesthetic Value —— 257

Author Index —— 275

Subject Index —— 279

Larissa Berger
Introduction

In philosophical discourse, many concepts with a long and rich tradition seem to share a common fate: they are so prominent that one could hardly ignore them when seriously attending to a certain debate, but just because they are so prominent it might seem somewhat obsolete to clarify their meaning. Surely, everyone in the discourse *has* a certain (more or less determinate) understanding of the relevant concept. Yet, once these understandings are made explicit it becomes clear that people are referring to quite different things (or to different aspects of the same thing). When it comes to the philosophical discipline of aesthetics, the concept of "disinterested pleasure" or simply "disinterestedness" surely has this fate. The thesis that beauty is constituted by, or is somehow related to, a feeling of disinterested pleasure (the thesis of disinterestedness) has been one of the most influential in philosophical thinking about aesthetics or beauty. Nick Riggle does not exaggerate when he speaks of "what is arguably the most influential idea about beauty, namely, that it essentially involves a kind of affective response that philosophers call 'disinterested pleasure'" (Riggle 2016, p. 2).[1] Unfortunately, what disinterestedness means is far from obvious, and it seems hopeless to try to pin down a universally accepted definition. To explore the horizon of "disinterestedness"—to differentiate different meanings of this term, single out commonalities and differences, and identify some misunderstandings—seems to be a much more promising project. Nothing more and nothing less is the aim of this volume. This, so I hope, will lead to a more *responsible* use of the word "disinterestedness." It will work against a kind of irresponsibility that has been identified by Miles Rind and that takes the following forms: "One consists in using the word with a sense that is neither its ordinary one nor any well-specified technical sense, but which rather waltzes about indeterminately. […] Another form of the vice consists in using the word 'disinterested' without care as to whether it makes an intelligible modification to the substantive with which it is combined. We may thank this habit for the pleonasm 'disinterested contemplation,' and the obscurantism 'disinterested perception.' Finally, there is the habit of using the noun 'disinterestedness' with-

---

[1] See also the following remark of James Shelley: "Much of the history of more recent thinking about the concept of aesthetic can be seen as the history of the development of the immediacy and disinterested theses." (Shelley 2017) Like the disinterested thesis, the "immediacy thesis," that is, the thesis that aesthetic judgments are not derived from principles and concepts, has one of its most influential historical roots in Kant.

out any clear thought of an act, disposition, or motive to bear the characteristic so described." (Rind 2002, p. 85)

A more responsible way of dealing with "disinterestedness" will also help us to demystify this notion. One myth surrounding disinterestedness was created by George Dickie for whom disinterestedness or "being distanced" is understood in terms of the aesthetic attitude and "simply mean[s] that one's attention is focused" on the aesthetic object (Dickie 1964, p. 57). This might be considered a myth insofar as most scholars—including Kant as the historic pioneer of disinterestedness—do not take disinterestedness to be (primarily) a characteristic of the *aesthetic attitude*.[2] Two other myths are the "myth of inactivity" and the "myth of the absent self." According to the former "not only is disinterested experience merely passive, rather than active but it is also detached from cognitive and moral concerns, *and from any other activity or experience*" (Gorodeisky in this volume, p. 135 fn). According to the latter in experiences of disinterested pleasure "the subject needn't do anything other than dispassionately stare at the object, bringing nothing of herself to the table other than awareness" (Riggle 2016, p. 4).[3]

One might suspect that, at least when it comes to its historical roots, the notion of disinterestedness is less mystical. Immanuel Kant has already been introduced as the historic pioneer of disinterested pleasure. Although he was not the first to use the concept—or its sibling "contemplation"—he can be considered the most important point of reference for its use. If any thought from his theory of beauty is still widely shared among contemporary aestheticians, it is his thesis that "[t]he satisfaction that determines the judgment of taste is without any interest" (KU: 204). One might be tempted to think that at least Kant's *own* notion of disinterestedness should be clear. In § 2 of the *Critique of Judgment* Kant defines "interest" as "[t]he satisfaction that we combine with the representation of the existence of an object" and "a satisfaction" that "always has at the same time a relation to the faculty of desire" (KU: 204). Accordingly, a disinterested pleasure or satisfaction would be one not taken in 'the representation of the existence of an object' and not related to the faculty of desire. But what does that mean? Indeed, Kant's take on disinterestedness is rather obscure, which might just add to this notion's mystical flavor. More than 200 years of Kant scholarship were not enough to settle a definite interpretation of Kant's thesis of disinterestedness. Rather, they have left us with a somewhat messy plurality of possible meanings of this thesis. Kant scholarship on disinterestedness would profit a lot from some clarity, even if that would only

---

[2] For a Kantian take on disinterestedness and "the illusion of aesthetic 'attitude,'" see Crowther 2010, pp. 71f.
[3] For a discussion of the "myth of the absent self," see Gorodeisky (in this volume), from whom I have also borrowed this terminology.

mean to identify and disentangle several (perhaps even incompatible) interpretations of the thesis of disinterestedness. Again, nothing more and nothing less is the aim of this volume.

Why then should we still hold onto the concept of disinterested pleasure, despite all mystification and unclarity? Why has this concept not only been historically successful, but is still appealing and interesting to both aestheticians and Kant scholars? First, the thesis of disinterestedness seems to capture something important about our experiences of beauty: they take us away from our daily needs, desires, and interests. Beauty (often) makes us linger without us wanting to do anything or to carry out any action—in beauty we experience a certain detachment from practical concerns.[4] Second, the thesis of disinterestedness fits with the (often implicitly accepted) requirement that we should appreciate beauty and art for their own sake and not because they satisfy any interests. Many of us might even have had the experience that (external) interests can block our aesthetic experiences or take the focus away from what matters aesthetically. Third, the thesis of disinterestedness fits with the intuition that when it comes to judging beauty we should abstract from our idiosyncratic conditions. It is a commonly held view that judgments of beauty are not solipsistic, but social or even universal (either in terms of a universal assertion or an invitation).[5] Since (most of) our interests are merely private, abstracting from them will help us to elevate our judgments of beauty to a social or even universal dimension. This is Kant's famous link between disinterestedness and universality. Finally, the thesis of disinterestedness might also help us to single out what is distinctive of or unique about aesthetic experiences. Even if one argued that disinterestedness was not sufficient to distinguish aesthetic experiences from other kinds of experience, it might still be a necessary feature. These are just some reasons why disinterestedness is still relevant and why it is worthwhile to clarify this notion and explore its role for both Kantian and contemporary aesthetics.

It is my hope that this volume might accomplish another goal, namely, to establish a dialogue between Kant scholars and philosophers working on contemporary aesthetics. Being a Kant scholar myself, I am deeply convinced that I can learn—and, indeed, have learned—a lot from contemporary takes on disinterestedness, and this knowledge has in turn helped me shape my understanding of Kant's thesis of disinterestedness. Conversely, I am convinced that contemporary discussions in

---

[4] Indeed, the thesis of disinterestedness might even speak to a certain ideal or longing of our times, namely, to free ourselves from all interests, desires, and needs that sometimes seem to take over our lives and push us around.

[5] For instance, Nehamas remarks that "when I am moved by a work of art and want to make it part of my life, I also want others to make it part of their life as well" (Nehamas 2007, p. 75).

aesthetics can profit a lot from a better understanding of its roots in Kant. By bringing together Kant scholarship and contemporary aesthetics, this volume hopes to establish a dialogue which might lead to a more *responsible* use of the word "disinterestedness," which will enable us to deal appropriately with the many puzzles surrounding it. The puzzle of how disinterestedness relates to universality (or intersubjectivity) is just one of the puzzles shared by contemporary aesthetics and Kant interpretation.

So far, this introduction was very abstract. Let me, thus, provide a more precise sketch of the horizon of disinterestedness by giving an overview of the different meanings of this notion as being discussed in this volume.

(1) To begin with, one might distinguish **negative and positive characterizations of disinterestedness.** These two characterizations can already be found in Kant: he claims, on the one hand, that one must be *in*different regarding the existence of the object and must *not* be dependent on it, and, on the other, that what matters is what one makes of the representation of the object in oneself (see KU: 204f.; see also Berger and Wenzel in this volume). Recently, Nick Riggle has suggested a similar twofold characterization of disinterest:

> Disinterest-: If a pleasure in an item is aesthetic, then it is not due to the way the item satisfies one's desires, needs, or worldly projects.
>
> Disinterest+: If a pleasure in an item is aesthetic, then it is due to sympathetic attention to, or contemplation of, the item for its own sake. (Riggle 2016, p. 3)

In this volume, Keren Gorodeisky takes up Riggle's distinction. Broadly speaking, she opts to understand the negative characterization in terms of the pleasure not being *practical*, i.e., independent of the will, the faculty of desire, the satisfaction of desires and so on. She spells out the positive characterization in terms of a certain form of active self-consciousness "that manifests itself—the pleasure of the appreciating self—as worthy of the object, and, as such, as justified" (Gorodeisky in this volume, p. 148).

(2) As already seen, Kant's negative characterization of disinterestedness comprises two components: independence from the object's existence and independence from the faculty of desire. Paul Guyer's interpretation of Kant and Mendelssohn refers mainly to the negative characterization in terms of its first component. On this interpretation aesthetic response is not concerned with the existence of the object but with **appearances and images (representations)**, that is, with how the object looks or sounds to us.

(3) Other authors mainly understand disinterestedness in terms of the second component of the negative characterization, that is, in terms of a **detachment**

from the practical realm. For instance, James Shelley interprets the thesis of disinterestedness such that "ascriptions of beauty do not motivate"—neither do they depend on nor result in a motive to act (Shelley in this volume, p. 269). Nick Zangwill differentiates several kinds of disinterestedness, all to be found in Kant and all related to desire: *basically disinterested* pleasure is not produced by a desire, whereas *productively disinterested* pleasure does not produce any desire. Zangwill labels the conjunction of both *disjunctively disinterested pleasure*. (He identifies a fourth kind of disinterestedness, so-called "noumenal disinterestedness," but argues that this is nothing but basic disinterestedness in disguise.) Lisa Schmalzried grounds her understanding of disinterestedness on Kant's conception of interest as put forward in his moral writings. Here, an interest is a determining cause of the will. She distinguishes two conceptions of disinterestedness, much in line with Zangwill's distinction between basic and disjunctive disinterestedness: On her "weak conception of disinterestedness," no determining cause of the will grounds the pleasure in the beautiful; on her "strong conception of disinterestedness," the pleasure does additionally not ground any interest.

(4) Schmalzried's interpretation implicitly hints at an intellectual understanding of interest, the latter being a conceptual or rule-bound determining ground of the will. An analogous interpretation of disinterested pleasure as **being independent from any rule-bound connection to the will** can be found in Gorodeisky's interpretation of Kant—here, disinterestedness is intimately connected to the pleasure's non-conceptuality (see also Lopes in this volume). (Such an intimate connection between disinterestedness and non-conceptuality is explicitly denied by Berger and Zangwill.)

(5) A certain detachment from the practical realm is also included in Thomas Hilgers' interpretation of disinterestedness. However, he interprets the latter as a characterization of the **aesthetic attitude.** For him, the "disinterested attitude" is characterized in terms of a person's disengagement from their "practical and interested involvements with the world" (Hilgers 2017, p. 3; p. 168 in this volume).

(6) In my contribution, I relate the thesis of disinterestedness to the pleasure being grounded in the free play of the faculties and to Kant's distinction between matter and form. Most importantly, I argue that the thesis of disinterestedness has a **phenomenological meaning:** it tells us that "the pleasure in the beautiful feels disinterested, that is, detached of any desiring" (Berger in this volume, p, 54). Thus, the independence from the faculty of desire has an impact on what it is like to experience this pleasure.

(7) Unlike Shelley, Dominic McIver Lopes does not take disinterested pleasure to be detached from all motives whatsoever. Rather, on Lopes' interpretation of

Kant, disinterestedness is a **strictly internal motive**, motivating merely its own continuation; it precludes all external motives, that is, all desires, where the latter are conceptually-laden. He models a related contemporary conception of disinterestedness by analogy to pain asymbolia: here, disinterested pleasure also provides merely internal motives because the so-called "care characterization" is absent, that is, a condition necessary for the motives to cause action. On Lopes' third take on disinterestedness, which he calls the "Kant Lite characterization," a disinterested pleasure is not merely an internal motive, but it motivates to perform acts of contemplation.

(8) Fiona Hughes focuses on the positive characterization of disinterestedness. Inspired by Kant, but going beyond him in important respects, she focuses on the **free play of the faculties** and claims that the latter is free from being determined by interests. Instead of excluding any interest whatsoever, disinterestedness is compatible with what she calls a playful negotiation of interests.

(9) Stefano Velotti also refers to Kant when focusing on the role of disinterestedness in terms of the **aesthetic principle of the faculty of judgment** or the determining ground (*Bestimmungsgrund*) of the judgment of taste. On his interpretation, disinterestedness does not concern actual judgments, which can, indeed, be mingled with interests. Rather, it provides the condition of possibility of aesthetic judgment. Velotti also opposes a certain psychological or empirical understanding of disinterestedness recently suggested by Bence Nanay. According to the latter, disinterestedness amounts to "distributed attention" (Nanay 2016, p. 26).

Let me conclude this brief introduction by some remarks on the structure of this volume. Following the aim of bringing together Kant scholarship and contemporary aesthetics, the volume comprises two main parts. In the first part, Kant's thesis of disinterestedness as put forward in the *Critique of Judgment* will be interpreted and explored. Paul Guyer relates Kant to his predecessor Moses Mendelssohn. Nick Zangwill and I each focus on the content of the thesis of disinterestedness and develop our original interpretation. Christian Helmut Wenzel and Stefano Velotti also each offer their own interpretation and explore its connection to other parts of the *Critique of Aesthetic Judgment:* Velotti relates his interpretation of disinterestedness to Kant's distinction between free and adherent beauty as well as his theory of art. Wenzel analyses the thesis of disinterestedness within the framework of the four moments of the *Analytic of the Beautiful,* and he relates it to the intellectual interest in beauty as well as Kant's theory of the sublime. The second part of the volume addresses disinterestedness within the framework of contemporary aesthetics. While all articles in this second part still refer to Kant, their focus is not on Kant interpretation, but either on the defense or the rejection of the thesis of disinterestedness within contemporary approaches to beauty.[6] Keren Gorodeisky and Thomas Hilgers both defend a version of disinterestedness. Gorodeisky argues against the "Myth of the Absent Self" by pointing out that disinterestedness contributes to what she calls "clarifying, evaluative, and transformative self-consciousness" (Gorodeisky, this volume, p. 138). Hilgers also focuses on the notion of the self. By drawing on his recent account of disinterested attitude,[7] he argues that the latter, understood in terms of a disentanglement from one's idiosyncratic perspective, enables the subject to lose her sense of the self, thereby gaining a sense of the other and ultimately achieving selfhood. Fiona Hughes and Lisa Schmalzried are both critics and advocates of disinterestedness. Hughes rejects a version of disinterestedness according to which we must preclude any interest whatsoever from experiences of beauty; but she defends a version according to which such experiences must not be determined by interests while possibly including a playful negotiation of the latter. Schmalzried focuses on human beauty and the so-called thesis of attractiveness. She argues that the latter is compatible with the weak claim that the pleasure in the beautiful must not be caused by any interest, but that it precludes the strong claim that the pleasure in the beautiful also must not give rise to any interest. Finally, James Shelley and Dominic McIver Lopes side with the critics of disinterestedness. While rejecting hedonism of aesthetic value, Shelley makes a strong case for judgments of beauty based on testimony and argues that these are not disinterested. Against this backdrop he also rejects disinterestedness with regard to aesthetic judgments of beauty, that is, judgments based on the beholder's own experience. Lopes likewise focuses on aesthetic value (and aesthetic hedonism), and argues that disinterestedness is neither helpful in answering the demarcation question—"what makes some values specifically aesthetic values?"—nor in answering the normative question—"why do aesthetic value facts lend weight to what one should do or think?" (Lopes in this volume, p. 236 and 238).

Abbreviations

All references to Kant's works are to Kant's Gesammelte Schriften, Ausgabe der Preußischen Akademie der Wissenschaften (Berlin: De Gruyter, 1902 ff.). Translations are from The Cambridge Edition of the Works of Immanuel Kant.

---

[6] In the headings of these sections I use the terms "disinterest advocates" and "disinterest critics," which I take from Keren Gorodeisky (in this volume).
[7] See Hilgers 2017.

The following abbreviation is used:

KU Kritik der Urteilskraft / Critique of the Power of Judgment

Literature

Crowther, Paul (2010): *The Kantian Aesthetic. From Knowledge to the Avant-Garde.* Oxford: Oxford University Press.
Dickie George (1964): "The Myth of the Aesthetic Attitude." In: *American Philosophical Quarterly* 1. No. 1, pp. 56–65.
Hilgers, Thomas (2017): *Aesthetic Disinterestedness. Art, Experience, and the Self.* New York and London: Routledge.
Nanay, Bence (2016): *Aesthetics as Philosophy of Perception.* Oxford: Oxford University Press.
Nehamas, Alexander (2007): *Only a Promise of Happiness. The Place of Beauty in a World of Art.* Princeton: Princeton University Press.
Riggle, Nick (2016): "On the Interest in Beauty and Disinterest." In: *Philosophers' Imprint* 16, pp. 1–14.
Rind, Miles (2002): "The Concept of Disinterestedness in Eighteenth-Century British Aesthetics." In: *Journal of the History of Philosophy* 40. No. 1, pp. 67–87.
Shelley, James (2017): "The Concept of the Aesthetic." In: Zalta, Edward N. (Ed.): *Stanford Encyclopedia of Philosophy.*

Part I **Disinterestedness in Kant**

Paul Guyer
Disinterestedness by Any Other Name: Kant and Mendelssohn

Abstract: Kant's characterization of the proper object of aesthetic judgment through his concept of disinterestedness in the existence of objects has a high philosophical cost, in view of his own insistence that existence is not a predicate. It is his way of getting at the claim that aesthetic response is concerned with representation, but other philosophers of the period, such as Moses Mendelssohn, made this point more straightforwardly. Mendelssohn's approach allows him to explain what he calls "mixed sentiment" and to resolve the paradox of tragedy.

1 Introduction

Some time ago, I argued that Kant's conception of the disinterestedness of judgments of taste was not his restatement of a view that was widely shared throughout the 18th century but rather the revival of a view, originating with Shaftesbury and Hutcheson, that had largely been rejected by intervening writers, who held in their different ways that there is something distinctive about aesthetic response and judgment but not that it is entirely independent from all ordinary human prudential and moral concerns, in a word, from all normal human interests.[1] Here, I want to refine my position. It remains true that neither British nor German writers between Hutcheson and Kant used the *word* "disinterestedness" or related terms in the exposition of their theories of aesthetic experience and taste. But the primary function of the concept for Kant is to point to the fact that aesthetic experience and judgments of taste expressing and evaluating such experience respond to the *representation* of beautiful or sublime works of nature or art, that is, with how such objects *appear* to us, in an ordinary, sensory sense of appearing, not Kant's transcendental sense of appearance, that is, how they *look* or *sound* to us, or what sorts of *images* they suggest to our imagination, and that our further aesthetic engagement with objects begins with the representation or appearance of ob-

---

1 See Guyer 1993, Chapters 2–3. Disinterestedness had earlier been held to be the defining feature of the 18th-century conception of the aesthetic by Jerome Stolnitz, e. g., "On the Origins of 'Aesthetic Disinterestedness'" (1961), and as such to be a crucial factor in the emergence of the modern conception of the arts by Paul Oskar Kristeller, in "The Modern System of the Arts," *Journal of the History of Ideas* (1951 and 1952), reprinted Kristeller (1980), pp. 163–227.

https://doi.org/10.1515/9783110727685-002

jects in this sense. And *this* conception of the aesthetic was certainly widely shared in the 18th century, although often stated in other terms, or perhaps better in precisely the ordinary terms I have just used. Moreover, this conception has continued to be central to many later aesthetic theories as well—Benedetto Croce's account of aesthetic intuition and Richard Wollheim's account of meaning in painting as beginning with the twofoldness of perceived marks on a canvas and the images those marks present to us being just two examples.[2]

Shaftesbury's original insistence that enjoyment of the beauty of an object should not depend on personal *possession* of an object and thus on an interest in it in that ordinary sense[3] was not controversial, so Kant's adoption of that point would also be non-controversial. And Kant's conception of disinterestedness has certain merits: in particular, his implication that *interest* in beauty can only be *indirect*, grounded in social or moral pleasures that are not part of our *immediate* response to the beautiful object of nature or art, provides a salubrious defense against excessive pragmatism or moralism, or didacticism, that is, against any theory that would collapse beauty or other aesthetic qualities into mere usefulness or moral instruction. It thereby leaves the way open for some art to appeal just to our senses and our imagination even if other art is also useful or morally instructive[4]. But Kant's theory also comes with high costs, including the theoretical cost of depending on a contrast between representation and existence that requires some fancy footwork in order to be reconciled with Kant's insistence that existence is not a predicate as well as the risk of excluding too much of the content of art from the proper object of taste. Other 18th-century aestheticians expressed the idea that aesthetic experience begins with representation in more ordinary terms and without some of the risks of Kant's way of doing it.

In what follows, I will first discuss the pros and cons of Kant's approach, and then look at one example of how a close contemporary and interlocutor of his, namely, Moses Mendelssohn, expressed this idea without some of these problems. Although Kant's central idea of aesthetic experience as that of the free play of the imagination may be more attractive to us now than Mendelssohn's perfectionist framework,[5] Mendelssohn's way of arguing that aesthetic experience begins

---

2 Croce 1922; Wollheim 1987.
3 See *The Moralists* (originally 1709), Part III, § II, in Shaftesbury 1999, Vol. II, pp. 102–103.
4 That Kant connects the empirical and intellectual interests in beauty only indirectly to what is supposed to be a basically disinterested response (*KU* §§41–42) is another reason why I resist Hannah Ginsborg's position that "normativity" should be considered part of the basic aesthetic response, even though what she has in mind is "epistemic" normativity. See Ginsborg 2015, especially Chapters 1–3 and 8.
5 *Contra* the position of Beiser 2009.

with representation may be a more straightforward way of introducing the basic point that aesthetic judgment begins from how we experience objects than Kant's problematic inference that aesthetic response does not concern the existence of objects from his peculiar definition of disinterestedness.

2 Kant's Conception of Disinterestedness

Kant begins the "Analytic of the Beautiful" with the statement that "In order to decide whether or not something is beautiful, we do not relate the representation by means of understanding to the object for cognition, but rather relate it by means of the imagination (perhaps combined with the understanding) to the subject and its feeling of pleasure or displeasure" (KU: 203). This suggests from the outset that aesthetic pleasure is pleasure that we take in the appearance of an object, how it looks or sounds, and how that appeals to our imagination, although here that sort of pleasure is contrasted only with a cognitive pleasure and interest in an object, that is, pleasure connected with classifying it, understanding it, learning a fact or theory from it, and so on.[6] Thus far Kant has said nothing that others such as Hutcheson and Hume did not also accept.[7] Kant introduces the concept of disinterestedness only in the next section, entitled "The satisfaction that determines the judgment of taste is without any interest" (KU: 204). What Kant means by the disinterestedness of the experience of beauty and the judgment of taste that may express it is stated, at least in part, in perfectly ordinary and non-controversial terms:

> If someone asks me whether I find the palace that I see before me beautiful, I may well say that I don't like that sort of thing, which is made merely to be gaped at, or, like the Iroquois sachem, that nothing in Paris pleased him better than the cook-shops; in true *Rousseauesque* style I might even vilify the vanity of the great who waste the sweat of the people on such superfluous things; finally I could even easily convince myself that if I were to find myself on an uninhabited desert island, without any hope of ever coming upon human beings again, and could conjure up such a magnificent structure through my mere wish, I would not even take the trouble of doing so if I already had a hut that was comfortable enough for me. All of this might be conceded to me and approved; but that is not what is at issue

---

6 In this paper, I will disregard Kant's suggestion that there is a properly aesthetic displeasure, although this has occasioned an extensive discussion of whether Kant posits a pure aesthetic judgment of ugliness. For my position in that debate, see Guyer 2005.
7 See Hutcheson, *An Inquiry Concerning Beauty, Order, &c.* (originally 1725), § I, Paragraph 13, in Hutcheson 2008, p. 25, and Hume, *An Enquiry Concerning the Principles of Morals* (originally 1751), Appendix I, in Hume 1998, p. 87.

here. One only wants to know whether the mere representation of the object is accompanied with satisfaction in me, [...]. (KU: 204–205)

(and whether, as Kant will shortly argue, the satisfaction in me can reasonably be imputed to other people as well). All of this is perfectly straightforward: the question whether you find the palace beautiful is not the question whether you approve of the circumstances under which or the reasons for which it was constructed, or whether you think you might find something good to eat there, but simply whether you like the way it looks (or sounds). Beauty lies in the way the object looks, not in its history, its use, its cost (monetary or social), and so on. The question for aesthetic theory would then be what exactly is our response to the way an object looks (or sounds), what mental activities do we perform upon such a representation, and, the way Kant structures the question, whether we can reasonably expect others to have the same response to such representations as we ourselves do, if so under what circumstances, and so on (the problem of taste).

To be sure, once Kant turns from his introductory examples of beautiful objects to the fine arts, especially to poetry (or literature more generally), which he regards as the foremost of the fine arts, his initial emphasis on how objects of taste *look* will have to be refined to accommodate objects of taste that are not directly presented to the senses. But that is not the complication with which I am concerned here. Rather, my concern is with Kant's complication of his initially non-controversial point by his contrast between the representation of an object and its existence. Kant precedes the passage just quoted with the statement that "if the question is whether something is beautiful, one does not want to know whether there is anything that is or that could be at stake, for us or for someone else, in the existence of the thing, but rather how we judge it in mere contemplation (intuition or reflection)" (KU: 204), and he fills in the conclusion, which I omitted in the previous quotation, with the words "however indifferent I might be with regard to the existence of the object of this representation" (KU: 205). We know perfectly well what Kant means when he says that we are concerned simply with whether the intuition of, reflection upon, or contemplation of the object is pleasing: do we like how it looks? or perhaps, in the case of poetry, the imagery that it evokes? does it stimulate our imagination, or, as he will say, set it into a harmonious free play? But we might not know what he means when he says that we do not want to know whether there is anything at stake for us in the existence of the object. For what it might mean for there to be something at stake in the existence of the object is ill-defined and, further, Kant has famously insisted, from his early book on *The Only Possible Argument for a Demonstration of the Existence of God* (1763) through the *Critique of Pure Reason*, that existence is not a proper predicate of objects at all. We might put the term "exists" in the grammatical position of a predicate in a sentence ("Socrates exists," or at least did exist), Kant allows, but it does not refer to any specific quality or add anything to our concept of the object in the way that a hundred and first dollar would add to a hundred dollars. In general, Kant says, "The modality of judgments is a quite special function of them, which is distinctive in that it contributes nothing to the content of judgment (for besides quantity, quality, and relation there is nothing more that constitutes the content of a judgment), but rather concerns only the value of the copula in relation to thinking in general" (KrV: A74/B100). In particular, *"Being* is obviously not a real predicate, i.e., a concept of something that could add to the concept of a thing. It is merely the positing of a thing or of certain determinations in themselves" (KrV: A598/B626).

Now, if one wanted to be tough-minded about it, one could simply say that since existence is obviously not a real predicate that adds to the concept of a thing, saying that our pleasure in beauty does not concern the existence of the beautiful object is not telling us anything about our experience of beauty at all, or at least not telling us anything we do not already know, namely, that this pleasure concerns how the representation of the object strikes us or what we can do with the representation. Kant's implicit definition of disinterestedness by its contrast to an interest in the existence of an object seems an unnecessary addition to the straightforward point that aesthetic pleasure is pleasure in the representation of an object or the representations it evokes. And certainly, it does not seem a promising strategy for Kant to *derive* the thesis that aesthetic pleasure is response to representation from an *antecedent* claim that a disinterested pleasure is not a response to the existence of an object when just what the latter means may not be well-defined.[8]

Nevertheless, we might also see a rationale for Kant's definition of disinterested as pleasure's independence from concern with existence. On Kant's account of modality[9] an assertion of the existence of an object does not add any particular quality to our concept of the object, but rather expresses a relation of the concept of the object to our entire body of "thinking" or thought, namely, it asserts that our

---

8 Here, I am departing from the approach of our editor, Larissa Berger, who takes Kant's definition of *Uninteressiertheit* (which I would suggest should be *Desinteresse* or *Interesselosigkeit*) as independence of concern with existence (and desire) to be the starting point of Kant's argument, from which aesthetic pleasure's concern with representation alone is derived (Berger 2022, pp. 127–135 and more). The passages she cites as evidence that Kant infers the concern with representation from the exclusion of pleasure in existence from KU §7, first paragraph, sentences 6 and 7 (KU: 205, at Berger p. 141) can just as easily be read in the opposite direction, and I would suggest that Kant is on firmer ground if read in this way.

9 On Kant's account of modality, see Abaci 2019.

entire body of thought provides adequate grounds for positing that this concept has an object. We might therefore suppose that saying that we have a stake in the existence of an object can mean that we can have *any* kind of reason for liking it, that *somewhere* in our entire response to the object there is a ground for liking it, and thus does not in any way *narrow down* the basis of our satisfaction in the object. However, the concept of the aesthetic *does* require that our grounds for liking an object be narrowed down, namely, to what our senses and imagination can do with the representation of the object, rather than whether the object itself is a good investment or a bad investment, exploitative or politically suspect, and so on.

So, Kant's characterization of a disinterested satisfaction in a beautiful object as one that has no stake in the existence of the object need not conflict outright with his claim that existence is not a "real" and therefore informative predicate of objects. Yet it also does not seem to add anything to what we already understand by understanding that our pleasure in beauty is a response to the representation of the object, or, we might say, our understanding of what Kant means by the denial that aesthetic pleasure concerns the existence of the object is entirely parasitic upon the latter. So, we might conclude that there is no great theoretical virtue in Kant's contrast between representation and existence, and that an account of aesthetic response as focused on our representation of objects without the addendum of the denial that it concerns existence would be theoretically preferable, at least on the ground of non-redundancy or economy. We will see that the aesthetic theory of Mendelssohn has this virtue, making the point that aesthetic pleasure concerns the representation of objects without the theoretically obscure conception of disinterest in existence.

There are also substantive problems in Kant's account of disinterestedness. The first is that Kant's insistence upon the disinterestedness of judgments of taste and the pleasure on which they are based is obviously connected with his insistence upon the "subjectively universal validity" of judgments of taste (KU: 215), that is, the claim that even though beauty is not an ordinary objective property but more like a disposition to produce a free play of imagination within the understanding's general constraint of "lawfulness" (KU: 241), any object that genuinely produces that response in one subject can properly be judged to be able to produce that response in any other optimally circumstanced subject. The problem that I have in mind is not the logical flaw in Kant's suggestion that disinterestedness is not merely a necessary but also a sufficient condition for subjectively universal validity (KU: 211), which ignores the possibility of sheer disinterested idiosyncrasy.[10]

---

[10] For this objection, see Guyer 1997, pp. 116–117. Berger accepts Kant's suggestion that the judgment of taste's claim to subjectively universal validity follows from the disinterestedness of the

The problem is rather with the insistence that any genuine response to beauty must be universally valid, which motivates the insistence upon disinterestedness. To be sure, if beauty were a genuinely objective property, like weight or velocity or age or chemical composition, then there would be a single correct value for such a property (at least relative to a particular inertial frame for some of these properties), on which all qualified observers should be able to agree. But if beauty is really an object's ability to stimulate a free play of imagination in a subject—Kant's version of the ontological displacement of beauty from object to subject on which most 18th-century authors agreed—then it is not clear why all people, even under optimal circumstances, should have this response to exactly the same objects. Surely the imagination must vary in all sorts of ways from one person to the next, so why should all and only the objects that set one person's imagination into free play do the same for everyone else? To be sure, other 18th-century writers who were influential for Kant, such as Hutcheson and Hume, also assumed that judgments of taste should have what Kant called subjectively universal validity, though they did not use this term, but that assumption was not universally made, and has come under fire in contemporary aesthetics. Alexander Nehamas, for one, has made a persuasive case that an individual's response to a work of art that she finds beautiful can be an on-going engagement with that work, and given the inevitable differences in individual psychology, history, tastes, etc., it is only reasonable to suppose that different persons will find different objects beautiful, that is, rewarding for their own on-going engagement.[11] Since Kant's insistence upon disinterestedness is so closely tied with his insistence upon subjectively universal validity, it is also vulnerable to objections to the latter.

Closely connected with Kant's insistence upon disinterestedness and universal validity is the formalism upon which he insists, at least in the initial argument of the "Analytic of the Beautiful." This is his view that in visual art, what is essential is always the "drawing" or spatial design, in Alberti's terminology the *disegno*, and that other properties such as color can never do more than "enliven" the formal features of the object, and that likewise in auditory art (music) it is the "composition," the formal structure of melody and harmony, that is essential, rather than the "agreeable tones of instruments," what is often called in analogy with the visual case "coloration" (KU: 225). Everything other than spatial and/or temporal

---

pleasure that it expresses (Berger 2022, e.g., p. 367) rather than treating disinterestedness as at best a necessary condition for subjectively universal validity. In any case, of course, Kant's claim that a representation that produces disinterested pleasure in one subject can reasonably be expected to produce it in all under ideal conditions does not follow from the conception of disinterestedness alone, but needs to be sustained by a successful deduction of judgments of taste (KU, §§21, 38).
11 Nehamas 2007.

form, not only other sensory qualities such as color or coloration but also semantic or referential content or any conception of the function or purpose of an object (see KU: 229–230), is extraneous to proper aesthetic response, and can even lead to an emotional response to objects that is "barbaric" (KU: 223)—and interested rather than disinterested. This approach seems not only to exclude much of what we find important in our response to art or even to natural beauty but also to present a problem for Kant himself when he comes much later in the "Critique of the Aesthetic Power of Judgment" to explain the "spirit" of works of art as due to their expression of "aesthetic ideas," that is, their expression of *content* in an imaginative way, content typically consisting of "rational" or moral ideas with which people would ordinarily have deep emotional associations and in which they would take deep interest (KU: 214–215). To be sure, Kant does have among his philosophical resources a highly abstract concept of form as *whatever* "allows the manifold of appearance to be ordered in certain relations" (KrV: A20/B34), which, even though it is introduced in the "Transcendental Aesthetic" of the first *Critique* to prepare the way for Kant's account of space and time as pure forms of intuition, need not be restricted to spatial and/or temporal relations—it could refer to whatever features, from colors to conceptual content, allow us to hold a manifold of experience together, and in the aesthetic case to whatever allows us to hold a manifold together by the free play of the imagination rather than in accordance with some ordinary, determinate concept functioning as a rule for the synthesis of that manifold. But although such a general conception of form could reconcile Kant's initial analysis of aesthetic experience with his later account of fine art, in the initial analysis Kant's concern with disinterestedness and his corresponding abhorrence of emotional involvement with beautiful objects pushes him to a much more restrictive interpretation of aesthetically significant form.[12]

Still, I also suggested earlier that there is a benefit to Kant's conception of disinterestedness, namely, its suggestion that our interest in beauty and art can be indirect rather than immediate. Here I have in mind Kant's account of the "empiri-

---

[12] Berger also accepts Kant's inference from the disinterestedness of aesthetic pleasure to his formalist conception of beauty, on the basis of the premise that any response to the "matter" of sensation is merely "agreeable" rather than a genuine response to beauty (Berger 2022, pp. 45, 750). But given Kant's abstract definition of form as virtually any kind of unifying relation, harmonious relations among colors, tones, or other "matters" of sensation should count as formal just as much as relations among shapes or temporal durations do. For an account of the abstractness of Kant's conception of aesthetic form, see Zuckert 2007, pp. 185–186; for the argument that Kant's abstract account of aesthetic form should include harmonious relations among "material" properties such as color, in addition to Guyer 1997, pp. 186–187, 190–210, see also Allison 2001, p. 136, and Hughes 2010, pp. 58–59. For a philosophical rather than interpretative effort to broaden Kant's restrictive application of his formalism, see McMahon 2007, pp. 5–12, and more.

cal" and "intellectual" interests in the beautiful that he appends to his "deduction" of judgments of taste, that is, his attempt to justify their claim to subjectively universal validity. By the empirical interest in art Kant means the satisfaction that we might attach to our primary, disinterested pleasure in beauty because that is a pleasure that can often be shared in social settings and that can promote sociability, and by the intellectual interest in the beautiful Kant means the moral interest that we can take in its existence, as a "sign" that the world is receptive to our own concerns, that is, makes the realization of our goals possible, an assumption that we have to make in order to make not merely our prudential but also our moral efforts rational (see KU: 296–303). As it happens, Kant associates the empirical interest in beauty with artistic beauty, and is suspicious of it because art can easily be used for self-aggrandizement, while he restricts the intellectual interest in beauty to natural beauty because of his explanation that the basis for this interest is our moral concern that nature be receptive to our moral goals (that we can in fact do what we ought to do). But the latter restriction is undercut by his own subsequent argument that *artistic* genius is a gift of *nature* (see KU: 307), which implies that the existence of artistic genius and genial art is also a sign that nature is receptive to our own human concerns; and Kant's suspicion of art because it *can* be used for self-aggrandizement surely ought to be tempered by recognition of the fact that it *is not* always used for this purpose—the history of art surely shows it to be used as often for the glorification of God, for example, as for aggrandizement of self. (No doubt many a medieval alter-piece donor used art for both purposes, but at least not solely for self-aggrandizement.) But the contingency of connection between the initial and primary response to beauty—the free play of imagination—and a further interest, whether in glorification of God or in personal self-aggrandizement, shows the value of Kant's conception of the indirectness of both empirical and intellectual interest in beauty. The point is that we may experience beauty without necessarily taking a further kind of interest in the beautiful object, thus without reducing our pleasure in beauty to the pleasure connected with that further interest, and we may also take such a further interest in the work without destroying or compromising the initial, perhaps we should say more purely aesthetic response to the object. There does not have to be either an interest in every beautiful object or an irremediable conflict between beauty and interest.

    Kant's concept of disinterestedness allows him to emphasize that aesthetic response at least begins with how things look or sound, or with the visual or acoustic images they may suggest to us, and in the end also allows him to suggest that our aesthetic experiences may be embedded in a rich context of human interests without sacrificing what is distinctively aesthetic about them. Still, his contrast between representation and existence also comes with philosophical costs. So, let us now look at an example of an aesthetic theory that make Kant's initial point, that aesthetic response is in the first instance a response to the representations afforded by objects, without using the concept of disinterestedness and being weighed down by some of its philosophical baggage.

3 Mendelssohn

Moses Mendelssohn was born five years after Kant but established his reputation with essays in aesthetics while he was still in his twenties. Indeed, Mendelssohn's work in aesthetics was largely completed before Kant ever spoke or wrote a word on the subject, and Kant does not mention Mendelssohn's name in his own main work in aesthetics, the first half of the *Critique of the Power of Judgment*, published three decades after Mendelssohn had completed his main work in the field. But as is often the case, Mendelssohn can be interpreted as the unnamed target of Kant's work;[13] in particular, Kant's insistence that taste that depends upon emotion is barbaric can be read as a rejection of Mendelssohn's view that sentiment, as we shall in the form of mixed sentiment, is a core component of aesthetic response. But that is a larger story;[14] here, we will focus on the issue of disinterestedness.

Mendelssohn entered the field of aesthetics in the wake of Alexander Gottlieb Baumgarten, who had baptized the field in his 1735 master's thesis[15] and published the first part of his never-to-be-completed textbook *Aesthetica* in 1750. Baumgarten treated aesthetic experience as a kind of cognition, and characterized beauty or the "goal of aesthetics" as the "perfection of sensory cognition" (Baumgarten 2007, § 14).[16] But Baumgarten's exposition is structured by a fundamental distinction between the beauty (or not) of *things*, as subjects of works of art, and of *cognitions*—as the sensory representations of those things:

> The general beauty of sensory cognition consists (1) in the harmony of thoughts, insofar as we leave aside their order and signification, into a unity, which is a *phaenomenon*. The BEAUTY OF THINGS AND OF THOUGHTS must be distinguished from the beauty of cognition, the first and foremost part of which it is, and from the beauty of objects and of material, with which, on account of the ordinary meaning of 'thing' [*rei*], it is often but incorrectly confused. Ugly things can, as such, be cognized beautifully, and more beautiful things can be cognized as ugly. (Baumgarten 2007, § 18)

---

13 For my attempt to sustain this assertion, see Guyer 2020.
14 I have told more of this story in Guyer 2020, Chapters 6–8.
15 Baumgarten 1983, § CXVI.
16 Quotations from Baumgarten are my translations from the Latin-German edition, Baumgarten 2007.

Baumgarten's paucity of terminology, that is, the multiple ways he is forced to use the terms "cognition" and "thought" (*cognitio* and *cogitatio*), make his argument a little hard to follow, but the final sentence makes clear what he is driving at: there is a distinction between things and the representations of them, therefore between the responses that we might have toward things represented, that is, the pleasure or displeasure that we might take in the things themselves, and the responses that we may take in the representation of them, the pleasure we might take in the perfection of the cognition or representation of the object or displeasure in its imperfection. Our response to the cognition or representation of a thing is the starting point of aesthetic response, not the perfection or imperfection of the represented thing itself. Baumgarten can thus make the point that aesthetic response begins with the representation of things without using Kant's concept of disinterestedness or his explanation of disinterested pleasure as concerned with representation rather than *existence*; he just needs the ordinary contrast between *representation* and represented *thing*.

Mendelssohn follows Baumgarten in this regard. Mendelssohn's first work in aesthetics, the letters *On the Sentiments* of 1755, begins with the argument that our pleasure in beauty must be grounded in a "positive power" or powers of the soul, not in something merely negative like the *indistinctness* or *confusion* of our representations (as if not Baumgarten then at least his predecessor Christian Wolff was thought to have held), and that this positive power of the soul is its ability to "preserve not simply representations, but rather representations combined and grounded in one another"—*representations*, not properties of the represented objects.[17] Mendelssohn then develops the distinction between representations and their objects in the *Rhapsody* added to the letters in 1761, stating that

> Each individual representation stands in a twofold relation. It is related, at once, to the matter before it as its object (of which it is a picture or copy) and then to the soul or the thinking subject (of which it constitutes a determination). As a determination of the soul, many a representation can have something pleasant about it although, as a picture of the object, it is accompanied by disapproval and a feeling of repugnance. Thus, we must indeed take care not to confuse these two relations, the objective and the subjective, with one another. (*Rhapsody*, Mendelssohn 1997, p. 132)

---

17 Moses Mendelssohn, *On Sentiments*, Fourth and Fifth Letters, in Mendelssohn 1997, pp. 19 and 23. Mendelssohn's *Philosophical Writings*, first published in 1761, collected a number of pieces he had published beginning in 1754, adding at that time a "Rhapsody, or additions to the Letters on Sentiments" (pp. 131–168). The collection was republished in 1771, with considerable revision. Dahlstrom translates the 1771 edition. Both editions are reprinted in the collected edition of Mendelssohn's work in Mendelssohn 1929, pp. 1–222 and 227–515.

Mendelssohn could have made his model clearer for the case of art if he had distinguished three terms rather than two, at least for the kind of mimetic or representational art with which he is chiefly concerned, namely, the represented object and two different kinds of representation, one the external object produced by the artist, the painting, poem, statue, etc., which is itself an external object although one that represents another object, and the other the mental or internal representation of the artistic representation and through that of the ultimate object—for example, a vase full of flowers, a painting of the flowers, and a mental representation of the painting of the flowers.[18] But the basic idea is clear enough: we can take pleasure (or not) in the way something is represented, in Mendelssohn's terms in the perfections (or imperfections) of the representations, which response is distinct from the pleasure (or not) that we might take in the perfections (or imperfections) of the object that is represented. The former pleasures are rooted in the exercise of the cognitive and conative powers of the mind, in our powers of knowing and desiring.[19] Mendelssohn does not yet distinguish *desire* from *approbation without desire*, or *Billigung*, as he will in the later *Morgenstunden* (1785),[20] which, as we will see, completes his account of disinterestedness without using the term "disinterested." But the distinction between representation and thing represented that he uses here is enough to allow Mendelssohn to explicate the central concept of his aesthetics, that of "mixed sentiment" or emotion, the key to his resolution of the "paradox of tragedy" that engaged so many writers of his period:[21] we can be pained by represented content but pleased by the representation of the content, or even more fully we can be pained by some represented content, but pleased by the exercise of both our cognitive and our moral capacities in response to it: "recognizing an action and disapproving of it are [both] affirmative features of the soul, expressions of the mental powers of knowing and desiring, and elements of [our own] perfection which, in this connection, must be gratifying and enjoyable." (*Rhapsody*, Mendelssohn 1997, pp. 133–134) All of this can be explained without the concept of disinterestedness or its explication by means of a contrast between representation and existence; as in Baumgarten, all that Mendelssohn needs is the ordinary contrast between a thing and a representation of a thing, with the possibility that we may have different responses to each. Equally importantly, Mendels-

---

18 Mendelssohn refers to the Dutch flower painter Jan van Huysum (1682–1749) in the (1757) essay "On the Main Principles of the Fine Arts and Sciences," Mendelssohn 1997, p. 174.
19 *Rhapsody*, Mendelssohn 1997, pp. 133–134.
20 Moses Mendelssohn, *Morgenstunden*, Lecture VII; in Mendelssohn 2012, pp. 53–57.
21 Beginning with Jean-Baptiste Du Bos, *Critical Reflections on Poetry, Painting and Music* (1719), translated as Du Bos 1748. For an extensive discussion of Mendelssohn's conception of mixed sentiments, see Pollok 2010, pp. 154–190.

sohn does not need the concept of disinterestedness to distinguish a genuinely aesthetic response from, for example, a moral response; rather, it will be the fact that our response to a representation involves *both* our cognitive and our conative powers rather than the latter alone that marks our response to the representation as genuinely aesthetic.

Rather than using a philosophical and contestable conception of disinterestedness to explicate aesthetic response, Mendelssohn provides examples of how our attention is focused on representations in the actual experience of art. In the *Rhapsody*, he writes:

> Another means of rendering the most terrifying events pleasant to gentle minds is the imitation by art, on the stage, on the canvas, and in marble, since an inner consciousness that we have an imitation and nothing genuine before our eyes moderates the strength of the objective disgust and, as it were, elevates the subjective side of the representation. It is true, the soul's sentient knowledge and capacities to desire are deceived by art and the imagination is so swept away that at times we forget every sign that it is an imitation and fancy that we truly see nature. But this magic lasts only as long as is necessary to give our conception of the object the proper vitality and fire. In order to have the most pleasure, we have accustomed ourselves to diverting attention from everything that could disturb the deception and directing attention only at what sustains it. However, as soon as the relation to the object begins to become unpleasant, a thousand factors remind us that we are looking at a mere imitation. Added to this is the fact that art adorns the representations with many sorts of beauties which strengthen the pleasant sentiments and help attenuate the unpleasant reference to the object. (*Rhapsody*, Mendelssohn 1997, p. 138)

There is a great deal going on in this passage. Underlying the whole passage is an assumption that is quite different from Kant's, indeed an assumption that, as I suggested, may have been Kant's target in his remark that any taste that relies on "charm and emotion" (*Reiz und Rührung*) is "barbaric" (KU: 223), namely, the assumption that the primary source of pleasure in our experience of art is an experience of emotion stimulated by the work of art. This includes emotion stimulated by the representation of events that we would certainly not like to experience in real life, such as the murders and suicides, eye-gougings, entombments of living victims, and so on, that are the stuff of tragedy. (Mendelssohn's focus on the paradox of tragedy is no doubt a reason for his focus on mimetic art even though his conception of mental representation is not identical to that of imitation.) But of course, the emotion produced by works of art cannot be purely negative, purely painful, for there would then be no explanation of why we would seek out the experience of art except perhaps sheer boredom, which would make negative emotions preferable to none at all, a view, associated with Jean-Baptiste Du Bos, that

Mendelssohn certainly rejects.[22] The emotion stimulated by a work of art must be mixed, at least partly pleasurable, and in fact predominantly pleasurable, in order to explain our attraction to art. In the last sentence of the passage, Mendelssohn suggests that the various sorts of beauties with which art adorns the representation of such events can be responsible for some of the transformation of the unpleasant emotions that the objects and events represented by art would themselves stimulate into mixed and overall pleasant sentiments. These sorts of beauties would presumably include the sorts of formal features that Kant focuses on in the "Analytic of Beautiful," beauties of drawing and composition but perhaps also features that Kant dismisses as mere charms, such as color and coloration. But this—a solution to the paradox of tragedy that might be considered akin to Hume's in his contemporaneous essay "Of Tragedy"[23]—is not the main thrust of the passage.

Rather, the central idea of the passage is just that in the experience of art we *know*, at least at some level, that we are dealing with an imitation or representation, and thus we can enjoy the "subjective side of the representation," or the exercise or "perfection" of our own "sentient knowledge and capacities to desire" as stimulated by the object. I think that we can best understand Mendelssohn's position if we assume that he is tacitly using the threefold rather than twofold distinction that I mentioned earlier, namely, that between the object represented by a work of art (for example, the blinding of Gloucester or the self-blinding of Oedipus), the artistic representation of that event (the relevant passages in *King Lear* or *Oedipus Rex*), and the subject's mental representation of the (in these cases fictional or legendary) events depicted by means of the artistic representation, occasioned by those representations (the response of a reader or auditor of the play). Mendelssohn's point is then simply that our knowledge at some level that our mental representation of the tragic event is being occasioned by an artistic representation of that event rather than by the actual occurrence of such an event before our eyes enables us to enjoy our own internal representation of the event and the exercise of our mental faculties with that representation rather than being overwhelmed by the negative emotions which the actual occurrence of such an event would cause. We do not need a special concept of disinterestedness to explicate this; the work is done by the knowledge that we are responding to a fiction rather than to a fact, that is, that our own mental representation is a response to an artistic representation of an event rather than to an actual event.

---

22 Mendelssohn, *On Sentiments*, Conclusion, Mendelssohn 1997, pp. 71–72. Mendelssohn acknowledges that this is a simplification of Du Bos' view at *Rhapsody*, Mendelssohn 1997, p. 136.
23 Hume 1987, pp. 216–225.

To be sure, such an account of aesthetic response requires some psychological sophistication. On the one hand, there is the problem that has been foregrounded in much recent discussion of fiction: how can we have an emotion without also having a relevant belief, for example, how can we have something like fear of a bear without also believing that there is actually a bear before us; thus how could we experience distress at the death of Cordelia without also believing that there really is, or was, a Cordelia, who was executed by the contemptible Edmund before she could be saved by the noble Albany? Conversely, how could our knowledge that we are being presented with a fiction not obviate all possibility of a genuinely emotional, even if mixed, response?[24] How could our response to a fiction be anything other than a response to the pure form and/or mere charms of the work of art, to the elegance of its plot and language and so on—just as Kant seems to suggest in the "Analytic of the Beautiful"? In general, for a philosopher working in the Leibnizian tradition, there should be no problem in assuming knowledge that is less than fully clear and distinct or at the forefront of our consciousness. But specifically, Mendelssohn proposes what we might think of as a "diachronic" solution to this problem: we go through a series of mental states, first thinking of the depicted events as if they were real or forgetting that they are fictional long enough to get suitably worked up, to experience "the proper vitality and fire," and then, just when the emotions stimulated in that state are about to become overwhelming, remembering that we are dealing with a fiction after all—"a thousand factors remind us that we are looking at a mere imitation" (*Rhapsody*, Mendelssohn 1997, p. 138). However, it might be better to think of or to attribute to Mendelssohn a "synchronic" solution, that is, a picture of our mental complexity that allows us to become emotionally involved with a work of fiction while maintaining the background knowledge that it is a work of fiction, that is, an artistic representation. It is not as if, while watching a play or film, one ever forgets that it is a fiction and then suddenly remembers it; one knows all along, at least in some dispositional sense of knowing, that it is a fiction and yet can be emotionally involved with it, specifically, enjoying a mixed sentiment stimulated by both the depicted events and the artistic qualities of the depiction. Of course, if the knowledge that one is dealing with a fiction is pressed too much into the foreground, say by the actors stepping out of their roles, the spell will be broken, just as it may be by too many commercials interrupting a TV drama or some technical interruption of the show, like a sudden pixilation of the image; but ordinarily, our minds are sufficiently complex to hold the emotional response and the knowledge that we are responding to a mere artistic representation in balance. A model

---

24 For a sophisticated response to these challenges, see Robinson 2005.

of levels of consciousness like this is what I mean can be readily accommodated in the Leibnizian tradition.

As I said, all of this can be understood without Kant's conception of disinterestedness, and writing in the 1750s and 1760s, decades after Shaftesbury and Hutcheson wrote and decades before Kant, Mendelssohn did indeed present his account of the mixed sentiments that are central to enjoyment of art without use of this concept. But as I mentioned earlier, in his final philosophical work, the *Morgenstunden* of 1785, Mendelssohn did introduce a distinction that is missing in his earlier work, namely, a distinction between *desire* and *approbation* (*Billigung*), and explicitly links this distinction to our ability to enjoy fiction. He introduces the distinction thus:

> It is customary to divide our psychological faculties into those related to cognition and those related to desire, and to count the sensations of pleasure and pain on the side of the desiderative faculty. But it seems to me that between cognition and desire lies approbation, or acclamation, which is the mind's own sense of pleasantness, which is actually far removed from desire. We contemplate the beauty of nature and art with delight and satisfaction but without the slightest fluttering of desire. Indeed, it seems that it is a particular feature of the beautiful that we contemplate it with quiet satisfaction and that we enjoy it even when we do not count it as one of our possessions or have any desire to possess it. Only then, when we consider the beautiful as having some possible connection to ourselves, or when we view it as a good worthy of possession, only then does there awaken within us the desire to possess it, a desire that is quite distinct from the enjoyment of beauty. And since the thought of its possession or of its having some other connection to ourselves does not always accompany the sense of the beautiful—and even when it does, the true lover of beauty is not always moved to look upon the beautiful with acquisitive longing—we may conclude from this fact that the sensation of beauty is not always associated with desire, and it can therefore not be considered to be an expression of our desiderative faculty. (Mendelssohn, *Morgenstunden*, Lecture VII, in Mendelssohn 2012, p. 53)

We need not concern ourselves here with why Mendelssohn introduces this distinction into the *Morgenstunden*, lectures on the existence of God, namely, to explain that God, a completely perfect being, can *approve* of the existence of the best of all possible worlds without *desiring* it, since desire is an *imperfection*.[25] We are concerned only with Mendelssohn's description of the enjoyment of beauty as often, and therefore in principle, distinct from a desire to possess the beautiful object. His presentation of this thought is reminiscent of the passage in *The Moralists* (1709) in which Shaftesbury first introduced the concept—but not the term—of disinterestedness into *moral* theory by an *aesthetic* analogy: there Shaftesbury ar-

---

[25] Pollok's treatment of the *Billigungsvermögen* (Pollok 2010, pp. 338–342) also concentrates on its potential for aesthetic theory rather than on its role in the theological argument of *Morgenstunden*.

gues that to desire to possess everything that one finds beautiful, such as a grove of fruit trees, would be "sordidly *luxurious*" just like desiring to eat all the figs or peaches growing there, in order to suggest by analogy that desiring to do the right thing only out of a desire for reward or fear of punishment is "mercenary" rather than virtuous (Cooper 1999, p. 103). But Shaftesbury does this without any contrast between representation and existence, and Mendelssohn too makes the point that approbation does not always lead to outright desire, and to action intended to satisfy desire, without any technical concept of disinterestedness. He does suggest that the quiet satisfaction we take in it and the fact that it does not lead to possessive desire is a "particular feature of the beautiful," perhaps, we might interpret him to suggest, even definitive of beauty, but he does not need Kant's contrast between representation and existence to make this point. He only needs the ordinary contrast between pleasure and approbation on the one hand and desire to possess on the other to make his point.

There are several further points about Mendelssohn's treatment of approbation or the "faculty of approbation" (*Billigungsvermögen*) that we should notice. One is that he associates approbation with the "formal" side of cognition: the truth or falsehood of a cognition, he states, is the "material" side of cognition, while "insofar as it arouses pleasure or pain and leads to approbation or disapprobation ... this I call the 'formal' side of cognition, because through it one differentiates one cognitive act from another" (Mendelssohn, *Morgenstunden*, Lecture VII, in Mendelssohn 2012, p. 54). This is a little confusing, because surely whether it causes pleasure or pain is not *sufficient* to distinguish one cognition from another; no doubt many cognitions can cause pretty much the same kind of pleasure, and many others the same kind of pain, and each instance of cognition cannot be distinguished from all others solely by the kind of pleasure or pain it causes. Rather, we must take Mendelssohn to mean that cognitions or representations can cause pleasure or pain independently of their truth or falsehood, presumably by a variety of their other features; and this leaves the door open to representations causing pleasure even when we know them to be false, which is the possibility we need for the aesthetic case of taking pleasure in fictions. By the same token, such representations need not lead to a desire to make them true, that is, to bring the kinds of objects they represent into actual existence. Desire can always be explicated as wanting to make something possible actual, as indeed Kant explicates it; but approbation does not have that result.

The second point to note is that Mendelssohn suggests that while sometimes approbation is not converted into desire simply because it would not be possible for us to realize the object of approbation and therefore it would be irrational for us to desire it, he also suggests that we can voluntarily indulge our imagination and therefore stop with approbation rather than desire:

> It is another matter, however, when we intend to exercise our faculty of approbation and therefore bring it to greater perfection. With this intention, a man loves to give free rein to his imagination. He refashions things so that they are in accord with his inclination, so that they put his sense of pleasure and displeasure into a congenial play [*ein angenehmes Spiel*]. He does not want to be informed but to be moved. He willingly lets himself be deceived, and he lets things be represented as actual that are not in accord with his better understanding of the truth. His reason remains silent so long as he is busy following the pleasing allure of every byway of his fancy. (Mendelssohn, *Morgenstunden*, Lecture VII, in Mendelssohn 2012, p. 56)

Here Mendelssohn explicitly suggests that we can keep in mind at some level that an artistic representation is a fiction and yet enjoy it by being emotionally involved with it. He also suggests that setting our imagination into play despite our knowledge of truth is the aim of art and of our engagement with art. He even uses the term "play," of which Kant would subsequently make so much to make this point.[26] But he does not have to use the concept of disinterestedness to make it. The ordinary contrasts between truth and imagination or fancy, and between pleasure or approbation and actual desire, are enough to do so.

On Mendelssohn's account, the difference between approbation and desire can be passive or active. Approbation can just stop short of desire; our approbation (or disapprobation) might be stopped short of desire, which ordinarily leads to action, by our knowledge that what is before us is a fiction, and there is nothing we can do to change its outcome (there is nothing we can do to save Desdemona, whom Shakespeare has destined once and for all for death; the proverbial yokel running up to the stage to try to save her can only interrupt the performance of the play); or we might intentionally create images or fictions—art—in order to produce approbation but not desire. The important point for us, however, is just that Mendelssohn's distinctions between representations and represented things, and between approbation and desire, allow him to say the important thing that Kant also has to say—namely, that aesthetic experience begins with our response to appearances and images—without the obscurities and problems of Kant's explication of his concept of disinterestedness.

---

[26] I have revised Dahlstrom's translation of this passage by rendering *angenehmes* as "congenial" rather than "genial" but also rather than the Kantian "agreeable" precisely in order to leave open the affinity of Mendelssohn's conception of *Spiel* with Kant's, which might be obscured by using "agreeable" since Kant contrasts the merely agreeable to the beautiful.

Abbreviations

Apart from the *Critique of Pure Reason*, all references to Kant's works are to Kant's *Gesammelte Schriften, Ausgabe der Preußischen Akademie der Wissenschaften* (Berlin: De Gruyter, 1902 ff.). References to the *Critique of Pure Reason* are to the standard A and B pagination of the first and second editions. Translations are from *The Cambridge Edition of the Works of Immanuel Kant*.

The following abbreviations of individual works are used:

KU   Kritik der Urteilskraft / Critique of the Power of Judgment
KrV Kritik der reinen Vernunft / Critique of Pure Reason

Literature

Abacı, Uygar (2019): *Kant's Revolutionary Theory of Modality*. Oxford: Oxford University Press.
Allison, Henry E. (2001): *Kant's Theory of Taste: A Reading of the* Critique of Aesthetic Judgment. Cambridge: Cambridge University Press.
Baumgarten, Alexander Gottlieb (1983): *Meditationes philosophicae de nonnullis ad poema pertinentibus/Philosophische Betrachtungen über einige Bedingungen des Gedichtes*. Heinz Paetzold (Ed.). Hamburg: Felix Meiner.
Baumgarten, Alexander Gottlieb (2007): *Ästhetik*. 2 Volumes. Dagmar Mirbach (Ed.). Hamburg: Felix Meiner.
Beiser, Frederick (2009): *Diotima's Children: German Aesthetic Rationalism from Leibniz to Lessing*. Oxford: Oxford University Press.
Berger, Larissa (2022): *Kants Philosophie des Schönen: Eine kommentarische Interpretation zu den §§1–22 der* Kritik der Urteilskraft. Baden-Baden: Karl Alber.
Cooper, Anthony Ashley (third Earl of Shaftesbury) (1999): *Characteristicks of Men, Manners, Opinions, Times*. Vol. II. Philip Ayres (Ed.). Oxford: Clarendon Press.
Croce, Benedetto (1922): *Esthetic as Science of Expression and General Linguistics*. 2nd ed. Douglas Ainslie (Trans.). London: Macmillan.
Du Bos, Jean-Baptiste (1748): *Critical Reflections on Poetry, Painting and Music*. 3 Volumes. Thomas Nugent (Trans.). London: John Nourse.
Ginsborg, Hannah (2015): *The Normativity of Nature: Essays on Kant's* Critique of Judgement. Oxford: Oxford University Press.
Guyer, Paul (1993): *Kant and the Experience of Freedom*. Cambridge: Cambridge University Press.
Guyer, Paul (1997): *Kant and the Claims of Taste*. 2nd ed. Cambridge: Cambridge University Press.
Guyer, Paul (2005): "Kant on the Purity of the Ugly." In: Guyer, Paul (Ed.): *Values of Beauty: Historical Essays in Aesthetics*. Cambridge: Cambridge University Press, pp. 141–162.
Guyer, Paul (2020): *Reason and Experience in Mendelssohn and Kant*. Oxford: Oxford University Press.
Hughes, Fiona (2010): *Kant's* Critique of Aesthetic Judgement: *A Reader's Guide*. London: Continuum.
Hume, David (1987): *Essays Moral, Political, and Literary*. 2nd ed. Eugene F. Miller (Ed.). Indianapolis: Liberty Fund.
Hume, David (1998). *An Enquiry concerning the Principles of Morals*. Tom L. Beauchamp (Ed.). Oxford: Clarendon Press.

Kristeller, Paul Oskar (1951): "The Modern System of the Arts: A Study in the History of Aesthetics Part I." In: *Journal of the History of Ideas* 12. No. 4, pp. 496–527.
Kristeller, Paul Oskar (1952): "The Modern System of the Arts: A Study in the History of Aesthetics Part II." In: *Journal of the History of Ideas* 13. No. 1, pp. 17–46.
Kristeller, Paul Oskar (1980): *Renaissance Thought and the Arts: Collected Essays.* Princeton: Princeton University Press.
McMahon, Jennifer A. (2007): *Aesthetics and Material Beauty: Aesthetics Naturalized.* New York and Abingdon: Routledge.
Mendelssohn, Moses (1929, 1971): *Gesammelte Schriften Jubiläumsausgabe.* Vol. I. Fritz Bamberger, Elbogen, Ismar, Guttmann, Julius, Mittwoch, Eugen, Bar-Dayan, Haim, Rawidowicz, Simon, Strauss, Bruno, and Strauss, Leo (Eds.). Reprinted Stuttgart-Bad Cannstatt: Frommann-Holzboog.
Mendelssohn, Moses (1997): *Philosophical Writings.* Daniel O. Dahlstrom (Ed.). Cambridge: Cambridge University Press.
Mendelssohn, Moses (2012): *Last Works.* Bruce Rosenstock (Trans.). Bloomington: Indiana University Press.
Nehamas, Alexander (2007): *Only a Promise of Happiness: The Place of Beauty in a World of Art.* Princeton: Princeton University Press.
Pollok, Anne (2010): *Facetten des Menschen: Zur Anthropologie Moses Mendelssohns.* Hamburg: Felix Meiner.
Robinson, Jenefer (2005): *Deeper than Reason.* Oxford: Oxford University Press.
Stolnitz, Jerome (1961): "On the Origins of 'Aesthetic Disinterestedness.'" In: *Journal of Aesthetics and Art Criticism* 20. No. 2, pp. 131–143.
Wollheim, Richard (1987): *Painting as an Art.* Princeton: Princeton University Press.
Zuckert, Rachel (2007): *Kant on Beauty and Biology.* Cambridge: Cambridge University Press.

Larissa Berger
What Is It Like to Feel Beauty? The Complex Meaning of Kant's Thesis of Disinterestedness

Abstract: Kant's thesis of disinterestedness (TD), as put forward in § 2 of the *Critique of Judgment*, functions as his entry into the realm of beauty. I aim to show that TD has a complex meaning which can be unfolded on several levels. To get a proper theoretical grasp on this thesis one needs to take into account the notions of the free play of the faculties, form and purposiveness without a purpose. But since these notions are only available much later after disinterestedness has been introduced, and moreover, since these notions are only derived from TD, I will argue that there must be a more intuitive grasp on TD. This grasp is phenomenological: the pleasure in the beautiful feels disinterested, that is, detached from any desiring.

"The satisfaction that determines the judgment of taste is without any interest." (KU: 204) Having just revealed that the judgment of taste is grounded in a feeling of satisfaction (*Wohlgefallen*) or pleasure, Kant introduces the criterion 'without any interest' or, simply, the criterion of disinterestedness to make this pleasure distinguishable from any other feeling. Hence, the thesis of disinterestedness (TD) is Kant's entrance into the realm of beauty, and it marks off the starting point of Kant's overall argument to eventually reveal the transcendental foundations of judgments of taste. Not only because of this function TD is of greatest importance, but also because it accounts for the uniqueness of aesthetic experience. It is by disinterestedness that experiences of beauty are first and foremost distinguishable from moral experiences and experiences of the agreeable. Moreover, since TD in one way or another implies that one frees oneself from desires and needs, this thesis disentangles experiences of beauty from daily, non-aesthetic concerns. It is this way of accounting for the uniqueness and autonomous status of aesthetic experience which, I assume, made TD such a powerful and attractive tool for philosophers working on aesthetics in the past and in the present. Because of this prom-

---

Note: A similar (but not wholly identical) German version of this article has been published under the title "Wie fühlt sich Schönheit an? Zur Phänomenologie des interesselosen Wohlgefallens bei Kant" in *Kant-Studien* (cf. Berger 2022c).

https://doi.org/10.1515/9783110727685-003

inent status, a comprehensive understanding of Kant's initial thesis seems highly desirable. However, what TD means remains an unsettled issue in Kant-scholarship. Sometimes it is suggested that disinterestedness just amounts to the pleasure in the beautiful having no relation to the will or faculty of desire.[1] As Zangwill puts it "pleasure is disinterested when the route from the representation of the object to the response of pleasure entirely bypasses desire" (Zangwill 1992, pp. 149 f.).[2] Since Kant claims that an interest "always has at the same time a relation to the faculty of desire" (KU: 204), such a bypassing of desire can hardly be denied as one aspect of TD. Yet, I will show that this is not TD's full content. In the secondary literature, the following different or supplementary meanings of TD have been suggested: the object of pleasure does not have to exist but can be purely imagined or illusionary;[3] we do not have, or do not apply, any determinate concept of the beautiful object and, since an interest is assumed to be bound to concepts, we have no interest in the object;[4] the pleasure is not in the matter of the representation (i.e., sensations), but in its form.[5] Although I agree at least with the last thesis, I will argue that neither of these interpretations of TD exhausts its full meaning. Rather, I will show that TD has a *complex meaning* consisting of several layers. Most importantly, I will show that one of these layers is *phenomenological*. I will proceed as follows: First, I will give a sketch of Kant's definition of "pleasure" as put forward in § 10 of the Critique of Judgment. Second, I will provide a reconstruction of his definition of "interest" as put forth in § 2, and third, I will give an overview of several formulations of TD introduced by Kant right after this definition. Fourth, by drawing on the notions of the free play and form I will unfold two theoretical meanings of TD. Finally, I will show that these theoretical meanings are not yet accessible to the reader in § 2 which opens up the way for a third meaning—namely, a phenomenological meaning. I will argue that it is this phenomenological meaning of TD which allows Kant to enter the realm of beauty in the first place.

---

[1] See, for instance, "objects of beauty are not primarily related to the will" (Matthews 1997, p. 25; cf. Crawford 1974, p. 25).
[2] Cf. similarly Zangwill's notion of basic disinterestedness in this volume, pp. 61-65.
[3] Cf. Makkreel 1997, p. 121; Wenzel 2008, p. 20; Crowther 2010, pp. 71 f. For an explicit rejection of this interpretation cf. Fricke 1990, p. 25; Longuenesse 2006, p. 197.
[4] Cf. Guyer 1979, pp. 187 f., 190 and 199 f.; Meerbote 1982, p. 73. I disagree with such an intellectual conception of interest, which will become clearer in the second part of this article.
[5] Cf. Fricke 1990, pp. 26 f.

1 Kant's Definition of Pleasure

In a recent publication Paul Guyer has argued against a "phenomenological model of pleasure," replacing it with a so-called "dispositional [...] account" (Guyer 2018, p. 162): "there is no distinctive way that pleasure and pain feel, pleasure just consists in the disposition to remain in the state one finds pleasing" (Guyer 2018, p. 149). Strikingly, Guyer seems to reject that pleasure has any phenomenal character whatsoever:

> To be sure, some cases of pleasure must involve distinctive sensations, for there is a characteristic way or range of ways that a good Bordeaux tastes, and a different way that a good Burgundy tastes, and each is enjoyable; but it is less plausible that there is a distinctive feeling of pleasure, whether always the same or not, *in addition to* the characteristic Bordeaux taste and Burgundy taste. (Guyer 2018, p. 163)[6]

I do not oppose the view that Kant's understanding of pleasure includes something like a disposition to remain in the state one finds pleasurable.[7] Yet, I argue that this disposition can only be properly understood by drawing on a phenomenological model of pleasure.[8] In § 10, Kant offers the following definition of "pleasure":

> The consciousness of the causality of a representation with respect to the state of the subject, for m a i n t a i n i n g it [the subject] in that state, can here designate in general what is called pleasure; [...]. (KU: 220)

The crucial feature of this explanation is the notion of *maintaining*. In my pleasure I become conscious of a representation causing to maintain my current mental state, that is, the state of pleasure.[9] So far, so good. But why does it matter to me that the representation causes the maintenance or preservation of my current state? It does matter in case I *want to remain* in my current state. This is the dis-

---

[6] When it comes to pain, Guyer admits that "perhaps there is room for an account of pain that combines a phenomenological and a dispositional aspect" (Guyer 2018, p. 163).
[7] For the combination of a functional and a phenomenological approach to Kantian pleasure cf. Berger 2022b, pp. 265–268.
[8] With the terms "phenomenology" and "phenomenological," I refer to the "what-it-is-likeness" of conscious mental states. I do not refer to the movement in the history of philosophy associated with figures like Edmund Husserl or Maurice Merleau-Ponty. For a reading of Kant's aesthetic theory in the light of Husserl's phenomenology, cf. Kuspit 1974.
[9] It might sound somewhat unusual that pleasure is defined as a kind of *"consciousness."* I take this to mean that pleasure is a mental state by which we become conscious of something. In the *First Introduction to the Critique of Judgment* Kant in fact defines pleasure as a mental state or "state of the mind" (*Gemütszustand*; EEKU: 230).

positional component of "pleasure": I want the representation to maintain my current state because I want to remain in that same state.[10] In these terms, pleasure makes up the opposite of displeasure, the latter being "a representation that contains a ground for [...] removing or getting rid of them [the representations]" (KU: 220). But now the question arises: why do I want to remain in my current state? The most obvious answer is: because it has a positive quality or phenomenal character—*it feels good.* Hence, the phenomenological model of pleasure. Let me very briefly mention two further reasons for adopting this model. The first reason draws on the fact that Kant provides his definition of "pleasure" only in § 10, while this notion is of greatest importance already in §§ 1–9.[11] This procedure makes good sense once we acknowledge that the pleasure in the beautiful is endowed with a specific phenomenal character, or to be more precise, that it is *essentially* characterized by the way it feels. For then we can see clearly that Kant does not need to define "pleasure" in the first place because everybody has an intuitive —namely, phenomenological—grasp on what pleasure is. Second, there is explicit textual evidence for the thesis that pleasure is essentially characterized by its phenomenal character. Having just introduced another definition of pleasure in the *First Introduction*, Kant remarks:

> It can be readily seen here that pleasure or displeasure, since they are not kinds of cognition, cannot be explained by themselves at all, and *are felt*, not understood; hence they can be only inadequately explained through the influence that a representation has on the activity of the powers of the mind by means of this feeling. (EEKU: 231 f., my emphasis)

Pleasure is '*felt*, not understood.'[12] Thus, it is primarily characterized by the way it feels and can only be inadequately understood by giving a (conceptual) definition (such as a dispositional one).

---

10 Thus, with regard to the pleasure in the beautiful Kant claims that "it has a causality in itself, namely that of m a i n t a i n i n g the state of the representation of the mind and the occupation of the cognitive powers without a further aim" (KU: 222).
11 Note that the definition of "pleasure" from the *First Introduction* has been removed from the official introduction.
12 In the *Observations on the Feeling of the Beautiful and the Sublime* Kant already notes: "To be sure, we do one another an injustice when we dismiss one who does not see the value or the beauty of what moves or charms us by saying that he does not understand it. In this case it is not so much a matter of what the understanding sees but of what the feeling is sensitive to." (GSE: 225) See also Kant's remark in the *Metaphysics of Morals* that "pleasure and displeasure cannot be explained for themselves" (MS: 212).

I suggest that the Kantian conception of pleasure can be reconstructed by a threefold notion of maintenance which, most importantly, encompasses the phenomenal character of pleasure:[13]

(i) Pleasure is a feeling with a positive quality (phenomenal character) and, thus, the subject wants to maintain it.
(ii) Throughout the feeling of pleasure, the subject becomes conscious that a representation x causes the maintenance of the subject's current state (i.e., the state with the positive quality).
(iii) Because the subject wants to maintain her current state (i) and because the subject is conscious of the representation x causing to maintain that state (ii), the subject wants to maintain the representation x.

It is the third notion of maintenance which, *prima facie*, poses problems for any conception of disinterested pleasure. For, how can we conceive of the fact that the subject wants to maintain a certain representation without attributing to her any kind of desire? Before turning to this question, we shall take a look at Kant's definition of "interest."

2 Kant's Definition of Interest

In § 2, Kant gives the following definition of "interest:"

> The satisfaction that we combine with the representation of the existence of an object is called interest. Hence such a satisfaction has at the same time a relation to the faculty of desire, either as its determining ground or else as necessarily interconnected with its determining ground. (KU: 204)

The first thing to note is that Kant explicitly understands pleasure as a kind of satisfaction (*Wohlgefallen*) or pleasure.[14] Hence, the threefold notion of maintenance

---

[13] The threefold notion of maintenance harmonizes well with Zuckert's thesis that pleasure is endowed with "future-directedness" (Zuckert 2007, p. 234; cf. 2002, p. 240).
[14] There are interpreters who doubt or deny the status of an interest as a kind of pleasure, e.g., Matthews: "For example, we may take an interest in something because we believe it will bring pleasure, although we may feel no pleasure on the occasion of our interest" (Matthews 1997, p. 21; cf. Guyer 1979, pp. 174 f.). Such interpretations contradict Kant's definition of interest in KU: 204 as well as other formulations such as: "a satisfaction in the e x i s t e n c e of an object or of an action, i.e., some sort of interest" (KU: 207); "to have satisfaction in its existence, i.e., to take an interest in it" (KU: 209). However, against the backdrop of the whole *Analytic of the Beautiful* things appear

applies to interests. Second, we can identify two conditions that a satisfaction or pleasure must fulfil in order to count as an interest. I call these the *condition of existence* and the *condition of desiring:*

An interest is a pleasure
- that we take in the existence of an object (*condition of existence*)
- that has a relation to the faculty of desire (*condition of desiring*).

Let me briefly explain the meaning of both conditions by drawing on the two different kinds of interest: the interest in the agreeable and the interest in the good.

Condition of desiring: The condition of desiring says that an interest has a relation to the faculty of desire. The latter is "a being's power to be, through its representations, cause of the actuality of the objects of these representations" (KpV: 9 fn.). Being the cause of the actuality (*Wirklichkeit*) of an object means nothing but causing the existence of an object, that is, *producing an object*. Thus, the *condition of desiring* basically says that we want to produce a certain object. In the definition of "interest" quoted above, Kant differentiates two relations to the faculty of desire: the pleasure can either be its determining ground or it can be otherwise 'necessarily interconnected with its determining ground.' The first of these relations applies to the agreeable. The pleasure in the agreeable is immediately felt in a sensation (*Empfindung*), for instance, the taste of chocolate.[15] Like every pleasure, the pleasure in the agreeable is characterized by the threefold notion of maintenance: The subject wants to maintain her current mental state which is characterized by a positive quality; she is aware that a certain representation (e. g., the taste of chocolate) causes the maintenance of this state; thus, she wants to maintain the representation (the taste of chocolate). However, a sensation cannot stimulate the subject over a longer period of time. The taste of chocolate vanishes quickly.[16] Therefore, in order to maintain her state of pleasure the subject needs to be stimulated by further sensations: she needs further stimuli of the same kind and, hence,

---

less clear. For instance, the headlines of §§ 3 and 4 suggest that interest is not itself a kind of pleasure, but an addition to certain kinds of pleasures; for here Kant claims that "[t]he satisfaction in the a g r e e a b l e [or the good] is combined with interest" (KU: 205; cf. KU: 207). In total, the Kantian text is ambiguous.

15 See: "The a g r e e a b l e is that which pleases t h e s e n s e s i n s e n s a t i o n." (KU: 205)

16 This effect might be most obvious in the case of tastes and sounds. But even with visual sensations we can understand that one single sensation, for instance, the sensation of a certain color, only strikes us for a short moment.

she desires to produce "objects of the same sort" (KU: 207).[17] This is how the pleasure in the agreeable becomes a determining ground of the faculty of desire. Things are different when it comes to the good. Here, the pleasure is "else [...] necessarily interconnected" with the determining ground of the faculty of desire (KU: 204). More precisely, "in the case of the upper [faculty of desire], it [the pleasure] follows only from the determination of the faculty through the moral law" (KU: 178).[18] In the case of the morally good the (upper) faculty of desire or, rather, the will is determined by the moral law. The will is enlivened by this determination and this enlivening activity of the will is experienced as a feeling of pleasure.[19] Hence, the pleasure in the good is nothing but an activity of the will as being felt. Understood this way the pleasure in the good obviously fulfils the *condition of desiring*.

Condition of existence: What does it mean that a pleasure is taken in 'the existence of an object'? Regarding the pleasure in the agreeable, I suggest the following: we take this pleasure immediately in a sensation. Kant identifies the latter as "what is real in an empirical representation" (KU: 203). Furthermore, something "real [...] corresponds to it" (KrV: A166).[20] Following Chignell, I take this to mean that the real objects in this world cause sensations as states of the subject.[21] In that way, a sensation is dependent on the existence of the real object corresponding to it. Since the pleasure in the agreeable is immediately taken in a sensation, it is likewise dependent on the existence of the object corresponding to this sensation. Hence, the pleasure in the agreeable is a *pleasure in 'the existence of the object'* because it is immediately taken in a sensation which is caused by an existing object. Again, things are different regarding the pleasure in the good. As argued above, this pleasure amounts to a determination of the will as being felt. A will being determined is nothing but a willing to produce something, that is, to cause the *existence* of an object.[22] Moreover, a willing always presupposes a purpose

---

17 Note that the subject does not need to have a definite concept of the agreeable object or, rather, the agreeable sensation. At the most basic level she will just want *more of this (whatever this is)*.
18 This quote focuses on the interest in the morally good. When it comes to the useful, that is, the "mediately good" (KU: 209), the will is determined by a hypothetical imperative in combination with a pleasure in the agreeable.
19 See: "The state of mind of a will determined by something, however, is in itself already a feeling of pleasure and is identical with it" (KU: 222).
20 Cf. KrV: A143/B182; A166/B207.
21 See: "Die Empfindung ist der subjektive Zustand, den die realen Dinge (äußere Gegenstände oder unser eigener Geist) in uns hervorrufen, welche als Dinge in der Welt (bzw. als Zustände unseres eigenen empirischen Ichs) einen objektiven Status innehaben." (Chignell 2015, p. 496)
22 Thereby, I do not want to imply that each determination of the will *de facto* results in an act of producing the corresponding object.

as the matter of the faculty of desire.²³ The "matter of the power of desire" is "an object whose existence is desired" (KpV: 21). Hence, a pleasure in the good, which is a felt activity of the will as being determined by a certain purpose, can be understood as a *pleasure in 'the existence of an object.'*

I take Kant's conception of interest in the *Critique of Judgment* to differ crucially from his conception of interest in the *Groundwork* and the *Metaphysics of Morals*. In the latter writings, an interest is characterized by a determination of the will, that is, the *upper* faculty of desire; such a determination of the will always proceeds by means of a law of reason.²⁴ This is an intellectual conception of interest in that it presupposes the application of concepts. By contrast, following § 2 of the *Critique of Judgment* an interest is merely characterized by a relation to the faculty of desire in general, that is, either the upper or the lower faculty of desire where the latter is not determined by concepts.²⁵ Kant here defends a broad conception of interest according to which also the merely sensible (non-intellectual) pleasure in the agreeable counts as an interest. Only by assuming this broad conception we can make sense, first, of "[a]greeableness" being "also valid for nonrational animals" (KU: 210).²⁶ Second, only this broad conception is in line with the pleasure in the agreeable being non-conceptual, where the latter marks off the main difference to the pleasure in the good. As Kant puts it, "[t]he agreeable, which as such represents the object solely in relation to sense, must first be brought under principles of reason through the concept of an end before it can be called good as an object of the will" (KU: 208). It is important to keep in mind that Kant makes use of the broad or non-intellectual conception of interest

---

23 Cf. MS: 384f., 389.
24 See: "the dependence of a contingently determinable will on principles of reason is called an interest" (GMS: 413 fn.; cf. 459); "a connection of pleasure with the faculty of desire that the understanding judges to hold as a general rule (though only for the subject) is called an interest" (MS: 212).
25 This broad conception is in line with Kant's conception of "practical pleasure" as being introduced in the *Metaphysics of Morals:* "That pleasure which is necessarily connected with desire (for an object whose representation affects feeling in this way) can be called *practical pleasure,* whether it is the cause or the effect of the desire." (MS: 212) Note that practical pleasure is contrasted with contemplative pleasure (i.e., the pleasure in the beautiful) by the *condition of existence:* "On the other hand, that pleasure which is not necessarily connected with desire for an object, and so is not at bottom a pleasure in the existence of the object of a representation but is attached only to the representation by itself, can be called merely contemplative pleasure or inactive delight. We call feeling of the latter kind of pleasure taste." (MS: 212)
26 Some interpreters take the interest in the agreeable to include a determination of the will by a law of reason (cf. Allison 2001, p. 91; Fricke 1990, p. 17; Guyer 1979, p. 187; Hilgers 2017, p. 17; Zammito 1992, p. 109; Zuckert 2007, p. 260). On this view, animals could not or, at least, only improperly have an interest in the agreeable (cf. Allison 2001, p. 361; Fricke 1990, p. 17; Zuckert 2007, pp. 259f.).

when it comes to the thesis of disinterestedness. For, against this backdrop, disinterestedness cannot merely amount to, or be grounded in, the non-conceptuality of the pleasure in the beautiful.[27]

In sum, an interest is characterized by the following (refined) conditions:

An interest is a pleasure
- that we take in the existence of an object (*condition of existence*)
   (a) by taking the pleasure immediately in a sensation, the latter being immediately caused by an existing object,
   (b) or by the pleasure being a felt willing to cause the existence of an object
- that has a relation to the faculty of desire (*condition of desiring*)
   (a) in terms of the pleasure determining the faculty of desire to produce more sensations of the same kind
   (b) or in terms of the pleasure being an activity of the will as being felt.

We shall keep in mind this understanding of interest when now turning to the thesis of disinterestedness.

3 Kant's Formulations of the Thesis of Disinterestedness

In its most general form, the thesis of disinterestedness (TD) says: "The satisfaction that determines the judgment of taste is without any interest." (KU: 204) In the course of § 2, Kant gives the following more specific formulations of TD:

TD1 But if the question is whether something is beautiful, one does not want to know whether there is anything that is or that could be at stake, for us or for someone else, in the existence of the thing, but rather how we judge it in mere contemplation (intuition or reflection). (KU: 204)

TD2 One only wants to know whether the mere representation of the object is accompanied with satisfaction in me, however indifferent I might be with regard to the existence of the object of the representation. (KU: 205)

TD3 One can easily see that to say that it is beautiful and to prove that I have taste what matters is what I make of this representation in myself, not how I depend on the existence of the object. (KU: 205)

---

27 For this latter interpretation, cf. Guyer 1979, pp. 187 f., 190 and 199 f.; Meerbote 1982, p. 73; Gorodeisky in this volume, pp. 140 f.

TD4 One must not be in the least biased in favor of the existence of the thing, but must be entirely indifferent in this respect in order to play the judge in matters of taste. (KU: 205)

One can differentiate two slightly different theses: a merely negative thesis on how the pleasure is not to be characterized, and a positive thesis on how it is to be characterized instead.[28] The negative thesis basically denies the *condition of existence:* one must be indifferent with regard to the existence of the object of pleasure. Furthermore, in TD3 Kant claims that one should not 'depend on the existence of the object.' Since the willing or desiring of an object surely implies a dependence on it (in terms of a need), this independence amounts to an indirect denial of the *condition of wanting*. Thus, both the conditions of existence and desiring are denied. In its strongest version, we can formulate the negative thesis of disinterestedness (TD-) as follows:[29]

TD- In a judgment of beauty, one must be indifferent regarding the existence of the object (denial of the *condition of existence*), and one must not be dependent on the existence of the object (denial of the *condition of desiring*).

The formulations TD1–4 also contain a positive thesis of disinterestedness (TD+). It says that we feel the pleasure in the beautiful in the 'mere representation of the object,' which is obviously meant to contrast with the *condition of existence*. Moreover, TD+ hints at a certain activity underlying the judgment of taste or, rather, the pleasure in the beautiful. I 'make' something 'of this representation in myself' and I 'judge it in mere contemplation (intuition or reflection).' Thereby, Kant somewhat obscurely hints at the free play of the faculties.

TD+ In a judgment of beauty, one only wants to know whether the representation of the object is accompanied with pleasure in me, and what matters is what I make of this representation of the object in myself, that is, in an activity of reflection.

---

[28] A similar distinction between a negative and a positive meaning of the thesis of disinterestedness has been suggested by McCloskey (1987, p. 35) and, within a systematic framework, by Riggle (2016, p. 3); cf. Gorodeisky (in this volume, pp. 139 f. and 145).

[29] This strong version of TD- only applies to pure judgments of taste. When it comes to impure judgments of taste, the pleasure in the beautiful gets mixed with a pleasure, or rather, an interest in the agreeable and, thus, the subject cannot be completely indifferent with regard to the existence of the object. However, in § 2, Kant is only concerned with pure judgments of taste.

In what follows, I will try to shed some light on these variants of TD and explore their meaning. Thereby, I will also touch on the question of whether Kant wants to defend the rather absurd view that we do not care at all for beautiful objects. Should I really be indifferent with regard to someone destroying Monet's *Poppy Field in a Hollow near Giverny* in front of my eyes while visiting Boston's Museum of Fine Arts?[30] And assuming that I want to maintain the representation corresponding to my pleasure (*notions of maintenance*), how can I be indifferent regarding the existence of the representation?[31]

4 Two Theoretical Meanings of the Thesis of Disinterestedness

4.1 A Pleasure Felt Immediately in an Activity of Reflection

In TD+ Kant hints at the fact that the pleasure in the beautiful is based on an inner activity ('what I make of this representation in myself'). We will see now that this is one key to understand the deeper meaning of TD. To do so, we shall ask in what the pleasure in the beautiful is taken as compared to the agreeable and the good.

The pleasure in the agreeable is felt immediately in a sensation. Since a sensation is caused immediately by an existing object, the pleasure in the agreeable is a pleasure in the *existence of an object*. Hence, a disinterested pleasure, that is, the pleasure in the beautiful, cannot be felt immediately in a sensation. This is confirmed by a passage from the *First Introduction:*

> In the aesthetic judgment of sense [i.e., the judgment about the agreeable] it is that sensation [of pleasure] which is *immediately produced by the empirical intuition* of the object, in the aesthetic judgment of reflection [i.e., the judgment of beauty], however, it is that sensation [of pleasure] which *the harmonious play of the two faculties of cognition* in the power of judgment, imagination and understanding, produces in the subject [...]. (EEKU: 224; my emphasis)

The pleasure in the beautiful is not felt immediately in an 'empirical intuition,' that is, a (objective) sensation, but in the 'harmonious play of the two faculties of cognition'—the free and harmonious play of imagination and understanding. Kant makes a similar claim in § 9:

---

30 Cf. Crawford 1974, p. 53.
31 See for this rather prominent problem Allison (2001, pp. 85f.) and Ginsborg (2008, p. 63).

> Now this merely subjective (aesthetic) judging of the object, or of the representation through which the object is given, precedes the pleasure in it, and is the ground of this pleasure in the harmony of the faculties of cognition; [...]. (KU: 218)[32]

The pleasure in the beautiful is based on a 'merely subjective…judging of the object,' which is nothing but the free and harmonious play of the faculties. Furthermore, this play of the faculties is a kind of 'judging' or, moreover, an activity of reflection. It is this activity at which Kant was hinting in TD+ with the notions of 'reflection' and 'what I make of this representation in myself.' I suppose that TD, at least partly, means that the pleasure in the beautiful is not felt immediately in the representation of the object, but rather in an inner activity of the subject. Of course, this does not mean that the representation of the object does not matter at all for the pleasure in the beautiful. For it is this representation that is dealt with in the free play of the faculties. But it is crucial to see that the pleasure in the beautiful is felt only indirectly in it. In that spirit, we can put forward the following provisionary reconstruction of TD:

TD_{R1a} The pleasure in the beautiful is
  i. a pleasure felt immediately in an inner activity of the subject
  ii. a pleasure felt only indirectly in the representation of the beautiful object.

Put his way TD does not suffice to detach the disinterested pleasure in the beautiful from the interested pleasure in the good. For the pleasure in the good is also felt immediately in an inner activity of the subject—namely, an activity of the will. As a felt activity of the will the pleasure in the good fulfils the *conditions of desiring and existence* and, hence, it qualifies for being an interest. In order to detach the disinterested pleasure in the beautiful from the interest in the good we have to add that the former is not felt in an activity of the will or the faculty of desire:

TD_{R1b} The pleasure in the beautiful is
  i. a pleasure felt immediately in an inner activity of the subject which is not an activity of the will or the faculty of desire
  ii. a pleasure felt only indirectly in the representation of the beautiful object.

---

[32] This quote is highly complex. For a detailed analysis, cf. Berger 2022a, pp. 500–503.

Characterized in this way, the disinterested pleasure in the beautiful is neither a pleasure in the existence of an object nor does it presuppose the desiring or willing of an object. But why does it not produce any desiring or willing?[33]

This latter questions relate to the above-mentioned question of whether we must really be completely indifferent with regard to the beautiful object. If I want to maintain my currently felt pleasure in the beautiful, I want to maintain the inner activity in which the pleasure is immediately taken, that is, the free and harmonious play of the faculties. However, as already noted, this pleasure presupposes a representation of the beautiful object, that is, something that the faculties can play with. Hence, I cannot be totally indifferent with regard to this representation. This becomes clear in the following passage:

> This pleasure is also in no way practical, neither like that from the pathological ground of agreeableness nor like that from the intellectual ground of the represented good. But yet it has a causality in itself, namely that of m a i n t a i n i n g the state of the representation itself and the occupation of the cognitive powers without a further aim. We l i n g e r over the consideration of the beautiful because this consideration strengthens and reproduces itself, [...]. (KU: 222)

The pleasure in the beautiful makes me to maintain 'the state of the representation itself'—I want the representation of the beautiful object to persist. Therefore, I linger in the presence of this representation, for instance, the presence of *Poppy Field in a Hollow.* Thus, I am far from being indifferent with regard to someone destroying this painting in front of my eyes. Put otherwise: I want the representation of the beautiful object to *stay present* and I *linger* in the representation's presence. However, I do not desire the object since I do not want to produce it or possess it or carry out any action with regard to it.[34] In that way, the pleasure in the beautiful is 'in no way practical.' I suggest that we can replace the two conditions for an interest with two conditions for a disinterested pleasure so that the latter still fits with pleasure's notions of maintenance:

A disinterested pleasure
– is not taken in the existence of the object, but the representation of the object must remain *present* to maintain the pleasure (*condition of presence*)

---

[33] Some authors explicitly defend the thesis that, despite not being based on any interest, the pleasure in the beautiful can give rise to an interest (cf. Allison 2001, p. 96; Crawford 1974, p. 53).
[34] It might appear that Kant's understanding of desire in terms of bringing about the existence of something is too narrow, since it does at a first glance not apply to activities such as running which do, however, not qualify as being disinterested. But even in a case such as running we can make sense of causing something's existence, for example, the existence of my physical or mental health.

- has no relation to desire, but one lingers over the representation of the beautiful object (*condition of lingering*).

It might seem odd that, on Kant's account, the *conditions of presence and lingering* do not include or imply any kind of desire. Why does my state of maintaining the representation of a certain object and lingering over it not include a desire for this object? Speaking with Kant, we could respond that a desire necessarily has practical implications in that we necessarily aim at bringing something about, causing something's existence or, at the least, carrying out any kind of action. Remember that for Kant the faculty of desire is nothing but "a being's power to be, through its representations, cause of the actuality of the objects of these representations" (CPrR: 9 fn.). A desire always includes the intention (broadly understood) to act accordingly (e.g., to produce something, buy something etc.), although this intention might not always lead to an action.[35] In the case of beauty, where just the continuing presence of the representation is required, no need to cause something's existence or to carry out any action with regard to the object arises in the first place. No action is needed, not even in terms of a mere intention to act. Of course, to accept this thought, we need to accept that merely lingering over the presence of the object does not qualify as an *action* or, to be more precise, that mere reflection is not a kind of action.[36]

Perhaps to some contemporary readers Kant's understanding of desire in terms of an intended action to bring something about might appear too restrictive. Still, I think we can make sense of desires being absent in the case of maintaining a representation and lingering over it. Systematically speaking, there seems to be a crucial difference between desires as being actualized and something like the disposition to desire something once the relevant object has disappeared. Consider the following example. While riding on a train, I am reading my copy of the third Critique. For my activity of reading to continue, it is important that my

---

[35] This intention must be understood broadly since, in cases of the lower faculty of desire, it is not conceptualized.

[36] In real-world cases, this might be a tricky issue. Imagine I go to Boston's *Museum of Fine Arts*. In an ideal Kantian beauty experience, I would just by chance stumble across Monet's *Poppy Field in a Hollow*, look at it, start to reflect on it and enter a state of pleasure in the beautiful. I would recognize that this is an experience of pleasure, but I would not intentionally decide to keep this experience alive or stay in front of the painting. It would merely happen to me. If, however, I intentionally approach this painting, intentionally stare at it because I assume to get pleasure form it and, thus, intentionally maintain my visual experience of it, this does not qualify as a beauty experience. Most real-world cases are probably to be situated somewhere in between these two cases. I might, for instance, intentionally approach the painting, but nevertheless be able to enter a state of the free play which maintains itself.

copy of the third Critique remains present and that I linger over the text (instead of looking out of the window etc.). Yet, I am experiencing no desire towards my copy of the third Critique. At the train station, while watching the train departing, I realize that I left my copy on the train. Immediately, I experience a desire to either get my old copy back or to buy a new one. Regarding desire, there is, obviously, a crucial difference between my state while reading my copy of the third Critique and my state after having lost it: whereas in the latter state, I surely have a desire as being actualized, in the earlier case, such a desire as being actualized is absent and one could, at best, say that I have a *disposition* to desire my copy of the third Critique to be actualized under certain circumstances. Similarly, while beholding *Poppy Field in a Hollow* and lingering over it, I experience no desire towards it —no desire gets actualized. Yet, when someone destroys the painting in front of my eyes, a desire to make the painting whole again is instantiated. Whereas in cases of the Kantian agreeable and the good a desire is always actualized, in the case of beauty such an actualized desire is absent, and we could at best account for a disposition to desire the object which would be actualized once the object has disappeared. Note, however, that whenever this disposition *is* actualized, the corresponding desire does not amount or contribute to the experience of beauty. Once *Poppy Field in a Hollow* gets destroyed in front of my eyes and I desire to make it whole again, I do not have a beauty experience.[37]

4.2 A Pleasure Taken in the Object's Form

We just saw that, despite being a pleasure felt immediately in an inner activity, the pleasure in the beautiful bears a connection to the representation of the beautiful object. With regard to TD, it is important to see which aspect of this representation matters. Kant makes the pleasure in the beautiful rely on the form of the representation and not on its matter. Remember that the pleasure in the agreeable is immediately felt in sensations, the latter being "the *matter* of the representations" (KU: 224; my emphasis). Understood this way, sensations are bound to the existing object and, thus, the pleasure in the agreeable meets the *condition of existence*. Un-

---

[37] This discussion might be understood in analogy to Kant's theory of inclination and respect (*Achtung*). Is it possible to perform an action x out of respect although I have a disposition in terms of an inclination to do x which remains, however, inactive? Put otherwise: can I be affected by a certain object or action x in terms of respect but not in terms of my (dispositional) inclination for x? Can I, analogously, experience a feeling of disinterested pleasure while beholding an object x although I have a disposition to desire x which, however, remains inactive? Perhaps these questions could only be answered by empirical psychology.

like sensations, the form of a representation is not being passively received, but it is achieved throughout an activity of synthesis carried out by the imagination.[38] In that manner, the form of a representation is not a mere effect caused by something existing, but it crucially depends on an inner activity of the subject. We shall remind ourselves of how the pleasure in the agreeable meets the *condition of desiring*. Sensations are merely momentary stimuli which cannot maintain the corresponding state of pleasure over a longer period of time. Since one wants to maintain the pleasure, one needs further stimuli and consequently desires to produce "objects of the same sort" (KU: 207). In contrast, the pleasure in the beautiful is based on the form of an object,[39] which is achieved by an activity of synthesis. And this activity can in some cases be maintained without further input, that is, further stimuli; this is what happens whenever the imagination is playing freely with forms. Therefore, the pleasure grounded in a form, that is, the pleasure grounded in the imagination's playing with forms, can be maintained without further input. Here is a second, deeper meaning of TD:

TD_{R2a} The pleasure is not based on the mere matter of the representation by which something existing is passively given to us but on the form of the representation which is achieved by an activity of synthesis carried out by the subject.[40]

This reconstruction of TD does not suffice to detach the pleasure in the beautiful from the interest in the good. Yet, one can apply the contrast of matter and form at another level. The pleasure in the beautiful has a twofold relation to the notion of form. In addition to being based on the form of the representation, the pleasure in the beautiful is also based on a mere form of purposiveness, that is, a (subjective) purposiveness without a purpose.[41] Purposes tell us "what the thing is supposed to

---

[38] For this contrast of matter and form, cf. KrV: A20/B34.
[39] Cf. KU: 223.
[40] Similar reconstructions of TD are found in Fricke (1990, pp. 25 ff.) and Crowther (2010, p. 72). For Zuckert TD consists in the pleasure of the beautiful being felt in a form which we are unable to subsume under a concept (cf. Zuckert 2007, pp. 262 f.).
[41] Of course, what exactly the latter means remains a highly controversial matter. Very briefly, I would tell the following story. Subjective purposiveness occurs whenever a given material (i.e., a manifold of sensations) fits with our faculties of cognition (i.e., imagination and understanding). This is the case whenever the imagination can synthesize the given material to a form and the understanding does or could apply a determinate concept. Here, imagination and understanding stand in "the disposition [...] for cognition in general" (KU: 238). Whenever such a disposition for cognition in general is instantiated on the occasion of a certain given material, the latter is called subjectively purposive. Crucially, in the case of beauty we become aware of the instantiation

be" (KU: 227), and purposiveness occurs whenever a given material fits together with 'what the thing is supposed to be.' In that way, purposes make up the *matter* of purposiveness.[42] A purpose would, at least potentially, qualify to determine the will—a concept of what a thing is supposed to be can determine our will to bring that very same thing about. This is exactly what happens in the case of the good: a purpose determines the will, and the will being determined is experienced as a pleasure in the good.[43] Therefore, if the pleasure in the beautiful were based on a purposiveness *with* a purpose, that is, on a purposiveness with matter, it would turn out to be a willing as being felt and, hence, an interest. Adding this to our reconstruction of TD, we end up with the following:

TD_{R2b} The pleasure in the beautiful
  i. does not rely on the mere matter of the representation by which something existing is passively given to us, but on the form of the representation which is achieved by an activity of synthesis carried out by the subject.
  ii. is based on a form of purposiveness, that is, a purposiveness without a purpose, and, thus, does not presuppose a purpose by which the will could potentially be determined.[44]

4.3 A Structural Problem

We reconstructed TD in terms of the pleasure in the beautiful (1) not being a pleasure in a mere sensation, but in an inner activity which is not an activity of the will, and (2) in terms of being independent of the two kinds of matter (i.e., the matter of representations and the matter of purposiveness). We have already seen that TD, understood in this way, does not imply complete indifference or ignorance with

---

of the disposition for cognition in general by means of our feeling of pleasure, that is, without applying the concept of a purpose (and even without applying any concept of the corresponding object). In this way, beauty instantiates a purposiveness without a purpose. For a detailed version of this view cf. Berger 2022a, pp. 604–612 and 643–648.

42 See: "Thus we can at least observe a purposiveness concerning form, even without basing it in a purpose (as the matter of the *nexus finalis*), and notice it in objects, although in no other way than by reflection." (KU: 220)

43 See: "Both [the useful and the morally good] always involve the concept of an end, hence the relation of reason to (at least possible) willing, and consequently a satisfaction in the e x i s t e n c e of an object or of an action, i.e., some sort of interest." (KU: 207)

44 Similarly, Crawford seems to interpret the deeper meaning of TD with regard to formal purposiveness (cf. Crawford 1974, pp. 38 f.).

regard to the beautiful object. For we want the representation of the object to remain present (*condition of presence*), and we want to linger over beholding that object (*condition of lingering*). Another challenge is harder to meet. We obviously take a strong interest in seeing or hearing works of art (e.g., we go to museums, concerts etc.). But TD precludes that the judgment of taste "ground[s] any interest" (KU: 205 fn.). Perhaps the best solution to this challenge lies in assuming a kind of meta-interest grounded in the judgment of taste. Despite being bound to the judgment of taste, this meta-interest does not itself amount to a *pleasure in the beautiful*. It falls under the following general class of meta-interests: since all pleasures contribute to our overall happiness, we take a general meta-interest (more precisely, an interest in the agreeable) in having pleasurable experiences.[45] By contributing to our overall happiness, we take such a meta-interest in experiencing pleasures in the beautiful. But, again, this meta-interest is not itself a (disinterested) pleasure in the beautiful.

There is still another challenge for TD. In the two reconstructions of its deeper meaning, we had to rely on the notions of the free play, the form of the representation and the formal purposiveness. But all of these notions are not yet available in § 2. These notions are only introduced in the course of the second and third moment. In general, it is not a big problem for a thesis or theory to unfold its full meaning successively. But in the case of TD things are not that easy. For, the notions of the free play, form and formal purposiveness are all derived from TD. Put otherwise, TD is the starting point of Kant's overall argument by which all latter theses are to be reached. Thus, there must be a meaning of TD which is already accessible on the stage of § 2. We seem to be in need of a further, theoretically less demanding meaning of TD. This becomes also clear once it is asked how Kant argues for TD in the first place.

Does Kant offer any argument for his thesis that the pleasure in the beautiful is disinterested? In § 2 as well as in the ongoing of the first moment Kant does not offer any explicit argument. This seems striking insofar as one might think that a desire would essentially belong to each kind of pleasure.[46] But maybe there is an argument implicitly included in the text. One such argument that has been suggested in the secondary literature—the so-called "elimination argument" (Crawford 1974, p. 42)—proceeds as follows:[47]

---

[45] See: "All satisfaction (it is said or thought) is itself sensation (of a pleasure). Hence everything that pleases, just because it pleases, is agreeable" (KU: 205 f.).
[46] See especially the entry "Lust" in Grimm's dictionary: "lust, *heftiges verlangen, begierde: appetitus*" (Grimm 1885, p. 1314).
[47] Cf. Allison 2001, pp. 90–94; Ameriks 2003, p. 294; and Schmalzried in this volume, pp. 220-222.

P1   All interest is either a pleasure in the agreeable or a pleasure in the good.
P2   The pleasure in the beautiful is neither a pleasure in the agreeable nor a pleasure in the good.
Therefore   The pleasure in the beautiful is not an interest (i.e., it is disinterested).

This argument fits well with the fact that Kant *de facto* contrasts the pleasure in the beautiful with the pleasures in the agreeable and the good. However, Kant never argues for there to be only two kinds of interest, that is, the pleasures in the agreeable and the good (P1).[48] Rather, he includes this assumption without further support in his definition of "interest:" "such a satisfaction has at the same time a relation to the faculty of desire, *either* as its determining ground *or* else as necessarily interconnected with its determining ground" (KU: 204, my emphasis). More importantly, it is not Kant's strategy to argue for TD by presupposing that the pleasure in the beautiful is to be detached from the pleasures in the agreeable and the good (P2). In fact, his argument goes the other way around: because the pleasure in the beautiful is disinterested it differs crucially from the pleasures in the agreeable and the good.[49] Considering Kant's overall account of the pleasure in the beautiful, there would be other criteria available to detach this pleasure from the pleasures in the agreeable and the good. For instance, unlike the pleasure in the agreeable the pleasure in the beautiful is grounded in an activity of reflection; and unlike the pleasure in the good the pleasure in the beautiful does not presuppose determinate concepts.[50] But the notions of the free play and non-conceptuality are derived from TD in the first place.[51] Hence, if we do not want to make Kant's argument circular, we cannot rely on the free play and non-conceptuality to

---

48 Cf. similarly Crawford 1974, p. 43. See also Kant's rather cautious remark: "especially *if we can be certain* that there are not more kinds of interest than those that are to be mentioned now" (KU: 205, my emphasis).
49 See especially the "comparison" of the pleasures in the agreeable, beautiful, and good in KU: 209.
50 See: "In order to find something good, I must always know what sort of thing the object is supposed to be, i.e., I must have a concept of it. I do not need that in order to find beauty in something. [...] The satisfaction in the beautiful must depend upon reflection on an object that leads to some sort of concept (it is indeterminate which), and is thereby also distinguished from the agreeable, which rests entirely on sensation." (KU: 207)
51 See: "But this universality cannot originate from concepts. For there is no transition from concepts to the feeling of pleasure or displeasure (except in pure practical laws, which however bring with them an interest of the sort that is not combined with the pure judgment of taste)." (KU: 211) Kant's argument for the free play starts from the premise that the pleasure is universal, where the latter thesis is derived from TD in § 6 (cf. KU: 211).

argue for TD. Crucially, this latter problem applies to *all* other arguments for TD one could conceive of. For instance, one could try to argue for TD by means of the free play of the faculties underlying the pleasure.[52] Kant seems to hint at such an argument in the following passage:

> That is b e a u t i f u l which pleases in the mere judging (thus not by means of the sensation of sense nor in accordance with a concept of the understanding). From this it follows of itself that it must please without any interest. (KU: 267)

Once he has established the free play of the faculties, Kant could argue that TD 'follows' from the pleasure being grounded in the free play (mostly, to prove that his reasoning so far was successful). However, to establish the free play as the grounding of the pleasure in the first place, Kant relies on TD.[53] Since the free play is derived from TD, the latter cannot be derived from the free play in the first place.[54]

All arguments for TD one could conceive of seem to fail. But should we conclude that Kant introduces TD as unsupported conjecture?

5 The Phenomenological Meaning of the Thesis of Disinterestedness

To see whether there is a less theoretically demanding meaning of TD already available in § 2 and whether there is some argumentative support for this thesis, we shall have another look at Kant's formulations of TD in § 2:

TD1 But if the question is whether something is beautiful, one does not want to know whether there is anything that is or that could be at stake, for us or

---

52 See the following diagnosis by Guyer: "the fact that the disinterestedness of aesthetic response is a consequence of its explanation as due to the harmony of imagination and understanding, rather than *vice versa*" (Guyer 1979, p. 169; cf. p. 178).
53 The same would hold true if one wanted to argue for TD by means of the pleasure in the beautiful being a pleasure in the form of the representation and the form of purposiveness.
54 One could imagine Kant's argument being turned upside-down. Here, Kant would start his argument by the presupposition that beauty experiences have their basis in what is called the free and harmonious play of the faculties, and from that he would conclude that experiences of beauty become manifest to awareness as a feeling of disinterested pleasure. However, it would be highly unconvincing to merely presuppose the free play of the faculties as the basis of beauty experiences. It is way more convincing to follow Kant's own argument and start off by beauty experiences as given to us, viz., by their disinterested character (cf. the following section).

for someone else, in the existence of the thing, but rather how we judge it in mere contemplation (intuition or reflection). (KU: 204)

TD2 One only wants to know whether the mere representation of the object is accompanied with satisfaction in me, however indifferent I might be with regard to the existence of the object of the representation. (KU: 205)

TD3 One can easily see that to say that it is beautiful and to prove that I have taste what matters is what I make of this representation in myself, not how I depend on the existence of the object. (KU: 205)

TD4 One must not be in the least biased in favor of the existence of the thing, but must be entirely indifferent in this respect in order to play the judge in matters of taste. (KU: 205)

Strikingly, Kant uses formulations like 'one does not,' 'one only wants to know,' 'one can easily see,' and 'one must not.' These formulations suggest that there is no doubt about the pleasure in the beautiful being disinterested; rather, it is suggested that TD is obvious and widely accepted.[55] Remember that, as shown above, pleasure in general is characterized by a certain phenomenal character. Since everyone knows what it is like to feel pleasure, Kant does not have to define pleasure in the first place. I suggest that it is similar with regard to the pleasure in the beautiful being disinterested. 'One can easily see' (or rather *feel*) that the pleasure in the beautiful is disinterested, because it is qualitatively experienced as disinterested. Thus, TD has a *phenomenological meaning*. Because of this latter meaning, Kant neither has to explain the meaning of TD nor put forward an argument for TD; his readers already have an immediate, namely, phenomenological awareness of what the pleasure in the beautiful feels like. Due to their own experiences of beauty, Kant's readers are aware that beauty feels disinterested.[56]

There is further support for TD's phenomenological meaning. The *Analytic of the Beautiful* is organized alongside the four moments of the table of judgment. The four moments of the *Analytic* each apply to the judgment of taste as well as the pleasure in the beautiful.[57] The first moment in which TD is introduced corresponds to the moment of *quality*. But what are we to understand by the quality of a feeling? The most obvious answer is that the quality of a feeling amounts

---

55 Guyer emphasizes that in § 2, Kant appeals to our "pretheoretic intuitions" (Guyer 1979, p. 174) and a kind of "common consent" (Guyer 1979, p. 176).

56 Wenzel briefly hints at a phenomenological meaning of TD (cf. Wenzel 2000, p. 80). Other authors explicitly deny such a phenomenological meaning, for instance Guyer (1979, pp. 203 f.), Kern (2000, p. 21) and Kulenkampff (1994, p. 74).

57 This is clear from the fact that in the second and third *Explication of the Beautiful* Kant determines the pleasure (and not the judgment) as universal and necessary (cf. KU: 219 and 240).

to its phenomenal character. Hence, the quality of disinterestedness would amount to a description of the pleasure's phenomenal character.[58]

The question arises of what it is like to feel disinterested pleasure. At this point, we should remind ourselves of the *conditions of existence and desiring*, which characterize an interest. It is questionable whether the condition of existence has any influence on the phenomenal character of an interest. By contrast, it is quite plausible that the condition of desiring has such an influence. This condition says that each interest has a relation to the faculty of desire. A desire is surely characterized by a certain way it feels—we *feel* a desire. Against this backdrop, we can understand the phenomenal character of a disinterested pleasure. Here, *we do not feel any desiring*. In these terms, we have an immediate grasp on TD because when having a pleasure in the beautiful, we do not feel any desiring. We shall add the following *phenomenological meaning of TD* (TDp) to our list:

TPp The pleasure in the beautiful has the phenomenal character of disinterestedness, that is, it feels detached of any desiring.

One could object that such a characterization of the pleasure's phenomenal character could only proceed by means of reflection on the concept of a desire. Thus, it would be far from being immediate. I admit that we can only *determine* the phenomenal character of the pleasure as "without any desiring" by means of the concept "desire." Yet, we do not have to determine our pleasure conceptually in order to account for its specific phenomenal character. For the latter, it suffices that the pleasure in the beautiful feels differently than an interest. The absence of an interest has a specific phenomenological character in its own right.

As mentioned above, TD marks off the starting point of the overall argument of the *Analytic of the Beautiful*. This thesis is Kant's entrance into the realm of beauty. More precisely, it is the phenomenological meaning of TD which provides this entrance. This latter meaning describes how beauty is *given* to us—namely, in terms of an experience of disinterested pleasure. By means of analogy to the second Critique, I suggest speaking of a *felt fact of disinterested pleasure* or a *felt fact of beauty*.[59]

---

[58] Again, this is explicitly rejected by Guyer: "In defining the 'quality' of aesthetic judgment Kant is not making a phenomenological distinction between different kinds of feelings of pleasure, but a distinction between the ways in which different instances of pleasure may be occasioned." (Guyer 1979, p. 171; cf. pp. 203 f.)

[59] I draw on Dieter Schönecker's notion of the "felt fact of reason," which he defended regarding the feeling of respect (cf. Schönecker 2013).

The following objection is perhaps not far to seek. Does not a phenomenological understanding of TD undermine Kant's transcendental approach? As is well known, the "main transcendental question" (Prol: 180) is "How are synthetic propositions *a priori* possible?" (Prol: 176). Since judgments of taste fall into the class of synthetic propositions *a priori*, the "problem of the critique of the power of judgment [i.e., the problem: How are judgments of taste possible?] belongs under the general problem of transcendental philosophy: How are synthetic *a priori* judgments possible?" (KU: 289). More precisely, it is the task of the transcendental critique of taste to reveal the conditions under which the judgment of taste (understood as a synthetic judgment *a priori*) is possible. To achieve this result, one must go beyond empirical descriptions of a certain phenomenon, that is, beauty experiences as empirically given. Against this backdrop, a phenomenological understanding of TD would only undermine Kant's transcendental approach if it would either turn the judgment of taste into a purely empirical judgment or if it would foreclose any possibility to proceed towards an uncovering of the conditions under which a judgment of taste is possible. The first thing to note is that the judgment of taste is a very peculiar kind of synthetic judgment *a priori:* It presupposes an empirically given pleasure felt by the judging subject and, in that respect, it is an empirical judgment; but it extends this pleasure *a priori*, that is, without any kind of empirical investigation, to all judging subjects—only with regard to this universality, it is a judgment *a priori*.[60] Thus, the judgment of taste includes an empirical element anyways, and it is this empirical element to which the phenomenological understanding of TD applies. But this does not interfere with the *a priori* component of the judgment nor does it make a transcendental analysis of the latter impossible. We should only be aware that the phenomenological understanding of TD is not itself part of the transcendental conditions of the judgment of taste. Yet, it can prepare the uncovering of these transcendental conditions. First, empirical investigations can have a kind of propaedeutic function for a transcendental investigation.[61] Second, and more importantly, a transcendental investigation can be dependent on an empirical starting point, especially in the realm of beauty. For in order to uncover the transcendental conditions of a phenomenon like beauty, one has to clarify in the first place what beauty is, and one has to delineate it from other phenomena. As seen above, this is exactly what TD, phenomenologically understood, does: it delineates the experience of beauty from the experiences of

---

60 See: "It is an empirical judgment that I perceive and judge an object with pleasure. But it is an *a priori* judgment that I find it beautiful, i.e., that I may require that satisfaction of everyone as necessary." (KU: 289)
61 See Kant's remark on Burke's "merely empirical exposition of the sublime and the beautiful" (KU: 277).

the agreeable and the good. Thus, instead of hindering any transcendental investigation, the phenomenological understanding of TD paves its way.

Let me finally emphasize that I am not arguing for the theoretical meanings of TD to be obsolete. It is not my claim that TD is to be understood exclusively in phenomenological terms. Rather, the two theoretical meanings of TD are important for a comprehensive understanding of TD. My claim is just that the phenomenological meaning has priority insofar as it is our first grasp not only on TD but also on beauty.

6 Conclusion

We have seen that the thesis of disinterestedness is endowed with a complex meaning which, most importantly, encompasses a phenomenological meaning. I have argued that this phenomenological understanding of TD is of greatest importance to understand its function as a starting point of Kant's investigations. In the first part of this article, I argued that pleasure in general comprises a phenomenal character, which can be illustrated by its notions of maintenance: Because the subject wants to maintain her current state which feels positively (*phenomenal character of pleasure*) and because the subject is conscious of the representation x causing to maintain that state, the subject wants to maintain the representation x. In the second part, I analyzed Kant's non-intellectual conception of interest which he puts forth in § 10: an interest is characterized by a *condition of existence* and a *condition of desiring*. Drawing on Kant's formulations of TD in § 2 I developed two theoretical meanings of this thesis: the pleasure in the beautiful (1) is not taken in a mere sensation, but in an inner activity which is not an activity of the will, and (2) it is independent of two kinds of matter (i.e., the matter of representations and the matter of purposiveness). However, we saw that these two meanings are not yet available in § 2. Moreover, Kant does not offer any argument for TD. This led us finally to a *phenomenological understanding of TD:* the pleasure in the beautiful feels disinterested, that is, detached of any desiring. This is the *felt fact of beauty* that opens up Kant's way into the realm of beauty.[62]

---

[62] I received helpful feedback and insightful comments on my theses concerning disinterestedness on many occasions. Amongst others, I would like to thank the participants of the conference "Disinterested Pleasure in Kantian and Contemporary Philosophy" held 2018 at the University of Siegen, participants of the Kant-Forum Rhein Main Sieg, the members of fiph Hannover, and the SublimAE Seminar at Institut Jean Nicod (Paris). I am also thankful for helpful feedback I received from Elke Elisabeth Schmidt and Dieter Schönecker.

Abbreviations

Apart from the *Critique of Pure Reason*, all references to Kant's works are to Kant's *Gesammelte Schriften, Ausgabe der Preußischen Akademie der Wissenschaften* (Berlin: De Gruyter, 1902 ff.). References to the *Critique of Pure Reason* are to the standard A and B pagination of the first and second editions. Translations are from *The Cambridge Edition of the Works of Immanuel Kant*; translations are altered when considered necessary.

The following abbreviations of individual works are used:

EEKU   Erste Einleitung in die Kritik der Urteilskraft / First Introduction to the Critique of the Power of Judgment
GMS   Grundlegung zur Metaphystik der Sitten / Groundwork for the Metaphysics of Morals
GSE   Beobachtungen über das Gefühl des Schönen und Erhabenen / Observations on the Feeling of the Beautiful and the Sublime
KU   Kritik der Urteilskraft / Critique of the Power of Judgment
KpV   Kritik der praktischen Vernunft / Critique of Practical Reason
KrV   Kritik der reinen Vernunft / Critique of Pure Reason
MS   Die Metaphysik der Sitten / The Metaphysics of Morals
Prol   Prolegomena zu einer jeden künftigen Metaphysik, die als Wissenschaft wird auftreten können / Prolegomena to Any Future Metaphysics That Will Be Able to Present Itself as a Science

Literature

Allison, Henry E. (2001): *Kant's Theory of Taste*. Cambridge: Cambridge University Press.
Ameriks, Karl (2003): *Interpreting Kant's Critiques*. Oxford: Oxford University Press.
Berger, Larissa (2022a): *Kants Philosophie des Schönen. Eine kommentarische Interpretation zu den §§ 1–22 der Kritik der Urteilskraft*. Freiburg: Alber.
Berger, Larissa (2022b): "On the Subjective, Beauty and Artificial Intelligence: A Kantian Approach." In: Kim, Hyeongjoo and Schönecker, Dieter (Eds.): *Kant and Artificial Intelligence*. Berlin and New York: De Gruyter, pp. 257–282.
Berger, Larissa (2022c): "Wie fühlt sich Schönheit an? Zur Phänomenologie des interesselosen Wohlgefallens bei Kant." In: *Kant-Studien* 113. No. 4, pp. 659–688.
Chignell, Andrew (2015): "Empfindung." In: Willaschek, Marcus, Stolzenberg, Jürgen, Mohr, Georg, and Bacin, Stefano (Eds.): *Kant-Lexikon*. Berlin and New York: De Gruyter, pp. 494–497.
Crawford, Donald W. (1974): *Kant's Aesthetic Theory*. Madison: University of Wisconsin Press.
Crowther, Paul (2010): *The Kantian Aesthetic. From Knowledge to the Avant-Garde*. Oxford: Oxford University Press.
Fricke, Christel (1990): *Kants Theorie des reinen Geschmacksurteils*. Berlin and New York: De Gruyter.
Ginsborg, Hannah (2008): "Interesseloses Wohlgefallen und Allgemeinheit ohne Begriffe (§§ 1–9)." In: Höffe, Otfried (Ed.): *Immanuel Kant. Kritik der Urteilskraft*. Berlin and New York: De Gruyter, pp. 59–78.

Gorodeisky, Keren (2023): "The Myth of the Absent Self: Disinterest, the Self and Evaluative Self-Consciousness." In: Berger, Larissa (Ed.): *Disinterested Pleasure and Beauty. Perspectives from Kantian and Contemporary Aesthetics*. Berlin and New York: De Gruyter, pp. 135–165.

Grimm, Jacob and Grimm, Wilhelm (1885): *Deutsches Wörterbuch, Sechster Band L. M.* Leipzig: S. Hirzel.

Guyer, Paul (1979): *Kant and the Claims of Taste*. Cambridge MA: Harvard University Press.

Guyer, Paul (2018): "What Is It Like to Experience the Beautiful and Sublime?" In: Sorensen, Kelly and Williamson, Diane (Eds.): *Kant and the Faculty of Feeling*. Cambridge: Cambridge University Press, pp. 147–165.

Hilgers, Thomas (2017): *Aesthetic Disinterestedness. Art, Experience, and the Self*. New York and London: Routledge.

Kern, Andrea (2000): *Schöne Lust. Eine Theorie der ästhetischen Erfahrung nach Kant*. Frankfurt am Main: Suhrkamp.

Kulenkampff, Jens (1994): *Kants Logik des ästhetischen Urteils*. Frankfurt am Main: Vittorio Klostermann.

Kuspit, Donald B. (1974): "A Phenomenological Interpretation of Kant's Apriori of Taste." In: *Philosophy and Phenomenological Research 34. No. 4, pp. 551–559.*

Longuenesse, Béatrice (2006): "Kant's Leading Thread in the Analytic of the Beautiful." In: Kukla, Rebecca (Ed.): *Aesthetics and Cognition in Kant's Critical Philosophy*. Cambridge: Cambridge University Press, pp. 194–219.

Makkreel, Rudolf (1997): *Einbildungskraft und Interpretation. Die hermeneutische Tragweite von Kants Kritik der Urteilskraft*. Paderborn: Ferdinand Schöningh.

Matthews, Patricia M. (1997): *The Significance of Beauty. Kant on Feeling and the System of the Mind*. Dordrecht: Kluwer Academic Publishers.

McCloskey, Mary (1987): *Kant's Aesthetic*. Basingstoke: The Macmillan Press.

Meerbote, Ralf (1982): "Reflection on Beauty." In: Cohen, Ted and Guyer, Paul (Eds.): *Essays in Kant's Aesthetics*. Chicago and London: The University of Chicago Press, pp. 55–86.

Riggle, Nick (2016): "On the Interest in Beauty and Disinterest." In: *Philosopher's Imprint* 16. No. 9, pp. 1–14.

Schmalzried, Lisa (2023): "Human Beauty, Attraction, and Disinterested Pleasure." In: Berger, Larissa (Ed.): *Disinterested Pleasure and Beauty. Perspectives from Kantian and Contemporary Aesthetics*. Berlin and New York: De Gruyter, pp. 211–229.

Schönecker, Dieter (2013): "Das gefühlte Faktum der Vernunft. Skizze einer Interpretation und Verteidigung." In: *Deutsche Zeitschrift für Philosophie* 1, pp. 91–107.

Wenzel, Christian Helmut (2000): *Subjektive Allgemeingültigkeit des Geschmacksurteils bei Kant*. Berlin and New York: De Gruyter.

Wenzel, Christian Helmut (2008): *An Introduction to Kant's Aesthetics. Core Concepts and Problems*. Malden: Blackwell Publishing.

Zammito, John (1992): *The Genesis of Kant's Critique of Judgment*. Chicago and London: The University of Chicago Press.

Zangwill, Nick (1992): "Unkantian Notions of Disinterest." In: *The British Journal of Aesthetics* 32. No. 2, pp. 149–152.

Zangwill, Nick (2023): "Disinterestedness: Analysis and Partial Defence." In: Berger, Larissa (Ed.): *Disinterested Pleasure and Beauty. Perspectives from Kantian and Contemporary Aesthetics.* Berlin and New York: De Gruyter, pp. 59–85.

Zuckert, Rachel (2002): "A New Look at Kant's Theory of Pleasure." In: *The Journal of Aesthetics and Art Criticism* 60. No. 3, pp. 239–252.

Zuckert, Rachel (2007): *Kant on Beauty and Biology.* Cambridge: Cambridge University Press.

Nick Zangwill
Disinterestedness: Analysis and Partial Defense

Abstract: Kant makes modest and ambitious claims with his idea of disinterested pleasure. The modest claim is that all aesthetic pleasure is disinterested. The ambitious claim is that all and only aesthetic pleasure is disinterested. I defend only the modest claim. I initially give a basic explication of what Kant had in mind by the doctrine. I then argue that if aesthetic pleasure were not basically disinterested, judgements of taste could not make the normative (or "universal") claims they do. Normativity is essential to judgements of taste; they would not be what they are without it. And basic disinterest is essential for normativity. Therefore, we cannot reject basic disinterestedness without rejecting judgements of taste altogether. I then distinguish various other notions of disinterest and argue that none of them allow Kant to make his ambitions claim.

1 Introduction

Kant's thesis that pleasure in the beautiful is disinterested is a cardinal doctrine of his *Critique of Judgment*.[1] My view is that some version of this doctrine is right, and importantly so. There are many who would have us abandon the thesis altogether. I shall attempt to dissuade them. However, it is true that we need to clarify what disinterestedness amounts to. And if we find that we can reconstruct the notion in a number of different ways, it may prove that some versions of the thesis do indeed go too far. We need to consider which version we ought to accept.

---

[1] I cite both the 1928 English translation by James Creed Meredith as well as the 2000 English translation by Paul Guyer and Eric Matthews. In citing the latter, I follow Hannah Ginsborg in preferring "pleasure" or "delight" to "satisfaction" since the latter suggest some desire that is satisfied (Ginsborg 2002). Furthermore, in accordance with the James Creed Meredith's translation, I distinguish "Gegenstand" from "Object," achieved in the Meredith English translation by small and capital letters in "object" and "Object" (see Kant 1928). Scholars do not agree about whether Kant makes a consistent distinction here. However, on *many* occasions, Kant takes a *Gegenstand* to be an object one might kick whereas he takes an *Object* to be something one might think about. I like to cite more than one translation partly because it is good to be reminded of the gap between original text and translation, and partly because different translations often bring out something different from the original.

Before we proceed with the attempt to give an account of the notion of disinterestedness itself, we must consider the *work* to which Kant puts the idea. He opens the "Analytic" of the *Critique of Judgment* with the announcement that "The judgment of taste is aesthetic" (KU-Guyer: 203). By this, he intends the plausible claim that a judgement of beauty is based on a response of pleasure or displeasure. This is why the claim that "The judgment of taste is aesthetic" is non-trivial.[2] It is "aesthetic" in the same sense that judgements about the niceness of Canary-wine are also "aesthetic." Kant's use of the word "aesthetic," therefore, does not coincide with the modern use according to which an "aesthetic" pleasure is the sort of pleasure on which judgements of taste or beauty are based. Pleasure in drinking Canary-wine is *not* "aesthetic" pleasures in the modern sense, but it is in Kant's sense. In this paper, however, I use the word "aesthetic" in the modern sense. By an "aesthetic pleasure," I simply mean a pleasure in beauty. This will make things simpler.

What follows Kant's opening announcement in the rest of the "Analytic of the Beautiful" is the attempt to say something about the *nature* of aesthetic pleasure. What *makes* a pleasure an *aesthetic* pleasure (or a pleasure in beauty)? This is where disinterestedness comes in: Kant employs the notion of disinterestedness in the attempt to *demarcate* aesthetic pleasure from other sorts of pleasure. Kant also seeks to connect disinterestedness with the "universal validity" that judgements of taste claim. The relation between these two projects is, as we shall see, somewhat complex.

Kant has a *modest* and an *ambitious* claim: the modest claim is that *all* aesthetic pleasure is disinterested. The ambitious claim is that *all and only* aesthetic pleasure is disinterested. The ambitious claim is correct if the classes of disinterested pleasures and aesthetic pleasures coincide. But if only the modest claim holds, then while all aesthetic pleasures are disinterested, some non-aesthetic pleasures might also be disinterested. Or to put it a different way, the modest claim is that the disinterestedness of a pleasure is a *necessary* condition of its being aesthetic; the ambitious claim is that it is a *necessary and sufficient* condition. Both modest and ambitious claims have been denied.[3]

I begin this paper by giving an initial explication of the notion of disinterestedness and of the modest and ambitious claims that Kant makes with the notion. I

---

[2] I refine and defend Kant's claim that the judgement of taste involves a response of pleasure or displeasure in Zangwill 1990, where I also defend the idea that judgements of beauty can be based on testimony and induction.

[3] In Zangwill 1995, I describe and partially defend Kant's view that pleasure in the agreeable is interested. In Zangwill 2013a, I partially defend Kant's claim that pleasure in beauty is disinterested against Nietzsche's interesting criticisms.

argue, on mostly Kantian grounds, that we should accept the modest thesis. However, I also argue that the reasons put forward in support of the modest thesis do not sustain the ambitious claim in the way that Kant thinks it does. So, I argue both for Kant and against him.

If the account I will present here is on the right lines, it will count as a reply to Paul Guyer's accusation that we must radically revise the account of disinterestedness that Kant gives in the *Critique of Judgment*.[4] I think that many of the problems that Guyer claims to unearth in what he calls Kant's "official definition" of disinterestedness are exaggerated. We can read Kant more charitably. I have not the space to run through all Guyer's criticisms, although I will reply to some of them. My procedure will mostly take the form of presenting what I hope is a clear and attractive positive interpretation of Kant's doctrine. We will find some minor flaws in Kant's presentation, but I will suggest ways of patching these up so that the modest project remains intact. I will then raise some problems for Kant's ambitious project later on. The problems, I will urge, are problems for what Kant wants to *do* with the notion, not with the use of the notion to characterize aesthetic pleasure.[5]

2 A Working Definition of (Modest) Disinterestedness

What, then, does Kant mean by calling a pleasure "disinterested"? When Kant introduces the idea of disinterested pleasure in § 2, he writes:

> The pleasure which we combine with the representation of the existence of an object [Gegenstandes] is called interest. Hence such a pleasure always, at the same time, involves a reference to the faculty of desire, either as its determining ground, or else as necessarily intercon-

---

4 Guyer 1979, Chapter 5, especially pp. 167–179.
5 If Kant came back from the dead, what would he say about the "dainty," the "dumpy," the "melancholic," the "unbalanced" and other aesthetic concepts (Sibley 1959)? One thing he might say is that we should first focus on aesthetic *pleasure* and *displeasure* and then expand and describe aesthetic *feeling* and *reaction* more generally. So, we should first focus on "beauty" before considering the "dainty," the "dumpy." If Kant can claim that aesthetic pleasure is disinterested, maybe he can go on to claim that the aesthetic feelings, reactions, or experiences that prompt us to judge that a thing is dainty, dumpy, melancholic, or unbalanced are also disinterested. Alternatively, perhaps Kant would categorize the dainty, dumpy, melancholic, or unbalanced as nonaesthetic and would see beauty and ugliness as his central concern. The dainty, dumpy, melancholic, or unbalanced might be relevant only as figuring in the representation of the object. If so, the ascriptions of these notions to things would not deploy the faculty of taste.

> nected with its determining ground. But if the question is whether something is beautiful, we do not want to know whether there is anything that is, or even could be, at stake for us or for someone else [...]. (KU-Guyer: 204)

That is the Paul Guyer and Eric Matthews translation. James Creed Meredith has:

> The delight which we connect with the representation of the real existence of an object [Gegenstandes] is called interest. Such a delight, therefore, always involves a reference to the faculty of desire, either as its determining ground, or else as necessarily implicated with its determining ground. Now, where the question is whether something is beautiful, we do not want to know whether we, or anyone else, are, or even could be, concerned in the real existence of the thing [...]. (KU-Meredith: 204)

And "where the question is whether something is beautiful" (KU-Meredith: 204),

> One only wants to know is whether the mere representation of the object [Gegenstandes] is accompanied by pleasure in me, however indifferent I may with regard to the existence of the object [Gegenstandes] of this representation. (KU-Guyer: 205)

Alternatively rendered in English by Meredith as:

> All one wants to know is whether the mere representation of the object [Gegenstandes] is to my liking, no matter how indifferent I may be to the real existence of the object [Gegenstandes] of this representation. (KU-Meredith: 205)

What we have here is two points rolled into one: first, there is the positive idea that delight in, or liking for the beautiful is simply a *direct response to a representation*. This claim is of the first importance for Kant (see KU: 267 and 289, for example). Second, there is the negative idea that in such a response, there is also an *indifference* or *lack of desire concerning* the existence of the object represented. These points are connected in that if the pleasurable response to a representation *did* involve a desire concerning the existence of the object represented, then this response would not be a *direct* response to the representation ("simple estimate," KU-Meredith: 289).

Why does Kant connect *desire* with the idea that interest is a pleasure in the representation of the existence of an object? The reason is that it is definitive of desire that it is directed to the existence of an object. That is what a desire is. (So, the "Hence" and "therefore" of the translations denote an analytic inference.) Although it may seem anachronistic, we could see Kant as embracing something like a functionalist theory of desire; he writes, in the Introduction to the *Critique of Judgment*:

the faculty of desire [...] [is] *the faculty for being through one's representations the cause of the reality of the objects [Gegenstände] of those representations* [...]. (KU-Guyer: 177 fn.)

Alternative translation:

the faculty of desire [...] [is] *a faculty which by means of its representations is the cause of the actuality of the objects [Gegenstände] of those representations* [...]. (KU-Meredith: 177 fn.)

According to Kant, desires tend to cause the existence of what they represent. So, desire and existence are connected. Moreover, they are not only connected one way, so that while all desires are directed towards the existence of a thing and tend to be its cause, there are also some mental states that are not desires, which are nevertheless directed towards the existence of a thing and tend to be its cause. Instead, the connection holds both ways, so that any pleasures in existence (that is, those that are interests) necessarily involve desire.

As a first attempt, then, it seems reasonable to interpret Kant's claim that aesthetic pleasure is disinterested, as the claim that *aesthetic pleasure is not pleasure in the satisfaction of any desire*. Or a little more exactly: aesthetic pleasure is disinterested because *it is not pleasure that is consequential on (that is, rationally caused by) the belief that a desire has been or may be satisfied*. This will be modified later on, but it will be worthwhile to consider this notion of disinterestedness before proceeding.

Some terminology will help focus things: a "representation" ("*Vorstellung*") is an intentional mental state that represents a state of affairs as obtaining or existing. The relevant states of affairs are typically objects or events that possess properties. I shall call a representation "non-aesthetic" when the properties ascribed to an object or event are *not* properties such as beauty, ugliness, grace, daintiness, or dumpiness.[6] For example, such properties will be properties such as physical and sensory qualities—a flower's shape, size, color, and smell, for example. In the case of works of art, this list of non-aesthetic properties will sometimes stretch to include semantic, representational properties, and perhaps art-historical properties.[7]

In these terms, Kant's doctrine of disinterestedness is at least the idea that there is a direct route from an input of non-aesthetic cognitive representation (it need not rise to the level of *belief*) or perceptual experience, to an output of aes-

---

6 Kant, of course, denies that beauty is a property of objects and that we have a concept of beauty (in §§ 6 and 7); that is a substantive thesis, and it does not affect the claim about non-aesthetic representation.
7 Here, I draw but make no attempt to justify a distinction between aesthetic and non-aesthetic properties. See further Chapters 1 and 2 of Zangwill 2001.

thetic reaction or response (pleasure, for example). The judgement of taste is based on such a reaction or response. We do *not* have an *indirect* function from an input of non-aesthetic representation or perceptual experience, *via* a desire or via the belief that a desire has been or is likely to be satisfied, to an output of reaction or response: aesthetic pleasure is a response *directly* to a non-aesthetic representation. (I take this to be compatible with what Kant says in § 9, which I discuss below.)

In a couple of later passages, this by-passing of desire is made explicit: aesthetic pleasure is said not to be "referred to any end whatever" (KU-Meredith: 236 fn.) or not "related to any end at all" (KU-Guyer: 236 fn.). Also, Kant writes

> [the pure judgment of taste] combines a delight or aversion immediately with the bare *contemplation* of the object [Gegenstandes], irrespective of its use or of any end (KU-Meredith: 242).

Alternatively translated as:

> [the pure judgment of taste] immediately connects pleasure or displeasure to the mere *consideration* of the object [Gegenstandes] without respect to use or to an end (KU-Guyer: 242, replacing "satisfaction" with "pleasure").

An example of a pleasure in the satisfaction of desire which contrasts with aesthetic pleasure is the pleasure of pride. Suppose that I am proud of my strength. Then whether I really am strong is far from irrelevant to me because I want to be strong. If I come to believe that I am not in fact strong, my pride will be undermined, and it will evaporate. Not so with aesthetic pleasure: there is no desire concerning existence because aesthetic response is not determined by beliefs about the satisfaction of desires. Suppose that I am pleased when I perceptually represent a flower or a building, but it turns out to be merely a hologram or image that deceives me. That image or appearance might still retain its beauty. *It*, the intentional Object of my representation, pleased me. I might be disappointed in other ways to find out that it lacks existence, but not aesthetically. Appearances suffice for judgements of beauty. (I defend the centrality of appearances in aesthetics in Zangwill 2013b.)

Risking anachronism, we might describe Kant's point in terms of the "causal-functional role" of aesthetic pleasure: the typical casual route runs from representation to aesthetic pleasure or displeasure, and it entirely by-passes desires and beliefs about desires. The *modest* disinterestedness claim is that aesthetic pleasure has such a desire-free role. The *ambitious* disinterestedness claim is that *only* aesthetic pleasure has this desire-free role.

This, then, is my initial conjectured interpretation of Kant's explication of disinterestedness in the *Critique of Judgment*. It is a consequence of the above interpretation that the fact that judgements of taste do not, in Kant's terms, involve a *concept*, is of no special significance when it comes to explicating disinterestedness. I mention this because Guyer places great weight on this in his book *Kant and the Claims of Taste*.[8] And many commentators follow him in this respect.[9] Guyer thinks that the conceptlessness of the judgement of taste is of a piece with disinterestedness. But, in fact, the conceptlessness of the judgement of taste is merely a consequence of the view that the judgement of taste is aesthetic (in Kant's sense) and not a "cognitive" judgement, and thus that beauty is not a real property of objects (see KU: 209, KU: 290 for textual confirmation of this point). For Kant, judgements of beauty are conceptless, just like judgements of the agreeable. Judgements of agreeableness do not involve a concept, yet they are not disinterested. So, Guyer and those who follow him cannot be right.

While pleasure in beauty and pleasure in the agreeable are both conceptless, the two pleasures differ in that the pleasure in the agreeable is not a direct response to a representation but pleasure in beauty is such a direct response. Pleasure in the agreeable, Kant thinks, always implies desire, either because it is based on desire or else because it generates desire, as we will see below. Either way, it is, as we might say, "muddy" with desire.

3 Pleasure and Judgement

Kant is not primarily making a point about the *judgement* of taste. As Kant introduces his notion of disinterestedness, it applies, in the first instance, to certain *pleasures* ("delight" KU-Meredith: 204 or "liking" KU-Meredith: 205). The crucial thing is a certain lack of connection between pleasure or aversion, and the "faculty of desire" KU-Meredith: 204). Both the title of § 2 and the "Definition of the beautiful derived from the first moment" (KU: 211; the translation is the same in Guyer and Meredith) make it clear that Kant is primarily concerned to say something about pleasure in the beautiful. We should not take Kant to be saying something primarily about the judgement of taste. This would be a misunderstanding, even though, as we shall see, Kant thinks that the universality of the judgement *follows from* the disinterestedness of the pleasure, because the judgement is based on such a pleasure.

It must be admitted that Kant does *sometimes* discuss disinterestedness in the context of the judgement of taste. But what he says is that judgements of taste are

---

8 Guyer 1979, Chapter 5, especially pp. 162–169.
9 For example, Kemal 1992.

impartial and *impure* when an interest "vitiates" (KU-Meredith: 223) or "spoils" (KU-Guyer: 223) them and when they are "tinged" by (KU-Meredith: 205) or "mixed" with (KU-Guyer: 205) interest. Such judgements, however, remain judgements of taste; but they are ones that are warped, skewed, or perverted by the alien interest. If so, perhaps § 2 should have been entitled "The delight which determines the judgement of taste *ought to be* independent of all interest." For only the delight determining *pure* judgements of taste is disinterested; and it seems to be a regrettable fact that not all judgements of taste are pure. Perhaps Kant is a little over-optimistic in his title. But the issue is not very important. The important point is that judgements of taste can be more or less perverted by interest, unlike pleasures in the beautiful. Whether a *judgement* of taste *is* based on an interest can be a matter of degree. There are two options here. One is to say that judgements that are interested or impure are partly based on a disinterested pleasure and partly based on some other pleasure. Another is to say that a judgement based on an interest is not at all a judgement of taste. Kant appears to lean towards the former when he writes:

> Hence judgments so influenced can either lay no claim at all to a universally valid delight, or else must abate their claim in proportion as sensations of the kind in question enter into the determining grounds of taste. (KU-Meredith: 223)

Alternative translation:

> Hence judgements that are so affected can make no claim at all to universal pleasure or as little claim as can be made when those sort of sensations are found among the determining grounds of taste. (KU-Guyer: 223, replacing "satisfaction" with "pleasure")

Here, it is a matter of degree whether a judgement is based on an interest or disinterested pleasure. An impure judgement of taste is improperly grounded, but it is still a judgement of taste.

However, whether a *pleasure* itself is disinterested is an all or nothing matter —unless we allow gerrymandered "conjunctive pleasures," which are the sum of an interested and a disinterested pleasure, to count as one pleasure.

That the disinterestedness of pleasure and of judgement are quite different can be seen by considering what Kant says about the case of morality. Kant thinks that moral *pleasure* is interested. But at one point he says that

> A judgment upon an object of our pleasure can be entirely *disinterested* yet still very *interesting*, i.e., it is not grounded on any interest, but it produces an interest; all pure moral judgments are like this. (KU-Guyer: 205 fn.)

So, even though an interest follows *as a consequence* of moral judgements Kant thinks that a moral *judgement* is disinterested in the sense of not being grounded on a desire. This is somewhat unusual or non-standard from the point of view of Kant's own usage. At any rate, the case of morality illustrates the fact that the disinterestedness of a pleasure and the disinterestedness of a judgement are two different things; for in the case of morality, Kant thinks that judgement is disinterested *unlike* pleasure. In *a* sense, moral judgement is disinterested because it is not based on an interest, whereas Kant thinks that moral *pleasure* is interested because it is inevitably connected with a desire. In the aesthetic case, by contrast, Kant thinks that *both* aesthetic pleasure and judgements of taste are disinterested (see KU: 300, quoted below). But even here, claims about pleasure and about judgement are different.[10]

In all this, it should now be obvious that Kant use the word "Interesse" as a technical term. The 18th-century German word did not mean exactly the same as the contemporary German word. And Kant seems to have his own idiosyncratic usage. And, of course, the English word "interest" is a long way from all these. For Kant, interest is a certain *species of pleasure*, namely, pleasure that is necessarily tied to desire; disinterested pleasure lacks that tie.

4 Kant's Further Views about Pleasure in Beauty

As the disinterestedness thesis was initially explicated above, the point is wholly negative. It says what aesthetic pleasure is *not*, not what it *is*. So, the thesis leaves room for a wide variety of positive views about its nature. It aspires to be relatively uncontroversial. What has been said thus far does not commit us to any special view of the nature of aesthetic feeling. In my view, some commentators introduce this too soon. It is assumed that the doctrine of disinterestedness is thoroughly impregnated with his further and more controversial views about the deep nature of pleasure in the beautiful and his view of how the judgement of taste is possible. As we will see below, he does think that disinterestedness entails universal validity (Kant asserts this in § 6). But as we shall see, there are problems in the way of deducing universal validity from disinterested.

In § 9, Kant begins to introduce us to his special view of the nature of aesthetic pleasure, and the view is developed in what follows in the *Critique of Judgment*.

---

10 It is also unhelpful to see the distinction between interested and disinterested pleasure as being somewhat like that between the way categorical and hypothetical imperatives motivate (compare Guyer 1979, pp. 162–169).

Very roughly, the view is that pleasure in the beautiful (aesthetic pleasure) arises from the "free play" of the cognitive faculties—apparently "imagination" and "understanding." When in the service of knowledge, the cognitive faculties are harnessed together, by means of rules. But pleasure in the beautiful, Kant thinks, arises from the cognitive faculties *on holiday*, without constraint from rules (see for example KU: 222).

This account of aesthetic pleasure proves to be crucial later in Kant's "deduction" of the judgement of taste. Kant appeals to our "cognitive powers"—to the "harmonious free play of the imagination and understanding"—as the *source* of judgements of taste. Here we see the elements of the solution that Kant eventually wants to provide for the overarching problem of how a judgement of taste is possible—of the justification of judgements that are both subjectively grounded as well as claiming universal validity. Kant's strategy, very roughly, is to rest his answer to this fundamental problem of the third *Critique* on the faculties of mind that he deploys in the first *Critique*. For Kant, aesthetic pleasure has its source in what is necessary for the cognitive faculties to function effectively; but our cognitive faculties are not arbitrary. There are some aspects of our cognitive faculties which any thinker or perceiver *must* possess. Kant thinks that the source of the possibility of judgements of taste lies in the general conditions of thought and perceptual experience together with the idea that the faculties of mind must be in the right "proportion" to generate knowledge (KU-Guyer: 219). It is beyond the scope of this paper to assess this grand plan. In many respects, Kant's views on taste develop the revolutionary British sentimentalist tradition, especially Hume. But in his view of the source of the possibility of taste, Kant in some respects reverts to older models of our aesthetic lives, bringing them nearer to cognition. Kant's deep account of aesthetic pleasure is at least very controversial and perhaps implausible.[11] But the claim that pleasure in the beautiful is disinterested merely describes a relatively *surface* feature of the judgement of taste, which is that it is grounded on such a pleasure, and it need not be bound up with Kant's *deep* explanation of the possibility of such a judgement.

Given Kant's account of the deep nature of aesthetic pleasure, it follows that the general ability to make judgements of taste is not something quite separate from our normal cognitive abilities. So, Kant's position falls somewhat across the contemporary meta-aesthetical boundaries. Often there is said to be a position, "cognitivism," according to which judgements of taste are cognitive judgements (beliefs aiming to match facts in the world); and that is contrasted with "non-cognitivism," according to which judgements express psychological states of some

---

11 See Malcolm Budd's insightful analysis and critique in Budd 2001.

other nature (perhaps attitudes or likings). But Kant's view probably has most in common with views that see judgements of taste as the expression of our perception of aspects.[12] For, the ability to see something as an X is dependent on our ability to have various cognitive states employing the concept of an X. Of course, that is not Kant's own view, but what it shares with Kant is the idea that aesthetic experience is to be understood in terms of our cognitive faculties when they are not functioning to produce knowledge of the world.

It is not plausible that aesthetic pleasure is directed to our own cognitive faculties, as some commentators think. That would be a strange counterintuitive view. On this point, I agree with Rachel Zuckert that it would make us overly "self-absorbed" in our aesthetic lives (Zuckert 2007, pp. 188–189; Guyer also discusses this issue see Guyer 2009, p. 205). Nevertheless, Kant's idea is that the operation and capability of those cognitive faculties can be a source of pleasure.

It seems that there ought to be, in Kant's book, a cleanly analytic phase, analyzing and describing aesthetic pleasure and the judgement of taste, and then a separate dialectical phase, in which the justification ("possibility") of those judgements, so described, is pursued.[13] Usually, Kant separates these, but it does seem that the positioning of § 9 is odd from this point of view. Perhaps he was impatient to get to the "de juris" part, especially given the supposed role of the entire book with respect to Kant's critical system. But the content hardly follows the official framework. The positioning of § 9 seems to be out of place in the book except as an advance *preview* of the solution Kant will later provide of the solution to the problem of how a judgement of taste is possible. The material of § 9 really has its natural place later in the book.[14]

I shall leave an assessment of Kant's controversial deep views of the nature of aesthetic pleasure entirely to one side in this paper. In my view, we can to a great extent examine and assess Kant's doctrine of disinterestedness without considering further questions about the nature of aesthetic pleasure. This may be thought to be a risky assumption to make. Indeed, I know of no commentator who has taken this route. (I hope not for good reason.) I draw confidence from the fact that Kant himself is clear that what it is which makes a pleasure interested or disinterested are the

---

[12] See, for example, much of Roger Scruton's *Art and Imagination* (Scruton 1974). Imagining that X without believing or knowing that X is crucial to Scruton's view of aesthetic perception.
[13] Henry Allison emphasizes this distinction in Allison 2001.
[14] Kant's form and content sometimes drift apart. What is the theory of art doing in the Deduction, for example? Ludwig's Wittgenstein's *Tractatus* (Wittgenstein 1922) is another book where the contents sometimes do not map onto the official formal framework.

[...] *relations* of representations to the feeling of pleasure and displeasure. (KU: 209, my emphasis; the translations of Guyer and Meredith are the same)

It is not as yet the *nature* of the pleasure; it is a wholly *relational* matter. It may be that some intrinsic feature of the pleasure explains the difference in extrinsic relations. But that is another question.[15]

5 From Normativity to Disinterest

Why, then, should we accept Kant's modest thesis that aesthetic pleasure is disinterested? Is Kant right?

It is the connection of disinterestedness with what we may call the *normative* claim of our judgements of taste that gives us what we need to vindicate Kant's modest thesis. The disinterestedness of aesthetic pleasure is implied by the fact that (at least some of) the judgements of taste we make on the basis of aesthetic pleasure lay claim to what Kant calls "universal validity" or "universal voice." Kant describes "universal validity" when he writes:

> when [someone] puts a thing on a pedestal and calls it beautiful, he demands the same delight from others. He judges not merely for himself, but for all men, and then he speaks of beauty as if it were a property of things. Thus he says that the *thing* is beautiful; and it is not as if he counted upon others agreeing with his judgment of liking owing to having found them in such agreement on a number of occasions, but he *demands* this agreement of them. He blames them if they judge differently, and denies them taste, which he still requires of them as something they ought to have; and to this extent it is not open to men to say: Every one has his own taste. This would be equivalent to saying that there is no such thing at all as taste, i.e. no aes-

---

[15] I am aiming to say what Kantian disinterestedness is, and what it leaves open. I say what it is not in Zangwill 1992. There I distinguish Kant's own notion from various more modern and far less interesting notions of disinterestedness. In particular, I distinguish Kant's notion from the one that George Dickie criticizes in his influential paper "The Myth of the Aesthetic Attitude" (Dickie 1964). Dickie's critique does not at all endanger *Kant's* doctrine of disinterestedness. The main reason for this is that Dickie's target is a view about a notion of aesthetic "attention" or "perception," not pleasure. Since "disinterest," for Kant, describes a kind of pleasure, not a kind of attention, Kant can easily evade Dickie's arguments. In a recent paper, Jessica Williams does not disagree with this point, but she would nevertheless find a place for attention in Kant's aesthetics (Williams 2021). She holds a double attention theory: first, we perceptually attend to the "form" of an object; and second, we attend to our own state of mind when we are pleased by something beautiful. I am happy to admit the former, for that would be part of the representation of the object, to which disinterested pleasure is a reaction. However, the latter means that we are attending to our own faculties, which is problematic for the reasons that Zuckert gives.

thetic judgment capable of making a rightful claim upon the assent of all men. (KU-Meredith: 212–213)

Alternative translation:

> if he pronounces that something is beautiful, then he expects the same pleasure of others; he judges not merely for himself, but for everyone, and he speaks of beauty as if it were a property of things. Hence he says that the *thing* is beautiful, and does not count on the agreement of others with his judgement of pleasure because they have frequently been found to be agreeable with his own, but rather *demands* it from them. He rebukes them if they judge otherwise, and denies that they have taste, though he requires that they ought to have it; and to this extent one cannot say, "Everyone has his special taste." This would be as much as to say that there is no taste at all, i.e., no aesthetic judgement that could make a rightful claim to the assent of everyone. (KU-Guyer: 212–213, replacing "satisfaction" with "pleasure")

I shall interpret the normativity that Kant describes rather simply, as the idea that some judgements of taste claim to be correct or appropriate, where this implies that the opposite judgement would be incorrect or inappropriate. This skates over some issues; but it will be adequate for the present discussion. (For further discussion and a defense of the normativity of the judgement of taste, see Zangwill 2019.)

The argument that we need in order to traverse the gap between disinterestedness and normativity is this: if aesthetic pleasure *were* dependent on whether we possessed a certain desire, then the judgement of taste we base upon it could not make claim to the agreement of those who lack that desire. The argument is: if aesthetic pleasure were based on a desire, then, as Kant says, the judgement that is grounded upon such aesthetic pleasure would be "very partial" (KU: 205, same translation; see also KU: 223). The validity of a judgement of taste would become relative to whether a person *happened* to possess the interest or desire. And with that, the normative claim would be lost. The implied argument, I suggest, is: we cannot require of someone who lacks a desire that they ought to have an aesthetic pleasure that they can have only if they have that desire. There is an "ought-implies-can" principle operative here: we can only require of someone what they are able to comply with. It is not fair to demand the impossible, in action or in feeling. Therefore, we cannot demand pleasure from someone who lacks the desire that would ground the pleasure.

This argument is not completely decisive. Perhaps "ought" does not always imply "can." Or perhaps there could be some assessment of desires that claims universal validity; and then pleasures based on such desires could have a derivative assessment. The normativity constraining desires might then spill over to the pleasures consequential upon them. But while this suggestion might seem tempting, its attractions fade once we consider the details. It is difficult to think of exactly which desires would be in question. Even if there are some desires that we all ought to have, there would be a risk that judgements of taste would then turn out to be disguised moral judgements. And it is difficult to think of morally vindicated desires that would pass on their worth to aesthetic pleasures that are grounded on them. For a number of reasons there is a lack of fit between the two. (For example, aesthetics is about appearances in a way that morality does not.) I invite the person who wants to take this line to come up with plausible suggestions that avoid these difficulties. In addition, intuition and phenomenological reflection support Kant in thinking that aesthetic pleasure is unlike pleasure in the satisfaction of desire.

So, we should accept the counterfactual conditional that if aesthetic pleasure were not disinterested, judgements of taste could not make the normative claim they do. This is important; for it is this normative claim that distinguishes judgements of taste from mere judgements of the agreeable—that is judgements of niceness and nastiness. It is not the case that any judgement of taste is as apt as any other; but as far as judgements of niceness and nastiness are concerned, pretty much anything goes. (In Zangwill 2018, and Zangwill 2019 I refine this claim.) Or as Kant puts it, with judgements of niceness and nastiness,

> no one is proposing to make his own judgment into a universal rule. (KU-Meredith: 337; see also 339.)

Alternative translation:

> no one has any thought of making his own judgment into a universal rule. (KU-Guyer: 337; see also 339)

But we *do* propose to do this with judgements of taste. (I discuss judgements of niceness and nastiness about food in Zangwill 2018.) Normativity is essential to judgements of taste; they would not be what they are without it. And disinterestedness is essential for normativity. Therefore, we cannot reject disinterestedness without rejecting judgements of taste. (This argument—from normativity to disinterest—is supplied on Kant's behalf; Kant's argument in the other direction—from disinterest to normativity—is examined in the next section and those that follow.)

There are skeptics who think that judgements of taste are defective in some deep way (for example, Bourdieu 1984 and Eagleton 1984). But if Kant is right about the modest disinterestedness doctrine, then the doctrine of disinterestedness is essential to an analysis of ordinary aesthetic thought and experience. It is true that the whole kind of thought might be systematically corrupt. But so long as we want a theory of aesthetic experiences and judgements of taste and as they actually are, we must retain the notion of disinterestedness. Skepticism about disinterestedness might be right. What cannot be done is to attack disinterestedness in isolation from the rest of our aesthetic life. For if Kant is right about disinterestedness, it is necessary for judgements of taste.

Note that many different sorts of aestheticians should want to respect the thesis that aesthetic pleasure is disinterested. It ought not to be a view that is peculiar to Kant. This is illustrated by the fact that something like Kant's idea can be found in Hume's classic essay "Of the Standard of Taste," where, on the one hand, Hume wants to see our judgements of taste as a matter of sentiment, but on the other, he describes various impediments to the true and healthy functioning of the aesthetic sensibility—such as inexperience or prejudice. These interfere with the direct aesthetic response to non-aesthetic input. Here is Hume:

> A critic [...] must preserve his mind free of all *prejudice* and allow nothing to enter into his consideration, but the very object which is submitted to his examination. (Hume 1985, p. 239)

And

> I must [...] consider [...] myself as a man in general, [and] forget, if possible, my individual being and my peculiar circumstances. (Hume 1985, p. 239)

In his doctrine of disinterestedness, Kant follows in the footsteps of his slumber-waking forebear![16]

6 From Disinterestedness to Normativity?

Thus far, things are going well for Kant. We have seen that the normativity of judgements of taste entails disinterestedness. That seems to be important and right. What is not so clear, however, is that disinterestedness entails normativity. Kant also has his eyes on this more problematic entailment. This is where problems and complications begin. We need to keep in mind the fact that Kant supposes that the step from disinterestedness to the "universal validity" of judgements of taste (their normative claim) is a simple one. In fact, Kant says that universal voice can be *deduced* from disinterestedness (KU: 211). Kant has disinterestedness do a lot of work!

---

[16] See Hume 1985, "Of the Standard of Taste," which is reprinted in many collections of Hume's essays and also in many aesthetics anthologies. Some other British sentimentalists had similar ideas; see Townsend 1999. I discuss Hume on taste in Zangwill 2001, Chapter 9.

There are two general worries: firstly, in principle, surely there might be *other* differences between people besides differences of *desire*. People might simply be disposed to respond differently.[17] The fact that someone responds in a certain way might not be traceable back to a desire or any other intentional state. The difference, for example, might be a consequence of a mere physical difference. Secondly, there may, for all Kant has shown, be other pleasures that are disinterested yet do not ground judgements that make a normative claim.

If Kant can argue from normativity to disinterestedness, as it has so far been analyzed, but not from disinterestedness to normativity, it would mean that although disinterestedness is a necessary condition of a pleasure's being aesthetic, it is not a sufficient condition. The modest thesis would be intact, but the ambitious thesis would be in jeopardy.

It is clear that if Kant is operating with the notion of disinterest, *as it has so far been characterized*, then he cannot deduce normativity, and his ambitious project therefore fails. However, it may be replied that what this shows is that Kant has a fuller or richer notion of disinterest.

Let us call the notion of disinterestedness which was described earlier "basic disinterestedness." Someone might think that, deep down, basic disinterestedness was all that Kant had in mind. But this cannot be right. It may turn out that this is all he *ought* to have meant. But let us stick with *de facto* questions for the moment. Many later passages show that Kantian disinterestedness is basic disinterestedness *plus something more*. What is this something more? Kant writes:

> All interest presupposes a desire *or calls one forth* [...] (KU-Meredith: 210, my emphasis.)

Alternative translation:

> All interest presupposes a need or produces one; [...] (KU-Guyer: 210.)

The consequence of this for the judgement of taste is that

> We have a faculty of judgment which is merely aesthetic—a faculty of judging of forms without the aid of concepts, and of finding in the mere estimate of them, a delight that we at the same time make into a rule for everyone, without this judgment being founded on an interest, *or yet producing one.* (KU-Meredith: 300, my emphasis.)

Alternative translation:

---

17 Paul Guyer notes this at Guyer 1979, p. 169. See also McCloskey 1987, pp. 25–26.

> We have a faculty of merely aesthetic judgement, for judging of forms without concepts and for finding pleasure in the mere judging of them which we at the same time make into a rule for everyone without this judgement being grounded on an interest or producing one. (KU-Guyer: 300, my emphasis, and "pleasure" is substituted for "satisfaction")

and

> of themselves, judgments of taste do not even set up any interest whatsoever. (KU-Meredith: 205 fn.)

Alternatively:

> the pure judgement of taste does not in itself even ground any interest. (KU-Guyer: 205 fn.)

Let us label the alternative here "productive disinterestedness" (see also Zangwill 1995 on this notion). Basically interested pleasure is pleasure that is produced by a desire, whereas productively interested pleasure is pleasure that produces desire. This generation may or may not also be *rational* causality; that is, the desire may or may not be *grounded* in the pleasure. This may be left open. Let us call a pleasure "disjunctively disinterested" when it is either basically or productively disinterested.

If Kantian disinterestedness is disjunctive disinterestedness, then, it seems that the earlier view of Kant's doctrine of disinterestedness should be modified by saying that not only is there no path from desire to disinterested pleasure, there is also none from disinterested pleasure to desire. A pleasure is an interest when it is connected with desire; but this connection can extend in two temporal directions.

7 The Agreeable and the Good

Has Kant abandoned his initial characterization? No, for two reasons. Firstly, my formulation of Kant's initial explication of disinterestedness in § 2 of the *Critique of Judgment* ignored the seemingly innocent qualification in the first quotation given in this paper:

> [...] *or else*, as necessarily implicated with its determining ground. (KU-Meredith: 204, my emphasis)

Alternatively rendered into English as:

> [...] or else as necessarily interconnected with its determining ground. (KU-Guyer: 204)

But this qualification allows for productively interested pleasure.

Secondly, at the end of § 2, Kant is himself helpful to warn us not to go wholly by his initial explication; he seems to be telling us that his initial explication is more like a working definition. He says that what he means by his claims about disinterestedness

> [...] cannot be better explained than by contrasting the pure disinterested delight which appears in the judgment of taste with that allied to an interest [...]. (KU-Meredith: 205)

Alternatively rendered into English as:

> We can find no better way of elucidating this proposition, however, [...] than by contrasting to the pure disinterested pleasure in the judgement of taste that which is combined with interest, [...]. (KU-Guyer: 205, replacing "pleasure" for "satisfaction")

He continues by arguing that as far as disinterestedness goes, pleasure in the beautiful contrasts with pleasure in the agreeable, on the one hand, and with pleasure in the good, on the other. So, one way of getting at what Kant *means* by "disinterested" is to consider his *arguments* over these subject matters. We can use what he later argues about the agreeable and the good to augment his initial account. And it turns out that this augmented account makes best sense of what Kant is aiming to *do* with the notion of disinterestedness—the ambitious demarcation project.

On the agreeable, Kant writes:

> I do not accord [the agreeable] simple approval, but inclination is aroused by it [...] (KU-Meredith: 207)

Alternatively rendered into English as:

> It is not mere approval that I give it, rather inclination is thereby aroused; [...]. (KU-Guyer: 207)

Furthermore,

> Now, that a judgment on an object by which its agreeableness is affirmed, expresses an interest in it, is evident from the fact that through sensation it provokes a desire for similar objects [...]. (KU-Meredith: 207)

Alternatively:

> Now, that my judgment about an object by which I declare it agreeable expresses an interest in it is already clear from the fact that through sensation it excites a desire for objects of the same sort, [...]. (KU-Guyer: 207)

It is *productive* interestedness that Kant has in mind when he argues that all pleasure in the agreeable is interested. That such pleasures generate desire is irrelevant to basic interestedness. All that is relevant for basic interestedness is that the pleasure is pleasure in the satisfaction of a desire; it is a question of what *grounds* the pleasure. But Kant thinks that pleasure in the agreeable is productively interested because it *generates* desire (see Zangwill 1995).

Furthermore, Kant thinks that is *why* pleasure in the agreeable is *not* a direct response to a representation. He thinks that although pleasure in the agreeable may not be grounded on the belief that we have got something that we desire, it is necessarily muddy with desire, unlike pleasure in the beautiful. If pleasure in the agreeable is necessarily such as to produce desire, of itself, that can only be because it is the kind of pleasure that stands in close proximity to desire. Pleasure in Canary wine may not satisfy a pre-existing desire, but it is "moreish" in that it provokes desire for similar wine, by itself, or it will do so in the right circumstances (when one is not sated, for example).

By contrast with pleasure in the beautiful, Kant also thinks that *moral* pleasure does generate an interest (KU: 222; see also KU: 271). I shall not discuss Kant's views on the agreeable and the good in depth in this paper (I do so in Zangwill 1995 and Zangwill 2022). But in these passages, we can see that Kant is not appealing to basic disinterestedness. Kant's claims and arguments over both the good and the agreeable clearly show that he intended more than basic disinterestedness, and that he at least had something like disjunctive disinterestedness in mind.

That is the good news. The bad news is that this disjunctive notion of disinterest does not get us much further with the problem of normativity. We saw that if disinterestedness is basic disinterestedness, Kant cannot deduce normativity from it. But even if he is operating with the wider disjunctive notion, normativity still cannot be deduced. The very strong connection Kant wants to uphold between disinterestedness and normativity is a problem whichever of these two notions of disinterestedness he deploys. For both basic and productive disinterestedness are characterized in terms of the particular sort of mental state—*desire*. But, as we have noted, people may differ in respects other than desire. So, invoking disjunctive disinterestedness cannot help Kant's ambitious project.

8 Noumenal and Dualistic Disinterestedness?

Kant sometimes seems to have in mind a stronger notion of disinterestedness, which is not restricted to ruling out an involvement with the particular mental state of desire. This idea of this sort of disinterestedness is not that no mental state of *any* sort determines aesthetic pleasure, but that no *idiosyncratic* mental state determines aesthetic pleasure. An idiosyncratic mental state is one the varies between people.

We might be encouraged to think that Kant has such a notion in mind from the passages where he appeals to the *freedom* of aesthetic pleasure. One place where this strand emerges is in § 6, where he is trying to argue that the normativity ("universal validity") of the judgement of taste follows from the disinterestedness of pleasure in beauty. He writes:

> For, since the delight is not based on any inclination of the Subject (or on any other deliberate interest), but the Subject feels himself completely *free* in respect of the liking which he accords the object [Gegenstande], he can find as reason for his delight no *personal conditions* [Privatbedingungen] to which his own subjective self might alone be party. Hence he must regard it as resting on what he may also presuppose in every other person; and therefore he must believe that he has reason for demanding a similar delight from everyone. (KU-Meredith: 211; the second emphasis is mine.)

An alternative English version is:

> For, since [the pleasure] is not grounded in any inclination of the subject (not in any underlying interest) but rather the person making the judgement feels himself completely *free* with regard to the pleasure that he devotes to the object [Gegenstande], he cannot discover as grounds of the satisfaction any *private conditions* [Privatbedingungen], pertaining to his subject alone, and must therefore regard it as grounded in those he can also presuppose in everybody else. Consequently he must believe himself to have grounds for expecting a similar pleasure of everyone. (KU-Guyer: 211; the second emphasis is mine, and "pleasure" is substituted for "satisfaction")

This is the argument that Kant uses in order to try to get from disinterestedness to universal validity. The argument would be invalid if disinterestedness were either basic or productive disinterestedness. However, in the quoted passage, he is not merely arguing that aesthetic pleasure must be based on what is present in everyone because it is not based on a *desire*, but because it is not based on *any personal or private condition*. Guyer and Matthews' translation "private condition" is better than Meredith's "personal condition" since the latter would rule-out the free play of the cognitive faculties that we all share, while the former serves only to rule out psychological respects in which we differ from each other. Kant also thinks that aesthetic pleasure is not based on what merely *happens* to be present in everyone, but on something which *must* (in some sense) be present in all of us. For Kant, the source of aesthetic pleasure is separate from anything that is a merely contingent feature of us. Aesthetic pleasure, he seems to be saying, is not a product of our "empirical psychology." With this, we find ourselves catapulted into the midst of Kant's notoriously difficult views on the self. Let us call the disinterestedness which would involve this freedom "noumenal disinterestedness." (Some of Kant's remarks in § 57 suggest this notion (KU: 340–341).)

We might think that if free aesthetic pleasure has nothing to do with the "empirical self," the notion of disinterestedness that emerges is one according to which aesthetic pleasure has complete and utter freedom from anything in the physical world. We might call that "dualistic disinterestedness." But it is not clear that noumenal disinterestedness would have to involve such a dualistic view of our mental life. For the sake of argument, assume that it would. Many philosophers think that a dualistic conception of mental states is problematic, mainly because it cannot explain the causal commerce of mental states with the physical world. But suppose that dualistic disinterestedness is not problematic on this score. Would Kant's inference to universal validity be any the better? It is not obvious that it would. Perhaps one person has dualistic pleasures while another has dualistic displeasures. We still have the problem of how one response can be more appropriate than the other. People can differ in respect of what is going on in their dualistic mental lives. Dualistic minds can differ psychologically in respects other than desire, and we cannot demand the impossible of those with particular dualistic mindsets. So, dualistic disinterestedness is as little help as basic or productive disinterestedness for the purpose of generating normativity. Even if dualistic disinterestedness were not problematic on general grounds, it is not clear how it yields normativity. If Kant has dualistic disinterestedness in mind, it will not help him.

We might also note that if Kant had dualist disinterest in mind, it would have to be an interactionist kind of dualism, because of Kant's commitment to the "inherent causality" (KU-Meredith: 222)/"causality in itself" (KU-Guyer: 222) of aesthetic pleasure. When we *"dwell* on the contemplation of the beautiful" (KU-Meredith: 222)/"*linger* over the consideration of the beautiful" (KU-Guyer: 222), this is presumably physically manifested. Whatever kind of disinterestedness Kant has in mind must accommodate this causality.

9 Free Disinterestedness

The idea of *free* pleasure need not imply dualistic disinterestedness. The idea of free pleasure seems, negatively, to be that aesthetic pleasure is not determined by, and does not determine, any idiosyncratic mental state (not just desire). And also, and positively, that it has its source in *me*—that I am its author. That does not imply, or not obviously so, that it is independent of the physical world. The idea of free aesthetic pleasure is that aesthetic pleasure is isolated from other aspects of our contingent mental life—not tied to them. It need not be way out in the dualist stratosphere. It is doubtful whether Kant could have meant anything like dualistic disinterestedness.

Since Kant is talking about freedom, we can try taking this in a "compatibilistic" rather than a "libertarian" way. Thus, we might say (negatively) that aesthetic pleasure is disinterested if it is not caused or determined by desires or other idiosyncratic mental states. It would not follow from this that it is wholly uncaused. It seems reasonable to suppose that aesthetic pleasure has causes. I quoted Kant saying that no "private condition" is the ground (and thus the cause) of aesthetic pleasure. But aesthetic pleasure need not be "free" in the sense of being undetermined by *any condition of a person*—mental *or* physical. But if Kant's reference to "private conditions" implies not just any *condition of a person*, mental or physical, but just idiosyncratic mental conditions of a person, then aesthetic pleasure may be "free" pleasure in that sense, which would mean that the pleasure could not be predicted and explained by someone knowing only the previous idiosyncratic mental facts about a person. That aesthetic pleasure is physically determined would be compatible with its being a free pleasure in this sense. Kant could say that the pleasure is free in that it does not have its source in previous idiosyncratic mental characteristics of the self, which is why it cannot be predicted and explained by invoking those mental facts. So, let us henceforth take free disinterestedness to be compatibilistic free disinterestedness.

The idea is not that aesthetic pleasure comes out of the blue mentally, emerging into our consciousness from subterranean physiological causes. That is not a form of freedom because the self is not engaged in producing the pleasure. The source of free aesthetic pleasure is not some previous "private" mental state that is a cause of the pleasure. Instead, the self is at least part of the source of free pleasure in the beautiful.[18] Free disinterestedness implies a psychological conception of the source of aesthetic pleasure, but not a source in previous "private" mental states.

How would such a notion of free disinterestedness' relate to the other notions? At first sight, this free disinterestedness seems to go further than basic or productive disinterestedness, but not as far as the extravagance of dualistic disinterested-

---

[18] See further Markosian 1999 and Markosian 2012 for a defense of compatibilist agent-causation views.

ness. Recall that basic disinterestedness is backward-looking, whereas productive disinterestedness is forward-looking. Kant writes that:

> the delight [...] of taste in the beautiful may be said to be the one and only disinterested and free delight; for, with it no interest, whether of sense or reason, extorts approval. (KU-Meredith: 210)

Alternatively rendered into English as:

> [the] pleasure of the taste for the beautiful is a disinterested and free pleasure; for no interest, neither that of sense nor that of reason, extorts approval. (KU-Guyer: 210, replacing "pleasure" for "satisfaction")

and

> All interest [...] being a ground determining approval, deprives the judgment on the object of its freedom. (KU-Meredith: 210)

Alternatively rendered into English as:

> All interest [...] no longer leaves the judgement on the object free. (KU-Guyer: 210)

This idea of free pleasure and free disinterestedness, then, is backward-looking, like basic disinterestedness. Free disinterestedness entails basic disinterestedness. But does basic disinterestedness entail free disinterestedness? We might think not, since basic disinterestedness is restricted to ruling out the determination of aesthetic pleasure by the specific mental state of *desire*, whereas free disinterestedness rules out its determination by *any* previous idiosyncratic mental state. It looks as if aesthetic pleasure could be basically disinterested but not a free pleasure if the determining were done not by a desire but by some other idiosyncratic kind of mental state. However, if we recall that basic disinterestedness also involved the underlying idea that aesthetic pleasure is simply a response to a representation, we can then see that the two notions probably coincide. For if aesthetic pleasure is determined, not by desire but by some other kind of idiosyncratic mental state, it would not be such a simple response, and is no longer free. Any idiosyncratic mental state that interferes with the route from representation to pleasure, deprives the pleasure of freedom. The idea of free aesthetic pleasure is in the end the same as the idea that aesthetic pleasure is a simple response to a representation. Hence, free disinterestedness just is basic disinterestedness in disguise. It seems, therefore, that all we have to worry about are basic and productive disinterestedness. This simplifies matters considerably.

However, this means that we have no new hope as far as normativity is concerned. There might be psychological differences between people just in their aesthetic responses, which are not traceable to other idiosyncratic psychological differences. Contrary to Kant, it cannot be assumed that if the aesthetic pleasure does not flow from idiosyncratic mental states, then it flows from the psychological capacities that we all share. For some divergences between people may not be due to any other mental differences. For example, they may be due to physical differences, such as different chemicals circulating around our brain. Thus, there can be divergence in pleasures between people where the diverging pleasures are basically and productively disinterested. And that means that normativity cannot be derived from any of the kinds of disinterestedness that we have encountered.

10 Coda

Disinterestedness implies a certain kind of independence of aesthetic pleasure from desire and other idiosyncratic aspects of our mental life. There are different notions of disinterestedness corresponding to different specifications of this independence. I separated basic, productive, dualistic, and free notions of disinterestedness. Basic disinterestedness is the most fundamental of these notions, and if any doctrine of disinterestedness is true, it is one deploying this notion. For this reason, my main concern was to establish the plausibility of the idea that aesthetic pleasure is basically disinterestedness. I did this by appealing to normativity. Normativity is a necessary condition of judgements of taste. And judgements of taste are grounded on aesthetic pleasure. Given this, we must accept any feature of aesthetic pleasure that is implied by the normativity of judgements of taste. The modest thesis that aesthetic pleasure is basically disinterested is essential to our understanding of judgements of taste because without basic disinterestedness, there is no normativity, and without normativity, there are no judgements of taste.

However, Kant also—more ambitiously—wants normativity to follow from disinterestedness. He wants disinterestedness to be sufficient as well as necessary for judgements of taste. But sadly, we found no notion of disinterestedness that yielded Kant's ambitious doctrine.

I hope to have suggested that it was a mistake for Kant to try and squeeze normativity out of disinterestedness. My own view is that if we seek a sufficient condition of aesthetic pleasure, we have no choice but to appeal directly to the normativity of the judgements that we base on those pleasures. How we explain it is another matter; but we should separate the analysis of judgements of taste from a philosophical explanation of their possibility. But this would short-circuit Kant's whole program of deriving normativity from disinterestedness.[19]

I have here offered *some* criticisms of Kant's ambitious project, but I should mention two matters that have not been discussed, and which are relevant to a full assessment of it.

Firstly, I have not discussed whether Kant is right to think that pleasures in the agreeable and in the good *are* interested. Perhaps there are non-aesthetic pleasures that are basically or productively disinterested.[20]

Secondly, we need to say something about the fact that we plainly do value the existence of things that we think are beautiful. I argued that pleasure in the beautiful is *basically disinterested*. But for all I have shown, pleasure in the beautiful might yet be *productively interested*. Kant needs to rule this out. He deals with this in §§ 41 and 42 of the *Critique of Judgment* where he discusses what he calls our "empirical" and "intellectual" interest in the beautiful. He attempts to give an account of the fact that we have desires about the existence of the things that we find beautiful that is consistent with pleasure in the beautiful being disinterested. If Kant's account in these passages fails and his position cannot be defended by other means, then productive disinterestedness would fail to mark the distinction between aesthetic and non-aesthetic pleasures; for aesthetic pleasures would have turned out to be productively interested. Guyer and others have criticized Kant on this point, and I have said nothing here in Kant's defense on this matter. Whether Kant's view that pleasure in the beautiful is productively disinterested is defensible is at present an open question, which requires serious critical discussion, and a discussion separate from anything that we have been through here.

In spite of everything, the more modest claim that *basic* disinterestedness is necessary for aesthetic pleasure has emerged unscathed, and I hope to have brought *its* centrality and importance into sharper focus. Kant's doctrine of

---

19 In the attempt to construct normativity, some philosophers might want to say that aesthetic pleasure is distinguished by its *content*. For example, they might say, with the "aesthetic realist," that aesthetic thought and experience represents the world as possessing mind-independent aesthetic properties. This is neither Hume nor Kant's way. One alternative to aesthetic realism is to distinguish aesthetic thought and experience by a kind of attitude to non-aesthetic contents (Hume's way). Or we might distinguish them by the array of psychological faculties underpinning pleasure in non-aesthetic representation (Kant's way). This raises complex and difficult questions that lie beyond the scope of this paper. (For discussion, see Zangwill 2003, reprinted in Zangwill 2015.)

20 See Zangwill 1995 for a discussion of the interestedness of pleasure in the agreeable and Zangwill 2022 for a discussion of the interestedness of pleasure in the good.

basic disinterestedness is well motivated. Let us not overplay Kant's failings when there are successes to celebrate.[21]

Abbreviations

All references to Kant's works are to Kant's *Gesammelte Schriften, Ausgabe der Preußischen Akademie der Wissenschaften* (Berlin: De Gruyter, 1902 ff.).

Translations are from *The Cambridge Edition of the Works of Immanuel Kant*, published as *Critique of the Power of Judgment*, trans. Paul Guyer and Eric Matthews, Cambridge: Cambridge University Press, 2000, and also from the translation by James Creed Meredith, published as *Critique of Judgement*, trans. James Meredith, Oxford: Oxford University Press, 1928.

The following abbreviations of individual works are used:

KU   Kritik der Urteilskraft / Critique of the Power of Judgment
KU-Meredith   Critique of Judgement, trans. James Meredith, Oxford: Oxford University Press, 1928.
KU-Guyer   Critique of the Power of Judgment, trans. Paul Guyer and Eric Matthews, Cambridge: Cambridge University Press, 2000.

Literature:

Allison, Henry (2001): *Kant's Theory of Taste*. Cambridge: Cambridge University Press.
Bourdieu, Pierre (1984): *Distinction*. London: Routledge and Kegan Paul.
Budd, Malcolm (2001): "The Pure Judgement of Taste as an Aesthetic Reflective Judgement." In: British
  Journal of Aesthetics 41. No. 3, pp. 247–260.
Dickie, George (1964): "The Myth of the Aesthetic Attitude." In: *American Philosophical Quarterly* 1. No. 1, pp. 56–65.
Eagleton, Terry (1984): *The Ideology of the Aesthetic*. Oxford: Blackwell.
Ginsborg, Hannah (2002): "Review of *Critique of the Power of Judgment* by Immanuel Kant, Paul Guyer, Eric Matthews." In: *Philosophical Review* 111. No. 3, pp. 429–435.

---

[21] A version of this paper was presented many moons ago at an American Aesthetics Society meeting at Asilomar, California. I then left the paper for nearly two decades while I pursued other philosophical topics. I even had a "revise and resubmit" for this paper from a history of philosophy journal around that time, but I never got around to resubmitting the paper. I hope that that what is published here is not too out of date! I am very grateful indeed to Rachel Zuckert for comments on a recent draft that were extremely interesting and insightful. Thanks also to Larissa Berger for constructive comments. I would like to add that I owe my interest in Kant's aesthetics to my teacher Ruby Meager, who taught me when I was doing my doctorate on metaethics at the University of London.

Guyer, Paul (1979): *Kant and the Claims of Taste.* Cambridge: Harvard.
Guyer, Paul (2009): "The Harmony of the Faculties: Recent Books on the *Critique of the Power of Judgment.*" In: *Journal of Aesthetics and Art Criticism* 67. No. 2, pp. 201–221.
Hume, David (1985): "Of the Standard of Taste." In: Miller, Eugene (Ed.): *Essays, Moral, Political and Literary.* Indianapolis: Liberty Press, pp. 237–238.
Kemal, Salim (1992): *Kant's Aesthetic Theory.* London: Macmillan.
Markosian, Ned (1999): "A compatibilist version of the theory of agent causation." In: *Pacific Philosophical Quarterly* 80. No. 3, pp. 257–277.
Markosian, Ned (2012): "Agent Causation as the Solution to All the Compatibilist's Problems." In: *Philosophical Studies* 157. No. 3, pp. 383–398.
McCloskey, Mary (1987): *Kant's Aesthetic.* Albany: SUNY Press.
Scruton, Roger (1974): *Art and Imagination.* London: Methuen.
Sibley, Frank (1959): "Aesthetic Concepts." In: *Philosophical Review* 68. No. 4, pp. 421–450.
Townsend, Dabney (Ed.) (1999): *Eighteenth Century British Aesthetics.* Amityville: Baywood Publishing.
Usher, Marius (2006): "Control, Choice and Convergence/Divergence Dynamics: A Compatibilistic Probabilistic Theory of Free Will." In: *Journal of Philosophy* 103. No. 4, pp. 188–213.
Williams, Jessica J. (2021): "Kant on Aesthetic Attention." In: *British Journal of Aesthetics* 61. No. 4, pp. 421–435.
Zangwill, Nick (1990): "Two Dogmas of Kantian Aesthetics." In: Woodfield, Richard *(Ed.): Proceedings of the 11th International Congress in Aesthetics 1988: Selected Papers.* Nottingham: Nottingham Polytechnic Press.[22]
Zangwill, Nick (1992): "Unkantian Notions of Disinterest." In: *British Journal of Aesthetics* 32. No. 2, pp. 149–152.
Zangwill, Nick (1995): "Kant on Pleasure in the Agreeable." In: *Journal of Aesthetics and Art Criticism* 53. No. 2, pp. 167–176.
Zangwill, Nick (2001): *Metaphysics of Beauty.* Ithaca: Cornell University Press.
Zangwill, Nick (2003): "Aesthetic Realism." In: Levinson, Jerrold (Ed.): *Oxford Companion to Aesthetics.* Oxford University Press. (Reprinted with revisions in Zangwill 2015.)
Zangwill, Nick (2013a): "Nietzsche on Kant on Disinterestedness." In: *History of Philosophy Quarterly* 30. No. 1, pp. 75–91.
Zangwill, Nick (2013b): "Clouds of Illusion in the Aesthetics of Nature." In: *Philosophical Quarterly* 63. No. 252, pp. 576–596.
Zangwill, Nick (2015): *Music and Aesthetic Reality.* London: Routledge.
Zangwill, Nick (2018): "The Yummy and the Yucky." In: *Monist* 101. No. 3, pp. 294–308.
Zangwill, Nick (2019): "Folk Aesthetics and Normativity: A Critique of Experimental Aesthetics." In: Cova, Florian and Réhault, Sébastien (Eds.): *Advances in Experimental Philosophy of Art.* London: Bloomsbury, pp. 289–307.
Zangwill, Nick (2022): "Kant on Pleasure in the Good." In: *Disputatio* 13. No. 62, pp. 181–188.
Zuckert, Rachel (2007): *Kant on Beauty and Biology.* Cambridge: Cambridge University Press.

---

[22] This text is printed with quite a few errors, unfortunately.

Christian Helmut Wenzel
Disinterestedness and Its Role in Kant's Aesthetics

Abstract: In this essay I explain the methodology of Kant's analysis of the judgment of taste. I focus on the very beginning, especially the footnote just before § 1. I explain how Kant thinks he is justified in being guided by certain logical functions to discover the "moments" of the judgement of taste. I show that "moment" (*das Moment*) here should be understood as "force" in terms of physics (Lat. *momentum*). I explain why he begins with Quality and not with Quantity, as one might expect on the basis of the *First Critique*. I then follow Kant's analysis and show how it leads to the first "explication" of beauty, i.e., that taste is based on disinterested satisfaction. Based on these results, I discuss the role disinterestedness plays in intellectual interest, autonomy, and judgments of the sublime.

1 Overview and Introduction

In his *Third Critique,* Kant introduces the judgment of taste and thereby beauty as something that is a kind of its own. He gives an account of taste according to which "satisfaction in the beautiful" (*Wohlgefallen am Schönen*) differs from all other kinds of "satisfaction" (*Wohlgefallen*), not in degree, but in kind.[1] It differs from "satisfaction in the agreeable" as well as from "satisfaction in the good." Thus, there are "three specifically different kinds of satisfaction" (KU: 209), beauty taking a middle position. Kant thereby tries to steer a middle course between empiricist accounts, such as the one offered by Burke, and rationalist accounts, such as Baumgarten's.[2] What allows him to steer this middle course is initially his way

---

1 "*Wohlgefallen*" is the original German for "satisfaction." Different translators have rendered it differently. "Satisfaction," "liking," "feeling of approval," and "pleasure" have been used. No translation is perfect. All these English expressions have their specific connotations that cannot be found in the original German. Which translation is best sometimes depends on the context and whether the English connotations are admissible or contrary to the original German and its connotations. One can choose to stick to one translation throughout to achieve uniformity, although this can at places appear odd and technical, or shift between translations according to context in order to be closer to the English language and achieve a smoother reading. The Cambridge Edition of Kant's works uses "satisfaction" throughout. I follow this edition.
2 Bart Vandenabeele (2012) argues that Kant's distinction between the beautiful and the agreeable is problematic and primarily directed at Burke, who does not draw this distinction. Nick Zangwill

of taking up the notion of disinterestedness (*Uninteressiertheit*). According to his account, satisfaction in the agreeable and satisfaction in the good are related to "interest" (*Interesse*), which involves desire, while satisfaction in the beautiful is free from such an interest. This freedom constitutes the "first moment of the judgment of taste." To substantiate his account and the claim that beauty is a kind of its own, Kant introduces several further "moments." As the "second moment of the judgment of taste," he reveals an implicit "claim to inter-subjective universal validity" (*Anspruch auf Allgemeingültigkeit*) in the judgment of taste. This claim is made in aesthetic reflection, or even self-reflection, in a "free play" (*freies Spiel*) of the two "faculties of cognition" (*Erkenntnisvermögen*, or *Erkenntniskräfte*): "imagination and understanding" (*Einbildungskraft und Verstand*). This claim opens the doors to his transcendental philosophy because any claim to *universality*, which is more than mere (empirical) generality, requires something *a priori*. He then reveals an *a priori* principle that is needed to support this claim to universality. This is the principle of "subjective purposiveness" or "purposiveness without purpose" (*Zweckmäßigkeit ohne Zweck*). Thus, he establishes an aesthetics that has an *a priori* ground of its own and can therefore be part of his transcendental philosophy. This theory of aesthetics is neither empiricist nor rationalist. It involves an *a priori* principle but it also requires something empirically given. Due to the claim to universality, it makes the *Third Critique* possible. As a fourth and last "moment" of the judgment of taste, Kant shows how the idea of a *sensus communis* can be seen to arise from the previous three moments, particularly from free play and its claim to universal communicability (*allgemeine Mitteilbarkeit*). The idea of the *sensus communis* has a complicated history dating back to Aristotle and Cicero. It involves intra-subjective as well as inter-subjective elements (Wenzel 2005, pp. 81–86, and Wenzel 2006). Kant argues that from his theory of aesthetics one can see how this idea of a *sensus communis* arises. But in order to get started with the whole analysis of the judgment of taste, it is crucial to grasp the way Kant takes up disinterestedness.

2 Disinterested Satisfaction in the Beautiful

The Analytic of the Beautiful comprises twenty-two sections, which are divided into four discussions devoted to the four moments of the judgment of taste. It is the

---

(1992 and 1995) gives more favorable accounts of Kant, especially regarding the agreeable. For broader accounts of the history of the notion of disinterestedness, see Guyer 1993, pp. 48–130, and Miles Rind 2002.

third moment that is the most important because it reveals the *a priori* principle that makes the *Critique of Judgment* possible. It is also the longest. It takes up eight sections. This third moment is arrived at via the discussion of the second moment, which reveals the subjective universality of the judgment of taste; and this second moment in turn is arrived at via the discussion of the first moment. Kant even speaks of a derivation. The explanation of the beautiful as based on a universal satisfaction (second moment), can be "deduced" (*gefolgert*) from "the previous" explanation (first moment) (KU: 211). Thus, there clearly is a development from the first to the third moment.[3] The fourth moment has, I think, a special position in Kant's system, but I will not dwell on this here.[4]

The first section is short and very dense. It is entitled "The judgment of taste is aesthetic" (KU: 203). Hence, it is primarily a *judgment* and not an object that is "aesthetic." I believe this title is directed at Baumgarten and his influential *Aesthetica* of 1750/1758. Kant's emphasis is on judgment. Many of the crucial results of the Analytic of the Beautiful are already hinted at in the very first few sentences of this section. § 1 introduces not only the subject of the study, but also justifies, although very briefly, the method of investigation. I will show that since we are concerned with disinterestedness and its role in Kant's aesthetics, it is helpful to pay close attention to the very first footnote that comes right at the beginning, even before § 1 begins: this is a footnote to the title of the investigation of the first moment. The topic of the first moment turns out to be quality and disinterestedness, and in that footnote Kant not only justifies his method, but also explains why he begins with quality and not as usual with quantity.

"Taste," Kant says, is the "faculty for the judging of the beautiful" (*Vermögen der Beurtheilung des Schönen*) and an analysis must reveal what this faculty involves and "requires" (*erfordert*) (KU: 203 fn.). The object of this analysis is the judgment of taste and its underlying power, namely, the "power of judgment" (*Urtheilskraft*). Of this power, Kant writes the following:

> In seeking the moments to which this power of judgments attends [*Acht hat*] in its reflection, I have been guided by the logical functions for judging (for a relation to the understanding is always contained even in the judgment of taste). I have considered the moment of quality

---

3 Bart Vandenabeele argues that "Kant (wrongly) holds that the universal communicability of aesthetic judgments logically follows from the disinterested character of the pleasure" (Vandenabeele 2012, p. 208). He has a point insofar as Kant in § 6 indeed speaks of "deduction" or "implication" (*gefolgert*) (KU: 211). But I think it is more a transition than a "logical" implication. I think Kant is primarily guided by the logical functions of judging. They impose an order. There are connections between the moments, but not strict logical implications.
4 See Wenzel 2006 and 2005, pp. 77–78, for an account of how Kant introduces ideas of exemplarity and the *sensus communis* in the discussion of the fourth moment.

first, since the aesthetic judgment of the beautiful takes notice [*Rücksicht nimmt*] of this first [*zuerst*]. (KU: 203, fn.)

Kant is rather poetic here. The power of judgment and the aesthetic judgment are anthropomorphized. Strictly speaking, powers and judgments do not "attend" or "take notice." It is human beings who do that. But it is clear that, metaphorically speaking, Kant wants to observe and follow the aesthetic judgment and its power in what it does, how it functions, and what these functions are based on. He wants to start where this judgment and power begin, so to speak. This beginning turns out to be the "moment of quality." But he does not say why he thinks the aesthetic judgment "takes notice" of the moment of quality "first." He offers no reason for this. I will offer one later. Furthermore, Kant says he is "guided" by the "logical functions for judging." But what exactly is meant by these "functions" and "moments" is not an easy matter, as I have already discussed elsewhere (Wenzel 2005, pp. 13–18). Some clarifications are necessary.

"Moment" (German *Moment*) can mean many things. Today, it usually means a moment of time. But it can also just mean a part or aspect of something. For Kant, it does not mean a moment of time but something closer to "part" or "aspect," and it means more than that. I think it is related to what the Latin "*movere*" (to move) and "*momentum*" mean in physics. In German, we have two different words: "*der Moment*" (masculine) and "*das Moment*" (neuter). The former means a moment of time, the latter *momentum*, i.e., weight, pressure, push, force, power, and influence. It is the latter that I think Kant has in mind, because he writes "*das Moment des Geschmacks*" and "*erstes, zweites, drittes, viertes Moment des Geschmacksurteils*," always using the *neuter* form. He does not use "*der Moment*," the masculine form, which would mean a moment of time. Kant has always been interested in the natural sciences, and we should take the Latin meaning seriously. Force and movement are what he meant. I suggest it is the faculties of cognition, imagination, and understanding that he has in mind as having a certain power or force that they can exert on representations (*Vorstellungen*), especially on intuitions (*Anschauungen*). At the end of the discussion of the first moment, Kant offers an "explanation of the beautiful," saying that taste is "the faculty of judging an object or a kind of representation through a satisfaction or dissatisfaction without any interest" (KU: 211).[5] This explanation is "deduced" (*gefolgert*) (KU: 211) from this first moment. I think we can take this as spelling out what the first moment turns out to be, or how it appears, namely, as disinterested satisfaction. But we must

---

5 Kant bases taste on a certain kind of satisfaction *or dissatisfaction*. I take passages like this to imply that there must be *a priori* grounds also for *negative* judgments of taste. See Wenzel 2012.

keep in mind what this satisfaction involves. The "moment" itself functions at a deeper, grounding level, while the experience of disinterested satisfaction is merely the tip of the iceberg.

We can learn about "Logical functions of judging" from § 9 of the *First Critique*. That section is entitled "The logical function of the understanding in judgments," and Kant there writes that "the function of thinking in [....] [a judgment] can be brought under four titles, each of which contains under itself three moments" (KrV: A 70/B 95). Thus, there is talk of "moments" already in the *First Critique*. The second of these titles is "quality of a judgment" and it "contains" the "affirmative," "negative," and "infinite" moments (KrV: A 70/B 95). Here in our text, the very first sentence of § 1, right after the title and the footnote we quoted above, says:

> In order to decide whether or not something is beautiful, we [...] relate the representation [...] to the subject and its feeling of pleasure and displeasure. (KU: 203)

Hence, I suggest that "the aesthetic judgment" of the beautiful "takes notice," as Kant says in the footnote, of the moment of quality *"first"* (whatever this moment turns out to be), because in such a judgment we "decide whether something is beautiful or not," and because the logical function of judging related to *quality* is exactly about affirmation and negation. This "logical function of judging" is applied in "deciding whether or not something is beautiful," and quality *therefore* comes "first" (both from the point of view of the aesthetic judgment and our analysis of it). "First" then has a temporal meaning regarding what is most apparent when one is asked whether one finds something beautiful. What is "taken notice" of "first," is the "yes" or "no" regarding a certain kind of satisfaction that we feel, or do not feel, when judging whether an object is beautiful or not. It is *this* that our judgment "takes notice of," or pays attention to, "first" (*zuerst Rücksicht nimmt*).

But this cannot be the whole story regarding quality. We have to say in what this kind of satisfaction consists. After the introductory § 1, Kant begins the analysis of the judgment of taste according to quality by turning directly to disinterestedness, as the title of § 2 promises: "The satisfaction that determines the judgment of taste is without any interest" (KU: 204). Thus, there is more to quality than just affirmation and negation. There is also content, i.e., a kind of satisfaction, which is disinterested satisfaction, pleasure, or liking (*Wohlgefallen*), through which we judge the object to be beautiful. When we investigate what is involved in finding something beautiful and pay attention to the experience itself, it is this kind of satisfaction and freedom (of interest) that strikes us "first." Universality and purposiveness are more fundamental systematically, but they will be taken up later in the course of the analysis.

We can now also explain why Kant in that footnote says that he is "guided" by (*nach Anleitung*) the "logical functions for judging." These functions have been introduced in the *First Critique* and are primarily about judgments of cognition and not judgments of taste. But Kant adds in the footnote in brackets, that "a relation to the understanding is always contained even in the judgment of taste" (KU: 203 n.) Hence, he feels justified in using this method of being guided by the logical function for judging as a way of analysis. This is crucial. Similarly, he adds in brackets in the first sentence of § 1 the phrase "perhaps combined with the understanding" (KU: 203). It is this link to the understanding that justifies the method. It is the second and third moments that later reveal universality and an *a priori* principle and thus give the full justification for a theory of "aesthetics" as part of his transcendental philosophy. Kant did not believe that such a theory of aesthetics was possible when he wrote the *First Critique* (see KrV: A 21/B 35, fn.). The moment of disinterestedness by itself does not provide this ground. It is too negative, as we shall see. It merely leads to, and does not by itself provide, universality and an *a priori* principle.

Now that we have at least roughly clarified some important methodological issues, we can turn to disinterestedness itself. For Kant, there are exactly three kinds of satisfaction: in the agreeable, the beautiful, and the good.[6] Only the satisfaction in the beautiful is free from "interest," that is, for Kant, not necessarily connected with desire and not concerned with the existence of the object. From today's point of view, this is a rather idiosyncratic use of the word, in German as well as in English. Kant gives the example of a palace and our being asked whether we find it beautiful (§ 2). Contemplating a palace, many considerations might come to mind that should not affect our judgment, such as its social function, its history, whether I would prefer good food instead, or the fact that I would not care about the palace if I lived alone on an island. All such considerations should play no decisive role. What matters is "what I make of this representation in myself" (KU: 205). The representation by itself (and what I make of it and how I do so) suffices. The existence of the object and our knowledge of it are not decisive.[7] This is different in the other two kinds of satisfaction. The "satisfaction in the agreeable" depends on sensation and the real existence of the object. It creates a desire, and we are therefore interested in the existence of the object and its capacity to satisfy that desire.[8] The "sat-

---

6 Henry Allison 2001, pp. 90–94, defends the completeness of this distinction. For a discussion of satisfaction and pleasure (*Lust*) more generally in Kant, see Thomas Höwing 2013.

7 This creates the question of whether an imagined palace is as good as a real one as far as beauty is concerned. So far, the answer might seem to be yes. But things change when we introduce intellectual interests, as we shall see later.

8 For a detailed discussion, see Zangwill 1995.

isfaction in the good" can be of two kinds, depending on whether the good is something useful and instrumental, or whether it is good in itself, i.e., the morally good. In both cases of what is "good," we depend on the existence of the object; in the former directly, as we depend on the existence as a means, and in the latter indirectly, as we depend on the existence as something to be brought about, namely, the existence of a moral act (§ 4). I think "existence" here does not mean the existence of the idea of the good, but the existence of a particular act to be brought about. If this reading is correct, we may be reminded of Erich Kästner's saying: "*Es gibt nichts Gutes, außer man tut es*" (nothing good exists, unless one does it).

Disinterestedness is thus primarily characterized in a negative way. Disinterested satisfaction is *without* interest; it does not depend on existence, desire, craving, appetite, or inclination, purposes or usefulness, or on the concept of the object. Kant gives many examples, such as drawings (*Zeichnungen*) that are "free" (*frei*) and "do not mean anything" (KU: 207). Disinterested satisfaction arises in contemplation. It also does not dependent on "charm" and "perfection," as Kant explains later (§§ 13 and 15), nor on ideals and standards (§ 17). This independence from perfection is additional to the independence from existence. It should not matter whether the object contemplated and judged is a house, a church, a horse, a human being, a European, or Chinese. A botanist knows a lot about flowers, but this knowledge should not be decisive when he makes a judgment of taste about a rose that he contemplates in his garden. This criterion of independence can be more difficult to satisfy when it comes to objects of art. How independent from concepts can our judgments of taste be, when we judge a fugue by Bach or a painting by Kandinsky? Do we not need some understanding? Is such a demand for independence easier to satisfy in modern art such as paintings by Kandinsky? In defense of Kant, we may say that concepts will play a role, but not a determining and decisive one.

So far, all of the characterizations have been negative. Kant hints at something positive, but he does not work it out until the discussions of the second and third moments. He says in § 2:

> It is readily seen that to say that it [the palace] is beautiful and to prove that I have taste what matters is what I make of this presentation in myself [...]. Everyone must admit that a judgment about beauty in which there is mixed the least interest is very partial and not a pure judgment of taste. One must not be in the least biased in favor of the existence of the thing, but must be entirely indifferent in this respect in order to play the judge in matters of taste. (KU: 205)

He does not say what this "making something of the representation in myself" consists in. But he speaks of "impartiality" and "playing the judge," and he hints at something positive. Indeed, he will later point out connections with autonomy

(§§ 31 and 32) and the Enlightenment (§ 40). What it means to make something of the representation in oneself will become more apparent and concrete when we learn more about free play, the demand for agreement, the belief in a universal voice, and various forms of purposiveness, which are revealed later in the second and the third moment.[9]

Due to satisfaction's independence, disinterestedness creates freedom. We are free from interests. It also creates room for contemplation, free play, and indirect connections with morality. But a fundamental difference with morality remains. Kant compares disinterested satisfaction with favor, or gratuity (*Gunst*) (see KU: 210), which is different from satisfaction grounded in a moral imperative. An object grants us a favor by allowing us to feel satisfaction in the beautiful. It provides us with a gift. We can also turn this around and say that it is we who grant the object a favor by finding it beautiful. It goes both ways, and Kant mentions both. If the object is an object of nature and not of art, Kant says that nature shows a trace (*Spur*) and gives us a hint (*Wink*) that we fit into nature (§ 42), which I think means that our hope to realize our moral ends will not be frustrated.[10] Nature then "figuratively speaks to us in its beautiful forms" (KU: 301). We may "marvel at it," be "unwilling for it to be entirely absent from nature" (KU: 299), and want to protect it. All this creates "intellectual interests," which are related to the existence of the object (in our wanting to protect it) or to the existence of other objects (in self-cultivation and moral acts). Kant later offers two whole sections to such connections, dealing with "empirical" and "intellectual interests in the beautiful" (§§ 41 and 42). But these interests are not part of the satisfaction of the beautiful itself. They arise later and are discovered later, in a second step, once beauty has been established in a particular judgment of taste. Empirical interests in the beautiful arise in society, when we communicate our feelings, which can be helpful in the development of "civilization" (*Zivilisierung*) and "humanity" (*Humanität*) (KU: 297). But since such empirical interests involve all kinds of empirical inclinations, beauty easily plays an "ambiguous" role in some sort of "transition" (*zweideutiger Übergang*) (KU: 298) from the agreeable to the beautiful. Kant is more optimistic

---

9 Fan Dahan points out that the "in myself" (*in mir selbst*) in the quoted passage above explains independence from the real existence of the object (Fan 2018, 40), and that the "making" (*machen*) reappears in § 5 (KU: 210). There, Kant explains how it is related to "favor" (*Gunst*). In matters of taste, we enjoy the "freedom to make anything into an object of pleasure ourselves" (KU: 210) (Fan 2018, 41).

10 I have suggested elsewhere that when finding nature ugly we might take this as a sign that we do *not* fit into nature and that our moral hopes will *not* be fulfilled. I have also argued that the judgment about the ugly should be seen as having *a priori* grounds, similar to the judgment about the beautiful. But this is a disputed issue. See Wenzel 2012.

regarding the "intellectual interest in the beautiful," especially when it comes to the beauty of nature, because there is less room for vanity in such a transition. There we do not show off in salons as we might do regarding beauty in art. We enjoy the beauty of nature more in solitude and with humility, and it is therefore a more reliable "mark of a good soul" (*Kennzeichen einer guten Seele*) (KU: 298). This is one major reason why Kant prefers (*Vorzug*) the beauty of nature to that of art. Kant emphasizes that such interests enter only in a second step once beauty has been established on its own grounds. By "established" I mean two things: primarily, beauty and taste, and secondly aesthetics as a theory of taste. It is desirable that taste and judgments of taste can exist on their own, independently of intellectual interests and other higher-level considerations. Then there will be the possibility of a "good soul." Kant's aesthetics makes this possible.

Part of such a second step is also the fact that "beauty is the symbol of morality" (§ 59). For such symbolism to work, beauty must have independent grounds and not depend on morality. It is our disinterestedness that makes this possible. Only if beauty is something on its own, maybe a gift, and not something dependent on morality, can it give support to morality. Otherwise, the relationship between beauty and morality would be circular. With the third moment, taste has its own *a priori* grounds, and this third moment is arrived at via the first moment, disinterested satisfaction. Thus disinterest (regarding existence) can give support to interest (regarding morality).

Regarding our intellectual interest in natural beauty, at the end of § 42 Kant gives the example of a nightingale and its song that we find beautiful and listen to "on a still summer evening, under the gentle light of the moon" (KU: 302). But once we find out that we have been deceived because it is not a bird that is singing but "a mischievous lad" who skillfully imitates the song using a reed, Kant says that "no one would long endure listening to this song" (KU: 302). Strictly speaking, I think this is not necessarily so. One might still be able to enjoy the melody. One's enjoyment might be independent of thinking whether what one hears is nature or art. One might even enjoy it more once one found out about the source. One might then think that there is a double as-if: a birdsong being natural beauty *as if* it were the beauty of art, and the lad's imitation being the beauty of art *as if* it were natural beauty (which in turn is beautiful as if it were the beauty of art). I think this would fit Kant's theory. The beauty of the song might still be enjoyable, as we today enjoy listening to a CD playing synthetic music that sounds like natural birdsong. But certain intellectual interests can no longer prevail, for instance, our interest in fitting into nature. If such interests are involved in our enjoying the song of the nightingale, then these interests would be frustrated by our finding out about the lad's trick. Thus, when Kant says "one would no longer listen," I think he means that the intellectual disappointment overshadows the satisfaction in the beautiful that we have, or might have, no matter whether we think it is produced by nature or art. I think in reality there is room for several aspects at the same time: for beauty generally, beauty of nature specifically, and an intellectual interest. It is only when the latter is very strong that it might happen that we "would no longer listen."

3 Disinterested Satisfaction and Dissatisfaction in the Sublime

The Analytic of the Sublime is short in comparison with the Analytic of the Beautiful. It is divided into only seven sections (§§ 23–29): The first (§23) is a "transition" from the discussion of the beautiful to that of the sublime, the second (§ 24) explains the division, the following three sections (§§ 25–27) investigate the "mathematical sublime" (§§ 25–27), and the final three sections (§§ 28–29) deal with the "dynamical sublime." This is followed by a lengthy "General remark on the exposition of aesthetic reflective judgments," which concludes the Analytic, after which comes the Dialectic.

Why the Analytic of the Sublime turns out to be so short can be seen from what Kant says at the end of § 23: first, the beauty of nature makes us discover a "technique of nature" (KU: 246) that is analogous to craft or art (*Kunst*). It "expands" (*erweitert*) our "concept of nature" (KU: 246) and makes us look for a reason *outside of us*. But the sublime confronts us with chaos and disorder, mere size and power, and makes us look for a reason *inside of us*. This reason inside of us is the idea of humanity and based on morality, an idea larger than the pyramids and more powerful than the ocean. But second, for morality, an *a priori* ground has already been given in Kant's moral philosophy. Hence the Analytic of the Sublime does not require an additional, new *a priori* principle, as the Analytic of the Beautiful did. Hence the Analytic of the Sublime has less of a task to accomplish. I think this second reason runs deeper than the first one that Kant himself offers (that beauty of nature makes us discover a technique of nature while the sublime does not). It explains why the Analytic of the Sublime is relatively short in comparison with the Analytic of the Beautiful. An object outside of us that we find sublime merely serves to help us discover something inside of us. It is purposive only in that limited sense. It is merely a trigger. This, I think, is the systematic reason why Kant, at the end of § 23, calls "the theory of the sublime a mere appendix" (KU: 246). The *a priori* principle of aesthetic judgment has been revealed already in the Analytic of the Beautiful.

The first sentence of § 23 draws a parallel between the beautiful and the sublime. I suggest this is related to disinterestedness: "The beautiful coincides with the sublime in that both please for themselves [*beides für sich selbst gefällt*]." (KU: 244) This "pleasing for itself" implies an independence. The beautiful *and* the sublime please not because they create and depend on a desire, as does the agreeable, nor because they rely on concepts, as does the good (but we will see that this is particularly problematic in the case of the sublime). They are independent of such interests. Nor are we interested in the existence of the object as given, as in the case of the agreeable, or as something to be achieved, as in the case of the morally good. The satisfaction is disinterested and purely aesthetic. It merely relies on aesthetic reflection. It "presuppose[s] [...] a judgment of reflection" (KU: 244).

In § 24, Kant sketches the division of the Analytic of the Sublime, saying that it follows the same principle as the division in the Analytic of the Beautiful. But unlike the Analytic of the Beautiful, the Analytic of the Sublime begins with the moment of *Quantity*, not with that of Quality.[11] Nevertheless, the Analytic of the Sublime reveals that the satisfaction in the sublime is also disinterested. Kant makes all these claims rather swiftly and without much justification. That we encounter disinterestedness should not come as a surprise, after having seen the parallels drawn already at the beginning of § 23. Just as in the Analytic of the Beautiful Kant simply took it for granted that our satisfaction in the beautiful is without interest ("if the question is whether something is beautiful, one does not want to know whether there is anything that is or that could be at stake [...] in the existence of the thing"; KU: 204), so does he here, regarding the sublime, also take this for granted: He simply observes in § 25 that "we have no interest at all in the object, i.e., its existence is indifferent to us" (KU: 249) when considering its mere magnitude and feeling satisfaction in extending our power of imagination. At the end of § 26, before the discussion proper of disinterestedness in § 27, he says that "everything that is to please the merely reflecting power of judgment without interest [*ohne Interesse gefallen soll*] must involve [...] subjective [...] purposiveness" (KU: 253). Disinterestedness is simply observed and taken as a fact, and then functions as a normative criterion (*gefallen soll*). No further justification is thought to be necessary.

I think it is primarily the feelings of pleasure or displeasure, and satisfaction or dissatisfaction, that are disinterested. Only in a derived way is a judgment or anything else "disinterested." A judgment is disinterested because the underlying

---

[11] Kant justifies this difference by observing that beauty is about the form of the object whereas the sublime is about formlessness (*Formlosigkeit*) and chaos. But I fail to see the connection to the question of what should come first.

feeling of satisfaction is. This is also the case when Kant says, in a long and compressed sentence at the end of § 24, that:

> this movement [of the mind, *Bewegung des Gemüths*, in the case of the sublime] is to be judged [*beurtheilt*] as subjective purposive (because the sublime pleases [*weil das Erhabene gefällt*]), thus this movement is related through the imagination either to the faculty of cognition or to the faculty of desire, but in both relations the purposiveness of the given representation is judged only with regard to this faculty (without an end or interest). (KU: 247)

In German, the expression "without an end or interest" (*ohne Zweck oder Interesse*) can be read as adverbial and referring to "judged." It can also be taken as adjectival and referring to "purposiveness," "representation," or "faculty." But as far as disinterestedness is concerned, I think it is basically the feeling of pleasure, or the reflective judgment or judging (*Beurtheilung*) based on it, that matters. Thus, Kant also begins his comment to § 26, thinking of both the beautiful and the sublime, with the phrase: "Since everything that is to please the merely reflecting power of judgment without interest [*ohne Interesse gefallen soll*] [...]" (KU: 253). It is pleasure or satisfaction that matters as being disinterested, or "without interest."

§ 27 is dedicated to "the quality of the satisfaction in the judging of the sublime" (KU: 257). But throughout the whole section Kant does not speak explicitly of disinterestedness, not even once, although this is what the section supposedly is about. Instead, based on his observations from § 26 and earlier, he describes our inability to perceive something absolutely large, and how this inability or inadequacy (*Unangemessenheit*), which is counter-purposive (*zweckwidrig*) for the imagination, turns out to be purposive for reason. It makes us discover an idea and a "rational vocation," and it "makes intuitable the superiority" of that vocation (KU: 257). A feeling of displeasure in one respect thus turns into a feeling of pleasure in another. It is this complex feeling involving both aspects that I think should be understood as disinterested and "pleasing for itself."

While Kant sees only *three* kinds of satisfaction in the Analytic of the Beautiful (§ 5), in the General Remark to the Analytic of the Sublime (after § 29), he speaks of *four* kinds of satisfaction, namely, regarding the agreeable, the beautiful, the sublime, and the good (see KU: 266). The satisfaction in the sublime has been added. He relates these four to quantity, quality, relation, and modality respectively. As I do not see by means of what shift of perspective he achieves this new classification, nor what purpose it serves, I cannot help but find it schematic and artificial.

In the General Remark at the end of the Analytic of the Sublime, Kant speaks of an interest regarding the sublime that is different from disinterested satisfaction in the beautiful. He speaks of an interest of the senses: "That is sublime which pleases immediately through its resistance [*Widerstand*] to the interest of the senses [*gegen das Interesse der Sinne*]." (KU: 267) He says this in contrast to the satisfaction in the beautiful, which he says in the immediately preceding sentence "must please without any interest." (KU: 267) Thus there is pleasure *without* interest (in the beautiful) and there is pleasure *in resistance to* an interest (in the sublime). The former is a lack of interest in the existence of an object; the latter is a "counter-interest," so to speak, to the proper function of the senses, or rather from their point of view. We did not encounter such a resistance to an interest in the Analytic of the Beautiful.

The satisfaction in the sublime is more complicated than the satisfaction in the beautiful. It involves reason and counter-purposiveness, both of which cannot be found in the satisfaction in the beautiful. It involves not only a disinterest regarding satisfaction and existence, but also a counter-interest regarding the senses and their interest. But aesthetically speaking, when thinking of our feeling of pleasure and displeasure, this feeling is without interest in the existence of the object, as is the satisfaction in the beautiful. Regarding the beautiful, it matters what we "make out of the representation" (in the free play of the faculties), and something similar can be said regarding the sublime. The idea of making something "out of" a representation is fundamental in Kant's aesthetics.

In § 28, we find another parallel between beauty and the sublime regarding disinterest, even though the expression "disinterested" is not used:

> Someone who is afraid can no more judge about the sublime in nature than someone who is in the grip of inclination and appetite can judge about the beautiful. (KU: 261)

Fear and inclination depend on the object's existence and are therefore not disinterested. If one "flees from the sight of an object," one cannot "find satisfaction in a terror," whereas if one finds such satisfaction (in the sublime), the "sight [...] [of the object] becomes all the more attractive the more fearful it is, as long as we find ourselves in safety" (KU: 261). For the satisfaction in the sublime to be disinterested, we must not be overcome by fear (as in the beautiful we must not be determined by inclination and appetite). We can also say: no interest, no fear to make us run away! Disinterest in the sublime rules out such fear.

Calling the satisfaction in the sublime "disinterested" can be seen to remain problematic in the following way. The sublime unfolds in two steps. Initially our senses are overwhelmed, but in a second step we turn inside ourselves and discover something larger and more powerful, namely, the idea of humanity. The first step by itself does not lead to any satisfaction or pleasure. It is only in the second step that this happens. But in that second step, *reason* plays a decisive role, and the satisfaction might then arguably not be purely aesthetic anymore. This objection can be countered in the following way. As there is a "free play" of imagination and *understanding* in the satisfaction of the beautiful, so there is a similar one in the sublime. As Kant says in § 27, there is a "free play" (KU: 258) of imagination and *reason* in the satisfaction of the sublime. The former play, in beauty, is harmonious, while the latter, in the sublime, is disharmonious. We may add that as in the former the understanding is not determining, so in the latter reason is not determining either. In that free play we merely become aware of this power of reason.[12] The play creates (*hervorbringen*) "a feeling that we have pure self-sufficient reason" (KU: 258.) That feeling of course requires that we have reason. Animals do not have this feeling if they do not have reason. But it is an aesthetic reflection that triggers this feeling and awareness, and in that sense, we may say that the sublime "pleases for itself," as Kant says in the very beginning of the discussion of the sublime: "The beautiful coincides with the sublime in that both please for themselves" (KU: 244). Nevertheless, this by itself is not pleasure (unless the second step enters the stage). Thus, it remains problematic to speak of aesthetic pleasure regarding the sublime, more so than regarding the beautiful.

Kant himself somewhat turns to this problem in the General Remark after § 29, when he points out that pure aesthetic judgments must be free from concepts (see KU: 270) and that if we were purely intelligent beings we would not have any experience of beauty or the sublime (see KU: 271). Thus, talk of "intellectual beauty or sublimity" is "not entirely correct," Kant says (KU: 271). Beauty and sublimity should not "rest on any interest" but "produce an interest" (of reason) (KU: 271). Thus, the aesthetic and the intellectual must be kept separate as far as their justifying grounds are concerned. The intellectual can only arise in a second step and on a higher level. Kant speaks of two different perspectives, or "sides." From the "aesthetic side (in relation to sensibility)" the satisfaction is "negative" (painful) and "contrary to this interest" (of sensibility); from the "intellectual side" it is "positive" (pleasurable) and "combined with interest" (of reason) (KU: 271). But then it will still be problematic to speak of aesthetic pleasure, because from the "aesthetic side" the satisfaction is "negative."

Relying on this complexity of purposiveness and counter-purposiveness in satisfaction with and without interest in the sublime, Kant points out a link to the feeling of respect (*Achtung*). The intellectual can be "represented" as sublime and "judged aesthetically," and this applies in particular to our feeling of respect,

---

[12] Fan Dahan discusses the role reason plays in judgments of the sublime (Fan 2018, pp. 54–67). In particular, he asks whether we may say that the judgment is purely aesthetic and that the satisfaction is disinterested. After all, no concept of the object (understanding), but the concept of our purpose and vocation (reason) needs to be involved. He sees the play between imagination and reason as *harmonious* insofar as reason transcends the limits of the imagination and imagination dedicates (*widmet*) itself to the free play (Fan 2018, p. 70).

which also involves some kind of force (*Gewalt*) that reason exerts on sensibility (KU: 271). Already in § 27, when discussing the moment of Quality, which is supposed to be disinterestedness, Kant begins that section by stating: "The feeling of the inadequacy of our capacity for attainment of an idea t h a t i s a l a w f o r u s i s r e s p e c t [*Achtung*]." (KU:257) It is the inadequacy of our power of imagination combined with our overcoming this inadequacy through the idea of humanity, that creates this link. On the moral side there is an inadequacy (for us as agents) regarding the moral law because we are not angels. On the aesthetic side there is an inadequacy (of imagination) regarding an object that we find sublime, due to its size and power, because we are still animals. The two are related, linked, and even interwoven, because the latter inadequacy makes us aware of the moral law, where we find an inadequacy again, namely, the former, which we experience in the feeling of respect. We are rational animals, not mere animals and not angels. I think Kant would say that our experiencing respect when perceiving an object that we find sublime is derived from our experiencing respect for the moral law.

Thus, our satisfaction in the sublime is *not* based on concepts of the object perceived, it is *not* interested regarding its existence, it is *contrary* to the interest of the senses, but it is *with* interest regarding reason—or rather from reason's perspective.

4 Conclusion

Disinterestedness has both positive and negative characterizations. Satisfaction in the beautiful is *without* interest insofar as it is *not* concerned with the existence of the object, as is the case in the satisfaction in the agreeable and the satisfaction in the good, which can be instrumentally good (as a means) or good in itself (as an end, which is the morally good and something to be brought about). This negative characterization depends on Kant's distinction between three different kinds of satisfaction, namely, the agreeable, the beautiful, and the good. Only the satisfaction in the beautiful is *free from* interest in the sense that it does not depend on the existence of the object. Kant later adds that satisfaction in the beautiful also does not depend on charm, perfection, or our knowledge of the object. These are all negative characterizations. The positive characterization consists in observing that there is something that we ourselves can do with a representation. This is the free play, which involves the claim to intersubjective universality and the principle of subjective purposiveness, which in turn leads to intellectual interests in the beautiful.

The theory of the sublime is a mere appendix because the *a priori* principle of purposiveness has already been established. Kant claims that regarding the sublime there is a kind of satisfaction without interest. He says: "The beautiful coincides with the sublime in that both please for themselves" (KU: 244). But the sublime is more complicated. It consists of two steps or levels. The first involves displeasure, and the second involves pleasure. Nevertheless, on that second level, there is a kind of independence of the object, insofar as we make something of the representation in ourselves: we discover reason within us. Thus, there is counter-purposiveness on the first level, regarding imagination and understanding; and there is purposiveness on the second level, regarding reason. Satisfaction with regard to reason is mixed with dissatisfaction with regard to imagination.

Kant develops his conception of disinterestedness by analyzing the judgment of taste under the guidance of the logical functions of judging. He thereby discovers the first "moment" of this judgment, under the heading of "quality," expressing affirmation or negation regarding beauty. When making a judgement of taste, we experience and affirm a certain kind of disinterested satisfaction or dissatisfaction (or, in the case of dissatisfaction, we experience dissatisfaction and negate satisfaction.) This method of analysis depends on the first *Critique* and the fact that even judgments of taste involve the understanding. It leads to the discovery of a claim to intersubjective universality and the discovery of an *a priori* principle, which in turn justifies the method.

For helpful comments, I wish to thank Herbert Hanreich, Paisley Livingston, Thomas Höwing, and Larissa Berger, and for a conversation over lunch, I wish to thank my students Wang Yian Hsiang and Konstantin Azarov.

Abbreviations

Apart from the *Critique of Pure Reason*, all references to Kant's works are to Kant's *Gesammelte Schriften, Ausgabe der Preußischen Akademie der Wissenschaften* (Berlin: De Gruyter, 1902 ff.). References to the *Critique of Pure Reason* are to the standard A and B pagination of the first and second editions. Translations are from *The Cambridge Edition of the Works of Immanuel Kant*.

The following abbreviations of individual works are used:

KU Kritik der Urteilskraft / Critique of the Power of Judgment
KrV Kritik der reinen Vernunft / Critique of Pure Reason

Literature

Allison, Henry (2001): *Kant's Theory of Taste.* Cambridge: Cambridge University Press.
Fan, Dahan (2018): *Die Problematik der Interesselosigkeit bei Kant. Eine Studie zur "Kritik der ästhetischen Urteilskraft."* Berlin and New York: De Gruyter.
Guyer, Paul (1993): *Kant and the Experience of Freedom: Essays on Aesthetics and Morality.* Cambridge: Cambridge University Press.
Höwing, Thomas (2013): *Praktische Lust: Kant über das Verhältnis von Fühlen, Begehren und praktischer Vernunft.* Berlin and New York: De Gruyter.
Rind, Miles (2002): "The Concept of Disinterestedness in Eighteenth-Century British Aesthetics." In: *Journal of the History of Philosophy* 40. No. 1, pp. 67–87.
Vandenabeele, Bart (2012): "Beauty, Disinterested Pleasure, and Universal Communicability. Kant's Response to Burke." In: *Kant-Studien* 103. No. 2, pp. 207–233.
Wenzel, Christian Helmut (2005): *An Introduction to Kant's Aesthetics: Core Concepts and Problems.* Malden: Blackwell.
Wenzel, Christian Helmut (2006): "Gemeinsinn und das Schöne als Symbol des Sittlichen." In: Hiltscher, Reinhard, Klingner, Stefan, and Süß, David (Eds.): *Die Vollendung der Transzendentalphilosophie in Kants "Kritik der Urteilskraft."* Berlin: Duncker and Humblot, pp. 125–139.
Wenzel, Christian Helmut (2012): "Do Negative Judgments of Taste Have A Priori Grounds in Kant?" In: *Kant-Studien* 103. No. 4, pp. 272–293.
Zangwill, Nick (1992): "Unkantian Notions of Disinterest." In: *British Journal of Aesthetics* 32. No. 2, pp. 149–152.
Zangwill, Nick (1995): "Kant on Pleasure in the Agreeable." In: *Journal of Aesthetics and Art Criticism* 53. No. 2, pp. 167–176.
Zuckert, Rachel (2007): "Kant's Rationalist Aesthetics." In: *Kant Studien* 98. No. 4, pp. 443–463.

Stefano Velotti
Making Sense: Disinterestedness and Control

Abstract: This essay aims to show how the transcendental aesthetic principle sought by Kant reveals itself not only as the principle of determination of aesthetic experience, both artistic and non-artistic, but also as a necessary principle for making sense of human experience in general. I begin by addressing some fundamental misunderstandings that still plague the study of Kantian disinterestedness, as well as by questioning its psychological redescription. Rejecting the thesis according to which works of art ought not to be considered examples of "free beauty" but only of "dependent beauty," the essay reconsiders the meaning to be attributed to "nature" as the "supersensible substratum" of our faculties. What emerges from my analysis here is a vision of Kant's transcendental as essentially *in the making*, at once both "natural" and "to be acquired." And yet, notwithstanding our moral responsibility to try to make sense of experience, we cannot pursue this end merely by clinging to what we can directly control.

1 Introduction

The requirement of disinterestedness in "the representation of the existence of the object" that Kant assigns to aesthetic judgment (KU §§ 2–5) is still mentioned, mostly in the non-specialist literature, as a claim to be considered anachronistic and inadequate as a matter of course. In such cases, no one usually takes the trouble to explain what is meant by the rejection of disinterestedness. Is it the rejection of aesthetic experience as such? Of the social distinction the alleged "disinterested judges" are thought to aim at? Of the lack of political engagement? Of the oblivion of the body, its emotions, its needs, and desires? Of its alleged "aconceptuality"? Of the separation of aesthetic experience or art from the rest of life? Of contemplation as an unacceptably passive attitude in regard to the society of the spectacle? Of its inadequacy in accounting for the interactivity and/or immersivity offered by digital media? Of formalism or aestheticism? Usually, detractors of the Kantian doctrine of disinterestedness seem concerned with rejecting one or more of these alleged consequences. I believe they are wrong. There are, as a matter of fact, many prominent interpreters who have shown convincingly that Kant's thinking about disinterestedness involves none of these consequences.

In this essay, I do not intend to go over, once again, the reasons why those views miss the mark. I will instead limit myself to recalling some key points that I think are sufficient to do away with these naive misunderstandings with the help of an essay written by one of the major interpreters of the third Kantian *Critique*, Emilio Garroni. Although Garroni's article was published over thirty years ago, it is still unknown in most scholarly circles, as it has only recently been made available in English (Garroni 2020). After reviewing briefly the interpretative assumptions necessary to any understanding of what the requirement of disinterestedness refers to (§ 1), I will try to examine some issues that to me seem to be more controversial and interesting, closely related to each other and to the interpretation of disinterestedness that is offered here: namely, an attempt to reread disinterestedness on empirical-descriptive bases and its limits (§ 2); the distinction between sense and meanings (§ 3); the value to be assigned to the distinction between free and adherent (or dependent) beauty (§ 4); and, finally, the question of whether or not aesthetic experience (aesthetic appreciation and the production of "beautiful things") is subject to our control (§ 5), or whether it is instead a by-product of other practices (§ 6) but can nevertheless be understood as linked to a moral duty (§ 7). The purpose of my essay is therefore first of all to clear the field of some misunderstandings that still plague discussions of Kantian disinterestedness, by way of distinguishing between actual judgments and their "principle of determination." This distinction allows us to show how disinterestedness cannot be reduced to a psychological redescription able to relinquish the transcendental. In fact, the transcendental principle sought by Kant reveals itself not only as the "principle of determination" of aesthetic experience, both artistic and non-artistic, but also as a necessary principle of every human experience, that is, for the exercise of the "power of judgment in general," both in its cognitive and non-cognitive use. Rejecting the thesis according to which works of art are not considered examples of "free beauty," but only of "dependent beauty," my essay reconsiders the meaning to be attributed to "nature" as the "supersensible substratum" of our faculties. What emerges is a vision of Kant's transcendental as essentially in the making, at once both "natural" and "to be acquired." Yet, I maintain, notwithstanding our moral responsibility to try to make sense of experience, we cannot pursue this end merely by clinging to what we can directly control.

2 Some Established Assumptions

Garroni's essay took its cue from a lexical issue: the unsystematic and therefore misleading Italian translation of a central term of the third *Critique* (Kant 1967), i.e., *Bestimmungsgrund,* the "determining ground" or "principle of determination" of aesthetic judgment. In fact, a new *Critique* may be justified only on the assumption that there is a transcendental *Bestimmungsgrund* of our faculty of judgment, which the previous two *Critiques* had not yet brought to light. The focus of the third *Critique* is obviously a normative question of principle, not a question of fact, as Kant immediately makes clear: "However, if one wants to give the origin of these fundamental principles and attempts to do so in a psychological way, this is entirely contrary to their sense. For they do not say what happens, i.e., in accordance with which rule our powers of cognition actually perform their role and how things are judged, but rather how they ought to be judged" (KU: 182).

Starting with the aforementioned terminological question, Garroni offers a quick survey of the third *Critique* as a whole[1], dispelling some common misunderstandings related to the notion of disinterestedness, which I will briefly summarize here:

a) *An "infinite judgment."* In the first Moment of the Analytic, Kant does not yet address the nature of the principle of determination of the judgment of taste, but merely asks whether every form of pleasure is exhausted by a pleasure arising from the satisfaction of a physiological or psychological need, or from the attainment of a practical (utilitarian or moral) purpose, or whether there is a *residual* pleasure irreducible to all possible interests on which other types of pleasure depend. In this inquiry, Kant not only characterizes as "infinite" the judgment of taste itself, but adopts an "infinite" procedure—neither affirmative nor negative—to carve out the room in which to place the new principle[2]:

---

[1] Garroni would subsequently retranslate Kant's work into Italian together with Hansmichael Hohenegger, with whom he wrote an extensive and important interpretive essay (Kant 1999).

[2] As is well known, in his critical inquiries, Kant always follows the thread provided by the table of judgments presented in the *Critique of Pure Reason* (KrV: A70/B95), where he brings all judgments "under four titles": Quantity, Quality, Relation and Modality. Each "title" contains "under itself three moments." In the Analytic of the Beautiful of the third *Critique*, Kant starts with quality, which contains three possible types of judgments: Affirmative, Negative, and Infinite. Under the heading of quality, in the first *Critique* Kant discusses infinite judgments at length, illustrating them with an analysis of the proposition, "The soul is nonmortal," which from a formal point of view could be treated as an affirmative judgment. But, he writes, "since what is mortal contains one part of the whole domain of possible beings, but what is immortal the other, nothing is said by my proposition except that the soul is one of the infinite multitude of things that remain if I remove all that is mortal. But the infinite sphere of the possible is thus limited only in so far as what is mortal is separated from it, and the soul is placed in the remaining space of its domain. But even with this exception this space still remains infinite, and more parts could be removed from it without the concept of the soul growing in the least and being affirmatively determined." (KrV: A72–73/B97–98).

> The infinite character of the pure aesthetic judgment simply signifies this: that its own principle, its *Bestimmungsgrund*, must be [...] a disinterested one, which is the opposite of the principles that determine the sensible pleasure or the purely practical one. Therefore, the beautiful, far from being that which "is not pleasurable," must be found in its *Bestimmungsgrund*, in that pleasure that "remains" (KU §8, B 26; AA 05: 216 "ihm noch übrig bleibt"), as Kant says, beyond the pleasure of the agreeable and the good, and is complementary to these other pleasures in the logical universe of possible pleasures (KU § 2, B 7; AA 05: 205; G/M 101). (Garroni 1989, p. 494)

b) *Disinterestedness concerns the aesthetic principle of the faculty of judgment, not the actual judgments.* Disinterestedness should not be interpreted in a "material" sense, as if it described a certain class of actual judgments, characterized by "an actual lack of interest and of intellectual content in the concrete aesthetic experience" (Garroni 1989, p. 496). The requirement of disinterest, in fact, does not concern actual judgments, but only their *Bestimmungsgrund*, the aesthetic principle as "feeling," "that allows us to conceive it as possible" (Garroni 1989, p. 496). Kant is quite explicit on this point in several places in his work, and Garroni (1989, p. 497) cites some of them, such as the following: "That the judgment of taste [...] must have no interest for its principle of determination [*zum Bestimmungsgrunde*] has been adequately demonstrated above. But from this, it does not follow that, having been given as a pure aesthetic judgment, an interest cannot be connected to it." (KU: 296) It is easy to see that what Kant is concerned with is the identification of a non-conceptual and not merely physiological *Bestimmungsgrund* but also the fact that nothing prevents actual judgments (our actual aesthetic experiences) from connecting to any other kind of interest.

c) *All sorts of interests are usually involved in a concrete aesthetic experience.* Limited to the issue of disinterestedness, after considering aesthetic ideas (to which I will return), Garroni reaches a first conclusion that puts out of play all the commonplaces on disinterestedness mentioned above:

> There is in fact [...] in every effective pure aesthetic judgment, insofar as it is determined by a pure aesthetic principle, also a cognition, whether true or false; there are also interests, attractions (even "repulsions," such as in the "sublime"), and emotions; and there is also [...] an intensification of intellectual activity, an activation of rational and ethical needs. (*And what else could not be involved in a concrete aesthetic experience?*) The purity of aesthetic judgment is not its separateness from the rest of the experience but consists exclusively of organizing all the different varieties of experiences under a *Bestimmungsgrund*, as a condition for the possibility or conceivability of that very judgment. (Garroni 1989, p. 499, my emphasis)

Therefore, Garroni concludes, alluding to Gadamer's interpretation of the third *Critique*, "there is no guilty 'aesthetic differentiation' in Kant" (Garroni 1989, p. 499).

3 Rereading Disinterestedness in a Psychological-Descriptive Way?

As is well known, many authors have spoken of disinterested judgments before Kant, both in the moral and in the aesthetic sphere, and others have taken up this theme in psychological terms after Kant (e.g., Edward Bullough with his notion of "Psychical Distance" at the beginning of the last century), without necessarily committing themselves to a definition of "aesthetic experience" or, even less, to the elaboration of a transcendental principle called to account for it. Kant himself invokes a common understanding of disinterestedness as impartiality at the beginning of § 6 of the second Moment of the Analytic, but it is clear that such a generic maxim—concerning our actual, empirical judgments—cannot legitimize the claim to the universality of aesthetic judgment. The legitimation of the peculiar subjective universality will only begin to be addressed from § 9 onwards. It is here that Kant rules out the possibility of proceeding by attempting to universalize a private feeling of pleasure, whatever it may be, by gradually *adding* some qualities that judges should possess, such as that of disinterested impartiality, along the lines of Hume. This commonsense reasoning, in fact, is bound up in a vicious circle: judgments can claim universality because they are impartial, that is, because they are supposed to be pronounced from a position that is not particular but, in fact, universal… The same holds for invoking, as a last resort, "the test of time," which remains a statement of fact that is in some cases pragmatically and culturally plausible but nevertheless logically untenable: one cannot, in fact, infer from the fact that a certain work survives over time (or continues to be generally appreciated over time) any proof of its aesthetic or artistic quality (or a legitimate claim of universal validity of its appreciation).[3] Survival over time or widespread generality of appreciation could both be due to heterogeneous factors unrelated to an aesthetic judgment.

A recent attempt to account for a paradigmatic case of aesthetic experience empirically is the one conducted in an interesting book by Bence Nanay (2016),

---

[3] Kant does not disregard Hume's perspective, but considers it an empirical criterion that, as such, is "weak and scarcely sufficient for conjecture": "The universal communicability of the sensation (of satisfaction or dissatisfaction), and indeed that which occurs without concepts, the unanimity, as far as possible, of all times and all peoples on this sensation in the representation of certain objects: though weak and scarcely sufficient for conjecture, this is the empirical criterion of the derivation of a taste, confirmed by examples, from the common ground, deeply buried in all human beings, of unanimity in judging the forms under which objects are given to them." (KU: 231 f.).

who—debunking George Dickie's crude theses aimed at dispelling "the myth of aesthetic attitude," behind which there would be nothing but the exercise of generic attention—recalls that there are different types of attention that Dickie did not consider. Nanay argues that "thinking of aesthetic attention as distributed attention does capture the original Kantian importance of disinterest in our aesthetic experiences" (Nanay 2016, p. 26). To be fair, Nanay does not believe that there is such a thing as one single aesthetic experience, only "varieties of aesthetic experience," which, the author admits, sounds "a little awkward" (Nanay 2016, p. 12). Perhaps to make this awkwardness more acceptable, one could resort to the Wittgensteinian concept of "family" and say that for Nanay, there is no class but only a "family" of aesthetic experiences, which would include "experiences of overwhelming beauty, experiences of strong emotions, experiences of strong identification with a fictional character, musical frissons, and so on" (Nanay 2016, p. 12). But what raises some suspicion about the claim that "distributed attention does capture the original Kantian importance of disinterest in our aesthetic experiences" is that Nanay insists that there cannot be "*principled* reasons to call some of these strong experiences encountered in an aesthetic context 'aesthetic experiences' and deny this label to others" (Nanay, 2016, p. 12, my emphasis). If he means that there are no rules or conceptual criteria for classifying our experiences as aesthetic, or that aesthetic elements inevitably enter into all of our experiences, the claim could be in line with Kantian thought. Nanay does not, however, exclude only conceptual "principled reasons," but any kind of principle, thus including that "determining principle" laboriously worked out by Kant. For this reason, however, I would say that not only does Nanay's argument not "capture the original Kantian importance of disinterest," but is, on the contrary, the very reverse of the Kantian thesis. Indeed, as we have seen, for Kant disinterest can only concern *the principle* of judgment, not a psychological description of our factual judgments.

Let us take a closer look at what Nanay means and at the consequences this psychological reinterpretation of the Kantian thesis may lead to. Nanay distinguishes four types of attention:
(i)   Distributed with regards to objects and focused with regards to properties.
(ii) Distributed with regards to objects and distributed with regards to properties.
(iii) Focused with regards to objects and focused with regards to properties.
(iv) Focused with regards to objects and distributed with regards to properties.
  (Nanay, 2016, p. 24)

Type i. is the most obvious form of attention, useful for classifying a multiplicity of objects possessing certain properties; type ii. would amount to wandering with one's gaze, without dwelling on anything in particular; type iii. would imply an intense concentration on a specific purpose; while type iv. would, according to Nanay, come closest to describing an aesthetic experience, focusing on a single object, and yet letting one perceptually and imaginatively peruse all its indefinite properties, without having already channeled them through conceptual purposes or immediate needs.

I am not persuaded that the second and third types of attention are wholly foreign to aesthetic experience, but this is not my point here. The problem is that in order to sum up this reduction of Kantian disinterestedness as an exercise of attention "focused with regards to objects and distributed with regards to properties," Nanay states that "[t]his may help us to give an answer to one of the most important questions about aesthetic experience, namely, *why should we care?*" His answer is "straightforward: because aesthetic experiences allow us to see and attend to the world differently: in a way that we don't, and couldn't, see otherwise" (Nanay 2016, p. 35, my emphasis). Granted, but what does "differently" mean here? "Defamiliarized" is Nanay's answer, in the wake of the Russian Formalists. Or rather, he notes, "If an object is unfamiliar, we do not know how to approach it, and we therefore tend to attend to a number of its properties to figure out what to do with it or what can be done with it" (Nanay 2016, p. 34). To be sure, an aesthetic experience typically allows one to discover properties (or, one could add, "affordances") that an experience already channeled by predefined or usual interests could possibly prevent one from discovering. And encountering objects that are unfamiliar, wonderful, unpredictable, unsettling, and otherwise unrelated to the already known is a necessary and enlivening part of our being immersed in contingency. But such unknown objects and such unfamiliar experiences cannot only disturb or disrupt the way we are organized; they must also be enlivening and a source of pleasure, on condition that they take place within a horizon of possible meaning. It must be possible to make sense of these experiences. Otherwise, it would not be possible to understand why not finding one's way in a "defamiliarized" world would be a desirable, gratifying, enlivening or advantageous experience. For Kant, in fact, as is well known, the free agreement of imagination and understanding (in relation to the demands of reason) concerns both appreciation and the production of aesthetic experiences:

> in an aesthetic respect, however, the imagination is free to provide, beyond that concord with the concept, unsought extensive undeveloped material for the understanding, of which the latter took no regard in its concept, but which it applies, not so much objectively, for cognition, as subjectively, for the animation of the cognitive powers, and thus also indirectly to cognitions [...]. (KU: 317)

Nanay's "unprincipled" account is thus missing an essential element that constitutes the heart of Kant's theoretical framework. For if an aesthetic experience were only defamiliarizing or unfamiliar, would it not be merely disorienting, bewildering, distressing, or even akin to a panic attack or psychotic episode? For Kant, seeing and attending the world differently is inseparable from that "disinterested pleasure" coinciding with the feeling of a "purposiveness without end" or "formal purposiveness." Not, then, an "unprompted eye" (Nanay 2016, p. 134) but rather the way a determinate experience (i.e., any singular empirical experience, spatio-temporally and conceptually conditioned) refers to an indeterminate horizon of sense, or rather, to a "cognition in general" as an indeterminate condition for attempting to *make sense* of any determinate cognition or action. If this is so, then, far from capturing "the original Kantian importance of disinterest in our aesthetic experiences" Nanay's account distorts it, making it unrecognizable.

Not addressing questions of principle and limiting oneself to empirically describing the psychological or attentional mechanisms of some members of the "family" of aesthetic experiences has a cost: it does not allow us to understand precisely "why we should care." An inquiry limited to only "varieties of aesthetic experience" without a consideration of aesthetic experience as such is not only "awkward," but I think it implies a dilemma: either it assimilates aesthetic experiences to disturbing moments of mere unpleasant disorientation—making it impossible to understand "why we should care"—or it tacitly relies on a notion of aesthetic experience for which it is unable to account. One can conceive of "varieties of aesthetic experience" as parts of a "family," but that family must have its own conceptually undetermined unity of sense, which Nanay claims not to admit. Yet Nanay's book offers other interesting insights to which I will return (§ 5). First, however, I must say something about this "unity of sense" of experience that anticipates "cognition in general" as a condition of all determinate cognition.

4 Sense and Meanings

As has been pointed out by some interpreters, by means of different arguments and interests (cf. in particular, Weil 1970; Garroni 1976, 1977, 1986, 1992, 2005; Guyer 2005a; Noë 2015), the most adequate understanding of the *Bestimmungsgrund* of aesthetic judgments, namely, the "free play of imagination and understanding" (to which Kant gives diverse but essentially almost equivalent names[4]), consists in accounting for our ability to orient ourselves in the world we share

---

[4] E.g., *"Gemeinsinn,"* "cognition in general (*überhaupt*)," "free schematism," "subsumption of the faculty of exhibitions to the faculty of concepts," "aesthetic faculty of judging," "faculty of judging in general."

in a sensible way,⁵ which is not at all the same as knowing, or even only thinking, but rather feeling, in a concrete and determined experience marked by multiple interests, the concomitant possibility of a disinterested "cognition in general." This is one of the ways in which the Kantian idea of a "free schematism" can be reformulated. In "free schematism," in fact, what counts is not so much the recognition of an object—that is, the reciprocal determination of a concept and a given intuition, according to a non-free objective schematism—as the fact that, by means of a determined object (experience, event, process…), the condition of every possible scheme and of every possible operation can manifest, exhibit or "exemplify" itself. This means the subsumption of the entire faculty of imagination under the faculty of concepts in the free play of imagination and understanding. Garroni (1977, 2005) has spoken in this regard of "meta-operativity" that is internal to every human operation but may also be expressed in some exemplary performances; Paul Guyer's term (2005b) is "metacognition"; and Alva Noë (2015) theorizes a "second level," or metalevel, that emerges within a "first level" in which our practices and activities unfold that are aimed at achieving a goal. It is because of this second level, inseparable from the first, that we can put "on display" the way we make sense of what we do (Noë 2015, p. 83, p. 124). Works of art are (or have been for at least the past two centuries) the most typical "objects" (works, events, processes…) in which this "meta-operative," "metacognitive," or "second level" condition is exhibited, or has been exhibited, in an "exemplary" way (see § 4 below)

It is not, therefore, *first and foremost* a matter of regressing properly to an "unprompted eye" (Nanay 2016, p. 134), or of accounting for the indefinite richness or interpretability of things, natural or artificial. Rather, it is a question of recognizing, at the bottom of our "faculty of judgment *in general*" (KU: 288, my emphasis), an indeterminate condition of sense (*Sinn* or *Gemeinsinn*), distinct from and inseparable from meanings (the *Bedeutungen* of concepts, KrV: A139/B179), which makes possible both "seeing and attending the world differently," as claimed by Nanay, as well as the indefinite interpretability of the real through the application or production of determinate concepts-meanings (what Guyer calls "the multicognitive interpretation of the harmony of the faculties," 2005a, pp. 77–110). This condition of meaning—this reference to "cognition in general" attested by a *Gemeinsinn*—is a

---

5 See the remarkable essay by Eric Weil, entitled "Sens et fait," which puts at the heart of the third *Critique* precisely the problem of sense: "il s'agit de la possibilité de s'orienter dans le monde: toute volonté concrète *présuppose* un monde sensé, en tant qu'elle est—et elle l'est en son essence—volonté d'action sensée" (Weil 1970, p. 88). But this presupposition of a sensible world is by no means the *guarantee* of a sensible world, or of a sense already given, but rather what might be called the necessity of a possibility of sense. On this essay by Weil, in the context of an interpretation of the transcendental as "epigenesis of reason," see Malabou (2016).

presupposition of all human knowledge or action (see especially KU: §21 and §40). But this does not mean, of course, that every human experience is an aesthetic experience. However, it happens that there are some experiences (typically but not exclusively those that we recognize as "artistic") in which this condition is "exemplified," without being prejudiced in its "principle of determination" by any interest.

5 Free and Adherent Beauty

From the very first section of the first Moment of the Analytic, Kant makes it clear that the same representation can be considered as logical or aesthetic depending on the principle of determination of judgment, and that just as a representation of our senses can be judged logically, it is possible conversely to judge aesthetically even a given concept: "even if the given representations were to be *rational* but related in a judgment solely to the subject (its feeling), then they are to that extent always aesthetic" (KU: 204, my emphasis). Shortly after this passage (which should be considered in the discussion regarding the accommodability of conceptual art in a Kantian framework), Kant adds that "It is readily seen that to say that [the object of representation] is beautiful and to prove that I have taste *what matters is what I make of this representation in myself*, not how I depend on the existence of the object" (KU: 205, my emphasis).[6] There are no classes of beautiful objects, and a fortiori there can be no classes of objects belonging to the sphere of dependent or free beauty.

It is immediately apparent, then, that *any* "representation of an object" can be judged aesthetically[7]—even a representation of a concept—and that the determining principle of the judgment of taste is normative but not prescriptive or doctrinaire: being a reflective, and logically singular, judgment, and not a determining judgment, it clearly cannot establish classes of objects. This does not mean, however, that those who judge aesthetically cannot usually recognize what kind of thing they are judging, and that this recognition cannot play a role in our judgment. But the merely reflective nature of judgment or what Kant terms its "heautonomy" (KU: 186), prevents us, in principle, from taking the illustrative examples that the philosopher offers (typically those in the third Moment of the Analytic) as probative

---

6 Although I agree with Lorand (1989, 2000) that there are not two *kinds* of beauty, I believe her arguments are flawed by her assumption that Kant presupposes two classes of objects, respectively susceptible to dependent or independent (kind of) beauty. It seems clear to me, even from the passage just quoted, that Kant does not take this position.

7 I leave aside, for reasons of space, the question of disgust, on which there is extensive literature.

or even as co-extensive with his thought. They may tell us something about Kant's personal taste or the taste of his time, or about "what he made of these representations in himself," but they cannot substitute for his thought. When this happens it is because some interpreters confuse *exemplarity in the strong sense*—an object, or a judgment about it, as "example of a universal rule that one cannot produce" ("die man nicht angeben kann," KU: 237)—with examples that would have a merely illustrative and "facilitating" task. Such examples could only be challenged if Kant had provided a principle of the judgment of taste of a conceptual kind.

This confusion has generated quite unnecessary disputes. Such a meticulous reader as Derrida, for example, showed his appreciation for the crucial notion of "exemplarity in a strong sense," only to focus his deconstruction, however, on illustrative examples that were not "exemplary in a strong sense." After stating that he was interested precisely in "the example [...] given prior to the law" (Derrida 1987, p. 51), i.e., "in a strong sense," he then seamlessly moved on to deconstruct Kantian thought from merely illustrative and occasional examples. Kant mentioned "the borders of paintings, draperies on statues, or colonnades around magnificent buildings" (KU: 226) as ornaments or *parerga*, from which Derrida drew the conclusion that for Kant, since "the draperies on statues" are mere ornaments, external to the representation, "[w]hat is represented in the representation would be the naked and natural body; [...] it alone would be essentially, purely, and intrinsically beautiful, 'the proper object of a pure judgment of taste'" (Derrida 1987, p. 57). While Kant's thought does not allow us, in principle, to classify which traits are salient and which are not in our aesthetic representations of objects, Derrida assumed the difference between ornamental and non-ornamental elements as an ontological distinction, between objects that would be "the proper objects of a pure judgment of taste" and those that would be improper, glossing over the fact that for Kant "what matters is what I make of this representation in myself," which also depends, of course, on one's culture of belonging. But Kant's purpose, of course, was not to prescribe rules for the exercise of taste, as he immediately makes clear in the Preface: "Since the investigation of the faculty of taste, as the aesthetic power of judgment, is here undertaken not for the formation and culture of taste (for this will go its way in the future, as in the past, even without any such researches), but only from a transcendental point of view, it will, I flatter myself, be judged leniently with regard to its deficiencies for the former end." (KU: 170)

Leaving aside the possible *uses* of philosophical texts, as distinct from their interpretation, something similar can be said to recur in the broad debate provoked by the Kantian distinction between free and adherent (or dependent) beauty, in which the latter seems to reintroduce the interest in the existence of the object that had been excluded in the first Moment.

The Kantian distinction has its own raison d'être—and in the face of the recurring accusation of formalism, comparisons of this distinction with Kendall Walton's anti-formalist article "Categories of Art" (Walton 1970) are crucial—but I think it has less relevance than it is given in some interpretations. A careful reader like Diarmuid Costello, for example, who has addressed this issue several times, in a recent article reiterates the thesis that "while we are in principle free to judge abstract (or any other kind of) art non-dependently, as pure visual array, we cannot judge its beauty *as artistic beauty* freely, even for Kant." Therefore "all works of art are dependently beautiful" (Costello 2021, p. 608). Let me explain here why I find this thesis unconvincing.

Costello begins by pointing out that for Kant it is possible to judge the dependent beauty even of natural products and not only of artificial products, which presuppose intentions and concepts for their production, and that, vice versa, it is possible, in principle, to judge as free beauty even an artistic product, but at the cost of considering it—in the case of visual arts—not "*as art*," but "as pure visual array" (Costello 2021, p. 608). I believe that the contrast between free and dependent beauty is misunderstood here, and risks assuming "art" to be a defined class of objects. We all know how futile attempts to properly define art, or the class of artworks, have been: they invariably turn out to be either uninformative or wrong (cf. Velotti 2008), and I think Costello would agree on this point. But I think that a closer examination of his article can dispel some confusion, which will then lead us to the last point—for me central, more problematic, and interesting—with which I intend to conclude this essay.

As Costello notes, Kant states that when faced with something we judge to be "beautiful" we need to know whether it is a product of nature or a product of art. This is empirical information that has important consequences, but obviously cannot be provided by the principle of aesthetic judgment. Arthur Danto, who in his later essays attempted to reduce Kantian aesthetic ideas to his notion of "embodied meanings" (cf. Costello 2008), gave such importance to this trivial circumstance that he believed he could base on it his argument for the supposed irrelevance of aesthetics for an understanding of art, constructing a philosophy of art that claims to be independent of aesthetic reflection.[8] To be sure, we are *usually* able to distinguish quite easily whether something is an artifact or a natural product. It may happen, however, that we come to believe that a natural product is a human artifact, or vice versa (as in the case of the imitation of the song of the

---

[8] But, I believe, unsuccessfully. Not surprisingly, in Chapter 7 of his major work, *The Transfiguration of the Commonplace* (Danto 1981), he is forced to fall back, inconsistently, on the Kantian notion of taste.

nightingale mentioned by Kant, §42, KU: 302, and later discussed by Danto), and many contemporary artists aim to minimize or to try to cancel their own intervention in their works (as in the cases of contemporary BioArt, Evolutionary Art, Generative Art and so on).

Costello supports the thesis that "all works of art are dependently beautiful" evoking Kant's statement that "art is distinguished from nature as doing (*facere*) is from acting or producing in general (*agere*), and the product or consequence of the former is distinguished as a work (*opus*) from the latter as an effect (*effectus*)," so that "only production through freedom, i.e., through a capacity for choice that grounds its actions in reason, should be called art" (KU: 303). Kant here is still not speaking specifically of the fine arts but only of those *téchnai* traditionally considered as liberal arts (some of which, according to him, are probably classifiable as sciences, and others as crafts). These arts all require a certain skill, not reducible to simple conceptual or propositional knowledge. From each of them may also emerge, to some extent, that spirit "in the aesthetic significance"—at which Kant only hints here, before he treats it extensively beginning in § 49—that we recognize, *if and when* we recognize it, in what we call beautiful art: "But it is not inadvisable to recall that in all liberal arts there is nevertheless required something compulsory, or, as it is called, a mechanism, without which *the spirit, which must be free in the art and which alone animates the work*, would have no body at all and would entirely evaporate" (KU: 304, my emphasis).

From these considerations relative to all the liberal arts, Costello concludes that for Kant only "something that, as a product of intentional agency, must be judged *in the light of the reasons* for which it was made, is to be judged accordingly" (Costello 2021, p. 608, my emphasis). The problem lies in the weight to be given to the expression "in the light of the reasons for which it was made." Is it to be understood, strongly, as "based on reasons"? In that case, however, it does not rely on the *Bestimmungsgrund* of the judgment of taste. Or does it figure just as a weaker "taking into account"? As already mentioned, an aesthetic judgment is typically a judgment given about a *recognized* object of a certain kind, certainly not unrelated to the rest of our experience: not only do we usually know with a good degree of certainty whether the object is an artifact or a natural product, but also whether it is identifiable as a church or a gas station, a flower or a mold, a poem or a warning label, a dog sculpture or a non-representational or decorative work. And if we judge such an object as free beauty, *we certainly do not forget what we know:* it is unthinkable that freely judging the beauty of a gas station, of a mold or of a film makes us see only "a visual array," or that freely judging a novel makes us appreciate only the sounds of the words, or that judging as free beauty a performance makes us perceive only movements of bodies in space, outside of any other information, context, tradition or expectation. It is not possible to forget⁹ or abstract from knowledge, cultural context, and the indefinite types of interest that attach to a judgment of actual taste, as if freely beautiful things or beautiful works of art were unexpected or miraculous appearances, unrelated to the forms of life in which we are immersed.¹⁰

The essential point that justifies the distinction between free and adherent beauty is another: it is whether such judgments are determined by an aesthetic *Bestimmungsgrund* or whether they are based on other principles. Products considered as dependently beautiful could presuppose properly aesthetic appreciations that have passed judgment,¹¹ and subsequently become objects of circumstantial and perhaps enlightening reconstructions and analyses of a technical, psychological, typological, morphological, historical, mathematical, ideological, or political type, without however a direct or primary reference to the principle of determination of the judgment of taste.¹² Thus, I find Costello to be in error when he states that "while we are in principle free to judge abstract (or any other kind of) art non-dependently, as pure visual array, we cannot judge its beauty as *artistic beauty* freely, even for Kant" (Costello 2021, p. 608).

I believe that underlying this misunderstanding is an underestimation of the relationship that Kant establishes, with respect to beautiful art, between art and nature. After distinguishing, as we have seen, between art (associated with *facere* and *opus*) and nature (associated with *agere* and *effectus*), Kant explicitly introduces the notion of beautiful art for the first time in § 45, and then titles the next section: "Beautiful art is an art to the extent that it seems at the same time to be nature" (KU: 306). Here he states that "the purposiveness in the product of beautiful art, although it is certainly intentional, must nevertheless not seem intentional; i.e., beautiful art must be regarded as nature, although of course one is aware of it as art" (KU: 316–317). This statement could be interpreted as a declaration

---

9 As I will argue below, that would be, by the way, a contradictory request: remember to forget!
10 Emine Hande Tuna offered good arguments that support this perspective: "In short, just as there are no rules for genius to follow in producing beautiful artworks, so too there are no rules that we can follow in appreciating them either. We judge a work of genius on the basis of an aesthetic idea and a rational idea. However, none of these ideas are fixed, and indeed they get further expanded once we judge the artwork. This expansion is possible because, in judging artistic beauty, even though we start with a concept (whatever it may be), this concept only occasions or triggers the aesthetic ideas; moreover, as I said, it does not determine the whole process". (Hande Tuna 2018, p. 172).
11 As Leo Steinberg recalls, "Art is cherished, or it does not survive. A succession of value judgments, embodied in acts of neglect or preservation, largely determines what we receive from the past" (2007, p. 311).
12 It seems to me that this interpretation of dependent beauty is not incompatible with the conclusion reached by Guyer after his broad recognition of the concept (Guyer 2005b).

of classicist taste, linked to the ancient adage *"ars est celare artem,"*[13] wherein the first occurrence of art would be beautiful, successful fine art, and the second would be the premodern notion of art as *téchne*. But it seems to me that this passage should not be read that way. It is not merely a matter of exercising *"sprezzatura,"*[14] i.e., of "masking" the technique, the study, or the "punctiliousness" of the artist, which would harm, according to Kant, the success of the work, but rather precisely to draw on the very nature of the "genius" ("in products of genius nature (that of the subject) not a deliberate end, gives rule to art," KU: 344). It is no coincidence that, introducing the notion of genius, Kant writes, in a first approximation, that "genius is the inborn predisposition of the mind (*ingenium*) through which nature gives the rule to art" (KU: 307). And it is nature (that of the subject) that must give the rule to art, Kant explains, because every art presupposes rules on the basis of which a product must be thought of as possible. Yet beautiful art does not allow the judgment of the beauty of one of its products to be derived from a rule "that has a concept for its determining ground [*Bestimmungsgrund*], and thus has as its ground a concept of how it is possible" (KU: 307). Since without a rule we cannot speak of art, then it is nature that must give the rule to art in the subject.

But what does "nature" mean here? Perhaps the most explicit and concise answer is to be found after the crucial discussion of the notion of aesthetic ideas in § 49, in n. 1 to § 57, where Kant writes that

> As a result of this, one can also explain **genius** in terms of the faculty of **aesthetic ideas**: by which at the same time is indicated the reason why in products of genius nature (that of the subject), not a deliberate end, gives the rule to art (the production of the beautiful). For [...] it is not a rule or precept but only that which is merely nature in the subject, i.e., the supersensible substratum of all our faculties (to which no concept of the understanding attains), and so that in relation to which it is the ultimate end given by the intelligible in our nature to make all our cognitive faculties agree, which is to serve as the subjective standard of that aesthetic but unconditioned purposiveness in beautiful art, which is supposed to make a rightful claim to please everyone. Thus alone is it possible that the latter, to which one can prescribe no objective principle, can be grounded on a subjective and yet universally valid principle a priori. (KU: 344)

The nature of the subject, understood as the *supersensible substratum of all his faculties*, is the subjective standard, "aesthetic but unconditioned," which not only constitutes that "universal rule that one cannot produce" ("eine allgemeine Regel die man nicht angeben kann," KU: 237, that is, which cannot be stated or made ex-

---

13 On the history of this adage, see D'Angelo (2014).
14 On this term coined by Baldassarre Castiglione, see again D'Angelo (2014).

plicit), but which moreover constitutes that "unity of sense of experience" insofar as it is distinct from *determinate meanings*, but is nevertheless exhibited exemplarily only through them, to which we referred in § 3 of this essay.

Determinate concepts, in fact, certainly play an indispensable role in both appreciation and production of works of genius, in the expression of aesthetic ideas (whether these are artistic or some other kind of expression) and in their meaningful recognition. It is for this reason, in fact, that taste has the last word with respect to the originality of genius, which moves on the limits of sense, extending (KU: 315) and forcing the understanding to revise and produce new concepts (KU: 317), but which without the feeling of "purposiveness without end" proper to *Gemeinsinn* could also produce "*Unsinn*" or non-sense.[15]

What matters, from this point of view, is not so much the exhibition of such concepts intended by the agency of the individual genius as what is rather produced *through* it but not *thanks* to it: thanks instead to the "nature of the subject," that is, to the agreement of all of the subject's faculties. After expounding the crucial notion of aesthetic ideas, Kant summarizes the results obtained, insisting that genius, in its production, certainly presupposes "a determinate concept of the product, as an end, hence understanding, but also a representation (even if indeterminate) of the material [*Stoff*], i.e., of the intuition, for the presentation of this concept, hence a relation of the imagination to the understanding" (KU: 317). And he hastens to specify that genius "displays itself *not so much in the execution of the proposed end in the presentation of a determinate concept as in the exposition or the expression of aesthetic ideas*, which contain rich material for that aim [...]" (KU: 317, my emphasis). He adds, and this is the point that interests us most here, "that the *unsought* and *unintentional* subjective purposiveness in the free correspondence of the imagination to the lawfulness of the understanding presupposes a proportion and disposition of this faculty that cannot be produced by any following of rules, whether of science or of mechanical imitation, but that only *the nature of the subject* can produce" (KU: 317–318, my emphasis).

What is essential, then, for the production and appreciation of a successful work of art (or for the exemplary expression of aesthetic ideas, whichever way they are expressed, through what we call fine art or in other cultural forms transmitted to us from our past, or yet unknown forms in the future) is precisely that matter (*Stoff*) which the imagination supplies to the understanding in an "unsought" (*ungesucht*) and "unintentional" (*unabsichtlich*) manner, prompting our

---

15 "To be rich and original in ideas is not as necessary for the sake of beauty as is the suitability of the imagination in its freedom to the lawfulness of the understanding. For all the richness of the former produces, in its lawless freedom, nothing but nonsense; the power of judgment, however, is the faculty for bringing it in line with the understanding." (KU: 319).

faculty of concepts to consider it and to reconfigure itself. But if this is the essential point, then it is clear that even beautiful works of art, although they are produced through a process aimed at "seeking" the best solution to give body to the "intentions" of the artist, can be successful works of art only through the production of an imaginative matter whose subjective purposiveness is not controllable by the subject, but is dependent on the principle constituted by the free play of imagination and understanding. Such play is free insofar as it remains "disinterested" and therefore "unsought" and "unintentional."

Costello is right to refer to the "semantic content" (Costello 2021, pp. 608–609) of works of art in relation to aesthetic ideas, and there is no doubt that, unlike natural beauty, in the case of works of art there are legitimate questions about the artist's intentions, the "aboutness" of the work or what the work expresses (Costello 2021, p. 608) (which, I would add, could also admit, if necessary, what contradicts the hypothetical intentions of the artist). But something essential is missing from his account here. For, through the concrete and singular expressions by which aesthetic ideas take shape, what is exhibited, in a symbolic or analogical way, is not so much—as Costello now also notes—"the concept of art." The latter, not being a determinate concept, could not in any case be intended as a purpose. But nor could "a far more varied set of concepts than simply that of art itself" (Costello 2021, p. 608). *Rather what is exhibited is experience itself in its indeterminate supersensible totality*, "cognition in general" as the possibility of the agreement of all faculties. Or, if you will, that "metaoperative," "metacognitive," or "second-level" condition of meaning that is the horizon of all determinate experience and of the "varied set of concepts" itself. If Kant intended to see in the expression of aesthetic ideas only the artist's intentions, the aboutness and expressiveness of the work, perhaps he would not call into question the "nature of the subject," but more importantly he could not also assign to nature the capacity to exhibit aesthetic ideas, as he admits as a matter of course: "Beauty (whether it be beauty of nature or of art) can in general be called the expression of aesthetic ideas," with the only difference that "in beautiful art this idea must be *occasioned* by a concept of the object, but in beautiful nature the mere reflection on a given intuition, without a concept of what the object ought to be, is sufficient for arousing and communicating the idea of which that object is considered as the expression." (KU: 320, my emphasis)

6 The *"Je-Ne-Sais-Quoi"* and the "Spirit, in an Aesthetic Significance"

> One says of certain products, of which it is expected that they ought, at least in part, to reveal themselves as beautiful art, that they are without **spirit**, even though one finds nothing in them to criticize as far as taste is concerned. A poem can be quite pretty and elegant, but without spirit. A story is accurate and well organized, but without **spirit**. A solemn oration is thorough and at the same time flowery, but without spirit. Many a conversation is not without entertainment, but is still without spirit; even of a woman one may well say that she is pretty, talkative and charming, but without spirit. What is it then that is meant here by "spirit [*Geist*]?" (KU: 313)

This is how Kant introduces the important § 49, in which he elaborates on the concept of aesthetic ideas. The examples he gives (art, a poem, a story, an oration, a conversation, "even a woman") are the examples we find most frequently in the vast literature that flourished, between the 17th and 18th centuries, on the notion of *"nescio quid"* or *"je-ne-sais-quoi,"* among whose authors we find Baldassare Gracián, Dominique Bouhours, Benito Feijoo, Pierre de Marivaux, and Leibniz. This literature was intended to counter rationalistic and academic aesthetics, which claimed to provide prescriptive conceptual rules for the production and appreciation of works of art. If beauty is identified with a specifiable order or harmony of some kind (if it is thought that compliance with laws, proportions, measures, rules, etc., or adaptation to specific purposes, guarantees its production and regulates its appreciation), then it is easy to understand why it can be contrasted with that special charm, enlivening and elusive, which would derive from, or be identical to, a certain *"je-ne-sais-quoi."* A contrast, in essence, between rules and perfection that can be intellectually appreciated, on the one hand, and an apparent but fascinating disorder that can be appreciated with feeling, with *"esprit"* or with taste, on the other.

Marivaux captured this contrast in the most brilliant way, synthesizing what had been debated for well over a century in an apologue interwoven with allegories and prosopopoeia: in the "abode of Beauty," we find a garden characterized by the "most exact symmetry" and by a shrewd "distribution of the parts." Beauty in person arouses the union of "admiration and respect" but also boredom.[16] Kant agrees: "All stiff regularity (whatever approaches mathematical regularity) is of itself contrary to taste: the consideration of it affords no lasting entertainment, but

---

[16] The notion of *"je-ne-sais-quoi"* has a long history, rooted in ancient rhetoric and theology. For a reconstruction, with an anthology of texts, see D'Angelo and Velotti (1997) and, on the relationship with Kant, Velotti (2003). Marivaux's 1734 text is included among those anthologized.

rather, insofar as it does not expressly have cognition or a determinate practical end as its aim, it induces boredom" (KU: 243). Although literarily effective, Marivaux's apologue did not set out to make explicit its philosophical implications. A few decades earlier, beginning with the *Meditationes* of 1684 (and subsequently in many other writings), Leibniz had opined on the difference between beauty and the *"je-ne-sais-quoi,"* with quite a different philosophical depth.

But despite the phenomenological affinities between the *"je-ne-sais-quoi"* and the "spirit, in an aesthetic significance" (KU: 313)—vitality, animation, provocation of thought, pleasure etc.—Kant could not hold onto the contrast between intellectual beauty and the *"je-ne-sais-quoi."* Unlike Leibniz, for Kant there is no longer a beauty made of order and explicit rules next to which there would be room for a more elusive feeling (consisting of clear and confused ideas), because the very idea of an "intellectual beauty" is inconsistent: "The designation of an intellectual beauty can also not be allowed at all, for otherwise the word 'beauty' would have to lose all determinate meaning" (KU: 366). Or, more precisely, *at the level of principles*, "there is no transition from concepts to the feeling of pleasure or displeasure" (KU: 212), as is instead admitted in Leibniz' "continuistic" model.

What remains in common between the *"je-ne-sais-quoi"* and the Kantian "spirit, in an aesthetic significance" is that, since neither one can be produced or appreciated by means of explicable, conceptual rules, they cannot, as such, even be properly taken aim at or sought after. Kant knows well that one cannot aim at originality, understood as *"Sonderbarkeit,"* because "one calls a product of art **mannered** only if the presentation of its idea in that product is **aimed** at singularity rather than being made adequate to the idea" (KU: 319, my emphasis).

The paradox of certain ends that get lost if one looks for them can be exemplified in many manners: "The *Cantos* [...] left me cold," writes, for instance, Iosif Brodskij about Pound, whose "main error was an old one: questing after beauty. For someone with such a long record of residence in Italy, it was odd that he hadn't realized that beauty can't be targeted, that it is always a by-product of other, often very ordinary pursuits" (Brodskij 1992, p. 70). Or, as the Romantic poet Giacomo Leopardi notes pertinently:

> When you seek only pleasure in something, you never find it: you find nothing other than boredom, and often distaste. In order to experience pleasure in any action or occupation, it is necessary to seek some purpose other than pleasure itself [...]. This happens (among a thousand examples that could be given) in reading. [...] And perhaps for this reason public spectacles and entertainments in themselves [...] are the most terribly tedious and tiresome things in the world, because they have no purpose but pleasure. This alone is desired, this alone is expected; and something from which pleasure is expected and demanded (like a debt) almost never gives it: it indeed gives the opposite. Pleasure (it is perfectly true to say) only comes unexpectedly; and it is found where we are not seeking it, and have no

hope of finding it. [...] In this respect, pleasure is similar to peace of mind [...] The very desire for peace of mind necessarily excludes it, and is incompatible with it. (Leopardi 2013, Z 4266–4267, 1827)

It seems, in short, that disinterested pleasure or a successful work cannot be produced intentionally and intelligently, and, in this sense, it escapes our control.

7 (Non)control and the Duty of Making Sense

Returning now to Bence Nanay's reflections on disinterestedness, we find a remark of his that goes exactly in this direction. One of the features that Nanay takes to be very important for his account of disinterested aesthetic experiences is that "we do not have full control over them [...] In this respect, aesthetic experiences are very different from the ordinary perceptual experiences of, say, color or shape" (Nanay 2016, p. 16). This observation—with which I agree—shows, according to Nanay, the limitations of those approaches that attempt to account for aesthetic experience through a "deflationary account" or of other approaches "that talk about 'valuing for its own sake'" (Nanay 2016, p. 30). Indeed, if aesthetic experience simply consisted of "the detection of the object's 'aesthetic and/or expressive qualities,' then why wouldn't we control whether we have an aesthetic experience?" (Nanay 2016, p. 30). He makes a similar objection to the second type of approach: "If my experience yesterday in the museum was of the very same properties of the artwork as today, what explains that I don't seem to be able to value this experience for its own sake (while I could do so yesterday)?" (Nanay 2016, p. 31). Nanay states that this is because "attending in a certain way is not something we can always force ourselves to do" (Nanay 2016, p. 32), but he also cautiously adds that he does not claim that his "account is the only possible account that is capable of explaining the fact that aesthetic experiences are not fully under our control" (Nanay 2016, p. 32 fn. 16).

In fact, I think it is possible to hypothesize another, more complex account of our lack of control, both over our aesthetic experiences and over the production of successful works of art. I think it is useful to turn to a contribution by Jon Elster entitled "States that are Essentially By-Products" (Elster 2016, pp. 43–109). As a first approximation, we can say that Elster defines "states that are essentially by-products" as those "mental and social states" that have "the property that they can only come about as the by-product of actions undertaken for other ends" (Elster 2016, p. 43). Many, but not all of these states are characterized, Elster notes, by deprivation. It is psychologically contradictory, for example, to plan to forget, since it would be a matter of remembering to forget, that is, remembering not to remember. It is true that in order to forget someone or something one may want to be distracted by, let us say, going to the movies, provided, however, that one goes to the movies to view the film, and not strictly speaking to be distracted. Or, again, it is impossible to obey the order to be spontaneous (i.e., without self-awareness), because obedience and spontaneity are in contradiction. So it is impossible, at times, to do things that we can do if we do not try to do them. For instance, it is impossible to want to be in grace (in the theological sense) or to want to have grace (without "affectation," in the aesthetic sense) by virtue of actions and artifices that aim at it; the techniques for displaying *"sprezzatura"* in Castiglione's *The Book of the Courtier* are always accompanied by the awareness of a circular reference to something imponderable, namely, "grace" itself. This is what Elster calls the "moral fallacy of by-products": "It is the fallacy of striving, seeking and searching for the things that recede before the hand that reaches out for them" (Elster 2016, p. 108).

In addition to this, there is also an "intellectual fallacy," which consists in the attempt to explain what is essentially a by-product "as the result of action designed to bring it about—even though it is rather a sign that no such action was undertaken" (Elster 2016, p. 43). We cannot go over Elster's fascinating and complex analysis in detail here,[17] but from what has been said so far, it seems clear to me that aesthetic experience and the "genial" (in the Kantian sense) production of a work of art occur precisely, respectively, as instances of states and products that are essentially by-products of actions undertaken for other ends. This is not to say that aesthetic experience, or the production of a work of art, happens to us in an entirely unexpected way: if we go to the theater or to the movies, if we walk along the beach or in the mountains, if we read a poem or a novel, if we attend an exhibition or immerse ourselves in an installation, we can reasonably expect this activity to induce an aesthetic experience. Just as, if we paint or write, photograph or dance, with great accuracy and dedication, we can reasonably anticipate that a work or performance *may* emerge with which we are aesthetically satisfied, and which can be appreciated inter-subjectively. Elster rightly notes that these states

> cannot be brought about intelligently and intentionally. They may [...] be brought about knowingly and intelligently, if the agent knows that as a result of his action the effect will come about in a certain way [one cannot perform an action *to* be admired, and yet you can deliberately elicit admiration,[18] if for example you act to achieve a certain goal, and at the same

---

[17] I have attempted to do so, also in relation to Kant's notion of disinterestedness, in Velotti (2003).
[18] Kant defines "admiration" as "an astonishment that does not cease when the novelty is lost," "which happens when ideas in their presentation *unintentionally* and without artifice agree with aesthetic satisfaction" (KU: 272, my emphasis).

time you believe you know or expect that you will be admired for it]. They may also come about intentionally and nonintelligently, if the agent achieves by fluke what he set out to bring about [a child orders me to laugh and gets what he wants not because I obey his order but because of the naivety of his request]. (Elster, 2016, p. 53)

It is possible, then, to distinguish between *willed effects* and *reasonably expected effects:* I cannot obtain an aesthetic experience or produce a successful work of art by aiming directly to obtain it, but if I expose myself to certain experiences or perform certain activities, I might reasonably expect to obtain certain results that are not obtainable if I aim directly to obtain them. In his conclusion Elster mentions *spontaneity,* which is a strange form of freedom that escapes the freedom of the will because it is necessarily disinterested, just like Kantian "free play." The attraction of states that are essentially by-products could consist not only in seeing things "differently," but in "the value we attach to freedom, spontaneity and surprise. Most centrally, by-products are linked to what befalls us by virtue of what we are, as opposed to what we can achieve by effort or striving" (Elster 2016, p. 109).

The third *Critique* is full of clues regarding the non-intentionality of aesthetic experience, as early as § VII of the Introduction (KU: 190), which is of crucial importance for the entire work: "Now if in this comparison the imagination [...] is *unintentionally* brought into accord with the understanding, as the faculty of concepts, through a given representation and a feeling of pleasure is thereby aroused, then the object must be regarded as purposive for the reflecting power of judgment" (KU: 190, my emphasis; cf. also KU: 218).

To conclude on this specific issue, I would like to point out the particularly significant choice of verb used by Kant to designate the activity of genius in giving expression to aesthetic ideas: "thus genius really consists in the happy relation, which no science can teach and no diligence learn, of finding ideas for a given concept on the one hand and on the other hitting upon the expression [*den Ausdruck zu treffen*] for these" (KU: 317). "*Treffen,*" "hitting upon" or "coming upon," also conveys the sense of an *encounter* that is not entirely dependent on my control, an agency that is also an event that escapes my intentions. Perhaps one could reinterpret in this way Anscombe's formula: "I *do* what *happens*" (Anscombe 2000, pp. 52–53). It is an exposure to the contingency of my experience that nevertheless must be able to make sense, in the horizon of a "cognition in general," without such a sense being guaranteed: one could say that it is the transcendental necessity of a possibility or, as Kant expresses it, of a merely exemplary necessity (KU §18).

8 Are We Responsible for Making Sense of Experience?

In conclusion, I would like to hint at one last problem. If aesthetic experience, as disinterested, is essentially beyond our direct control, and if it is an exemplary experience of making sense, does this mean that the possibility of making sensible experiences is outside of the domain of our responsibility?[19] Answering this question articulately would require another essay, but I think that in order to set up a plausible answer, we can mention a passage that, in its location after the quasi-deduction of *Gemeinsinn* made in § 21, may prove surprising. In fact, Kant asks himself in § 22 "whether taste is an original and natural faculty, or only the idea of one that is yet to be acquired and is artificial" (KU: 240). The question is intimately paradoxical and has puzzled some of his readers. Kant has just offered a quasi-deduction of a new transcendental principle of the faculty of judgment and now asks whether taste is a faculty that could still "be acquired" and in this sense would be "artificial." We know, of course, that a transcendental principle is not innate (or a subjective predisposition "for thinking, implanted in us along with our existence by our author"), but is rather "selfthought" (*selbsgedacht*, KrV § 27, B 167), and that Kant places his research into the a priori conditions of possibility of experience within the framework of a "system of **epigenesis** of pure reason" (KrV § 27, B 167). But the question posed in § 22 seems to indicate that the entire transcendental apparatus, although it cannot be derived from experience, is nevertheless dynamically constructed, feeding on empirical, historical, biological, cultural, and contingent experience.

In her remarkable book, for instance, Malabou (2016) considers the debate over whether the transcendental is natural or fabricated ("factitious") to be pointless, insofar as it would be the very development of the transcendental, from the first to the third *Critique*, to be epigenetic[20]. Without specifically calling into ques-

---

[19] The Swiss artist Thomas Hirschhorn has insisted that "the artist is responsible even beyond his own responsibility. That is what art is: to be responsible for that which we cannot be responsible for." And again: "The artist is responsible for everything and even for what he cannot control or predict [...]. I must be responsible for that for which I am not responsible" (Hirschhorn 2013, p. 82, p. 376).

[20] It is not possible to summarize here the grand tour de force undertaken by Malabou in her book (2016). To give just a hint of the direction of her perspective, I quote only the conclusion of Chapter 13: "The Kantian critical enterprise combines a structural and an evolutionary view of reason in a whole. There's no need to choose between the two. The dynamic of transcendental philosophy proceeds both from the formal anteriority of the a priori—the archeological dimension—and from its modifiability through successive corrections—the teleological dimension. The permanence

tion epigenesis in this context, Garroni arrives at the conclusion that the faculty of judging is not even a faculty in all senses of the term, since it is "self-constructed" inasmuch as it invests with its character all the other faculties, and therefore the very status of the transcendental outlined in the previous critical works. The "nature" of the principle is "in the making" (Garroni 1992, pp. 210 and 227), precisely because it is the condition of possibility of every other use of our faculties, as well as of philosophical discourse itself. That condition cannot therefore be, circularly, only "cultural," "artificial," or "[something] to be acquired," but neither is it even only "natural" or "original," as if it were a guarantee of sense that, making everything indistinctly sensible and justifiable, would not allow us to take seriously cultural differences and conflicts, not only in relation to "other cultures" but also to "our own" (Garroni 1992, pp. 245–270). For Garroni, making sense emerges, after all, as an *aesthetic-ethical risk* that we ought to run, without yearning for a "supreme meaning" or a triumph of a supposedly universal sense (what has been called, e.g., "the end of history"). I would say that making-sense is an aesthetic-*ethical* duty because we *ought* to attempt to actualize our moral plans within the contingent "territory (*territorium*)" of experience (KU: 174), without any guarantee that the domain of nature (internal and external to the subject) is hospitable to them. The "favor [*Gunst*] in which we take nature in" (KU: 350) in our aesthetic judgments is the way we happen to make sense of it as "favorable" also for possible further purposes. Thus, it is an *aesthetic*-ethical risk because our faculty of judgment should allow "the transition *from the manner of thinking* in accordance with the principles of the one [a ground of the unity of the supersensible that grounds nature] with the principles of the other [a ground that the concept of freedom contains practically]" (KU: 176, my emphasis). And, finally, it is an aesthetic-ethical *risk* because not only do we not know to what extent the contingency of nature comes to meet our plans (KU: XXXVI), but also because we may err by excess, allowing ourselves to make "artificial" sense of everything with a "tolerance" that would make everything equally senseless.

There is no doubt that this reading of the *Critique of the Power of Judgment* constitutes a premise for an overall revision of the transcendental, shedding a new light also on the two preceding Critiques[21]. But how to reconcile something that is not in our control with the risky aesthetic-ethical *duty* of making sense?

---

and mobility of form are thus combined in a single economy: the system of the epigenesis of pure reason."

[21] In addition to the remarkable works already mentioned by Garroni and Malabou, I think some other essays in the moral and political field also go in this direction, starting with the reflections of Arendt (1992) (although not always accurate in the reading of Kant) and Ferrara (2008) and, more recently, of Vaccarino Bremner (2021).

Sensible experience occurs when we feel that what happens has a comprehensible connection with the rest of our possible experience in its elusive totality, with the space of accumulated experience and with the horizons of our expectations. Our recurring plunge into the senseless and into the absurd, along with our suffering from it, is precisely what confirms to us the inevitability of this need for control over our experience which, although clearly indispensable, paradoxically cannot be satisfied by clinging to what we can directly control.

Abbreviations

Apart from the *Critique of Pure Reason*, all references to Kant's works are to Kant's *Gesammelte Schriften, Ausgabe der Preußischen Akademie der Wissenschaften* (Berlin: De Gruyter, 1902 ff.). References to the *Critique of Pure Reason* are to the standard A and B pagination of the first and second editions. Translations are from *The Cambridge Edition of the Works of Immanuel Kant*.

The following abbreviations of individual works are used:

KU Kritik der Urteilskraft / Critique of the Power of Judgment
KrV Kritik der reinen Vernunft / Critique of Pure Reason

Literature

Anscombe, Gertrude E. M. (1957, 2000): *Intention*. Cambridge: Harvard University Press.
Arendt, Hannah (1992): *Lectures on Kant's Political Philosophy*. Ronald Beiner (Ed.). Chicago: University of Chicago Press.
Brodskij, Iosif (1992, 1997): *Watermark*. New York: Penguin.
Costello, Diarmuid (2008): "Danto and Kant: Together at Last?" In: Stock, Kathleen and Thomson-Jones, Katherine (Eds.): *New Waves in Aesthetics*. London: Palgrave McMillan, pp. 244–266.
Costello, Diarmuid (2021): "Conceptual Art and Aesthetic Ideas." In: *Kantian Review* 26. No. 4, pp. 603–618.
D'Angelo, Paolo (2014): *Ars est celare artem. Da Aristotle a Duchamp*. Macerata: Quodlibet.
D'Angelo, Paolo and Velotti, Stefano (1997): *Il 'non so che.' Storia di un'idea estetica*. Palermo: Aesthetica.
Danto, Arthur (1981): *The Transfiguration of the Commonplace*. Cambridge: Harvard University Press.
Derrida, Jacques (1978, 1987): *Truth in Painting*. Chicago and London: The University of Chicago Press.
Elster, Jon (1983, 2016): *Sour Grapes. Studies in the Subversion of Rationality*. Cambridge: Cambridge University Press.
Ferrara, Alessandro (2008): *The Force of the Example. Explorations in the Paradigm of Judgment*. New York: Columbia University Press.
Garroni, Emilio (1976): *Estetica ed epistemologia. Riflessioni sulla Critica del Giudizio di Kant*. Rome: Bulzoni.

Garroni, Emilio (1977): *Ricognizione della semiotica.* Rome: Officina.
Garroni, Emilio (1986): *Senso e paradosso. L'estetica, una filosofia non-speciale.* Rome and Bari: Laterza.
Garroni, Emilio (1992): *Estetica. Uno sguardo-attraverso.* Milan: Garzanti.
Garroni, Emilio (2005): *Immagine, linguaggio, figura. Osservazioni e ipotesi.* Rome and Bari: Laterza.
Garroni, Emilio (2020): "Kant and the Bestimmungsgrund/'Principle of Determination' of Aesthetic Judgment (1989)." In: Schlüter, Gisela (Ed.): *Kants Schriften in Übersetzungen.* Archiv für Begriffsgeschichte. Sonderheft 15, pp. 491–502.
Guyer, Paul (2005a): "The Harmony of the Faculties Revisited." In: Guyer, Paul (Ed.): *Values of Beauty. Historical Essays in Aesthetics.* New York: Cambridge University Press, pp. 77–109.
Guyer, Paul (2005b): "Free and Adherent Beauty: A Modest Proposal." In: Guyer, Paul (Ed.): *Values of Beauty. Historical Essays in Aesthetics.* New York: Cambridge University Press, pp. 129–140.
Hande Tuna, Emine (2018): "Kant on Informed Pure Judgments of Taste." In: *The Journal of Aesthetics and Art Criticism* 76. No. 2, pp. 163–174.
Hirschhorn, Thomas (2013): *Critical Laboratory. The Writings of Thomas Hirschhorn.* Lisa Lee and Hal Foster (Eds.). Cambridge and London: The MIT Press.
Kant, Immanuel (1781, 1787, 1998): *Critique of Pure Reason.* Paul Guyer and Allen W. Wood (Trans.). Cambridge: Cambridge University Press.
Kant, Immanuel (1790, 2000): *The Critique of the Power of Judgment.* Paul Guyer and Eric Matthews (Trans.). Cambridge: Cambridge University Press.
Kant, Immanuel (1967): *Critica del Giudizio.* Alfredo Gargiulo (Trans.); revised by Valerio Verra. Rome and Bari: Laterza.
Kant, Immanuel (1999): *Critica della facoltà di giudizio.* Garroni, Emilio and Hohenegger, Hansmichael (Eds.). Torino: Einaudi.
Leopardi, Giacomo (1898, 2013): *Zibaldone.* Michael Caesar and Franco D'Intino (Eds.). New York: Farrar, Strauss, and Giroux.
Lorand, Ruth (1989): "Free and dependent beauty: A puzzling issue." In: *The British Journal of Aesthetics* 29. No. 1, pp. 32–40.
Lorand, Ruth (2000): *Aesthetic Order. A Philosophy of Order, Beauty and Art.* New York and London: Routledge.
Malabou, Catherine (2014, 2016): *Before Tomorrow. Epigenesis and Rationality.* Cambridge and Malden: Polity Press.
Nanay, Bence (2016): *Aesthetics as Philosophy of Perception.* Oxford: Oxford University Press.
Noë, Alva (2015): *Strange Tools. Art and Human Nature.* New York: Hill and Wang.
Steinberg, Leo (1972, 2007): *Other Criteria: Comparisons with Twentieth-Century Art.* Chicago and London: The University of Chicago Press.
Vaccarino Bremner, Sabina (2021): "On Conceptual Revision and Aesthetic Judgment." In: *Kantian Review* 26. No. 4, pp. 531–547.
Velotti, Stefano (2003): *Storia filosofica dell'ignoranza.* Rome and Bari: Laterza.
Velotti, Stefano (2008): *Estetica analitica. Un breviario critico.* Palermo: Aesthetica Preprint.
Walton, Kendall (1970): "Categories of Art." In: *Philosophical Review* 79. No. 3, pp. 334–367.
Weil, Eric (1970): "Sens et fait." In: Weil, Eric (Ed.): *Problèmes kantiens.* Paris: Vrin, pp. 57–107.

Part II **Disinterestedness With and Beyond Kant**

(a) **Disinterest Advocates**

Keren Gorodeisky
The Myth of the Absent Self: Disinterest, the Self, and Evaluative Self-Consciousness

Abstract: A notorious concept in the history of aesthetics, "disinterest," has begotten a host of myths. This paper explores and challenges "The Myth of the Absent Self" [MAS], according to which in disinterested experience, "the subject need not do anything other than dispassionately stare at the object, bringing nothing of herself to the table other than awareness" (Riggle 2016, p. 4). I argue that the criticism of disinterest experience grounded in MAS is skewed by two false assumptions: about the nature of the clarifying, evaluative, and transformative self-consciousness (which the disinterest critic takes to be at the heart of the profundity of beauty) and about the nature of the self. By bringing out the falsehood of these two assumptions, and by clarifying the core commitments of disinterest, the paper proves that the disinterest critic is in no superior position to the disinterest advocate regarding the explanation of the profound role of beauty in human life.

The protagonists of Oliver Jeffers' *The Day the Crayons Quit* are Duncan's crayons. They are quitting their jobs as crayons because of over-exhaustion (blue), because they are used only to draw the outlines but never to color (black), or because they are used only by Duncan's sister but never by Duncan (pink). "Disinterest" would clearly be a protagonist in the book *The Day the Philosophical Concepts Quit*, quitting its job as a philosophical concept because of over-exhaustion and perhaps also because of misuse or unfair treatment. After all, "disinterest" is a notorious concept in the history of philosophy.

Like all concepts with such a pedigree, "disinterest" has begotten a host of myths. Some of these have been adopted and developed by a number of its own advocates (when they themselves forgot or misunderstood the genuine sense of the term), and some were imposed on the term by its detractors (due to their own misunderstandings). Two such myths have been central in the literature: "The Myth of Inactivity" (and detachment) [henceforth MI][1] and the "Myth of

---

[1] According to MI, not only is disinterested experience merely passive, rather than active but it is also detached from cognitive and moral concerns, *and* from any other activity or experience. In Monroe Beardsley's words, aesthetic experience is characterized by "*Felt Freedom.* A sense of release from the dominance of some antecedent concerns about past and future" (Beardsley 1982, p. 288). It is, George Dickie writes when explaining Beardsley's view, "detached from past and fu-

the Absent Self" [henceforth MAS]. Even though some of my arguments will bear on MI, I will not discuss it in this paper. My focus is on MAS.

Nick Riggle formulates MAS succinctly. On his reconstruction, in disinterested aesthetic experience, "the subject need not do anything other than dispassionately stare at the object, bringing nothing of herself to the table other than awareness" (Riggle 2016, p.4). On this picture, the self is "diminished, obscured or excluded" (Riggle 2016, p. 7) from disinterested experience *because* this experience is independent of the satisfaction of the self's existing desires, needs, or values [henceforth, "desires, etc."].

Surprisingly, the dispute between the disinterest advocate [henceforth, "advocate"] and the disinterest critic [henceforth, "critic"], we will learn below, does not concern primarily the nature of aesthetic experience, but rather different understandings of the self and self-consciousness.[2] I will argue first, that, without further explanation, the critic's view is not superior to the advocate's view but rather inferior to it when it comes to explaining the genuine character of experiences of beauty and their significance in human life, and, second, that this is primarily because of the confusions regarding the self and self-consciousness that seem to mar the critic's criticism of disinterest. At the very least, the critic owes us explication of his view's advantage over the advocate's view since the most natural reading of his criticism suggests that it is based on a confused understanding of self-consciousness, the self, and the core commitment to a Kantian form of disinterest implies.

Before I start, a few clarifications are called for.

I have no wish to defend the whole tradition of disinterest, particularly not what was made of this notion in the long 20th century. Theories of disinterest such as Jerome Stolnitz' and Monroe Beardsley's (that are grounded (respectively) in the concepts of "sympathetic attention" and "detachment" or "isolation")[3] are

---

ture experiences and from any other possible or actual present experience" (Dickie 1988, p. 7). What stands behind this myth, I suspect, is a core commitment of the disinterested theorist to the contrast between disinterested experience and willing and desire. But commitment to this contrast (I believe but will have no space to defend in this paper), implies neither inactivity nor detachment from other activities and experiences. In fact, there is no way to understand disinterested pleasure, or for that matter, any pleasure or appreciation, as either merely passive or as disconnected from other (actual, and not merely possible) activities and experiences.

2 The disagreement also concerns conflicting understandings of motivation, the activity of certain (affective) experiences, and the relation of activity and passivity more generally, but I will not discuss these in this paper.

3 E.g., Beardsley 1982; Stolnitz 1960.

notorious for a reason, and will not be defended on these pages.[4] Moreover, those particular accounts of disinterestedness are *not* entailed by a core commitment to disinterest, a core commitment that I will present by loosely drawing on Immanuel Kant's notion of the disinterest pleasure in the beautiful.

Yet, the paper is systematic, not historical. Rather than a reading of a historical figure or tradition, this is an attempt to explore what is entailed by a basic commitment to the view that experiences of beauty are disinterested in a Kantian spirit, the nature of the self-consciousness that constitutes them, and the nature of the self.

But if I do not aim to give a reading of Kant or to engage in any historical reconstruction, why reconstruct the DA's core commitment by drawing on Kant's notion? One reason for this strategy is that Kant is often taken to be the philosopher who did most to reorient the notion of disinterest in a way that has been most influential on later developments *and* criticisms of the notion. Even though most of the 20th and 21st criticisms of disinterest draw heavily on features that were developed and attributed to the notion *after Kant*, they are standardly described as criticisms of "Kantian Disinterest" or of accounts that the critics take to continue Kant's notion (e.g., Korsmeyer 2004, Riggle 2016, Cavedon-Taylor 2021). Given that, understanding the "Kantian" core commitment is crucial for a clear grasp of "disinterestedness" and the limitations of the criticisms that it has attracted over the years.

1 Riggle's Criticism

Some texts, literary, philosophical, and otherwise, inspire and deserve continual engagement and discussion. Nick Riggle's paper, "On the Interest in Beauty and Disinterest," is one of them. Riggle here aims, correctly and valuably, to revive the tradition of thinking about encounters with beauty as profound (Riggle 2016, p. 2). He nicely brings out a genuine dimension of (at least) a certain kind of aesthetic experiences, particularly, those experiences portrayed by some 20th century literary authors, such as Marcel Proust, John Williams, and Rainer Maria Rilke.[5] Sometimes, perhaps even often, aesthetic encounters with beauty are profound insofar as they bring to the forth our sense of self: "Aesthetic experience can bear on—

---

[4] For criticisms of these views as well as arguments distinguishing these views from 18th-century accounts of taste, see, for example, Dickie 1964, 1974 and 1997; Rind 2002; and Shelley 2017.
[5] In the following, I will suggest in passing some of the disagreements between Riggle's reading and my reading of the passages he draws on, but because nothing substantial hangs on these disagreements, they will not be discussed in detail.

highlight, clarify, transform—our sense of self [and] can bear on our evaluative sense of our lives [...]" (Riggle 2016, p. 9).

So far, so good—even great. Riggle's argument that aesthetic experiences can highlight, clarify, and transform our sense of self, and can bear on our evaluative take on our lives is correct and valuable. Our paths diverge, though, regarding, first, what is required for such evaluative self-conscious and transformative aesthetic experiences, second, the nature of the human self, and, third, the advocate's ability to account for such profound aesthetic experiences.

Riggle complains that, without further explanation, the advocate cannot account for the profundity of aesthetic experience since she cannot account for the way that many engagements with beauty *answer to* existing individual desires, etc., and are aesthetically valuable largely due to this. According to Riggle, disinterested experience is "incompatible with or effaces our self-awareness" (Riggle 2016, p. 11). But I will show that critic owes us a clarification of this criticism since it is most naturally understood as grounded in two mistaken presuppositions, which even the critic would find unpalatable. These are the assumptions that (1) the satisfaction of the self's existing desires, etc., is required for clarifying, evaluative, and transformative self-consciousness,[6] and could afford such self-consciousness on its own, independently of assessing *what is desirable* or *valuable*, and (2) the self[7] is wholly determined by its actual psychology—it is reduced to the set of its existing desires, needs, and commitment to values.[8] If the critic is not commit-

---

[6] Suffices it to say here that this self-consciousness is an experience in which the self has a clearer understanding of herself, an understanding that allows the self to evaluate its stances on the world, and possibly to transform them. More on this below.

[7] I will often speak of the "concrete self" and the consciousness of the concrete individual rather than about "personal self-consciousness" (other than in quotation marks) deliberately. As we will see in what follows, part of what seems to motivate the critic's worry is his impression that the advocate does not portray aesthetic experience as personal enough, even though this experience is, according to the critic, all too personal, and profound for this reason. While I will attempt to show that disinterested aesthetic experience can and often does implicate the concrete self (e.g., Keren) and ground self-consciousness of e.g., me as Keren, I will not argue that the advocate agrees with the critic that aesthetic experience is "personal" since the very dichotomy between the personal and the impersonal, as the critic posits it, is confused.

[8] The critic's criticism appears to be based on two further misguided assumptions (but, given space limitations, I would not be able to argue for this in this paper): the assumptions that (3) self-awareness that is grounded in the satisfaction of existing desires, etc., is capable of manifesting the *concrete* human self, and that (4) there are exclusively two kinds of self-consciousness: self-consciousness of ourselves as rational, universal selves—"impersonal self-consciousness"—and self-consciousness of ourselves as the concrete individual that we are—"personal self-consciousness." But (3) is false because the concrete human self is a non-conjunctive whole and thus cannot be manifested by an experience that is grounded merely in the satisfaction of *some* desires, etc.

ted to these false assumption, he must reformulate and clarify his criticism. Until then, his view is not superior to the advocate's, but in fact, as I show below, inferior to it.

In short, while I will show that the advocates *can* account for the way that aesthetic experience evaluatively bear on the appreciator's concrete self and life, my main strategy consists in turning the table on the critic: I will argue that, on its most natural reading, the critic's own view cannot account for what he aims to explain, namely, how aesthetic experience can involve clarifying, evaluative, and potentially transformative self-consciousness. The burden is now on the critic. We have yet to hear why interested experience is a better characterization of aesthetic experience than a disinterested one.

2 Kantian Disinterestedness

But first things first. What does a commitment to disinterest in a Kantian spirit look like?

It is (virtually) a truth universally acknowledged that any disinterest thesis worthy of the name has both "negative" and "positive" dimensions: advocates and critics agree that the view should be explained both in terms of the "dis" of disinterest, namely, in terms of what this experience is independent of ("interest"), but also in terms of what it positively consists in. And it is uncontroversial that the negative dimension of disinterest consists of some kind of independence: disinterested experience is widely regarded by both advocates and critics as independent of the will and the faculty of desire generally and as independent of the satisfaction of pre-existing desires, etc., particularly.[9]

Riggle formulates the negative dimension of disinterest as follows:

Just as the self is not composed of independently existing parts, properties, and characteristics, so a genuine self-consciousness of the concrete human self cannot be composed out of various acts of consciousness of the self's different properties, etc., including the self's existing desires, etc. Finally, the dichotomy underlying (4) is false. When properly understood, disinterested experience is a self-conscious experience in which we are aware of ourselves as concrete, human individuals *to the extent* that we are rational-affective selves, sharing in rational-affective capacities with others. There are no two kinds of aesthetic self-consciousness. Rather, aesthetic self-consciousness is neither "personal self-consciousness" nor "impersonal self-consciousness" because it is both (non-conjunctively). The critic's distinction between the personal and impersonal is muddled. For a related challenge to this distinction with regard to (ethical) virtues, see Brewer 2009.
9 This is included in Riggle's reconstruction of the advocate as "Disinterest-."

> Disinterest-: If a pleasure in an item is aesthetic, then it is not due to the way the item satisfies one's desires, needs, or worldly projects. (Riggle 2016, p. 3)

While Riggle claims that the independence of disinterested experience from the faculty of desire and willing, and from particular desires, needs, and values is responsible for the self's attenuated presence in disinterested experience (Riggle 2016, p. 4), I will show in this section that neither kind of independence entails that the concrete individual self is absent from the relevant experience. Correctly understanding disinterested experience's independence from desire and willing shows it to be compatible with an experience in which the concrete appreciating self is involved, and through which it is reflected. (This will be made even clearer in § 4.)

So, what does it mean to claim that an experience is independent of interest or desire?

In contrast to his predecessors, Kant reorients the notion of disinterest to refer to a kind of experience that is independent—in the relevant sense to be explained below—not only of individual, private and/or idiosyncratic desires, etc., but of *any* desire, want or need; in one word, independent of any interest.[10] The characterization of aesthetic experience as "disinterested" is Kant's primary way of articulating the fact that this experience is an exercise of taste, not of willing or desiring. More specifically, this label serves to articulate the receptive rather than productive character of aesthetic experience[11] and its independence from a *rule-bound* connection to desire. Kant's notion of "interest" diverges from its colloquial use: he characterizes interest as "a connection of pleasure with the faculty of desire that the understanding judges to hold as a *general rule*" (MS: 212, my italics).[12] Aesthetic experience, then, is disinterested partly in being a pleasurable experience that is independent of a *rule-bound connection* to desire. A proper appreciation of beauty is not rule-bound insofar as it is not, and should not be mediated by a rule, principle, general desire, or general conception under which the beautiful

---

[10] On this difference between Kant and his predecessors, see Shelley 2017.
[11] Kant clearly argues that the imagination in aesthetic experience is "productive" rather than merely "reproductive" and "associative" (KU: 240). What I am arguing here is compatible with this claim insofar as I use "productive" (as I explain below) to refer to the characteristic of a capacity that is the cause of its own objects (e.g., EEKU: 230), not to a characteristic of an activity that is contrasted with mere reproduction and association.
[12] In the *Groundwork*, he clarifies that this is a rule of *reason*, whether the pleasure is pleasure in the agreeable or the good. Interest is *that by which reason becomes practical*, i.e., a cause determining the will. "One says of rational beings only that they take an interest in something; non-rational creatures feel only sensuous impulses" (GMS: 459–460 fn.).

object that is given to us immediately through feeling is subsumed, or one to which it fits (in contrast to all cognitive judgments, both theoretical and practical). More particularly, it has no rule-bound relation to *desire* (as interested experiences do). Why?

I now turn to propose three interpretations of this view and to support them briefly by reflection on our practices around beauty. All these interpretations yield plausible and fairly uncontroversial characterizations of aesthetic experience, and, pace the critic of disinterest, do not prevent experiences that are so independent from implicating and manifesting consciousness of the concrete experiencing subject or her concrete "perspective."[13] As such, they raise a question on MAS.

First, aesthetic experience is independent of a rule-bound connection to desire (i.e., interest) insofar as it is immediate and non-inferential (even if it is responsive to reasons for appreciating the object).[14] No matter how much background knowledge and understanding we often need, and legitimately use in order to put ourselves in a position to appreciate any particular beautiful object,[15] the very act of appreciating it is not inferred from this knowledge or from any general repre-

---

[13] In the last few decades, feminist critics have pursued a version of MAS, arguing that disinterested theories mask the fact that they are formulated from and for a white male appreciative perspective insofar as they obliterate both the different perspectives from which different appreciators appreciate, and awareness to one's own gender and situation (e.g., Korsmeyer 1993, vii–viii; Korsmeyer 2004, Chapter 4; Eaton 2020). These criticisms are part of important philosophical approaches that are correct to remind us that, as a historical fact, many historical theories were designed from a perspective of a white man with this perspective in mind, even if this perspective is sometimes masked. Yet, they are wrong that the disinterest advocate masks this perspective *by* obliterating concrete gendered perspectives because her view does not imply such an elimination of concrete perspectives. Rather, on my reconstruction of the core commitment of Disinterest, Disinterested experience is compatible both with the involvement of a particularly situated, gendered, concrete appreciator in this very experience, and with the appreciator's awareness of her gender, historical, and social situation, etc. Disinterested experience is incompatible only with the idea that this experience is grounded and explained by the satisfaction of existing desires and needs, but, as I argue, this does not entail the elimination of the concrete self. As Korsmeyer—one of the critics—herself stresses, Disinterest is compatible with perspectivism: "Even a successfully disinterested stance [...] does not necessarily cancel out discrepancies of perspective that different perceivers take to an artwork. That is, there may be a variety of perspectives on a work, all of which qualify as disinterested. [...] The alert viewer is aware of how a work invites appreciative points of view, but that point of view is not necessarily adopted" (Korsmeyer 2004, p. 56).

[14] On the non-inferential *yet reasons-responsive* character of aesthetic appreciation, see Gorodeisky and Marcus 2022.

[15] Though it often goes unnoticed, Kant is clear that such background knowledge is often required and is legitimate, for example, in his discussion of dependent beauty (KU: 230–231), and in his discussion of the important role of succession and predecessors in aesthetic criticism and artistic production (KU: 283).

sentation under which the particular beauty at stake falls: it is not a conclusion arrived at merely by recognizing how an individual fits a general description. Though not exclusive, this is a common view in aesthetics. I take it that most disinterest critics can agree with this sense of independence from interest.

Second, aesthetic appreciation is independent of rule-bound connection to desire in terms of the standards of appropriateness of this realm, which are explained partly by the kind of responsiveness that beauty (but not empirical facts, good actions, agreeable objects, or useful objects), calls for. To grasp this, consider first the pleasures one might take in a newly purchased good chair, in a pampering hot bath, or in one's successful negotiations with the mayor's office to defund the police in town. One is not called on to treat the chair, the particular hot bath, or this specific action *as* the individual chair, the particular hot bath, or the specific action that they are, on their own terms. Rather, to enjoy them as good or pleasant is to enjoy them in light of their fitness to the norms that are grounded in the very concepts "chair," "hot bath," or "combating racism." These pleasures are felt as they satisfy a (general) desire for *a* good chair, for *a* pampering bath or for fighting racism. In these "interested" cases, your enjoyment could be fully appropriate (can meet standards of appropriateness in its realm) when you enjoy the objects/actions because and insofar as they meet general norms or satisfy general desires, for example, when you enjoy the chair as *a* good chair (one that is a good chair merely *because* it perfects what it shares with all good chairs). If we ask you, "why are you so happy with the new chair?" we will most likely be satisfied with the answer, "because it is such a good chair" or "because it is so sturdy and comfortable, as all good chairs should be." There is no room to wonder at, let alone criticize, your explanation of your liking in these general terms—it is a good explanation of one's pleasure in the usefully good. The same goes for moral actions. Suppose that your negotiations with the mayor aim to fight the systematic racism exhibited by police brutality in town. And suppose that fighting racism is morally good. In this scenario, explaining your pleasure merely in general terms, grounded in the goodness of *any* action that combats racism, by saying, for example, "phew, I am so thrilled—another steppingstone in the fight against racism," or "this is so satisfying—a little less racism in our town," is fully appropriate. There is no room for wonder about these answers, let alone criticism: "really, are you proud of your negotiations merely as an act of fighting against racism?" Enjoying an action/object as fitting the general description that shows it to be either morally good or useful meets the standards of appropriateness in this realm of the good.

With beauties, it is different; they do call on us to treat them, not only as instantiating general kinds or as satisfying rule-bound desires for something general, but also as the individuals that they are. Explaining aesthetic pleasures merely in terms of general norms or rule-bound desires is inappropriate, a good reason for doubt, criticism and/or other reactive attitudes. Consider the pleasure one takes in reading John Williams' novel *Stoner* (a novel that Riggle discusses). Even though *Stoner* is a 20th-century American novel, and even though being so exerts constraints on its beauty and on how to appreciate it, responsively enjoying it as a beautiful object cannot be reduced to enjoyment grounded *merely* in its fitness to the external norms of the goodness of such novels, or in the satisfaction of a general desire. Enjoying the novel merely as a *John Williams novel* rather than as the particular—and distinctive—novel that it is is a failure to properly appreciate it because it is a failure to be responsive to what it merits. This is a failure to meet the standards of appropriateness in this realm.

Even if the disinterest critic may first resist, this way of understanding the independence from interests does not strike me as controversial. Think how common it is to ask, if someone indeed enjoys *Stoner* merely *a* William's novel, "really, do you love it only because it is a John Williams novel?" Such appreciation is likely to be wondered at, often to be doubted, and even criticized. Reading the novel only in terms of what it shares with others, in light of a general description that applies to all of them, or as grounded in your general desire to read *a* Williams novel is being irresponsive to it: it is to fall short of being appropriate to it and thus of meeting the standards of appropriateness in this field (as exchanges of the sort I just presented show). While appreciating beauties is constrained by the norms of the categories to which they belong,[16] their values as beautiful are never reduced to those, and apt appreciation of them cannot be grounded merely in those. Beauties give substance to their own norms of appreciation and should be appreciated (at least partly) in light of these norms. In this respect, beauties are like persons, who should not be responded to *merely* in light of general norms and rational desires (e.g., for respecting them *as* rational beings), but also as the individual persons who they are, in terms that are constituted by their own free individuality.

That aesthetic experience is independent of rule-bound desire or "interest," then, is explained partly by the kind of *responsiveness* beauty calls for, responsiveness that constitutes the standards of appropriateness in the realm of beauty.[17] As Kant puts it, responsiveness to beauty requires that we be attuned to the *beautiful object's own claim on everyone's pleasure* (KU: 282), just as responsiveness to my partner's love for me requires that I love him as the individual who he is, not merely as *a partner*.

---

16 This much was famously argued for by Walton (1970).
17 On the different standards of appropriateness governing beliefs, actions, emotions and acts of aesthetic appreciation, see Gorodeisky 2021b.

On the disinterest advocate's view, proper appreciation of beauty is independent of interests *in these two senses*, which most disinterest critics could and should accept. For this independence of interest is both faithful to our common practices around beauty, and compatible with the involvement of the concrete appreciator (including her gender and situation) in the engagement with beauty that the disinterest critic emphasizes. We need a further argument, not yet given, if the critic is to show that independence of interests is incompatible with the involvement of the concrete self.

Note, though, that, in line of the systematic rather than historical character of the paper, I am not committed to finding this notion of disinterest in any actual figure (even though I do believe that it is faithful to Kant's notion). I am saying instead that this is a perfectly good way to understand a central aspect of a Kantian commitment to disinterest, which a (contemporary) advocate of disinterest could endorse, thus portraying disinterest aesthetic experience as involving and manifesting the concrete individual appreciator.

What about aesthetic experience's independence of the faculty of desire in general?

To endorse this independence is to deny that aesthetic experiences are *productive* rather than receptive (even if their receptivity, as I will suggest below, is both rational and active). In contemporary parlance, engagements with beauty and exercises of the faculty of desire have *different directions of fit*. Desire belongs to a *productive* capacity: it is the capacity "for being, through its representation, the cause of the reality of the objects of these representations" (EEKU: 230). Here are two marks of a productive capacity (of desiring and willing): first, the objects of this capacity are those that are to be brought about or actualized rather than those that are received or experienced as already actual (as the objects of empirical knowledge, emotional understanding, and aesthetic appreciation are). For example, to intend to get my son vaccinated against COVID-19 as soon as the vaccine is approved for kids younger than 12 is to desire that which I will bring about by taking him to get the shot. In contrast, to appreciate Michaela Cole's TV show *I May Destroy You* is to appreciate that which is already actual and need not be actualized.

Second, exercises of a productive capacity are normatively grounded in the worth or the point of what is to be actualized, and they reflect, not the world as it is already actual, but the world as it would be as actualized. Desires and willings are justified insofar as their actualizations are worthy or have a point, as a means to other actions, virtuous, pleasant, morally right, or good in another respect. For example, my intention to get my son vaccinated is justified (or not) by the goodness of that which is to be actualized—his getting the vaccine—and the world as so actualized—the state of the world in which he is vaccinated. But acts of appreciation (and empirical knowledge and emotions) are different: they are normatively grounded in the worth of their (already) actual objects, *not* in the state of the world when they themselves (the acts of appreciation) are actualized. What justifies my aesthetic appreciation of *I May Destroy You* is *not* the fact that my actualized appreciation is a means to another end or that it is *itself* good, pleasant, etc., but the fact that the *show* (as actual independently of my appreciation) is (in a reductive summary) a probing exploration of rape, sexual consent, trust and accountability and a sharp and beautiful portrait of the life, loves and friendships of Millennial blacks in London as embedded in the story of the hilarious, moving, and loving writer Arabella. This distinction between the productive and the receptive is another reason why Kant and others stress that the disinterested pleasure in the beautiful, an exercise of aesthetic appreciation, is independent of, and different from the practical, productive capacity for desiring and willing.

Hence, I see no reason for the disinterest critic not to accept aesthetic experience's independence of the faculty of desire in general, and no reason to think that this independence is incompatible with an experience that involves and manifests the concrete, individual appreciator.[18] The critic's criticism, insofar as the so-called "negative" aspect of disinterest is concerned, requires further support.

What about the positive aspect of disinterest?
Riggle reconstructs it as follows:

> Disinterest+: If a pleasure in an item is aesthetic, then it is due to sympathetic attention to, or contemplation of, the item for its own sake. (Riggle 2016, p. 4)

I am not sure what is meant by "sympathetic attention" (a term often used by 20th-century disinterest advocates, and repeated in Riggle's reconstruction). Kant himself uses neither of the terms in this phrase. Instead, while he characterizes the (interested) pleasures in the agreeable and the good as "practical," and dubs the pleasure in the *sublime* "contemplative" (e.g., KU: 292), for the most part, he labels the pleasure in beauty a pleasure "of reflection" (e.g., KU: 292), where reflection, as

---

[18] This is the first step in showing that we need *not* pursue "the reinstatement of desire in theories of aesthetic pleasure" (Korsmeyer 2004, p. 56) in order to gain and celebrate the specific perspective of the concrete appreciator in aesthetic experience. The independence from desire is an articulation of the receptive rather than productive nature of aesthetic experience, not of the elimination of the concrete self. Moreover, the very attempt to reinstate desire with the goal of gaining the perspective of the concrete appreciator is misguided since, like other varieties of MAS, it also presupposes that the self is reduced to her existing sets of desires, etc. In IV, I show that it is not.

elsewhere in his corpus, most likely stands for an act of the mind that involves a comparison between the mind and what is given to it or between different aspects of the mind (e.g., KrV: A260/B316, EEKU: 211).[19]

However, at least in one discussion, the term "contemplative" serves to characterize the pleasure in beauty (cf. MS: 212). If not being practical is the negative characterization of disinterest, and being "contemplative" and "reflective" is its positive dimension then, the following passage is one of the most explicit characterizations of the Kantian Disinterest +:

> Now it is similar with the pleasure in the aesthetic judgment, except that here it is merely contemplative and does not produce an interest in the object, while in the moral judgment it is practical. *The consciousness of the merely formal purposiveness in the play of the cognitive powers of the subject in the case of a representation through which an object is given is the pleasure itself.* This pleasure is also in no way practical, neither like that from the pathological ground of agreeableness nor like that from the intellectual ground of the represented good. *But yet it has a causality in itself, namely that of* **maintaining** *the state of the representation of the mind and the occupation of the cognitive powers without a further aim. We* **linger** *over the consideration of the beautiful because this consideration strengthens and reproduces itself*, which is analogous to (yet not identical with) the way in which we linger when a charm in the representation of the object repeatedly attract attention, *where the mind is passive*. (KU: 222; the emphasis is in the original, though the italics are mine)

Disinterested pleasure is here characterized *positively* as having active, committed, rational, and conscious internal causality. But this pithy summary clearly requires explanation.

Notice first that Kant here distinguishes the disinterested pleasure in beauty from the interested pleasure in the agreeable, not only as "contemplative" rather than "practical" but also as *active* rather than passive. Though in feeling both kinds of pleasure, the subject tends to continue the engagement with that which pleases, the pleasure in the agreeable is passive vis-a-vis this self-maintenance. In contrast, disinterested pleasure is not passive (as the Myth of Inactivity has it) but active in maintaining the subject's engagement with the beautiful object.

In what sense is it active? Disinterested pleasure is active in part because it *itself* is the ground for its self-maintenance: it has *internal* rather than external causality. Interested pleasures, we learn here and elsewhere (e.g., EEKU: 230–231) have merely an *external* causality: they could not be reproduced independently of bringing about their objects through actions. Zoe cannot continue to enjoy her just act of volunteering in administrating COVID-19 vaccines unless she continues to volunteer (perhaps at different centers in different times). Joe cannot continue

---

[19] On Kant's notion of reflection, see Gorodeisky 2021a.

to enjoy his hot bath unless he prepares himself another one. The maintenance of interested pleasure depends on a causality that is *external* to them: it depends *on the practical causality of the will*, which is required to bring about an action, and then another one of the same kind or to produce another agreeable object and then another one. Without this causality, which is external to these pleasures themselves, those pleasures would cease (in spite of their future-directed trajectory, namely, in spite of their subject's tendency to be motivated to have more of the same pleasures).

Disinterested pleasure is the only pleasure that has an *internal* and active causality. This is partly what it means to say that it is not practical, independent of the faculty of desire. Disinterested pleasure has *itself* the power of self-maintenance: it continues the subject's pleasurable, appreciative engagement with the beautiful object until she—the appreciating subject—judges otherwise (that the object is not beautiful, and so not worthy of appreciative pleasure). Disinterested pleasure does not need the will for self-maintenance. Why? A promising answer is that this is partly because of its own conscious, active and rational character (which Kant explains partly by its connection to the free play of the imagination and the understanding). The disinterested pleasure in beauty may be actively and internally self-maintaining insofar as it is the "consciousness" (as Kant calls it in the above passage) of this (pleasurable, understanding, and imaginative) engagement as merited by the object, that is, in virtue of involving recognition of its fittingness to the object. In the rest of this section, I elaborate on this explanation of the active and conscious character of disinterested pleasure, that is, explain this gloss on Disinterest +.

In the passage I cited above, Kant contrasts the internal causality of disinterested pleasure with the passivity of the pleasure in the agreeable. Disinterested pleasure actively maintains itself insofar as it is an act of self-consciousness that presents itself (the pleasure itself) as not just causally elicited from the object but as *merited* by it. I take it that this is why Kant regards it as an act of responsiveness to the beautiful object's "own claim to everyone's satisfaction" (KU: 282): we do not simply find our engagement with beauty as fitting to the object through feeling, but we *recognize* this fittingness to be called for. Hence, in contrast to the pleasure in the agreeable, disinterested pleasure is actively *taken* in an object as it is a "consciousness" of the whole pleasurable, disinterested engagement with the object as *necessary* to the object: "Of that which I call **agreeable** I say that it **actually** produces a pleasure in me. Of the beautiful, however, one thinks that it has a necessary relation to satisfaction." (KU: 236–237) Unlike the pleasure in the agreeable, and like beliefs, intentions, and other exercises of rationality, aesthetic pleasure is actively felt, as it is constituted by the recognition (the "consciousness" which is "the pleasure itself") that it is "necessary" to the beautiful object. For the disinterest advocate, aesthetic pleasure is as much self-consciousness as a consciousness of the object, precisely revealing their *mutuality* or *fitness* to each other (which Kant sometimes dubs "subjective" or, as in this passage, "formal" purposiveness). Disinterested pleasure is self-maintaining, then, in part because it is grounded in recognizing the object as worthy of itself, even if such recognition is implicit or inchoate at first. And it involves a commitment to actively continue the engagement with the beautiful object until it is experienced otherwise, as not worthy of this pleasure:[20] "The consciousness of the merely formal purposiveness in the play of the cognitive faculties is the pleasure itself because it contains a determining ground of the activity of the subject with regard to the animation of its cognitive powers, thus an internal causality" (KU: 222). This is plausibly why Kant claims that the disinterested pleasure in the beautiful is "a special feeling and distinctive receptivity that requires a special section under the properties of the mind" (EEKU: 207).[21]

This reconstruction is not my main argument against the disinterest critic. Instead, it is designed only to demonstrate that an advocate of disinterest can be committed to Disinterest + on which disinterested experience is constituted through an *active*, rational, and committed form of *self-consciousness* that manifests itself—the pleasure of the appreciating self—as worthy of the object, and, as such, as justified. When I enjoy *Stoner*, when I enjoy *I May Destroy You*, when I enjoy the view from the Blue Ridge Parkway, I do not simply enjoy a fleeting pleasure, exhausted by the here and now, but am rather enjoying those that I take (however inchoately and implicitly) to deserve my appreciative pleasure open-endedly—or at least until I experience them as undeserving. Such aesthetic pleasures are committal and open-ended because they involve consciousness of the normative fitness between the self and the object. If it did not involve any such consciousness of normative fit, however inchoate this consciousness may first be, I would never be able to explain when asked, for example, "why do you appreciate *Stoner*?" But we *are* often able to respond to this question, saying, "because of the so ordinary and uneventful yet riveting life of William Stoner," or "because of the plain but moving language." Even if we cannot answer in these ways, we are expected to respond with answers that reveal the applicability of the question itself, for example by saying "I am not sure why I like it, let me think about it"

---

[20] For a full argument to the conclusion that aesthetic pleasure is constituted by an active rational commitment and is, to this extent, an exercise of rational agency, see Gorodeisky 2018.
[21] Nicholas Dunn very nicely explains that Kant's view of this pleasure as a special feeling that "is dependent only on reflection" and "connected with it in accordance with a principle *a priori*" (EEKU: 249) suggests that "feeling itself functions as a distinct (and non-discursive) mode of judging" (Dunn MS, p. 11).

or "I don't really know why, why do you?." Such answers show the applicability of the "why" question that asks for normative grounds[22] and entails that our experience itself already involves consciousness of something in the object that merits our pleasurable experience.[23]

And in any case, just as Disinterest -, as reconstructed above, is compatible with the involvement of the concrete appreciator in the experience of beauty, so is Disinterest +. In fact, this way of understanding Disinterest entails that the concrete appreciator *is* actively involved in the experience of beauty. How? In and through feeling disinterested pleasure, the self recognizes that her own pleasurable experience is particularly fitting to the object, and is actively committing herself to a continual appreciation of it. The disinterest critic owes us an argument that supports what presents itself as an unsupported claim, namely, the claim that in disinterested experience "the subject need not do anything other than dispassionately stare at the object, bringing nothing of herself to the table other than awareness" (Riggle 2016, p. 4). This is no doubt the Myth of the Absent Self, but it is *only* a myth.

It is particularly strange that the critic regards disinterested experience as one in which the subject brings "nothing of herself to the table other than awareness," given that the Kantian advocate emphasizes its *affective* nature. Not only is Disinterest compatible with the concrete self's involvement and consciousness in disinterested experience, as I have shown above, and not only does Disinterest + entail that disinterested experienced is active and self-consciousness, as I just explained, but as disinterested *pleasure*, aesthetic experience necessarily involves and manifests the self. After all, as a *feeling*, disinterested *pleasure* is the subject's own receptivity to a particular object; a "modification" or "determination" (e.g., EEKU: 223) of the *subject*, in Kant's terms. Like all other affects, pleasure makes a special reference to the *feeling subject*. Aesthetic engagement is clearly an engagement with and *about* the beautiful object at stake (EEKU: 223), but it could not be under-

---

22 I take it that this is partly manifested in Kant's view of aesthetic appreciation as grounded in the high faculty of the power of judgment and in his emphasis on the ubiquitous conversations and arguments about beauty.

23 The claim is *not* that every aesthetic appreciation is responsive to reasons. I might appreciate a shade of violet color for no other reason than its particular color, which *as such* merits appreciation. This in no way undermines the applicability of the rational "why" question (which asks for normative ground) to aesthetic appreciation, just as the fact that some actions are performed for no reason does not undermine the applicability of a similar "why" question to action. In both cases, the relevant responsiveness to reasons is *not* a matter of a positive answer to the rational question "why," but of the *applicability* of this question (cf. Anscombe 2000, p. 25). Moreover, even though I appreciate this shade of violet for no other reason than this very color, my appreciation is constituted by my sensitivity to this shade of color as meriting appreciation.

stood in isolation either from the self (e.g., KU: 204) or from the particular object that the self is taking in and is taken by (e.g., EEKU: 223, KU: 279). As Anton Ford nicely puts it, beauty is a part of a "bipolar relation between the object and the subject of judgment" (Ford 2010, p. 397).

Recall too that Kant argues that beauty is not an ordinary predicate (e.g., KU: 288): not a concept that you predicate without manifesting, expressing, and staking your*self*. In articulating my engagement with beauty, it is my pleasure "that accompanies the representation of the object and serves it instead of a predicate" (KU: 288). This is a reminder that judging beauty is *not* reporting facts about the world but an expression of the *self's* affective engagement with the world. *Feelings*, including aesthetic appreciation, are neither mirrors of the world nor of the self, but reflections of the self's (bi-polar) exchange with the world.

Notice that affective reflection, and so too aesthetic self-consciousness, is not to be confused with modes of accessing ourselves, as if from outside.[24] Our feelings are *not* evidence of who we are, as if we are in touch with ourselves through feeling third-personally, as we *may* be in touch with some other people (who do not tell us their mind), and with objects. Rather than evidence or access to the self, feelings essentially involve the self since they are immediate self-manifestations. They are immediate self-conscious engagements with the world.

Recall that this way of drawing on Kant is not meant as a close interpretation but as a way of showing what core commitment is open to a Kantian disinterest advocate. If she indeed continues Kant's spirit, she may well hold that, in disinterested experience, I take pleasure in a beautiful object *not* because it satisfies any of my *existing* desires, etc., but because, through this pleasure itself, I am both conscious of my pleasurable experience as merited by, and so fitting to the object, and committing myself to continue this pleasurable engagement with the object open-endedly, through this pleasure's own capacity for self-maintenance. As such, this reconstruction *is* evidence that the disinterest critic's characterization of disinterested experience as an inactive, dispassionate staring that involves nothing of the self other than its passive awareness is incompatible with the core commitment of Kantian disinterest unless you add to it further layers of commitment that do not belong to it as such. Nothing in the commitment as presented above prevents disinterested experience from involving and revealing the concrete subject engaged with beauty. It denies *only* that such self-consciousness and involvement are *due* to this experience's satisfaction of existing desires, etc. This is a central point of disagreement between the disinterest advocate and critic. As I will show in the next section, the two approaches also presuppose different models

---

24 Cf. Merritt 2021 and Moran 2001.

of self-consciousness: while the disinterest critic holds that clarifying, evaluative and potentially transformative consciousness of yourself as the concrete individual you are depends on the satisfaction of existing desires, needs or values, the advocate believes that such consciousness is not only independent of such satisfaction but in tension with it. And this disagreement is closely related to their disagreement regarding the self.

3 Self-Consciousness: What is Valuable vs. What is Already Valued

While the Kantian disinterest advocate understands aesthetic self-consciousness as unmediated by any evidence or satisfaction of existing desires, etc., the most natural understanding of the critic suggests that, on his view, aesthetic self-consciousness is possible *by virtue of the appreciator discovering* that she has a particular need or desire that the beautiful object satisfies and thus reflects: the subject "sees herself in the beautiful objects by seeing her ideals reflected there" (Riggle 2016, p. 13), namely, *in virtue of* beauty's satisfaction of some of the subject's desires, needs or interests. The critic further claims that the disinterest advocate cannot account for the self-consciousness that is so often part of aesthetic experience *because* she denies that this experience satisfies the self's existing desires, etc. This claim indicates what appears to be the critic's underlying assumption: self-consciousness cannot be had unless some of the self's existing desires, etc. are being satisfied.

But why assume that we cannot become conscious of ourselves and our values (in a clarifying, evaluative, and transformative way) unless some of what we already desire and value is being satisfied? This assumption is unsupported. While we *may* come to an awareness of ourselves this way (*by* recognizing the satisfaction of our existing desires, values or needs) *sometimes*, since this mode of awareness is grounded not in a reflection on *what is to be desired or valued* but merely in an observation of what is in fact already valued and desired, it is in tension with the kind of evaluative, transformative self-consciousness that the disinterest critic finds in the experience of beauty. Since evaluative, transformative self-consciousness requires critical reflection and consideration of the world, it could only be had through an experience or act that involves assessment of what is *of value*, independently of what we already value (or desire). Moreover, the critic's position appears to be based on a confused understanding of the self insofar as he argues that in disinterested experience, the self is "bringing nothing of herself to the table other than awareness" (Riggle 2016, p. 4) *because* this experience satisfies none of her existing desires, etc. This seems to assume that the self just is its actual psychology: it is reduced to a given set of desires and interests. But this is an error. The self determines its own psychology. To be a self is to form oneself, freely, actively, and individually, in responsiveness to what each self takes to be worthy of belief, desire, feeling, appreciation, and valuing more generally. The disinterest critic may, upon reflection, recognize this error and accept the alternative conception of the self as genuine, but, as it stands, he is saddled with a dilemma: either revise your view such that it would not be committed to this erroneous picture of the self, or show that it is not erroneous.

Note first that the satisfaction of existing desires is neither necessary for evaluative, transformative self-conscious experience, nor is it sufficient for it. Rather, such satisfaction is in tension with such self-consciousness: a genuine evaluative stance towards one's life in the search of clarity, critical reflection, and (possibly) transformation—in short, the kind of self-consciousness that Riggle advocates as part of the profundity of beauty—cannot be grounded merely in what one *already* believes, feels, desires, and values. The point is to be clearer on whether what one believes, feels, and values *should be believed, felt, and valued*; whether those attitudes should be maintained and endorsed, or rather disavowed. To be evaluatively clearer on one's commitments, values, and the way to live one's lives, one should (metaphorically speaking) look "away" from what one already believes, feels, desires, and values, and asks instead what *to* value (etc.).[25] But we cannot become clearly and evaluatively conscious of ourselves by actually satisfying what we already value and desire, as if this satisfaction gives us evidence that this is what we indeed value, evidence without which we cannot be "clear" on our lives and values. This is mistaken. We are conscious of our life and are capable of evaluating and transforming it when we consider the reasons for valuing this but not that. And this requires that we look, as it were, *away from ourselves* and towards the world. The disinterest critic's model of self-consciousness is shaped, to put it metaphorically, by the "wrong direction of gaze."

---

25 Self-consciousness that is grounded in consideration of the *world* is often described as "transparent," and attitudes and experiences that are constituted by this self-consciousness are labeled "transparent." Cf. Moran 2001, pp. 60–65. The term "transparency" comes from Roy Edgley, who nicely explains it: "My own present thinking, in contrast to the thinking of others, is transparent in the sense that I cannot distinguish the question 'Do I think that P' from a question in which there is no essential reference to myself or my belief, namely 'Is it the case that P?' [...] I cannot distinguish them, for in giving my answer to the question 'Do I think that P?' I also give my answer, more or less tentative, to the question 'Is the case that P?'" (Edgley 1969, p. 90). Gareth Evans uses the "outward looking" metaphor that I sometimes use in this paper, for example, in arguing that "[i]n making a self-ascription of belief, one's eyes are, so to speak, or occasionally literally, directed outward—toward the world" (Evans 1982, p. 225).

Of course, if the relevant self-consciousness is to be clarifying, evaluative, and potentially transformative, the self, including the self's existing beliefs, feelings, desires, and values could not drop out of the picture, a point to which I will return shortly. But it is not the values that need to fit themselves to what the self finds herself to already value. Rather, the self has to fit herself to *what is of value.*

This is exactly what the disinterest advocate proposes. In disinterested experience, we do not value beautiful objects *because* they satisfy our existing desires, etc. Rather, we value the beautiful object even though it does not satisfy what we already desire and value.[26] When engaging with beauty, we do not ask ourselves if it satisfies existing desires, etc., but rather *whether it is valuable.* We raise nothing other than the question that we should be asking if we are to gain evaluative clarity over our lives, and alter our attitudes and self. While the critic struggles to explain the connection between beauty and the evaluative self-consciousness that he correctly finds to be often kindled by beauty, the disinterest advocate can easily account for the connection between them: *beauty is a fertile ground for evaluative clarity and transformative self-consciousness because we find it to be valuable and worthy of valuing even though it does not necessarily satisfy what we already value.*[27]

In short, the "transparent" model of self-consciousness required for any genuine evaluative and transformative self-consciousness speaks in favor of the disinterest advocate's model of aesthetic self-consciousness, and against her critic's model. If Riggle is right that beauty is profound (partly) because it often grounds clarificatory, evaluative, and transformative self-consciousness, then it is much more likely that the experience of beauty is *disinterested:* an experience directed *away* from what the self already desires and values; an experience in which we ask ourselves and apprehend through feeling *what is to be valued* (aesthetically). This suggests the disinterest advocate's superior explanatory power: a clearer grasp of what is required for evaluative self-consciousness and of the character of disinterested experience shows that the advocate can better explain than the critic *why* beauty has such close connection to evaluative self-consciousness. She can better

---

26 This is partly why Kant claims that we "favor" beauty (e.g., KU: 210): we value it even though it need not satisfy anything we already value. And in doing so, it favors us. While beauty favors us in many different ways, one of these is beauty's way of grounding clarifying, evaluative self-consciousness.

27 Intuitively, this kind of "outward look" or openness seems to be required also by beauty itself: beauty calls on us to be attuned to it, and open to accept it on its own terms, not merely in terms that we bring to it from an external source. As Alexandra Grundler instructively suggests, the disinterest critic's inverse picture seems on the face of it strange, as if appreciators have "an aesthetic eye pre-directed inward" (Grundler MS, p. 11).

explain the profundity of beauty. The critic's criticism of the disinterest is not valid without further revisions.

This means that the satisfaction of desires, etc., is not a sufficient condition for evaluative self-consciousness. One cannot be evaluatively clearer on one's life without a consideration of *what is of value*. Nor is it necessary, I am now going to show. The disinterest critic's (at least seeming) assumption that we cannot become self-conscious independently of the satisfaction of our existing desires, etc., is unsupported in part by a common phenomenon: as a matter of fact, we do often come to self-consciousness in such a way. I turn now to introduce a few of many cases that prove this.

Consider, first, Imani Perry, a scholar of African American studies. In a recent interview, Perry recalls how upon reading Peter Wood's *Black Majority* (a history of the Black population in pre–Revolutionary War South Carolina) in college, she "was hooked. The book pulled [her] away from math and into African-American studies" (Perry, *NYRB Newsletter*, July 17, 2021). Whether or not it was an aesthetic experience does not matter for our purposes. What matters is that the book clearly had a transformative impact on Perry's life: it allowed her to understand what she wants, values, and believes, paved the way for her professional trajectory, and anchored the commitment that still underlies her work today:

> My work is based in a belief that the kinds of stories we learn and share are important for the world we co-create every day. And that belief requires a rigorous contemplation of what we have at our disposal, what is missing, and what we must imagine or re-imagine over and over again. The histories and stories of the oppressed are the closest we get to understanding the core of the human condition. (Perry, *NYRB Newsletter*, July 17, 2021)

Yet, there is no indication and no reason to believe that Perry had already had this belief before reading *Black Majority*; that she had already valued shared stories as crucial for everyday life and for the fight against oppression; or that she had already desired to pursue a career studying African American culture in the distinctive way she does. On the contrary, the way she relates this pivotal moment of her life suggests that this clarificatory and evaluative moment of self-consciousness and transformation was not grounded in what she had *already* valued, desired and believed but rather allowed her to *form* the belief that the kinds of stories we learn and share are crucial for the construction of our everyday world, to commit herself to exploring and sharing the stories of the oppressed, and to form a desire to pursue this commitment as part of her professional career *for the first time*. Reading the book allowed her to understand, for the first time, that these *are* true, valuable, and desirable and that these are a commitment and a desire suitable for her to pursue.

This is, of course, only one example, but since the satisfaction of existing desires, etc., is not a requirement on evaluative-transformative self-consciousness but is rather in tension with it, examples abound. Consider next Zadie Smith's momentous turn from disliking Joni Mitchell's music to loving it. Smith's marvelous reflection on her pas-de-deux with Mitchell's music is an insightful exploration of the way in which some of our deepest aesthetic loves (those powerful enough to change who we are) catch us "unprepared," surprised, and even reluctant, given that they *do not* satisfy any of our existing desires, etc., or fit neatly into our background and existing commitments.[28] "The first time I heard her, I haven't heard her at all. My parents did not prepare me," she opens the essay. The first time she heard "Joni" at a college party, she was so unprepared for her music that she heard her voice as a "piercing sound, a sort of wailing—a white woman wailing, picking out notes in a non-sequence. Out of tune, or *out of anything I understood at the time as a 'tune'*" (Smith 2018, p. 101; my italics). Not only did her music satisfy nothing that Smith had already desired or valued; it was so jarring to her that hearing it after college in the car with her would-be-husband, she found it so "annoying," she thought, "No, I can't hear it. It's horrible" (Smith 2018, pp. 102–103). But this thought and feeling occurred only seconds before the music suddenly dawned on her, and turned into an object of aesthetic admiration; she resented the music only seconds before she was so open and attuned to it— rather than to her existing preferences and interests—that she has fallen in love with it, and allowed it to change her; to change the person she had been before this moment of sudden and surprising attunement with it:

> As I remember it, sun flooded the area, my husband quoted a line from one of the Lucy poems; I began humming a strange piece of music. Something had happened to me. In all the mess of memories we make each day and lose, I knew that this one would not be lost. I had Wordsworth's sensation exactly: "that in this moment there is life and food/For future years." (Smith 2018, p. 103)

Smith's beautiful reflection on aesthetic appreciation probingly explores the very possibility of such a complete, yet surprising transformation—a transformation for which one's background and existing psychology does not prepare one:

---

[28] Titled "Some Notes on Attunement," it first appeared in the *New Yorker* in 2012 and was then collected in Smith's *Feel Free* (Penguin Random House, 2018). For a similar sentiment on strong, transformative aesthetic experiences that fit into nothing in the self's background, history, and set of existing preferences, see also Patricia Hampl's illustrative portrayal of being arrested by a Matisse on the first pages of *Blue Arabesque: A Search for the Sublime* (2007). After writing these pages, I learned that Rita Felski instructively draws on both of these writers' aesthetic experiences to explain the attachments she thinks are integral to aesthetic experience (see Felski, 2020).

> But when I think of that Joni Mitchell-hating pilgrim [...] I truly cannot understand the language of my former heart. Who *was* that person? Petulant, hardly aware that she was humming Joni, not yet conscious of the transformation she had already undergone. How is it possible to hate something so completely and then suddenly love it so unreasonably? How does such a change occur? (Smith 2018, p. 104)

This reflection is too subtle, powerful, and beautiful to be summed up. So, I will not do so, but I will present yet another one of Smith's passages, a passage that brings out, as the disinterest advocate does, the crucial role of openness to complete otherness in aesthetic appreciation. No matter how important the gradual cultivation of taste for the reception of particular beauties is, "we also have to be open to them" (Smith 2018, p. 107). Independently of what one already prizes, vulnerability and attunement to otherness are central for transformative acts of aesthetic appreciation:

> With Joni, it was all so easy. In a sense, it took no time. Instantaneous. Involving no progressive change but, instead, a leap of faith. A sudden, unexpected attunement. Or a returning from nothing, or from a negative, into something soaring and positive and sublime. (Smith 2018, p. 110)

> [L]oving Joni Mitchell does not require an acceptance of absurdity. I am speaking of the minor category of the aesthetic, not the monument of the religious. But if you want to effect a breach in that stolid edifice the human personality I think it helps to cultivate this Kierkegaardian sense of defenselessness. (Smith 2018, p. 112)

> Put simply: you need to lower your defenses. (I don't think it is a coincidence that my Joni epiphany came through the back door, while my critical mind lay undefended, focused on a quite other form of beauty). Shaped by the songs of my childhood, I find it hard to accept the musical "new," or even the "new to me". (Smith 2018, p. 113)

William Stoner, whose life is strewn with moments of self-revelation, exhibits the same truth. On the very first pages of the novel, Stoner stumbles upon a clarificatory, evaluative, and transformative moment of self-revelation that will radically change the course of his life, redirecting it from a farm life in Missouri to the life of a university professor. This happens in Archer Sloan's English course, the very first English course Stoner has ever taken, which "has troubled and disquieted him in a way nothing had ever done before" (Williams 2009, p. 10). Stoner "pondered the words that Archer Sloan spoke in class, as if beneath their flat, dry meaning he might discover a clue that would lead him where he was intended to go" (Williams 2009, p. 11). But this transformative moment of self-consciousness was *not* made possible by the satisfaction of Stoner's existing desire to pursue English studies, and his existing commitment to value the life of the mind. He had not had such a desire and such a commitment before his enrollment in the course.

Rather, his experiences in the course grounded this momentous transformation by allowing him to *form* this desire and this commitment to value, which he could not have had independently of something like this course.[29]

Consider Riggle's own examples too, which speak, I believe, against what seems like the assumption undergirding his criticism, rather than in favor of it. While he seems to assume that we cannot become conscious of ourselves in a clarifying, evaluative, and transformative way unless some of our existing desires are satisfied, Riggle also suggests that the literary portrayals of aesthetic experiences that he discusses support this assumption. If I understand him correctly, he thinks that at least two of the passages he discusses (retelling Bathilde Amédée's experience of the church steeple in Combray in Marcel Proust's "In Search of Lost Time", and William Stoner's experience of turning the basement in his newly owned home into a study in *Stoner*) show that experiences of beauty that facilitate evaluative and transformative self-consciousness are grounded in the satisfaction of these appreciators' *existing* needs, desires, or values. Should not this convince us that the satisfaction of one's existing desires, etc., is necessary for evaluative, transformative self-consciousness?

I believe not. Note first that, even if Riggle's interpretations of those characters' experiences is correct, this can demonstrate *neither* that such profound experiences *must* be grounded in the satisfaction of existing desires, etc. (that such satisfaction is a necessary condition for this self-consciousness), nor that it is this satisfaction that *accounts* for their evaluative and transformative self-consciousness. *If* it were a correct reading of these literary passages, it would, at best, have shown a significantly more minor claim, namely, that such evaluative and transformative self-consciousness *can* be grounded in experiences that satisfy the appreciators' existing desires, etc. Even if the interpretations were apt, it would still leave open the question of whether the relevant experience affords this self-consciousness *because* it satisfies the appreciator's existing psychology. However, it is, at most, a question whether Bathilde's and Stoner's experiences are indeed grounded in the satisfaction of their *existing* desires, needs, or values: in fact, I believe that the relevant passages make no such suggestion.

Stoner's experience of working on his study (whether an aesthetic experience or not) is indeed one of a number of pivotal, revelatory moments that Stoner ex-

---

[29] These examples prove not only that the satisfaction of existing desires, etc., is not a necessary condition of evaluative-transformative self-consciousness but also that the self-constitution, which I show in the next section to be the heart of who we are, is *not* the self-constitution of some "universal," "impersonal" self, as opposed to the "personal" self. Rather, these examples show that each of us *personally* is not who she is by the set of desires, etc., that she already has, but by constituting those through acts of being in touch with what is valuable, desirable, etc. More on this below.

periences in the novel: "it was himself that he attempted to define as he worked on his study" (Williams 2009, p. 100). But there is no indication that it is transformative *because* it satisfies Stoner's existing desires, etc. There is no indication that it satisfies any existing desires, etc. We are reading instead about an experience that *awakens him to desire* and *to value*. The content of Stoner's new evaluative desires and commitments are not fully specified (either for the reader or for Stoner). Perhaps working on his study inspires Stoner to cultivate himself, or to wish for a glowing period of aging, as "the wood paneling glowed with the richness of age" (Williams 2009, p. 100), or to wish for some (mental, emotional, and physical) space for him to think and to study. It was an experience of "defining" himself, of forming himself in light of these new evaluative wishes, which were "locked" hitherto—these were not desires that working on his study simply satisfied since they were not active until this moment, not ones he had endorsed and committed himself to, but rather desires and values that he *could* have committed himself to, had he been less blind to these values. It is exactly the experience of preparing his study that *allows him for the first time to recognize these as desires and commitments to have, endorse, and cultivate.*

Bathilde—the narrator's grandmother in Marcel Proust's *In Search of Lost Time*—is no different. I will be brief about her as Alexandra Grundler, in a fine paper on disinterest, has already convincingly argued that Proust's portrayal of Bathilde does *not* suggest that her love of the chapel's steeple is grounded in the satisfaction of her *existing* "desires, needs, and worldly project" (Riggle 2016, p. 8). Grundler has persuasively argued that Bathilde's appreciation is "disinterested in the relevant sense" (Grundler MS, p. 10), and that, for this reason, the disinterest critic's picture of her is unjust. For the critic seems to portray Bathilde *not* as being *open* to accept whatever is beautiful because it is beautiful but rather as if she were "scanning the rooftops, seeing many buildings that do not live up to her pre-set standard of aesthetic love, and finally, viewing the church of Saint-Hilaire with a sense of relief that she found just what she was looking for (Grundler MS, pp. 11–12). Is that faithful either to Bathilde's experiences or to those of any familiar aesthetic appreciator? Grundler convincingly argues that Bathilde should instead be read as having an open, searching eye. She is willing to seek open-endedly until she is surprised by finding an object that is lacking in the common "vulgarity, pretension and niggardliness" (Proust 1981, p. 69) that tire and disappoint her elsewhere. The narrator stresses that only when the steeple unexpectedly strikes her as lacking in those characteristics, she falls for it, "without quite knowing why" (Proust 1981, p. 69). Falling for it and being attuned to it in such a way, she is unconcerned with whether others would understand her appreciation or instead laugh at her. It is most faithful to the novel that we recognize that she is willing to stake herself for her love for the steeple because she takes her love to be called for and merited by *it*, the steeple itself, independently of whether she already values these characteristics. Grundler concludes her alternative reading of Bathilde's appreciative engagement, writing

> Far from looking to satisfy her "desires, needs, and worldly projects," Proust describes Bathilde as so present in her aesthetic contemplation of the church that "she would absorb herself so utterly in the outpouring of the spire that her gaze seemed to leap upwards with it…" To my ears, this sounds precisely like what the disinterest theorists are describing when they speak of "pure contemplation" (Grundler MS, p. 12).

I am left merely to echo Grundler's way of hearing the relevant passages from Proust.

Obviously, in all these cases, the recognition of these beautiful objects as beautiful and of these ways of living and aspects of life as valuable is not sufficient for the momentous transformation. To be transformative, the subject needs to acknowledge not only that these are to be valued, desired, and pursued but also that, among the many valuable forms of life and values one may pursue, these particularly beckon them or have a particular claim on them. If that is what the disinterest critic means when arguing that the profundity of aesthetic experience is tied to the particular person engaged with beauty, then the advocate could gladly agree with him. She agrees that, among all the beautiful objects and all the valuable ways of living, those particular beauties that each of us spends most time with, and those particular ways of life that each of us ends up pursuing have a particular allure for each one of us, even when we acknowledge that they are no less valuable than others. But this does *not* imply that those profound experiences of beauty that support evaluative and potentially transformative self-consciousness must be grounded in the satisfaction of one's existing (so-called "personal") desires, etc. And, as I argued in the last section, while the disinterest advocate is committed to aesthetic experience being independent of the satisfaction of existing desires, etc., she could embrace and even celebrate the thought that disinterested experience is one in which the concrete person engaged with beauty is actively implicated. Though independent of the satisfaction of existing desires, etc., and though not an exercise of the faculty of desire, disinterested experience can involve the subject, and reflect her fitness or unfitness for valuing what she hitherto has not valued.

How is that possible?

4 Not Found but Founded: The Self

In brief, the disinterest advocate can embrace the thought that the self is implicated in an experience that is independent of the satisfaction of the self's existing desires, etc., primarily because the concrete individual subject is *not* reduced to the set of her existing desires, etc. Rather, the self is actively and responsively self-constituting herself in light of what she regards as to-be-valued (or to-be-believed, felt, appreciated, etc.), however inchoately this regard may be at first. Let me introduce and explain this argument.

The disinterest critic would probably doubt that the advocate can truly allow the subject to be an active part of disinterested experience if she denies that this experience satisfies the subject's existing desires, etc. For he seems to assume that the concrete self cannot be implicated in any experience, unless the experience satisfies, and by so doing discloses, her existing desires, etc. But this is a gross mistake for a number of reasons, the chief of which is the misguided understanding of the human self that it assumes, a misguided understanding from which I suspect even the disinterest critic would like to distance himself.

Our own self, who each of us is, is not something that we simply find ourselves saddled with, something we are passive about: we are not the given set of beliefs, desires, commitments, emotions, and aesthetic loves that we actually already have. Rather, to have a self is to "own" it by constituting it.[30] We "own" our self by (metaphorically speaking) self-creation: no matter how much of our life and our character is shaped by factors that are external to us and are not under our first-person authority, to be a self is to form ourselves in responsiveness to what we find called for, appropriate, or in some sense suitable.[31] As I will explain in the rest of this section, if the self were not so constituted—by our free agency, that is, by our *taking* our states and attitudes to be apt, called for, or fitting rather than by *finding* ourselves with them—there would be no sense to subject our character, values, actions, and other attitudes, such as certain emotions, desires and acts of aesthetic appreciation, to rational criticism, praise, blame, and reactive attitudes.

This is why the disinterest critic's assumption that the concrete self that is engaged with beauty cannot be involved and reflected in this experience unless the

---

[30] This view is inspired by Stuart Hampshire, Charles Taylor, and Richard Moran.
[31] Cf. Charles Taylor on the requirement to reinterpret and redescribe our situation while assessing its significance in order to alter our evaluative commitments and our own self (1985, p. 101). As he argues, "what I have called strong evaluation," which is, for him, open-ended questioning and adjustment of our desires, commitments, emotions, etc., in light of reassessing the world, "is an essential feature of a person" (Taylor 1985, p. 45).

self's existing desires, etc,. are satisfied is ungrounded. The concrete self is not reduced to its actual psychology. Rather, she is who she is in and through determining her own psychology, and so she can be present in, and revealed through an experience that is independent of the satisfaction of her existing desires, etc., an experience by which *she determines herself to value what she had not necessarily valued before or through the reaffirmation of a former evaluative commitment.*

On the view I propose (but only sketchily and briefly defend),[32] the (mental) life of the self is not a passive fact the subject can only observe, or access on the basis of some evidence, or perhaps by introspection. Nor am I related to those of my reasons-responsive attitudes and characteristics, like many of my desires, emotions, commitments to values, beliefs, and acts of aesthetic appreciation, *fundamentally* by noticing their satisfaction or, more generally, in the same way I know facts about the world. Rather, those states, attitudes, and characteristics are constituted by our own acts of taking them to be appropriate, warranted, or otherwise called for, and are known by us as such. In Hampshire's words, my consciousness that, say, "the object is dangerous, or of its saddening features, *constitutes* my fear of it, or my sadness about it" (Hampshire 1965, p. 95)—that is, this consciousness constitutes my emotions.

This is true of the self as a whole: just as "from my point of view, [my desires, emotions and attitudes] are not facts to be learnt" (Hampshire 1965, p. 105), so my whole individual self is not a mere fact about me to be found and observed on the basis of some other facts about me (e.g., particular desires and needs). The self is essentially self-created through acts that embody questions about what to believe, to do, to feel, to desire, to value, to appreciate, and to be. To put it in a slogan (inspired by Stanley Cavell),[33] *the self is not something that I find but that which I found.* I am not an object to myself but irreducibly an *I*.

This view of the self is well-supported. If it were false, it would be very hard to account for the responsibility we have over these attitudes and for the fact that they are always open to a question about their normative grounds, to criticism if they are found to be ungrounded, and to reactive attitudes. To the extent that these attitudes are subject to a "why" question concerning their normative grounds, to rational criticism, praise, blame, and reactive attitudes, they are *constituted* by our taking them to be either appropriate or inappropriate. To form a belief or a desire, to feel an emotion, to appreciate beauty, and to be committed to a value—when those are believed, desired, felt, valued, or appreciated *for a reason*, as they typically are—is to *take* these to be appropriate or called for or fitting

---

[32] I can here only hint at the view but have argued and developed it in Gorodeisky 2022.
[33] Cavell 1989.

(again, however implicit and inchoate this "take" initially is). Otherwise, they could not have been subject to (1) the normative-explanatory "why" question that asks not only about their causal factors, but also about their *normative grounds* (e. g., "why do you like *Stoner*?" Why are you rooting for the *Tigers*?), (2) rational criticism ("do you really believe the COVID-19 vaccines change one's DNA?" "You shouldn't grieve England's loss in the European Championship!" "Why do you dislike *BoJack Horsman*? It is good!"), and (3) reactive attitudes. But these attitudes (etc.) *are* subject to such a question, criticism, praise, blame, and reactive attitudes. Beliefs, acts of appreciation, our commitments to values, and many of our emotions and desires can so much as be subject to these to the extent that they are formed by our taking them to be apt in some sense.

The disinterest critic challenge suggests that he is either blind to or overlooks this self-constitution and so the genuine character of the human self. His argument that disinterest advocates fail to account for the way the concrete self is implicated in the experience of beauty *because* they deny that this experience satisfies existing desires, etc., entails that he takes the concrete self to be a matter of her actual psychology. Relatedly, it assumes that to be aware of herself, the self needs to have a glimpse of her actual, existing states and attitudes.

But, as we saw, I am not what I happen to find myself to have but what I found as myself.[34] And partly for this reason, the fundamental mode of self-knowledge cannot be a mode of observing what states and attitudes the self already has.[35] Given that the self is self-constituting, to know oneself is to maintain or discontinue this self-constitution by endorsing or disavowing our states or attitudes as either proper or not.

To review: criticism of disinterest seems to be based on a misunderstanding of the self, and the critic's own alternative is self-defeating since he aims to explain but fails to capture the kind of clarifying, evaluative and transformative self-consciousness that experiences of beauty often ground. The disinterest critic faces a dilemma: either he needs to revise his challenge of disinterest theories such

---

[34] The disinterest critic might retort that this self-constitution is true only of what he would call the "universal" or "impersonal" self, rather than the "personal" self. But this distinction is misguided. As I mentioned in fn. 28 above, the "personal" self, the "who" that each of us is, is equally self-constituting rather than a matter of her existing psychology. Who each of us is not a matter of what each of us happens to find herself with but what she takes to be apt, what she endorses as hers, however inchoately. This was particularly evident in the examples of Imani Perri, Zadie Smith, Stoner, and Bathilde above: they show that we cannot even pursue what Riggle calls "personal ideals" merely on the basis of existing desires, etc., but only on the basis of taking some ideals to be ideals—to be valuable and desirable while beckoning us.

[35] For other reasons why we must think of self-knowledge this way, see Moran 2001.

that it would not be committed to an erroneous picture of the self, or he proves that this picture is not erroneous. But the last disjunct is very implausible. We are still waiting, then, for a revised version of the criticism. Until then, the disinterest advocate's view suggests itself superior to the critic's view both in its fitness to the experience of beauty, and in its power to explain why this experience is often profound in the way the critic claims it is.

5 Conclusion

A curious implication of the arguments of this paper is that the best way to understand what is meant by a disinterested engagement with beauty, and a central way of understanding how it accounts for the profundity of many of our engagements with beauty is to focus on the role of the self and self-consciousness in this kind of experience. Riggle's pressing exploration of the experience of beauty productively helps to bring this out, and also to bring out the core disagreement between the disinterest advocate and its critic: at bottom, the main dispute between them is less about the experience of beauty and more about the self and self-consciousness.

Given that, my arguments have focused on the form of the self and on aesthetic self-consciousness. Yet, I hope that they help substantiate the view that the central commitment to distinguish disinterested experience from the satisfaction of existing desires, interests or values not only leaves room for but in fact celebrates the ample role of the concrete self and of self-consciousness in aesthetic experience and that, by virtue of this and its faithfulness to the phenomenon, disinterest is a fine characterization of aesthetic experience, worthy of endorsement by all aestheticians.

Jeffers' *The Day the Crayons Quit* has a sequel: *The Day the Crayons Came Back Home.* I hope that *The Day the Philosophical Concepts Quit* would also have a sequel: *The Day the Philosophical Concepts Came Back Home.* Perhaps "disinterest" will never be fully rested, remaining always a little bit over-exhausted. Yet, she might feel less mistreated or misunderstood and find reasons to return home.

Abbreviations

Apart from the *Critique of Pure Reason*, all references to Kant's works are to Kant's *Gesammelte Schriften, Ausgabe der Preußischen Akademie der Wissenschaften* (Berlin: De Gruyter, 1902 ff.). References to the *Critique of Pure Reason* are to the standard A and B pagination of the first and second editions. Translations are from *The Cambridge Edition of the Works of Immanuel Kant*; translations are altered when considered necessary.

The following abbreviations of individual works are used:

EEKU Erste Einleitung in die Kritik der Urteilskraft / First Introduction to the Critique of the Power of Judgment
GMS   Grundlegung zur Metaphysik der Sitten / Groundwork of the Metaphysics of Morals
KU   Kritik der Urteilskraft / Critique of the Power of Judgment
KrV   Kritik der reinen Vernunft / Critique of Pure Reason
MS   Die Metaphysik der Sitten / Metaphysics of Morals

Literature

Anscombe, Gertrude E. M. (2000): *Intention*. Cambridge: Harvard University Press.
Beardsley, Monroe (1982): *The Aesthetic Point of View*. Ithaca: Cornell University Press.
Brewer, Talbot (2009): *The Retrieval of Ethics*. Oxford: Oxford University Press.
Cavell, Stanley (1989): "Finding as Founding." In: Cavell, Stanley: *This New Yet Unapproachable America*. Albuquerque: Living Batch, pp. 77–118.
Cavedon-Taylor, Dan (forthcoming): "Life Through a Lens" In: Sophie Archer (Ed.): *Salience: A Philosophical Inquiry*. London: Routledge.
Daywalt, Drew and Jeffers, Oliver (2013a): *The Day the Crayons Quit*. New York City: HarperCollins Children's Books.
Daywalt, Drew and Jeffers, Oliver (2013b): *The Day the Crayons Came Home*. New York City: HarperCollins Children's Books.
Dickie, George (1964): "The Myth of the Aesthetic Attitude." In: *American Philosophical Quarterly* 1. No. 1, pp. 56–65.
Dickie, George (1974): *Art and the Aesthetics: An Institutional Analysis*. Ithaca, NY: Cornell University Press.
Dickie, George (1988): *Evaluating Art*. Philadelphia: Temple University Press.
Dickie, George (1997): *Introduction to Aesthetics: An Analytic Approach*. Oxford: Oxford University Press.
Dunn, Nicholas (MS): "Kant on Judgment and Feeling."
Eaton, Anne (2021): "Feminist Aesthetics." In: Hall, Kim Q. and Ásta (Eds.): *Oxford Handbook of Feminist Philosophy*. Oxford: Oxford University Press, pp. 295–311.
Edgley, Roy (1969): *Reason in Theory and Practice*. London: Hutchinson.
Evans, Gareth (1982): *The Varieties of Reference*. Oxford: Oxford University Press.
Felski, Rita (2020): *Hooked: Art and Attachment*. Chicago: Chicago University Press.
Ford, Anton (2010): "Reply to Irwin." In: *Classical Philology* 105. No. 4, pp. 396–402.

Gorodeisky, Keren (2018): "Aesthetic Pleasure as an Exercise of Rational Agency: A Kantian Account." In: Shapiro, Lisa (Ed.): *Pleasure: A History.* Oxford: Oxford University Press, pp. 167–194.
Gorodeisky, Keren (2021a): "Reflection." In: Wuerth, Julia (Ed.): *The Cambridge Kant Lexicon.* Cambridge: Cambridge University Press, pp. 374–377.
Gorodeisky, Keren (2021b): "Must Reasons be Either Theoretical or Practical? On Aesthetic Criticism and Appreciative Reasons." In: *Australasian Journal of Philosophy* 100. No. 2, pp. 313–329.
Gorodeisky, Keren (2022): "Aesthetic Agency." In: Ferraro, Luca (Ed.): *The Routledge Handbook of the Philosophy of Agency.* London: Routledge, pp. 456–466.
Gorodeisky, Keren and Marcus, Eric (2022): "Aesthetic Knowledge." In: *Philosophical Studies* 179. No. 8, pp. 2507–2535.
Grundler, Alexandra (MS): "The Virtue of Disinterest in Aesthetic Life."
Hampl, Patricia (2007): *Blue Arabesque: A Search for the Sublime.* New York: Mariner.
Hampshire, Stuart (1965): *Freedom of the Individual.* Princeton: Princeton University Press.
Korsmeyer, Carolyn (1993): "Introduction: Philosophy, Aesthetics, and Feminist Scholarship." In: Korsmeyer, Carolyn and Hein, Hilde (Eds.): *Aesthetics in Feminist Perspective.* Bloomington and Indianapolis: Indiana University Press, pp. vii–xv.
Korsmeyer, Carolyn (2004): *Gender and Aesthetics: An Introduction.* New York and London: Routledge.
Merritt, Melissa (2021): "Feeling and Orientation in Action: A Reply to Alix Cohen." In: *Kantian Review* 26. No. 3, pp. 363–369.
Moran, Richard (2001): *Authority and Estrangement: An Essay on Self-Knowledge.* Princeton: Princeton University Press.
Perry, Imani (2021): *NYRB Newsletter.* July 17, 2021.
Proust, Marcel (1981): *In Search of Lost Time: In Swann's Way (Volume I).* Scott Moncrieff and Terence Kilmartin (Trans.). New York: Random House.
Riggle, Nick (2016): "On the Interest in Beauty and Disinterest." In: *Philosophers' Imprint* 16, pp. 1–14.
Rind, Miles (2002): "The Concept of Disinterestedness in Eighteenth-Century British Aesthetics." In: *Journal of the History of Philosophy* 40. No. 1, pp. 67–87.
Shelley, James (2017): "The Concept of the Aesthetic." In: Zalta, Edward N. (Ed.): *Stanford Encyclopedia of Philosophy.*
Smith, Zadie (2018): "Some Notes on Attunement." In: Smith, Zadie: *Feel Free.* London: Penguin Books, pp. 100–116.
Stolnitz, Jerome (1960): *Aesthetics and Philosophy of Art Criticism.* Boston: Houghton Mifflin.
Taylor, Charles (1985): *Philosophical Papers: Volume I, Human Agency and Language.* Cambridge: Cambridge University Press.
Walton, Kendall (1970): "Categories of Art." In: *Philosophical Review* 79. No. 3, pp. 334–367.
Williams, John (2009): *Stoner.* New York: New York Review of Books.

Thomas Hilgers
Aesthetic Disinterestedness Revisited

Abstract: In this article, I revisit the account of disinterestedness that I introduced and defended in my book *Aesthetic Disinterestedness: Art, Experience, and the Self.* After briefly spelling out some key features of this account, I address several objections to it that recently have been raised by commentators on my book. These objections force me to spell out further (a) the relationship between the world that an artwork presents and the world that its recipients occupy, (b) the specific nature of an artwork's meta-perspective, and (c) the moral dimension of disinterestedness.

There is a long list of objections raised against the claim that aesthetic experiences are essentially disinterested. On theoretical grounds, such objections have been raised by philosophers, cultural theorists, sociologists, literary scholars, and others. On practical grounds, they have been raised by certain works of art. That is, some artworks seem to have challenged the given claim by means of asking their recipients to respond to what they present in an interested manner. Of course, the success of all such objections ultimately depends on how exactly we spell out the claim that aesthetic experiences are essentially disinterested. More precisely, their success depends on how exactly we understand the notion of disinterestedness. In my book *Aesthetic Disinterestedness: Art, Experience, and the Self*, I introduced and defended a novel account, which was meant specifically to meet the most serious objections against the claim that our aesthetic engagements with artworks are disinterested (Hilgers 2017). During the last few years, other philosophers have discussed my account in an insightful manner and have formulated several interesting objections against it. In this article, I will address some of these in order to revisit and clarify my original account. I will proceed in four steps. First, I will briefly spell out some key features of the account I defended. Second, I will address an objection raised by Samantha Matherne, which forces me to say more about the relationship between the world that a work of art presents and the world that the work's recipients occupy. In light of objections raised by Richard Eldridge and Lisa Schmalzried, I will then discuss the specific nature of an artwork's meta-perspective, and finally, I will take up Carol Gould's challenge regarding the possibly problematic moral dimension of disinterestedness.[1]

---

[1] In my book, I focused on the aesthetic experience of art. My explanation for why such an expe-

1 Disinterestedness

The account that I introduced and defended is deeply influenced by the aesthetic theory that Kant spelled out in his *Critique of the Power of Judgment*. Following Kant, I assume that

> an artwork *asks* a person to engage with it in such a way that her sensuous, affective, and conceptual capacities enter a play-like state of interaction. This state affects a person in three related ways: it makes her temporarily lose the sense of herself, it makes her gain a sense of the other, and ultimately, it makes her achieve selfhood. The aesthetic engagement with an artwork does the first, because it includes the adoption of a disinterested attitude. That is, while aesthetically relating to what it shows, we disengage ourselves from our practical and interested involvements with the world, and forget about our own past and future, about our own needs and ends. When adopting such an attitude, though, we not only lose our sense of self, but also become fully involved with the presence of what a work shows. In other words, we become immersed in its presentation, absorbed in its appearance, and we adopt perspectives on it different from our own. (Hilgers 2017, p. 3)[2]

Adopting a disinterested attitude, then, first of all means disengaging from one's own specific perspective and relating to things in a non-practical manner. The aim of my book was to spell out what exactly this means, to show why such a disengagement must make one temporarily lose the sense of one's own specific self, to counter important objections against this claim, to explain how works of art establish conditions of reception that make one adopt a disinterested attitude towards what they show, and to explain why even our engagements with works from contemporary performance and installation art remain disinterested (at least, in a certain way).

---

rience typically must be disinterested relies on a particular understanding of art. Lisa Schmalzried was right to point out that this explanation cannot be applied (at least, not en bloc) to the experience of natural beauty (Schmalzried 2020, p. 172). Indeed, there are important differences between our aesthetic engagements with artworks and our aesthetic engagements with natural beauty, but there are also similarities. In particular, I take it that both are disinterested, insofar as they are non-practical and make one temporarily lose the sense of one's own specific self. In contrast to an artwork, though, natural beauty does not show a world, and does not ask its spectators to engage with it from particular perspectives. Therefore, a different story has to be told regarding our aesthetic experiences of natural beauty. I will not tell this story here, but I acknowledge the necessity to develop it. I further acknowledge that Schmalzried was right to doubt that my analysis clarifies the experience of human beauty. I do believe, though, that it clarifies the aesthetic experience of architecture (Hilgers 2017, pp. 137–141).

[2] For my interpretation and discussion of Kant's account of disinterestedness, see Hilgers 2017, pp. 15–39.

Obviously, the notion of an attitude or a perspective is of great importance for my account. How exactly, then, do I conceive of an attitude or a perspective? Following philosophers such as Elisabeth Camp, I take it that a person structures her propositional relations to things, other people, and herself according to certain categories, principles, interests, and goals. In order for her to count as a rational agent, and in order for her to share a common world with all other such agents, some of these categories, principles, interests, and goals must be universal. Others depend on a person's specific historical, cultural, and social context, and then, of course, there are idiosyncratic interests and goals related to a person's particular biography. Collectively, all of these constitute a person's fundamental perspective, by means of which she continuously organizes her propositional states, and thereby relates to everything in a particular way. Moreover, a person often adopts specific perspectives for a limited amount of time, depending on a given situation. Following a pragmatist outlook, I claim that a person's fundamental as well as specific perspectives are usually connected to her various practices. I further claim that we can still relate to something while disengaging from our practical relations as well as from the idiosyncratic and context-relative aspects of our perspectives. Succeeding in this disengagement is what I call "adopting a disinterested attitude." Artworks typically ask us to adopt such an attitude towards what they show. In the following, I further spell out my understanding of art by discussing an objection raised by Samantha Matherne.[3]

2 Worlds

In her review of my book, Samantha Matherne states that there is a problem with my claim that artworks are presentational works that show worlds different from the ones we live in:

> To begin, I worry that his claim that works of art establish an "aesthetic sphere" threatens to misconstrue the relationship art can have to our world. Hilgers suggests that the "world" of a work of art is typically a "fictional" one that is separate from the world in which we live (the exceptions he notes are experimental theater and performance art) (119). However, it seems to me many works of art serve as "mirrors" for our world and are thus continuous with it. [...] his aesthetic conception of art appears to occlude one of the most powerful aspects of art, viz., its ability to show us the world that we live in, but are so often blind to. (Matherne 2020, pp. 54–55)

---

[3] For a more detailed discussion of my understanding of a perspective, see Hilgers 2017, pp. 12–15.

This objection calls for two clarifications: 1) what exactly am I saying when I claim that the world an artwork shows is different from the one its recipient lives in, or rather occupies? 2) In what sense can a recipient's adoption of a disinterested attitude still include a relation to the world she occupies? Beginning with my first clarification, let me explain how I conceive of a presentational work in general, before focusing on the particular kind of presentational work that I take an artwork to be. When talking about presentational works, I am primarily thinking of artifacts such as paintings, sculptures, photographs, films, novels, theater performances, and so on. The main characteristic of a presentational work is that it shows something *as* something. More precisely, it shows something *as* perceived from a particular perspective. Even when showing a historically factual event, a presentational work will always show it according to its specific point of view; it will always show it *as* this or that, instead of just replicating it. In general, there are many perspectives that a work asks its recipients to adopt while engaging with it, but there is only one "meta-perspective" that ties everything together (Hilgers 2017, p. 26). If a recipient cannot construct this perspective, whose categories, principles, interests, and goals are meant to structure her overall experience of what the work shows, then she cannot relate to the given work *as* to the work that it is, for a work's identity is tied to its meta-perspective. When speaking of an artwork's world, I am referring to everything the work shows *as* perceived from the perspectives it unfolds—specifically, of course, as perceived from its meta-perspective. I do not deny that there often might be referential connections between such a world and the world that we, as the recipients of the work, inhabit. I am even willing to accept Matherne's metaphor of the work as a mirror, as long as we keep in mind that such a mirror is colored, or rather perspectival. Consequently, a work never simply shows reality but rather shows it *as* seen from some perspective (Hilgers 2017, pp. 24–27).

However, when stressing the difference between an artwork's world (or rather its aesthetic sphere) and the recipient's world, I certainly had more in mind. Indeed, there typically exists a metaphysical wall between what a work shows and the world that we, as its recipients, live in. Following some key insights from Ernst Tugendhat's reading of Heidegger's existential analytic of *Dasein* and from Stanley Cavell's philosophy of film, I began spelling out this claim by means of discussing the ontology of film and the nature of cinematic experiences, and by then applying the results of this discussion to other art forms. In a nutshell, the argument goes as follows: the world that we inhabit is a world of practical engagement and mutual acknowledgment. That is, I can—and typically do—engage with the things and people that I perceive around me in a practical manner, constantly asking myself practical questions, such as "what could I do with this" or "what could this do to me." Moreover, I am visible to other people, just as they are visible to me.

They can, in principle, at least, acknowledge my presence, as I can acknowledge theirs. Sitting in a movie theater—to take the scenario from which I originally built up my argument—the situation is different. I cannot practically engage with what I perceive on screen, and my own presence cannot be acknowledged by it. According to the account of practical self-consciousness that I rely on, this implies that I must lose the sense of my own specific self while watching a film. It also implies that I, strictly speaking, relate to something that is not situated within the world that I actually live in, for this world, as said before, is a world of practical engagement and mutual acknowledgment. This does not imply, though, that my having such a disinterested experience may not lead to a change in my relations to things and people situated in the world I inhabit. It only implies that I cannot practically relate to whatever I see happening on screen (Hilgers 2017, pp. 121–133).

All of this holds true not only with respect to fictional films, such as *Le Mépris*, *Jules et Jim*, or *Le samouraï*, but also with regard to documentaries, for they also show us something *as* seen from a particular perspective that we can neither engage with in a practical manner nor can feel acknowledged by (at least, not while actually perceiving it on screen). According to my understanding of what it means to live in a world and of what it means to have a sense of one's own specific self, this implies that, for the most part, we are not relating to things and people situated within the world we occupy and are not having a sense of our own specific self when watching a documentary. This is not to say that a documentary may not teach us something about the world we live in (Hilgers 2017, p. 162). Moreover, it is important to keep in mind that I conceive of a person's aesthetic engagement with an artwork as a dynamic process constituted by three moments: losing the sense of oneself, gaining a sense of the other, and achieving selfhood. In this manner, there is a self-reflective and self-determining moment included in our engagements with artworks, and this moment may kick in already before the actual reception of a work has ended (Hilgers 2017, p. 126).

So far, I have attempted to clarify my understanding of an artwork in order to show that it not only is compatible with, but rather affirms Matherne's claim that the recipient of a work of art often can learn something about her own world or life from her experience of that work. However, I suspect that there ultimately is a conflict between our positions, for it seems that Matherne assumes there to exist artworks that ask their recipients to adopt very particular "personal, practical, or political" perspectives towards the world they actually live in (Matherne 2017, p. 54). More precisely, and in light of her examples, it seems to me that she assumes there to exist artworks with messages, and this is something I deny. That is, I deny that artworks tell us exactly how to live or how to behave. As Matherne herself points out, I defend a normative conception of art. In my view, not all presentational works qualify as artworks. Every film, for instance, is a presentational work, and thereby asks its recipients to adopt a disinterested attitude, but not every film, just as not every painting or novel, qualifies as an artwork. Rather, many films are works of entertainment, communication, or propaganda. It may sound strange to argue that a work of propaganda asks its recipients to adopt a disinterested attitude towards what it shows. Does such a work not call for the exact opposite? Is it not its goal to make us adopt particular interests and objectives, and to act accordingly? It certainly is, but a work of propaganda attempts to achieve this goal by first disengaging us from our own perspectives, and it is this maneuver that I call "making us adopt a disinterested attitude." Some may argue that instead of relying on the controversial difference between interested and disinterested attitudes, it may be more productive to distinguish between different kinds of interested perspectives—namely, between those tied to particular actual people and those tied to particular presentational works. This is a plausible objection, but I still consider it to be fruitful to single out the moment of disengagement from one's own fundamental perspective and call it "the adoption of a disinterested attitude." Specifically, if we pay attention to the non-practical nature of this attitude, such a move allows us to point out a shared and important moment of our engagements with all presentational works.[4]

In order for a presentational work in general to qualify as an artwork, its perspective must be truly unique and illuminating. However, I further take it that we can never fully construct an artwork's meta-perspective, for there always remains something to be discovered here. What an artwork presents, and how it does so, prevents us from arriving at a smooth and final synthesis of all its elements. It asks us to remain active, stimulating our freedom and making us look for further relations. Obviously, my understanding of the kind of aesthetic response an artwork asks for is deeply influenced by Kant's notion of a free and harmonious play between our cognitive capacities (Hilgers 2017, p. 22). However, it is also influenced by Adorno's aesthetic theory, specifically by his insistence that a work of art has a dissonant form or structure, and consequently a "broken unity of meaning"

---

4 Lisa Schmalzried correctly states that everything I have to say about the conditions of reception obtaining in the case of film can be applied to the experience of any film, no matter whether it qualifies as an artwork or not. She further writes that I should have said more about the specific form and/or content of artworks in order to distinguish them successfully from other kinds of presentational works (Schmalzried 2020, p. 173). I would not know how to make this distinction by specifying some particular content. However, I am convinced that one can succeed in making it by pointing out some necessary characteristics of an artwork's form, and I actually attempted to achieve this in my book—specifically, in Paragraph 5 of section I.1. In the following, I repeat a few key points from my discussion there.

(Adorno 2009, p. 297). Therefore, I conclude that an artwork's meta-perspective must remain a projection and can never be related to a world-view or a message:

> Due to an artwork's wealth, multiperspectivity, and dialecticity, the engagement with it must remain an open-ended process of re-articulating and creative synthesizings. Rather than culminating in final conceptualizations or the construction of world-views, it instead culminates in a self-reflective process in which our own specific perspectives become a topic of concern for us. [...] they [artworks] leave us ample space for relating freely to what they present; they allow our capacities to *play* with what they show, and motivate a kind of awakening process of thinking and self-reflecting. (Hilgers 2017, pp. 3–4)

In fact, Matherne hits the nail on the head when she writes: "Insofar as Hilgers defends a 'normative' conception of art, he may, in fact, embrace the possibility that his view will disqualify many politically-inflected or representational works as works of art" (Matherne 2020, p. 55). Indeed, I whole-heartedly embrace this possibility, which again reveals the Kantian-Adornian heritage that my account of art relies on and that nowadays is too often (and hastily) disregarded as elitist, antiquated, or ideological. This is not at all to say that I am opposed to works of entertainment or communication as objects of reception or of research, but it is to say that I am opposed to dropping the distinction between entertainment, communication, propaganda, and art. Concerning the topic of disinterestedness, it is further crucial to stress that it is not only artworks that ask for the adoption of a disinterested attitude towards what they show. Rather, all presentational works typically do so—at least, to some degree. Works of art, however, do more: they make their recipients temporarily lose their sense of self, they make them gain a sense of the other, and ultimately, they allow them to achieve selfhood.

3 Perspectives

I claim that the adoption of a disinterested attitude and the temporary loss of one's sense of self are necessary in order to gain a sense of the other. When it comes to our engagements with artworks, gaining a sense of the other must include more than just seeing things from another person's perspective, for without some further qualification, such a seeing would be too trivial a matter. As said before, an artwork's perspective must be unique and illuminating. I take it to be a widely shared belief that we can learn something from works of art, i.e., that they can make us see something important, which we might have missed otherwise. Obviously, Matherne shares this belief, and so do I. How exactly, though, can one distinguish between an illuminating and a deceptive perspective? Which perspective is trustworthy, and which is not? Richard Eldridge has challenged me on this difficult issue:

> The implication here is that we often enough suffer from cliché and inattentiveness, and that art's heightening of attention—its animation of our sensibilities—can address this condition effectively. Here, oddly, in his wish to avoid formalism, Hilgers does not say as much as he might about how and why we might come to trust a work's perspective. [...] It would have been good to hear more about exactly how this enlightenment, strengthening, and purification take place via the experience of a trustworthy work, beyond the fact of simply entering into its new perspective—good to hear more about what makes its perspective worth our trust. (Eldridge 2017)

In response to Eldridge, I do not have a theory of trustworthy or illuminating perspectives to offer. In my view, this whole problem is related to the age-old question of artistic truth, i.e., to the question of whether works of art can provide us with a special kind of insight. This question has been discussed, at least, since the time of Aristotle's *Poetics*, even though Aristotle himself did not write about works of fine art in general, but rather about poetry and specifically tragedy. In fact, though, I doubt that one could come up with a definition that all trustworthy and/or illuminating perspectives fall under, apart from an empty definition such as: "An illuminating perspective is neither deceptive nor stereotype, but rather allows one to discover some noteworthy feature of reality, which one typically does not recognize." This is a truism. The real task is to reveal concretely a given perspective's epistemic power. If I, for instance, claim that a novel, such as Kafka's *The Trial*—to take an example from my book—or a film, such as Malick's *The Thin Red Line*, opens up illuminating perspectives, and others disagree with me, then I must make them discover the supposedly noteworthy features for themselves by means of making them adopt the relevant perspectives (towards the work's diegetic world as well as towards our own world). This is not to say that an illuminating perspective must make one discover some hitherto unnoticed object or fact. It may do so, but it may also make one discover some relation or structure that allows one to make more sense of the world one occupies and of the life one lives—or rather, to understand both better.

What is the condition, though, that a perspective must satisfy in order to make more sense of a world or a life? I guess there is no condition to satisfy here apart from the condition of actually making more sense. However, making sense of something is no solipsistic activity. That is, a person can hardly make sense of something, and thereby understand it, without others being able to share this understanding. How could I have succeeded in making sense of something if nobody else could recognize my success? More precisely: how could I reasonably distinguish between understanding and misunderstanding something independently of some inter-subjective criterion, and what else could this criterion consist of but the agreement of others with my understanding?[5] I am suggesting that a given perspective only allows one to understand better one's world or life if it allows others to do the same. Apart from our agreement that an artwork's particular perspectives are illuminating, there is no guarantee that they actually are. Moreover, every participant in the relevant discourse can challenge our agreement anew and reopen the argument. What Kant, then, holds to be true regarding the question of whether an object is beautiful or not, also holds true regarding the question of whether an artwork's perspectives are illuminating or not. I cannot convince someone of *The Thin Red Line*'s epistemic value by restating the film's argument, for the film makes no argument—at least, not the kind that could be reproduced independently of adopting the film's perspectives. In order to judge the film, then, one must try out its perspectives, and one can only fully do so by means of watching the film *as* it asks to be watched. At times, we do not get an artwork's perspectives right. At times, we miss some of its suggestions. It is not the philosopher who is particularly gifted and educated to get things right here. Rather, this is the domain of the critic. Of course, nothing speaks against a philosopher also being a critic, but I take there to have been few who succeeded in both tasks. In any case, being capable of describing an artwork in such a way that others come to feel its epistemic power is a different task than describing an artwork's perspectival form in general.

One might object that there is a certain tension between my claim that a work of art unfolds illuminating perspectives, which allow one to understand one's world and life, and my claim that an artwork's meta-perspective must remain a projection. Moreover, Lisa Schmalzried has wondered why I insist that a work of art never allows us to construct fully its meta-perspective, and why I insist that only artworks, and not works of entertainment or communication as well, allow us to achieve selfhood (Schmalzried 2020, p. 173). Again, the reason for my insistence here relates to my adherence to Kant's understanding of the aesthetic experience as a free play. By denying us a finished product, or rather a precise and final synthesis of all its elements, and by confronting us with questions and puzzles, a work of art forces us to remain active, i.e., to continue perceiving, thinking, and reflecting. In other words, it profoundly and continuously motivates the free performance of our capacities. According to Kant, this is one of the main reasons why the aesthetic experience of beauty gives us pleasure, and this pleasure is different in kind from the one we feel when effortlessly consuming some work of entertain-

---

[5] I take this to be a version of Wittgenstein's famous argument against the existence of a private language.

ment. The pleasure we feel when aesthetically engaging with an artwork relates to the actuality of our freedom. Since I assume that achieving selfhood involves our freedom's actuality, I take it that artworks can contribute to this achievement in a way that works of entertainment, communication, and certainly propaganda cannot. This is not to say, though, that we can achieve selfhood only by aesthetically engaging with artworks. As is well known, Kant took the experience of natural beauty and of the sublime to play an important role in the realization of our freedom. Moreover, there may be other activities, such as philosophizing, and certain social interactions that also have a great role to play here.

But how can we resolve the mentioned tension? How can an artwork unfold illuminating perspectives, on the one hand, and possess a projective meta-perspective, on the other? How can it help us to understand our own world and life without offering a world-view? First, I take it that in contrast to a world-view, an artwork's illuminating perspectives do not render everything within a world intelligible, closing it off from any doubt or question. They may make us understand something better, but simultaneously must motivate us to ask further questions and to continue striving for a better understanding. In other words, they must motivate the free performance of our capacities, instead of putting such activity to an end. The understanding, then, that an artwork has to offer is always a starting and never a closing point. Moreover, there must remain an uncertainty regarding an artwork's perspectives. Since its meta-perspective is open and projective, we can never be sure that we correctly identified what we take to be illuminating about it or about its subordinated perspectives, which it ties together. As long as an artwork remains alive, there remains something about it to be discovered, and there remains the possibility that we have not yet understood what there is to understand. In contrast to a work of propaganda, an artwork never gives us a precise order for how to see things. It never condemns us to passivity, but rather emancipates us as perceiving, thinking, and reflecting beings. That is, it emancipates us as autonomous agents. This deeply Kantian and highly normative account of art is certainly exclusive, but is also worthwhile defending (Hilgers 2017, pp. 24–39 and 156–160).

4 Disinterestedness and Morality

Carol S. Gould criticized my account for neglecting "the moral problems that arise from disinterest" (Gould 2018, p. 371). In support of her criticism, she turns to an artwork that I myself discussed, namely, Marina Abramović's performance *Lips of Thomas:* "Obviously, every member of the audience faced a practical, moral dilemma: should one jump to her aid to prevent her from harming herself, or should one follow the rules of the art game by conforming to the etiquette expected of the audience at a performance" (Gould 2018, pp. 371–372). In fact, Gould describes the situation similarly to the way that I described it, and I see no real disagreement between us. Indeed, *Lips of Thomas* challenges my account, because it is an artwork that forces its spectators, or rather its participants, to ask themselves practical questions, and thereby keeps them from adopting a disinterested attitude in a straightforward manner. I have never denied this fact, nor have I denied that Abramović's performance addresses its spectators as moral agents, potentially posing a moral dilemma for them (Hilgers 2017, pp. 152–153). So, contrary to my claim that artworks typically ask us to adopt a disinterested attitude, *Lips of Thomas* is widely regarded as a work of art *and* encourages its spectators to adopt an interested attitude towards what it shows. What is my solution to this problem?

I take it that we do not ask ourselves practical questions as spectators of a performance in the same way that we ask ourselves such questions in the context of our daily lives. That is, as spectators of a performance, or of any other work of art, we ask ourselves such questions in an explicitly self-aware manner, reflecting on our thought process while actually performing it:

> A contemplative-reflective relation towards one's own actions could qualify as a disinterested one, if it makes one describe and evaluate one's actions from a perspective that is not one's own. On a different level, then, not only might reflection and contemplation come back into the picture, but also aesthetic disinterestedness. Moreover, works of art that disable straightforward disinterested engagement often still rely on disinterestedness as the main paradigm constitutive of artistic experiences. [...] They intentionally break with an aesthetic paradigm [...] and by doing so they prove the continuing importance of that very paradigm. (Hilgers 2017, p. 155)

However, Gould's deeper worry seems to be related to works of art that somehow confront us with evil: "Where does evil fit into a theoretical structure such as that of Hilgers?" (Gould 2018, p. 372). In response to this question, we need to make an important distinction: on the one hand, there may be presentational works that show something evil happening within their fictional worlds. On the other hand, there may be presentational works that ask their recipients to adopt an evil perspective towards what they show. I see no reason why the first kind of presentational work could not in principle qualify as a work of art. Of course, an artwork can show something morally appalling. Some will take this to imply that a recipient cannot, or should not, adopt a disinterested attitude towards what this work shows. This assumption arises from the usual association of disinterestedness with cold detachment. According to my account, though, the adoption of a disinterested attitude does not exclude the feeling of emotions, the having of affects and interests, or the making of moral judgments (Hilgers 2017, pp. 70–81). Rather, it only excludes a practical relation towards what one immediately perceives, and asks for a temporary disengagement from the idiosyncratic and context-relative aspects of one's own perspective. In fact, I take there to be an affinity between the adoption of a disinterested attitude and the adoption of a moral one (Hilgers 2017, p. 23 and pp. 156–160). Therefore, I see nothing problematic with adopting a disinterested attitude towards something morally appalling happening within an artwork's diegetic or fictional world. The more difficult question is whether we could, or should, adopt a disinterested attitude towards what a work shows if it asks us to adopt an evil perspective, i.e., if it asks us to apply principles, categories, interests, and goals that we justly consider to be immoral. In other words, the difficult question goes: should we ever (even temporarily) adopt an evil perspective? Moreover, could a work that asks us to adopt such a perspective ever qualify as an artwork? In contemporary aesthetics, this question is typically discussed as the question of whether a work's moral defect is always an aesthetic defect. This is an old debate. Hume already addressed this problem and defended one possible solution to it:

> But where the ideas of morality and decency alter from one age to another, and where vicious manners are described, without being marked with the proper characters of blame and disapprobation; this must be allowed to disfigure the poem, and to be a real deformity. I cannot, nor is it proper I should, enter into such sentiments; and however I may excuse the poet, on account of the manners of his age, I never can relish his composition. (Hume 1985, p. 246)[6]

In general, I am in agreement with Hume. Being asked to affirm immoral categorizations or judgments creates pain instead of pleasure. Following Tamar Szabó Gendler and Elisabeth Camp, I briefly discussed the topic of "imaginative resistance" in my book.[7] At times, one may resist adopting a given perspective for a good reason (Hilgers 2017, p. 37). Assuming that an evil perspective is deceptive instead of illuminating, such resistance seems to be well justified with respect to evil perspectives. A work that asks us to see things affirmatively as they ought not to be seen is dangerous and may lead us astray. It contradicts the epistemic power of artworks and does not allow one to understand better one's own world and life—at least, not in the way that works of art do so.[8] A presentational work that asks us to adopt an evil perspective towards what it shows can be highly intelligent and aes-

---

6 For a good introduction to the contemporary debate on this topic, see Gaut (2007).
7 For the topic of imaginative resistance, see Gendler (2000).
8 We must keep in mind here the difference between a work itself being illuminating and a study or a discussion of a deceptive work being illuminating by means of identifying and describing the relevant deception. Of course, we can learn something from a deceptive work, but only if we are fully aware of its deceptive nature.

thetically innovative, but there is a good reason for us to resist it or, at least, to keep our distance. Moreover, such a work is likely to open up a closed world-view instead of an open and projective meta-perspective, thereby denying its recipient the kind of pleasure related to the free performance of her capacities. In other words, it most likely denies a recipient's capacities to play freely with each other and does not contribute to her emancipation as an autonomous agent. Leni Riefenstahl's *Triumph of the Will* may serve as a standard example here. The film might be an aesthetically interesting and propagandistically effective work, which deserves the attention not only of historians and political scientists but also of film and media scholars. It is no work of art, though. In response to Gould's challenge, then, I conclude that an artwork may ask us to perceive something evil, but may never ask us to embrace it. Once again, then, the exclusionary nature of my normative account of art shows itself. The extraordinary and specific value that we typically ascribe to works of art would remain mysterious if we did not hold on to such an account (Hilgers 2017, pp. 4–5 and pp. 156–160). In this article, I have hopefully been able to spell out further some of the reasons for holding on to my particular account.

Literature

Adorno, Theodor W. (2009): *Ästhetik (1958/59)*. Posthumous Writings. Div. IV/3. Frankfurt am Main: Suhrkamp.
Eldridge, Richard (2017): "Aesthetic Disinterestedness: Art, Experience, and the Self." In: *Notre Dame Philosophical Reviews*. http://ndpr.nd.edu/news/aesthetic-disinterestedness-art-experience-and-the-self, last accessed on Jan. 29, 2023.
Gaut, Berys (2007): *Art, Emotion and Ethics*. Oxford: Oxford University Press.
Gendler, Tamar Szabo (2000): "The Puzzle of Imaginative Resistance." In: *The Journal of Philosophy* 97. No. 2, pp. 55–81.
Gould, Carol S. (2018): "Hilgers, Thomas. Aesthetic Disinterestedness: Art, Experience, and the Self. New York and London: Routledge, 2017, ix +190 pp.." In: *The Journal of Aesthetics and Art Criticism* 76. No. 3, pp. 370–372.
Hilgers, Thomas (2017): *Aesthetic Disinterestedness: Art, Experience, and the Self*. New York and London: Routledge.
Hume, David (1985): "Of the Standards of Taste." In: Hume, David: *Essays: Moral, Political, and Literary*. Revised Edition. Eugene F. Miller (Ed.). Indianapolis: Liberty Fund, pp. 226–249.
Matherne, Samantha (2020): "Review of Thomas Hilgers, *Aesthetic Disinterestedness: Art, Experience, and the Self*." In: *Philosophy in Review* 40. No. 2, pp. 53–55.
Schmalzried, Lisa (2020): "Thomas Hilgers: Aesthetic Disinterestedness—Art, Experience, and the Self, London/New York: Routledge 2019, 190 S.." In: *Zeitschrift für Ästhetik und Allgemeine Kunstwissenschaft* 65. No. 2, pp. 169–173.

(b) **Something in Between**

Fiona Hughes
The Playful Negotiation of Interests: Kant in Conversation with Fried and Winnicott

Abstract: Kant's idea of aesthetic disinterestedness is still significant as a challenge to the view that we are condemned to determination by interests. Although Kant may appear to argue that we must in fact wholly exclude all interests, his position is best understood as proposing this as an ideal. Nonetheless, even this could invite either cynicism or complacency. Drawing on Kant's idea of the "play of the faculties" and building on the distinction between having, and being determined by, an interest, I propose an alternative understanding of disinterestedness *as* a playful negotiation of interests. Both Michael Fried's "absorption"—requiring separation from the world—and Donald Winnicott's "play"—a form of contemplation requiring interruption—contrastively inform my thinking of a dynamical relation between disinterestedness and interests. In conclusion, I argue that the capacity for playful negotiation is a necessary condition for the possibility of the rational assessment of interests.

1 Introduction

In this paper, I argue that Kant's idea of aesthetic disinterestedness is still significant as a challenge to the view that we are condemned to determination by interests—both our own and those emanating from the world around us. Although Kant may appear to support the view that in judging aesthetically, we must wholly exclude any relation whatsoever to interests, on closer examination his position is best understood as that this goal is an ideal. I develop Kant's idea of the "play of the faculties," arguing for an alternative understanding of disinterestedness as a playful negotiation—not an absolute exclusion—of interests. It will become apparent that disinterestedness and having interests are difficult to pin down. I propose both can be better understood by eschewing a binary position and taking a dynamic approach focusing on the interstices and exchanges between disinterestedness and interests. I will argue not only that having interests does not necessa-

Acknowledgement: I am grateful to Larissa Berger, Louise Crawford, Tony Garelick, Stéphan Guéneau, Maggie Iversen, Jules Lubbock, Alan Montefiore, Jörg Schaub, and John Walshe as well as to an anonymous reviewer for De Gruyter for their extremely interesting and helpful comments on this paper.

https://doi.org/10.1515/9783110727685-009

rily undermine aesthetic judgement but further that aesthetic judgement offers a way of negotiating interests *so* that they are not determining.

If we read Kant's account of disinterestedness as requiring—either in fact or as an ideal—the total exclusion of interests, the radical discrepancy between goal and reality threatens to undermine our intentions, however genuine they may be. Failing to see how we could ever achieve a goal so removed from experience, we may fall victim to the skeptical position that disinterestedness is beyond our capacity and thus meaningless.[1] On the other hand, aiming at an absolute exclusion of interests may render us tone-deaf to ways in which interests pervasively shape our views of the world, for instance, in unconscious bias, but also in ways that are positive and at times necessary, for instance, in our commitment to principles. If, in contrast to these polar opposites, we read disinterestedness as freeing us up from being determined by interests through our capacity for play, as I will argue in an extension of Kant's account of aesthetic judgement, we can accept that as humans we are—for better and for worse—shaped by interests while not concluding we are fated to succumb to them.

The second section of this paper addresses Kant's official account of disinterestedness presented in § 2 of the First Moment of the Analytic of the Beautiful. Kant appears to argue that disinterestedness requires the exclusion *in fact* of any interest whatsoever. However, drawing on the "Analytic of the Beautiful" more widely, both Guyer and Allison argue that for Kant we can never be certain that we have in fact excluded interests. Consequently, the exclusion of interests must operate hypothetically (Guyer) or as an ideal (Allison). If either Guyer or Allison is right, disinterestedness as the exclusion of all interests should be understood as an unachievable goal which nonetheless shapes our experience. At the end of this section, I contrast having an interest from being determined by an interest, a distinction I build on throughout the rest of this paper.

In the third section, focusing on the key idea of play, I develop an alternative account of disinterestedness as compatible with interests so long as we are not determined by them. Distinguishing between play and games reveals how play negotiates while not necessarily rejecting rules. I argue that Kant's account of free-play implies a negotiation of rules as well as moral principle and its attendant interest. Using the examples of "child's play" and free jazz, I further argue that play understood as a primordial form of negotiation can render interests non-determining.

---

[1] This, I think, is the point of many attacks on disinterestedness. Berleant (1994), for instance, argues there is a core of truth to disinterestedness but that it would be better to get beyond this way of framing the question.

While my account of disinterestedness as playful negotiation draws on Kant, it differs from him in a number of respects.

I go on to discuss two ideas, neither of which are interpretations of Kant but both of which are productive for understanding the stakes arising from the contrastive models of disinterestedness discussed in this paper. In the fourth section, I consider the art historian Michael Fried's idea of absorption, according to which criterion artworks should not engage in relations with the spectator. I explore how this model for art, as exhibiting a contemplation detached from the world and the interests arising in it, bears several parallels with Kant's official position on disinterestedness as absolutely excluding interests.

In the fifth section, I consider Winnicott's psychoanalytical idea of play. For Winnicott, play allows for and even requires the possibility of interruption. Play —indeed, to adopt Fried's terms, absorption in play—is not destroyed by interruptions so long as they are not over-riding. I suggest that Winnicott's account shows how play not only tolerates but incorporates interruptions *so that* and not just *so long as* they are not determining. This makes for a dynamic rather than a binary relation between contemplation and interruption, which is instructive for my idea that aesthetic judgement not only can tolerate interests but also can negotiate them so as to render them non-determining.

In the sixth section, I examine the implications of Kant's account of the relation between aesthetic judgement and world for the idea of disinterestedness. His official version of disinterestedness implies withdrawal from the world in order to attain the exclusion of all interests. I argue that Kant's more systematic account of the relation between aesthetic judgement and world cannot be understood as a withdrawal from the world. I examine his claim that aesthetic judgement helps understanding "find its way about in nature," arguing this implies that aesthetic judgement operates as an orientation through which making sense of the world is possible. If the world does not need to be abandoned, then we are capable not only of accommodating interests alongside aesthetic judgement: the latter can negotiate the former so as to render them non-determining.

In conclusion, I briefly discuss the relation between the aesthetic negotiation of interests I have proposed and the rational assessment of interests. My account does not aestheticize our ability to resist determination by interests, even though I argue that the capacity for aesthetic play is a precondition for the possibility of rational assessment. Nor am I suggesting that aesthetic absorption is unachievable or unnecessary, just that it need not be pure.

2 Kant's Official Account of Disinterestedness: The Exclusion of Interests

§ 2 of the "Analytic of the Beautiful" offers Kant's most explicit account of the character of disinterestedness. Aesthetic judgement is determined by a liking that is "devoid of all interest" [2] (KU: 204). That this strong view of disinterestedness as exclusion of interests is proposed by the First Moment as a whole and represents Kant's official position is made clear by his repetition of the same phrase in the concluding statement:

> Taste is the ability to judge an object; or a way of presenting it, by means of a liking or disliking devoid of all interest [*ohne alles Interesse*]. The object of such a liking is called beautiful. (KU: 211)

Kant begins § 2 by defining interest as a liking—indeed, a desire—bound up with [*verbinden*] the presentation of an object's existence (KU: 204). To have an interest is to desire either to possess something or to bring about a state of affairs, be that moral, immoral or amoral. By contrast, the liking characteristic of aesthetic judgement is not bound up with a desire for the existence of an object and qualifies as a form of contemplation (KU: 204).[3] Kant goes on to state that there can be no mixing of interest with aesthetic liking (KU: 205).[4] The case seems clear. If we are to achieve aesthetic contemplation, we must *in fact* eliminate any relation to interests. As a result, Kant can be seen as the champion of a judging that achieves detachment from our normal involvement with the existence of objects.

However, for Guyer, it is always uncertain that we have in fact achieved an aesthetic judgement (Guyer 1979, p. 205[5]). Meanwhile, Allison specifically distinguishes between *de facto* aesthetic judgements and the standard for those judgements,

---

[2] Unless otherwise signaled, I use Pluhar's translation of the *Critique of Judgment*.
[3] Guyer (1978, p. 453) argues against Kant that desire does not entail interest: "it is not obvious that a delight in the existence of a particular object is identical with a desire for experience of further objects of the same sort, or even entailed by such a desire; so it is not clear that the desire which Kant describes as being aroused by the agreeable must be connected with an interest as he has defined it."
[4] Kant is referring to what he later calls pure, in contrast to adherent, beauty (KU: 229). This paper is focused on pure judgements of taste. See fn. 23.
[5] "Establishing that a pleasure is disinterested is a matter not of incorrigible introspection, but of hypothesis and conjecture about causal connections in one's mental history." The uncertainty of aesthetic judgement is "due at least in part to the general uncertainty of empirical self-knowledge, and not to any problem unique to aesthetic judgment." (Guyer 1979, p. 205-6).

which must be recognized as pure and ideal (Allison 2001, p. 110[6]). As disinterestedness is the characteristic quality of aesthetic judgements, it follows that the absolute exclusion of interests from the pleasure we take in the beautiful (and the sublime) is unachievable in fact. In what follows, for economy of expression, I will refer to the non-achievability of disinterestedness as its "ideal" status, even though not all *de facto* non-achievability is ideal and not all ideals are identical. Admittedly, it is difficult to find evidence for the ideal status of disinterestedness in the first Moment. However, if we accept—as Kant clearly intends—that the Four Moments of the Analytic of the Beautiful are mutually necessary, then it is valid to find that evidence elsewhere.[7] The ideal status of disinterestedness is implied, for instance, by Kant's presenting both the universal voice (KU: 216) and common sense (KU: 237) as ideas. Disinterestedness speaks with the universal voice of common sense, which is an idea or presupposition. With this precision, Kant's official position still makes the strong claim that disinterestedness requires the absolute exclusion of all interests, but only as an ideal.

There is, however, a small and almost imperceptible detail in § 2, which, I believe, opens up the possibility of a different perspective on disinterested aesthetic pleasure. Towards the end of the section, Kant insists that we must not be "in the least" *eingenommen* in favor of the thing's existence (KU: 205). Reporting on 18th-century usage, Adelung gives the primary meaning of *eingenommen* as "to be taken over by something external" (Adelung 1811[8]). Translating *eingenommen* as "biased"—as do Pluhar, as well as Guyer and Matthews—invites the conclusion that the exclusion of all interests is required because to have an interest is to be biased. However, if we take the more finely tuned sense of *eingenommen* as being taken over, its negation implies that our pleasure in a beautiful thing must not be *determined* by interests, which could still be influential in a non-determining way. Both Allison and Guyer mention that Kant rules out determination by

---

6 Allison argues this specifically in relation to the "universal voice" in the Second Moment. However, as I will argue, this clearly has implications for disinterestedness.

7 Evidence in support of the interconnectedness—and not just the mutual necessity—of the four Moments comes when in § 9, Kant refers as a constituent part of his current argument to universal communicability, which is taken up as a theme in the Fourth Moment (KU: 217).

8 Adelung: "Von außen herein nehmen (taken in from outside)" and, more narrowly, "taken in by someone else," for instance, on account of their (perhaps only apparent) qualities. For the less historically adjacent Grimm brothers (1838) *eingenommen* is: "occupatus, captus, für oder gegen etwas einnehmen," i.e., busy or engaged with (but also, literally, taken into possession by), captured, for or against something. The correlative noun *Eingenommenheit* is: "propensio aut offensio, vorgefaszte neigung oder abneigung," that is, "propensity or aversion, preconceived inclination or disinclination." While neither a propensity nor an aversion need be determining, they connote strength of influence.

interest (Guyer, 1979, p. 196; Allison 2001, p. 96[9]). Nonetheless, neither they—nor Kant—develop the idea of determination as the key to how disinterestedness could be compatible with interests so long as they are not determining of our pleasure. There is a fine but, I believe, significant distinction between the ideal of being absolutely interest-free and the goal of being free from determination by interests. In what follows, I develop an alternative account of aesthetic disinterestedness as requiring that interests are not determining, rather than that they are absent.

3 An Alternative View of Disinterestedness as a Playful Negotiation of Determination by Interests

In this section, I will show how Kant's account of the play of the faculties can be developed into an alternative view of disinterestedness as the playful negotiation of interests. I first establish how the play of the faculties contributes to disinterestedness as a negotiation by the imagination of understanding so as to show up only *possible* determination under a concept. As a next step to establishing a model of disinterestedness as negotiation, I develop a phenomenology of play as primordial negotiation among possibilities, showing that this need not exclude rules. I go on to draw out how Kant implies that aesthetic play allows for the negotiation of the possibility of—though not determination by—cognitive rule-following, morally determining principles and moral interest. The argumentative progression from rules and laws to interests is that they all can be species of determination. I propose two "facts," namely, that interests are (i) pervasive and (ii) overlapping. On the basis of (ii) I argue that interests need not be determining despite (i). I consider the risk my thesis could pose to a fight-back against interests, arguing this is addressed by the thesis that play renders interests non-determining.

We have to wait until § 9 in the Second Moment to learn that aesthetic judgement requires both imagination and understanding in "free play (*in einem freien Spiele*)."[10] Their distinctive contributions are: "imagination for the composition (*Zusammensetzung*) of the manifold of intuition, and understanding for the

---

9 The question of whether or not aesthetic judgement can lead to interest is not my topic here (Allison 2001, pp. 94–97; Guyer 1978).
10 Kant also refers to the "harmony of the cognitive powers" (KU: 218). The harmony in question is playful. See Hughes 2007, pp. 296–299, on "contrapuntal exemplarity."

unity (*Einheit*) of the concept that unifies the representations."[11] Such free play is an exercise of "cognition in general" (KU: 217).

While imagination takes priority in aesthetic judgement, it has to work cooperatively with understanding.[12] If we focus on the requirement that understanding contributes "the unity of the concept" within "*cognition in general*," it may seem that understanding is determining and that taste is a subspecies of knowledge (Baz 2005[13]). However, the distinctive contribution of imagination in aesthetic judgements to "cognition *in general*" ensures there is no determination under any particular concept as would be required for knowledge (KU: 217).

How does this peculiar balancing act work? Imagination's role of composing representations within an intuition first introduced in the *Critique of Pure Reason* at A99 as the "running through and the holding together" of the manifold in an intuition is a necessary condition not only of epistemic but also of aesthetic judgement (KU: 217[14]). But were understanding to unify the manifold under a concept, this would result in a determining epistemic judgement, thus destroying the aesthetic character of the judgement (KrV: A103). Consequently, it can only be the *possibility* of unification under a concept that is required for the play characteristic of aesthetic judgement. Understanding is constrained by imagination which holds in check the former's normal function of determining an intuition under a concept.[15] This is an initial example of what I call "negotiation."

We now need to establish how the play of the faculties contributes to Kant's account of disinterestedness. While at the outset of the First Moment—the principal topic of which we have seen is disinterestedness—superficially it appears that imagination and *not* understanding is under consideration, closer examination reveals a more complex story:

> If we wish to decide whether something is beautiful or not, we do not use understanding to refer the presentation to the object so as to give rise to cognition; rather, we use imagination

---

[11] Here, I prefer Guyer and Matthew's "composition" for *Zusammensetzung*. Pluhar's "combination" would better translate *Verbindung* implying the unifying activity of understanding. KrV: B129.
[12] Epistemic judgement also requires a cooperation of the faculties as its subjective condition, although in that case understanding takes priority in determining unification under a concept (KU: 218). See Hughes 2007, pp. 169–206.
[13] For a critique of Baz' interpretation, see Hughes 2006.
[14] My translation.
[15] Imagination is able to achieve this because of its role as mediating between different mental orientations. Mediation among faculties is characteristic of imagination in all its guises but comes to the fore as the principal cognitive activity in aesthetic judgement (Hughes 2007, pp. 147–151).

(*perhaps in connection with understanding*) to refer the presentation to the subject and his feeling of pleasure or displeasure. (KU: 203, my emphasis)

Thus, some form of cooperation between the faculties is already mooted and all that is ruled out is determination under a concept of understanding so as to give rise to knowledge. It is only in § 9, as we have seen, that Kant explicitly claims that judging something as beautiful *requires* both imagination and understanding. But, as the play of the faculties is a necessary condition of aesthetic judgement, a characteristic feature of which is disinterested contemplation, *and* as Kant already moots the possibility of a co-operation of the faculties in § 1, we can safely conclude that disinterestedness requires a play of the faculties.

According to Kant's official account of disinterestedness it would follow that the play of the faculties aims at the idea or ideal of excluding all interests. *Prima facie*, it seems odd to claim that a playful state of mind aims at the absolute exclusion of anything, including interests. One way of explaining this unease would be to object that excluding all interests would require a determining rule alien to the concept of play and to the freedom of imagination which makes it possible (KU: 240). The rule would be of the form: in order to attain the state of disinterestedness we *must* aim to exclude any interest whatsoever. Such a prescriptive and negative rule, the objection would go, is surely at odds with a play of the faculties which is "free" exactly because it is not determining. However, this objection is too dependent on lexical definition. It is true that requiring a rule to bring about the exclusion of interests would be contrary to Kant's notion of play. However, being disinterested may not require a determining rule or even an intention to bring about an ideal. Perhaps an exclusion of interests could arise from a shift in perspective as the result of a change in priorities without the deployment of any prescriptive rule.

A more convincing way of making sense of the unease about the compatibility of free play with an absolute exclusion of interests arises from examining the phenomenology of play. Typically, when we play, we let one perspective or another come to the fore or recede into the background as a form of exploration. Play is distinct from games, which are determined by rules. The rules of a game are, we must suppose, arbitrary in respect of their genesis but once established, they are determining. Think of the off-side rule in football. The rule is subject to change over time, but at any one time the current interpretation is determining. Play, in contrast, is the condition of the possibility of freedom to improvise within a game. Usually, there will be some element of play within a game whatever the competence of its participants. Certainly, in order for a competitive game to be played well, players must do more than simply abide by determining rules. Play within a game emerges through some degree of improvisation within rules. Play, consequently, does not require the elimination of determining rules and is compatible with them as operative at some level.

However, there is a more radical model of play that operates not so much within the rules, as on the margin in the emergence of rules. This is the deeper level of play I am trying to get at, one that is the condition of the possibility of any actual playing. At this pre-cognitive and pre-moral level, play *is* primordial negotiation as an exploratory movement among possible patterns of activity. This existential level of negotiation-play is an open-ended orientation uncovering and, potentially, bringing into being emergent possibilities as experientially—not just logically—possible.[16] Think of children playing, while inventing and subverting possible rules as they go along. "From now on, we'll skip backwards...... Now we'll hop on the left foot..." These proto-prescriptions remain in the realm of the possible because they are dreamt up as emergent ways of seeing the world, not pinned down as actual rules establishing stable constraints. Such intuitive and inventive imagining of rules shows up a capacity for playful negotiation of a range of possibilities that is often concealed—or lost—in adult life. Aesthetic pleasure is a "mature" (possibly repressed or more conventionally acceptable) corollary to child's play, bringing to the fore what is usually unremarked on, namely, an ongoing fluctuation of possibilities out of which every clear-cut experience emerges. Another example is free jazz improvisation, where someone—let us say, Ornette Coleman—does not so much follow (even creatively) the existing rules and, rather, alludes to—"quotes"—and, at the same time, subverts more traditional ways of making music—including other non-traditional styles of jazz—while creating new patterns of playing and hearing. Coleman plays at the threshold of, not within, the rules: his music is a playful negotiation of possibilities we have not yet heard, which even he, perhaps, had not fully grasped until he found himself playing them. Both "child's play" and Coleman exemplify what I mean by negotiation of—not just escaping determination by—rules.

During this phenomenological excursus I have established that play need not exclude rules, even though it cannot succumb to determination by them. But I have also shown how a more radical form of play is exploratory in relation to rules. I will argue that aesthetic judgement not only need not entirely exclude but can also resist determination by interests.[17] For now, I return to Kant, drawing out how he

---

16 See § 6 on exploratory orientation.
17 This argumentative transition in my account does not require that all interests entail concepts operating as rules but only that interests potentially initiate patterns of behavior which could be pinned down as rules. Guyer (1979, p. 187) and Fricke (1990, p. 16) argue that, for Kant, interests entail concepts, making the transition from not determined by rules to not determined by interests direct.

does not exclude any relation to rules and laws and only determination by them from aesthetic judgement. At the beginning of this section, we saw how his account of aesthetic play entails a relation to understanding, but not determination under a concept. Determination under a concept is the unification of sensory intuitions under a rule. Understanding is the faculty of rules insofar as it is the source of concepts which operate as "functions" or rules for unification of intuitions (KrV: A68/B93). That understanding is required in aesthetic judgements thus implies that the latter and their characteristic play of the faculties stand in some relation to rules. I propose that while determination by rules is excluded in aesthetic judgement, determinability under rules—that is, the *possibility* of rule-following—is not.[18] A beautiful thing could under other circumstances be determined as a cognitive object. This possibility is recognized insofar as aesthetic judgement is an expression of cognition in general. The play between imagination and understanding allows determination under a rule to be negotiated as a possibility rather than either actualized or denied. Insofar as aesthetic judgement is not governed by rules and only reflects on the possibility of rules, it is more akin to the emergence of rules within child's play and free jazz than it is to a rule-governed competitive game within which play is tolerated. Consequently, free play is not only compatible with the possibility of rules: a state of free play treats rules as only possible *such that* they are rendered non-determining.[19] This is what I mean by negotiation.

But how do we get from rules to interests? Answering this requires establishing the link between aesthetic judgement and the determinations of moral reason. Admittedly the latter are laws, but because like rules, these are species of determination, they can be examined in a parallel way. Subsequently, I will turn to interests, which can but need not operate as determinations.

Aesthetic pleasure is distinct from moral liking, which is law-governed insofar as it is based on determining practical ideas of reason and thus cannot be an exercise of free purposiveness or play (KU: 292[20]). Nonetheless, Kant claims that beauty is a symbol of morality (KU: 351–354). This implies that an aesthetic presentation allows for reflection on moral principles in an exploratory or playful way. For instance, a poem or a painting opens up perspectives from which a moral principle can be indirectly exhibited, rather than arguing from principle to particular as would be necessary for a determining moral judgement (KU: 179). Kant also suggests that aesthetic judgement facilitates the realization of moral principles in the empirical world in positioning reflective judgement as intermediary between

---

[18] See David Bell 1992 on aesthetic judgement and rule-following.
[19] This is what makes play important for resisting determination by interests more generally. See the Conclusion.
[20] See Hughes 2010, p. 108.

reason and understanding (KU: 176–179; EEKU: 206–208). Schiller, explicitly drawing on Kant's notion of play, presents aesthetic judgement as transitional between nature and reason such that "aesthetic play" facilitates the emergence of morality within the empirical world (Schiller 1982, pp. 207–209[21]). Indeed, Kant's idea of "the free lawfulness of imagination" may suggest that imagination makes possible a transition from the lawfulness of understanding to the freedom of reason (KU: 240). Finally, Kant suggests play is compatible with the determining power of practical reason in presenting aesthetic ideas as distinct from but analogous to rational ideas (KU: 342[22]). All these are expressions of Kant's view that aesthetic judgement is conducive to the possibility of moral law, while not being determined by it.[23]

But what, if anything, does the compatibility of aesthetic judgement with possible determination by reason contribute to our understanding of the relation in which disinterestedness stands to interests? One explicit link is that our liking for the good—which *qua* moral is governed by the determining power of reason —gives rise to interest (KU: 207). This is the point at which the thesis proposed in this paper most directly converges with Kant, for his account implies that if aesthetic judgement is compatible with determining moral principles, then, by extension, it is in some way compatible with an interest in the good. Certainly, Kant contrasts liking based on an interest with disinterested liking (KU: 207). However, if beauty can be a symbol of morality and aesthetic ideas emulate rational ideas, then aesthetic judgement must be capable of coexisting with—even negotiating the realization of (as Schiller clearly thinks)—an interest in the good. The distinctiveness of the two likings at the level of principle does not entail their incompatibility within experience.

At the end of the previous section, I argued on etymological grounds that disinterestedness may only require that we are not determined by interests. I have now argued that for Kant play *is* compatible with cognitive rules, moral principles, and moral interest so long as these are not determining. Going beyond the internal logic of Kant's argument—while building on his account of play—I have offered an

---

[21] Twenty-seventh Letter, 3. Schiller makes the link between play and disinterestedness but follows Kant's official line in presenting play as an ideal unrealizable within our sensory existence (Schiller 1982, pp. 205–211).

[22] On the relation between aesthetic judgement and reason, see Hughes 2010, p. 19.

[23] It is crucial to my position that these claims are true of pure beauty. Certainly, Kant holds that the ideal of beauty is compatible with, indeed, relies on moral ideas and that adherent beauty depends on concepts of perfection (§§ 16 and 17). But in these cases, the standard for human beauty is determined by an idea of what humanity or some object should be. Pure beauty cannot be determined by a concept, a rational idea or a moral interest and only thus can stand in a distinctively symbolical, not subsidiary, relation to morality. Consequently, I am arguing that association with interests does not undermine *pure* judgements of taste.

account of play as negotiation, where these terms conjointly capture an implicit exploration of emergent possibilities deeply embedded throughout experience.

I now propose that disinterestedness, understood as a form of negotiation-play, relates not only to rules but also to non-moral interests. While negotiation of cognitive rules and moral principles is clearly distinct from negotiation of non-moral interests, the salient parallel I draw is that all these forms of negotiation resist determination through the exercise of play. Just as in a playful state of mind, cognitive rules and moral principles are treated as possible, that is, rendered non-determining, non-moral interests can also be treated as possible in the sense of operating in the background as potentialities rather than as actual determinations. In trying to build up a picture of what this playful response to the possibility of determination under interests would look like, I now focus on establishing that having interests need not be determining. This is a first step toward establishing my stronger thesis that aesthetic judgement can negotiate interests.

I might, for instance, care about an artwork in part because it allows me to make a philosophical point more persuasively. It would be odd if I did not at all care about the existence of an artwork I find philosophically or in some other way illuminating. An art historian will almost certainly take an interest in the provenance and conservation of a work on which she has expertise. However, so long as advantages derived from the existence of the artwork do not determine the pleasure taken in it, they need not—although, of course, they could—undermine the aesthetic status of judgements made about it.[24] Arguably, some such interests are always at some level or another intermingled with aesthetic pleasure—for instance, gaining a degree of satisfaction from being the sort of person who likes this kind of artwork. But the intermingling of interests with a playful state of mind makes achieving aesthetic contemplation challenging, not impossible.[25]

It can, admittedly, be argued that simply to have an interest is to be determined by it. The way Kant sets up his argument in §2 may suggest he holds such a view. I do not deny that to have an interest is to be influenced or to have

---

[24] Aesthetic judgement requires "a direct liking (*Wohlgefallen*) for the object" (KU: 227). (Pluhar's translation is here preferable to CUP's "immediate satisfaction," which is not consistent with Kant's section titles at KU: 211 and 213.) It also eschews determination by an interest in the existence of the object (KU: 204). Some interests, e.g., information about an artwork, may be incorporated within free play, while others, e.g., being hungry, may still be operative despite free play. For a discussion of the role of the object in taste, see Hughes 2023.

[25] Challenges include retaining aesthetic focus while taking into consideration exhibition notes supplied by curators alongside works.

an inclination, for this is what it is to have an interest.[26] What I deny is that to have an interest entails that I am taken over by that interest.

In further support of establishing a gap between having and being determined by an interest, I now draw attention to two facts that are, I believe, supported by reflection on experience:
(i) The pervasiveness of interests: interests are widespread throughout experience.
(ii) The plurality of interests: interests very rarely stand alone and typically overlap with one another.

The plurality of interests as overlapping does not preclude that any one interest—or combination of interests—is determining. Overlapping interests may reinforce rather than compete with one another with the result that determination by an interest is strengthened. Nonetheless, our capacity for operating with a plurality of interests suggests that to have an interest is not necessarily to be determined by it. Thus, despite (i), we may be capable of disinterestedness.

Imagine you are on the way to an art exhibition by an artist whose work you have enjoyed in the past. Just as you arrive, you realize you are hungry. That you choose to prioritize your anticipation of aesthetic pleasure over hunger does not entail you are no longer hungry. You still have an interest in eating, but you are not determined by that hunger. Later you will prioritize your hunger, just not now. Moreover, your pre-existing interest in the artist—you almost always find her works inspiring, and you have read up about this exhibition in advance—need not determine, though it will certainly influence, whether or not you experience aesthetic pleasure when faced with the artworks. And however enthralled you are by the artworks, if someone you care about unexpectedly calls on your mobile phone looking for help, you do not have to retrieve your interest in their welfare in the way you will retrieve the coat you left in the cloakroom. Human investments still operate even in a state of aesthetic play. It could be objected that, as soon as you respond to the request for help, you switch or flip from disinterested to interested, from a state of excluding interests to one of determination by them. It is certainly true that you shift your priorities. But the point I am making is that you could not make this transition if it were not the case that even when you were caught up in disinterested pleasure you still had interests even though they were not determining of your pleasure in the artwork. While successfully resisting being overwhelmed—taken over or determined (*eingenommen*)—by these interests, you

---

26 See V-Anth/Friedländer: 581–588.

did not have to achieve a state where you stood in no relation whatsoever to other commitments and needs in order to take disinterested pleasure in the artworks.

Through these examples, I am suggesting that the way in which interests operate can be more complex than either that interests are determining of my pleasure or that they are excluded by it. I can have several interests—competing, reinforcing, or running parallel to one another—yet it is not necessary that they destroy my capacity for disinterested appreciation. The mere having of—and thus being influenced by—interests does not entail we are determined by them. Thus, it is possible to achieve a playful state of mind while having interests. Indeed, it is not just that interests are compatible with disinterestedness: play negotiates interests so as to render them non-determining for instance when I resist hunger in favor of aesthetic pleasure. As in my earlier examples of child's play and free jazz, playfulness can trump determining interests. I will further develop this stronger version of my thesis in my discussion of Winnicott.

However, despite the phenomenological complexity I have argued for, if I cannot—even as an ideal—aim to wholly exclude interests, do I not inevitably end up in hock to my interests? Moreover, does not my proposed alternative version of disinterestedness muddy the waters so as to undermine the motivation for resisting interests? If so, would it not be best to stick with the official version of disinterestedness as the exclusion of all interests at least as an ideal?

In response to these important concerns—which haunt me while writing this paper—it is necessary to reemphasize what is meant by "determination" by interests. Determination by an interest means to be taken over by it (*eingenommen*) so that my pleasure is entirely motivated by it. I become an advocate for my interest. This would certainly preclude free play and, consequently, disinterestedness. However, if it is possible that I can have an interest and yet not be taken over by it, then, the interest need not be determining even though I am influenced by it. Having an interest in an object and its existence need not dictate that I like it only appetitively or, indeed, morally. I am capable of experiencing a play of the faculties *despite* having some interest in the object.[27] Indeed, I am in the course of arguing, play-as-primordial-negotiation *renders* interests non-determining.

---

[27] Without this possibility, it would be necessary to deny that the art market is even in principle compatible with aesthetic appreciation of artworks. While the art market certainly distorts aesthetic value, it is possible for a commercially successful artist to produce genuinely aesthetic works. This is not to deny that there are also many valuable aesthetic works that receive no success in commercial terms. Commercial interest and aesthetic value are distinct, though not necessarily incompatible.

4 Fried and Absorption: The Exclusion of the World

The art historian Michael Fried distinguishes between, on the one hand, art that absorbs the spectator by not taking anything about the external world into consideration and, on the other hand, "theatrical" or "literalist" art that incorporates elements of the world and its concerns within the artwork. For Fried absorption is the mark of successful art, whether in the late 18th century or in the late 20th century. In this section, I will show how Fried's claim that absorption excludes the spectator and the surrounding world implies the exclusion of interests, thus converging with Kant's official account of disinterestedness.[28]

For Fried, in order to "make meaning" or achieve "meaningfulness *as such*" the absorptive artwork must stand apart both from what surrounds it and from its beholder, even though the latter is rapt in the face of it (Fried 1998, p. 162). In contrast, what Fried calls "theatrical" or "literalist" art rejects clear boundaries between the artwork and its surroundings, so that the artwork takes its meaning from what is around it—the theater in which it appears.

> Literalist sensibility is theatrical because, to begin with, it is concerned with the actual circumstances in which the beholder encounters literalist work. (Fried 1998, p. 153)

Fried claims that "the very best recent work" is anti-theatrical, whereas theatrical works are often "ingratiating and mediocre" (Fried 1980, p. 5). In *Absorption and Theatricality* (1980) Fried carefully situates the rise of an explicit theoretical theme of "absorption" both historically and geographically within late 18th-century France, especially in response to works by Chardin, Greuze and David and as a reaction against the previously dominant and theatrical Rococo.[29] However, in *Art and Objecthood* (1998) Fried applies the contrastive axis of absorption and literalism to the later 20th century. Modern absorptive art includes the large-scale metallic abstract sculptures of Roland David Smith and Anthony Caro, along with the formal or atonal music of Elliott Carter. Meanwhile, modern theatrical art includes John Cage, composer of aleatoric or chance-controlled music such as 4'33", as well as Robert Rauschenberg. Fried also includes within literalism minimalist artists

---

28 While Fried's target is artworks and their meaning, Kant's is aesthetic receptivity. Nonetheless, both raise questions as to how the aesthetic stands in relation to the surrounding world.
29 Absorptive art was prevalent earlier, for instance, in the 17th-century works of Poussin and Rembrandt. However, it was only in the 1750s that absorption was proposed as a *desideratum* (Fried 1980, p. 52).

such as Donald Judd, Sol Le Witt, and Carl André (Fried 1998, p. 157). What Fried criticizes in these artists is embraced by much contemporary art: namely, a commitment to exploring the interstices between art and world *through* the artwork.

The paintings of Chardin, Fried argues, pay no heed to the beholder and *only thus* engender the viewer's absorption in the artwork.[30] In so arguing, Fried commits himself not only to a distinction between artwork and world—something he argues is missing in the "literalist" works of, for instance, Tony Smith—but to their separation (Fried 1998, pp. 157–160). In so doing, he sets up a fork between, on the one hand, art free of any influence by external interests and, on the other, art that is not art at all due to being wholly determined by external interests. Once he has assumed—rather than argued for—the absoluteness of this distinction, he concludes that theatrical art leaves no room at all for absorption. Consequently—but only because of this assumed premise—it is necessary that the world is not only other than but also excluded from absorptive art, whereas in theatrical art, according to Fried, the world entirely takes over the artwork. For Fried, this amounts to a "war" about the possibility of art as such (Fried 1998, p. 160).

Fried quotes revealingly from Diderot, whom he draws on for the distinction between theatricality and absorption:

> Whether you compose or act, think no more of the beholder than if he did not exist. Imagine at the edge of the stage, a high wall that *separates* you from the orchestra. Act as if the curtain never rose. (Fried 1980, pp. 94–95; Diderot 1758, p. 231,[31] my emphasis)

Exclusion of the world is necessary for the inwardness required for aesthetic experience. Interpreting David's work (from the end of the 18th century) as one of the highest achievements within absorptive art, Fried writes:

> Only the most inward and spiritualized action, David seems to have come to feel, escaped being theatrical; only action that no longer engaged with the world, either physically or temporally, could express its meaning purely, self-sufficiently, other than as theatre. (Fried 1980, p. 230 fn. 59)

The main parallel I draw with Kant's official position on disinterestedness is that Fried's reading of absorption amounts to a contemplation requiring the absolute exclusion of any considerations arising from outside the artwork. These external concerns or pressures are what Kant calls interests. For Fried, the fact that theat-

---

30 The "paradox," as Fried sees it, is that the beholder can "be stopped and held precisely there" only if "the fiction that no one is standing before the canvas" is achieved. This amounts to "the supreme fiction of the beholder's nonexistence" (Fried 1980, p. 108).
31 Fried's page reference is to Diderot's original edition.

rical artwork incorporates everyday concerns entails it is determined by what are, again in the terms of this discussion, interests.[32] Absorbed art, by contrast, operates in an aesthetic bubble, where the artwork resists any convergence with the everyday. For Fried, any muddying of the waters between artwork and the everyday necessarily results in the determination of the artwork by non-aesthetic concerns, that is, by interests.

Applying the distinction argued for in this paper, an artwork may incorporate and be influenced by—as well as reflect on—interests external to the artwork without being determined by them. One of Fried's own examples of theatricality, Cage's aleatoric music, provides an alternative perspective to the usual one on everyday phenomena. We attend to everyday sounds differently when we listen to them in a concert hall rather than when they are taken for granted as background within everyday life. The aleatoric artwork may have the same content as ordinary everyday experience but it does not have the same frame. In a 1957 lecture, *Experimental Music*, Cage described music as "a purposeful purposelessness or a purposeless play"—the Kantian resonance is evident—which is "an affirmation of life—not an attempt to bring order out of chaos nor to suggest improvements in creation, but simply a way of waking up to the very life we're living" (Cage 1973, p. 12). Experience of 4'33" leads to an intensification of and reflection on otherwise unremarked sounds, not a simple repetition of them. In § 6, I will argue that Kant's broader account of the relation between aesthetic judgement and world does not require the latter's exclusion.

Another parallel between Kant's official account of disinterestedness and Fried is that the latter's notion of absorption as wholly cut off from the world is an ideal he thinks is rarely if ever achieved. In the brief and somewhat surprising conclusion to "Art and Objecthood," Fried announces:

> In these last sentences, however, I want to call attention to the utter pervasiveness—the virtual universality—of the sensibility or mode of being that I have characterized as corrupted or perverted by theatre. We are all literalists most or all of our lives. Presentness is grace. (Fried 1998, p. 168[33])

---

[32] For Fried, absorption is "interest" in an object. (See, for instance, Fried 1998, p. 167 on the temporality of interest.) In Kant's terms Fried's absorbed interest is "disinterestedness." The point that I am making is that for Fried, absorbed art excludes the external world, which in Kant's terms requires excluding *its* "interests."

[33] This echoes the equally enigmatic opening reference to Perry Miller: "The abiding assurance is that 'we every moment see the same proof of a God as we should have seen if we had seen Him create the world at first.'" (Fried 1998, p. 148) This explains how absorptive art qualifies as "grace." No wonder Fried thinks we rarely, if ever, achieve absorption.

Fried's prescription is that we should strive to achieve absorption even though it is only rarely achievable. This implies that art should aim at absolutely excluding the interests of the everyday world, even though this is mostly impossible.

A further intriguing parallel with Kant—as well as with the thesis of this paper—is the seriousness Fried affords to play. He considers paintings by Chardin depicting children engrossed in play as emblematic of absorption (Fried 1980, pp. 46–51). Playing is depicted "not as time wasted but of time *filled.*" This is "a new unmoralized version of distraction as a vehicle of absorption" (Fried 1980, p. 51). Fried's account of absorption, including the specificity of the attention he pays to play, is fascinating as a reading of the 18th-century paintings under discussion, as well as persuasive in bringing to the fore absorption as a crucial theme for painting and for art more generally. Where I disagree is with the way in which he defines absorption as entailing exclusion of engagement with the world. For Fried, it follows that if a work is engaged with the world, it cannot be absorptive. This rests on an unnecessary polarization of the range of possibilities available.[34] Certainly, engaging with the world *could* lead to a work failing to be absorptive, but this need not be the case.[35]

5 Winnicott: Play and Interruption

For the psychoanalyst Donald Winnicott, interruption is not only compatible with but productive for play as a contemplative and exploratory state. While not all interests are interruptions, I will argue that his model reinforces my thesis that aesthetic judgement need not be determined by and, further, is capable of a playful negotiation of interests. For Winnicott, interest first arises as a singular attachment to the breast, but is gradually generalized into a variety of attachments to self and others, as well as engagements within the world (Winnicott 2005, p. 6).[36] By facilitating the development from an overpowering internal interest to-

---

[34] Fried remarks on a suggestion that Chardin shows "a natural pause in the action which, we feel, will recommence a moment later" (Referring to Châtelet and Thuillier 1964, p. 204). I feel that if he had developed this theme alongside his idea that we are all literalists most of our lives, he could have proposed a less extreme model of the distinction between attention and distraction. He would also have come closer to Winnicott, whom I discuss in the next section.
[35] Due to the space available, I have offered only one counter-example, namely, John Cage. However, his aleatoric work is so "theatrical" in Fried's terms that showing how this work is not determined by the world is exemplary for how theatrical works need not fail to achieve absorption.
[36] Compare this to my discussion of how interests are typically plural. For Winnicott, the generalization of interest breaks the dominance of a singular interest.

wards the negotiation of potentially overpowering external interests, play is crucial for how we relate to interests.

Famously, Winnicott claims that the transition from dependence to maturity requires the "good enough" mother. This is not the claim that it is sufficient to have a mother who does not quite "make the mark," but, rather, that it is necessary to have a mother who does not try to be wholly sufficient for the baby and understands—though not necessarily intellectually—the importance of weaning. The mother needs to be willing to "fail" in accordance with some absolute ideal of the satisfaction of the baby's needs. This is necessary if the older child and adult is to move beyond the assumed omnipotence of totally controlling her environment towards accepting her own lack of total control and imperfection.

The relevance of the "good enough" mother for our discussion is that play also requires coping with imperfection:

> What matters is the near-withdrawal state, akin to the *concentration* of older children and adults. The playing child inhabits an area that cannot be easily left, nor can it easily admit intrusions. (Winnicott 2005, p. 69)

The nuances "*near*-withdrawal," "cannot be *easily* left," and "nor... *easily* admit intrusions" reveal that the child's playing, while requiring that the child is not taken over by intrusions, is not perfectly sealed off from what is going on around her. Winnicott often worked therapeutically with mothers accompanied by their child. The therapist set up an area where the child could play apart while the adults conversed. The surrounding situation for the child's play is the main therapeutic activity, namely, the exchange between the mother-figure and the therapist.[37] On the face of things, the child's play is set up as a diversion so as to give the adults room to get on with their therapeutic work. However, Winnicott's method is much more complex, for he also aimed at a therapeutic exchange with the child. This required the child's absorption in play combined with the interruption of that play by the therapist. Tellingly, interruption of play is necessary for the efficacy of the child-therapist exchange. Rather than a picture of either isolated absorption or being simply prey to the intrusions of the world, Winnicott shows us how play can be productively combined with interruption by events arising outside it. We must assume that any successful therapeutic interruption opens up a vista beyond playful contemplation while not undermining the general mood of the latter so as to allow return to it. Consequently, play is not wholly detached from its worldly context and even requires interruption by it as long as the latter does

---

[37] Winnicott is careful to say that the mother-figure need not be the biological mother. In one case, it is clear that the "good enough mother" is the father (Winnicott 2005, pp. 24–25).

not demand a brutal shift in focus, as would be the case if some pressing interest suddenly took over the child's attention.

My understanding of this complex situation is that the interruption orchestrated by the therapist functions as a bridge between contemplation and engagement with the world and its interests. Playful contemplation ensures the child has a "safe space" where the effects of the outside world are held at bay, while the interruption ensures that the resistance to reality afforded by play is not merely a rejection of, and can initiate a shift within, reality. At least, this is what I, as a non-expert, find productive within the model Winnicott offers. In the terms of this paper, play allows the child a space where she is not determined by her normal concerns. Yet, while the orchestrated nature of the interruption is such that it does not undermine the beneficial effects of play, at the same time the interruption of play ensures there is no escape from reality. The child is encouraged—indeed, educated—to tolerate the intrusion of interests external to play while also developing strategies (in my terms, a capacity for negotiation) so as not to be overwhelmed by those interests.

Seeing the therapeutic exchange as constructing a bridge between contemplation and the everyday through the intermediary of playful interruption, is reinforced by Winnicott's account of the status of objects central to the play-space. The transitional object (TO)—such as a teddy or other toy—is a bridge between the original singular interest in the breast and the generalization of interests in later childhood and adulthood.[38] The TO "is outside the individual, but it is not the external world" (Winnicott 2005, p. 69). Winnicott makes it clear that the TO operates as a "potential space between": "the child gathers objects or phenomena from external reality and uses these in the service of some sample derived from inner or personal reality... and lives with this sample in a chosen setting of fragments from external reality" (Winnicott 2005, p. 69). In play something from the external world is taken up in such a way that it serves the needs of the inner world. But the "transitional object" is still at some level part of the real world and needs to remain so in order to fulfil the needs of the inner world. Thus, the child "invests chosen external phenomena with dream meaning and feeling" (Winnicott 2005, p. 69). In order to qualify as transitional, the toy needs to be both real and not real at the same time, otherwise it could not afford the transition between subject and world which is its designated role. The way in which worldly objects are transformed within play allows elements of reality to occupy a liminal space where they are neither determined by their normal use nor merely interior.

---

[38] "In health, however, there is a gradual extension of range of interest, and eventually the extended range is maintained, even when depressive anxiety is near." (Winnicott 2005, p. 6)

More specifically, the TO must be both inside and outside the world; otherwise, it could not contribute to the transition from dependence to maturity aimed at in the therapeutic exchange between therapist and child.

Winnicott's model of play and the Transitional Object highlights an in-between zone, a relation between interiority and exteriority, that neither achieves pure absorption nor is theatrically lost in the world. It is necessary that something from the world can be taken up within playing, and yet is neither determining for play nor negated as part of the world. Winnicott's playing is a space where the world is temporarily—i.e., temporally—held back but not denied and only thus can it operate as transitional in the development from omnipotence to reality. Winnicott's subtle and complex account converges with my thesis: just as contemplation is capable not only of tolerating but of negotiating interruptions, aesthetic judgement is capable not only of coexisting with but of negotiating interests.

6 Aesthetic Judgement in Relation to the World: Playful Orientation

In § 3, I outlined how Kant's idea of playfulness opens up the possibility of an alternative version of disinterestedness that not only escapes determination by but negotiates—rather than excludes—interests. In discussing Fried and Winnicott, we have discovered not only parallels with the two versions of disinterestedness discussed in §§ 2 and 3, respectively, but also two very different perspectives on the relation between contemplation and the surrounding world. I will now argue that Kant's broader account of aesthetic judgement implies a way of making sense of the world compatible with my alternative version of disinterestedness as a playful negotiation of interests and not with the official version.

For Fried absorption requires withdrawal to an inwardness "no longer engaged with the world" (Fried 1980, p. 230). It follows that absorption requires the exclusion of interests arising in the world. Correlatively, Kant's official position in insisting that aesthetic judgement withdraws from interests implies withdrawal from the world. For Kant, desiring implies a relation to the world. Wanting something appetitively entails I have an interest in whether or not it exists in the empirical world (KU: 205–207). Moral interests also aim to bring about something within the empirical world. Certainly, moral principle gives rise to an interest and not vice versa. However, moral interest seeks to exercise a principle in the "real" world, that is, within the dynamic relations among objects, events, and persons.[39] This is why in claiming that the good gives rise to an interest, Kant says I have "a liking for the existence of an object or action" (KU: 207). Consequently, if the distinctiveness of aesthetic pleasure requires that we stand in no relation whatsoever to interests, it follows that we must withdraw from the world within which interests arise.

In contrast both to Fried and to Kant's official position, I will show that Kant's broader account of aesthetic judgement neither requires nor permits that a stage curtain is drawn down so as to shut out the world. In this respect, Kant converges with Winnicott, for whom playful contemplation does not entail total isolation from the world and even requires a degree of interruption by it.

There are various ways in which Kant shows that he does not exclude the world from aesthetic judgement. I mentioned above that aesthetic judgement is a bridge between understanding, the faculty that makes possible the determination of objects within empirical experience, and reason, which determines our actions in respect of moral principles. As both cognition and, as I have just shown, morality imply a relation to the world, it is difficult to see how the bridge between them could not do so, even if only indirectly. I have also argued elsewhere that aesthetic judgement is subjective in the precise sense that it concerns the subject's reflection on the *relation* between subject and the world of objects (Hughes 2007). In this section, I take up Kant's claim that without the principle of aesthetic judgement, "the understanding could not find its way about in nature" (KU: 193).[40] I will draw out how this situates aesthetic judgement in relation to the world and has implications for the relation between disinterestedness and interests.

The claim that the principle governing aesthetic judgement helps understanding find its way about in nature—that is, the empirical world—suggests that aesthetic judgements contribute to making sense of the world in some way or other. We saw in § 3 that aesthetic judgement is compatible with the possibility of rule-following. I propose that "orientation" captures an exploratory sense-making that does not rely on an overarching principle operating as an already-established foundation. But orientation is also not wrapped up in the world as it makes possible exploration of the world with a view to discovering principles or rules not

---

39 This is the sense in which I use "world" throughout this discussion.
40 Pluhar's translation of "ohne welche sich der Verstand in sie nicht finden könnte." "sie" refers to "die Natur." This claim arises in the Introduction to the *Critique of Judgement* where Kant specifies he is referring to "the principle of a formal purposiveness of nature, in terms of its particular (empirical) laws, for our cognitive power" which judgement is dependent on in its "reflection on nature" (KU: 193). In short, the *principle* grounding aesthetic judgement is required for the application of understanding in respect of the range of empirical laws of nature. I will not analyze this extremely important and complex claim here, as I have already done so elsewhere (Hughes 2006).

given by it. An exploration of both particulars and principles allows patterns to emerge, opening up the world through an ongoing sense-making.

Aesthetic judgement cannot make sense of the world as a totality because the principle of reflective judgement is strictly indeterminate and can only ascend from singular phenomena to a universal (KU: 179). However, aesthetic judgement exhibits the possibility of sense-making in general. Insofar as a harmony between mind and world is exhibited in *this* case where the object is deemed beautiful, it is at least possible that the world will make sense more generally (Hughes 2007, pp. 277–310). For the singular instance to offer this promise for experience in general, it is crucial that the beautiful thing is contingent (KU: 191).[41] A playful relation is "found" (*angetroffen wird*) between the mental faculties and "a *given* representation (*eine gegebene Vorstellung*)" (KU: 217, my emphasis). We are "prompted (*Anlaß*)" by something that leads us into this mental state (KU: 219). In other words, we have to wait until we find something beautiful and cannot judge it so just by willing or thinking it so.[42] The orientation proposed here requires a capacity for discovery combined with receptivity. Aesthetic judgement gives understanding a foothold within empirical nature by showing that the mind's transcendental structures not only in principle, but also in practice, can make sense of a singular contingently given thing. Hence, in aesthetic judgement we are not cut off from the world: we explore the world as to its *possible* comprehensibility and coherence, which is indeterminately demonstrated in this particular and actual instance. This is true both of our aesthetic response to nature—for instance, in our appreciation of a beautiful landscape—and of works of art. In both cases, beauty shows up the mind's capacity for taking in and making sense of a singular given in the world. While an instance of natural beauty exhibits the way in which the mind is capable of making sense of something given in the natural world, a beautiful artwork shows up the mind's capacity for making sense through intervening in the cultural world.

Aesthetic judgement is neither merely "inside" nor "outside" the world; neither determined by the world and the interests pervasive in it nor an outright escape from or rejection of them. Aesthetic play experiments on and expands the world, whether by seeing it differently or by making it different. All aesthetic phenomena worthy of being called "beautiful" achieve this through invoking a playful-

---

[41] We encounter the beauty of the object as contingent—we did not define it as beautiful in advance—yet, once we apprehend it as displaying characteristics qualifying as beautiful, the pleasure we take in it is necessary (KU: 236).
[42] Certainly, it is the *way* in which something affects us that is crucial in giving rise to a play of the faculties. But while the existence of an object is not sufficient for aesthetic judgement, it is necessary that something affects us appropriately. Hughes 2023.

ness of mind.⁴³ For Kant, the playfulness of mind *is* a playful relation to an object and its surrounding world (KU: 217).⁴⁴

How does this account of playful orientation in relation to the world reinforce my account of the negotiation—rather than the exclusion—of interests? If aesthetic judgement operates playfully in relation to the world, then it is also capable of operating playfully in relation to interests arising within that world. The capacity to reflect aesthetically allows us to hold off as merely possible—yet not simply deny—the interests that often take us over, that is, when they determine our views and actions. Playful negotiation of interests requires an orientation to the world open to different perspectives: an orientation among a range of potential orientations.

Kant's more systematic account of aesthetic judgement, thus, does not replace the world with a *mise en scène* behind a theater curtain where interests have been wholly overcome, but no more does it passively copy its sense from the world. Aesthetic judgement opens up the world by exploring singularities while being directed towards a possible—but only possible—determination under a rule or principle. As a form of playful orientation, aesthetic judgement makes possible an opening up of our relation to rules and interests. As such, aesthetic judgement is a necessary—though not sufficient—condition of open and rational engagement with the world *as an ongoing negotiation*. I will explore this claim further in my Conclusion.

7 Conclusion: Aesthetic Disinterestedness as Preparatory for the Rational Evaluation of Interests

If I am right that interests are pervasive and yet they do not destroy the possibility of disinterestedness, then I think we need to re-evaluate whether proposing an ideal of the absolute exclusion of interests is the best way of ensuring they do not undermine our aesthetic judgements. If it is not possible to eliminate interests entirely, adopting such an ideal may be in bad faith even if our intentions are good. Indeed, aiming to exclude interests—even ideally—could undermine our capacity for effectively dealing with them. Recognition of the role played by interests is a

---

43 See § 3 above.
44 See Hughes 2010, pp. 149–153 on the idea of a dual harmony.

first step to ensuring they do not inappropriately take over our aesthetic judgements.

I believe this may have broader ramifications for the role of interests within our lives. My alternative account of disinterestedness suggests that it is at least in principle possible to have interests and yet not be determined by them. This goes further than merely coping with interests. Just as the player of a game can improvise around rules, we can not only break free from determination by our interests but also hold up those interests as merely possibly determining even though we cannot entirely break free from having them. Consequently, just because we have interests is not to say that interests wholly determine who we are and what we do. If this is true for aesthetic judgements then it may also be true that, more generally, we can negotiate interests such that they are not determining. While it would not be possible to make this further argument adequately here, the key step for preparing the transition between aesthetic disinterestedness and the negotiation of interests more broadly would be to explain how the capacity for aesthetic judgement contributes to the assessment of interests.

Certainly, affirming or rejecting interests requires more than playful negotiation. Assessment of interests requires the application of principles as well as consideration of various empirical factors. However, as a prior condition of rational evaluation of our relation to interests—deciding whether they should be maintained or rejected—it is necessary that an interest is acknowledged at the same time as treated *so as not to* already determine our judgements and actions, that is, it must be negotiated as possible and not simply actual or indeed necessary. The alternative account of disinterestedness I have proposed shows that this conjunction is possible.

Kant makes clear that some interests are necessary and, indeed, obligatory, for instance our interest in the good. Other non-moral interests, I would add, are also necessary, for instance, the fulfilling of needs conducive to survival and social solidarity. Aesthetic disinterestedness, as I have presented it, is an open and reflective frame of mind, allowing interests to be considered as possibilities rather than as already mandatory. Open-minded thinking is not, of course, restricted to aesthetic judgement. However, the *capacity* for the latter is a condition for loosening the ties of determination by interests as a prerequisite for open-minded assessment.

Kant associates judgement with a "broadened way of thinking [*Denkungsart*]" that allows us "to think from the standpoint of everyone else" (KU: 294–295). Crucially, he identifies aesthetic judgement with what is essential in judgement (KU: 193). Aesthetic judgement renders us capable of speaking with a "universal voice," that is, of thinking beyond individual interests (KU: 216). This is the reason why aesthetic judgement is quintessential for judgement in general for, without a universal voice, judgements would not be valid. It is through providing a condition of the possibility for open-minded thinking that our capacity for aesthetic judgement qualifies as a necessary element of reasoning in the broad sense of the term referring to "our cognitive power as a whole" (Pluhar 1987, p. xxxviii). Aesthetic judgement's specific contribution to the tripartite character of reason—as cognitive, moral, and aesthetic—is in thinking through particulars without a determining universal (KU: 167–168). Our capacity for aesthetic judgement exhibits *in principle* a general capacity for open-minded thinking that is, as yet, undetermined by the principles of reason or cognition. Consequently, aesthetic judgement's contribution to reason in general is distinct from—but also a complement to because preparatory for—determination under principles. This is why, for Kant, aesthetic judgement "opens up prospects advantageous to practical reason" (KU: 169).

The point I am making is this: our *capacity* to make disinterested aesthetic judgements is necessary for rationality in general. The capacity for aesthetic judgement makes possible *actual* aesthetic judgements. But it is not the case that specific aesthetic judgements are necessary for rationality, even though they can be educative (Schiller 1982, *passim*). It is the capacity for aesthetic judgement that renders interests non-determining in preparation for a decision as to whether or not they should be sustained. This capacity is exhibited in actual aesthetic judgements, which, consequently, are the expression and not the source of our capacity for disinterestedness. Certainly, this capacity has to be exercised in actual aesthetic judgements in order to qualify as such. However, it is the judgmental capacity that makes aesthetic judgements possible that is at work *throughout* our reasoning insofar as we are able to facilitate a degree of emergent determinacy, which is necessary for open-minded thinking.[45]

In case it may still be suspected I am proposing that in cognition and moral action we negotiate interests only by taking an aesthetic stance, let me reinforce that this is not my position. The relevance of aesthetic judgement for rationality in general is, firstly, that as a capacity for playful negotiation, it is *preparatory* for the evaluation of interests. Secondly, aesthetic judgements as expressions of that capacity are *exemplary* of the possibility of recognizing the role of interests in our lives without succumbing to determination by them. Importantly, the account of aesthetic judgement proposed here is not a complacent acceptance of the influence of interests. To aim at negotiating rather than being determined by interests is to adopt a standard of eternal vigilance which may be even more demanding than aiming at the goal of the absolute exclusion of interests, which could suggest that exclusion of interests is a state which we could achieve.

---

[45] This is related to my argument in Hughes 2006 that the principle of purposiveness in general is exhibited in but not identical to aesthetic judgements.

I wish also to rebut another possible objection, the reverse of the one to which I have just responded. Just as I am not aestheticizing rationality, I am not denying the distinctiveness of aesthetic judgements. We are capable of focusing on an artwork—or some natural phenomenon—such that we achieve a level of concentration not subsumed by the interests of everyday life.[46] This is one of the wonders of how artworks and nature can absorb us as well as a benefit for our rationality in general. Nonetheless, the disinterested aesthetic judge can acknowledge interests—not only those presented as part of the content of the artwork but also their own—while freeing up those interests so she neither denies nor is overwhelmed by them. Disinterestedness as the playful negotiation of interests is an ongoing process or orientation rather than a pure state.[47] In this way, aesthetic judgement reveals our capacity for resisting the pathological condition of determination by interests, yet we need not resort to relying on the idea that interests can be wholly removed, which would amount to denial in danger of merely concealing interests and thus qualifying as another form of pathology.

Abbreviations

Apart from the *Critique of Pure Reason*, all references to Kant's works are to Kant's *Gesammelte Schriften, Ausgabe der Preußischen Akademie der Wissenschaften* (Berlin: De Gruyter, 1902 ff.). References to the *Critique of Pure Reason* are to the standard A and B pagination of the first and second editions. Translations are from *The Cambridge Edition of the Works of Immanuel Kant*, Pluhar's translation of *Critique of Judgment*, or my own.

The following abbreviations of individual works are used:

KU	Kritik der Urteilskraft / *Critique of Judgment*
KrV	Kritik der reinen Vernunft / *Critique of Pure Reason*
V-Anth/Friedländer	Vorlesungen Wintersemester 1775/1776 Friedländer (AA 25) / *Anthropology Friedländer 1775/1776*

Literature

Adelung, Johann Christoph (1811): *Grammatisch-kritisches Wörterbuch der Hochdeutschen Mundart.* https://woerterbuchnetz.de/?sigle=Adelung#0, last accessed on Mar. 10, 2023.
Allison, Henry (2001): *Kant's Theory of Taste*. Cambridge: Cambridge University Press.

---

[46] This is especially marked when an artist is absorbed in creation.
[47] See Hughes 2007, pp. 154–155 for a discussion of judgement as process.

Baz, Avner (2005): "Kant's principle of purposiveness and the missing point of (aesthetic) Judgements." In: *Kantian Review* 10, pp. 1–32.
Bell, David (1992): "The Art of Judgment." In: Chadwick, Ruth F. and Cazeaux, Clive (Eds.): *Immanuel Kant: Critical Assessments*, Vol. IV. London: Routledge, pp. 26–27.
Berleant, Arnold (1994): "Beyond Disinterestedness." In: *British Journal of Aesthetics* 34. No. 3, pp. 242–254.
Cage, John (1973): *Silence*. Middletown: Wesleyan University Press.
Châtelet, Albert and Thuillier, Jacques (1964): *French Painting from Le Nairn to Fragonard*. James Emmons (Trans.). Geneva: Skira.
Diderot, Denis (1758, 1995): "Discours de la poésie dramatique." In: *Ecrits sur le théâtre volume 1 : le drame : Entretien sur Le Fils naturel (Dorval et moi) suivi de Discours sur la poésie dramatique*. Paris: Pocket.
Fricke, Christel (1990): *Kants Theorie des reinen Geschmacksurteils*. Berlin: De Gruyter.
Fried, Michael (1980): *Absorption and Theatricality: Painting and Beholder in the Age of Diderot*. Berkeley: University of California Press.
Fried, Michael (1998): *Art and Objecthood*. Chicago: University of Chicago Press.
Grimm, Jacob und Wilhelm (1838): *Deutsches Wörterbuch*. http://dwb.uni-trier.de, last accessed on Jan. 29, 2023.
Guyer, Paul (1978): "Disinterestedness and Desire in Kant's Aesthetics." In: *The Journal of Aesthetics and Art Criticism* 36. No. 4, pp. 449–460.
Guyer, Paul (1979): *Kant and the Claims of Taste*. Cambridge and London: Harvard University Press.
Hughes, Fiona (2006): "On Aesthetic Judgement and our Relation to Nature: Kant's Concept of Purposiveness." In: *Inquiry* 49. No. 6, pp. 547–572.
Hughes, Fiona (2007): *Kant's Aesthetic Epistemology: Form and World*. Edinburgh: Edinburgh University Press.
Hughes, Fiona (2010): *Readers' Guide to Kant's Critique of Aesthetic Judgement*. London and New York: continuum.
Hughes, Fiona (2023, forthcoming): "Analytic of the Beautiful." In: Baiasu, Sorin and Timmons, Mark (Eds.): *The Kantian Mind*. London: Routledge.
Kant, Immanuel (1899–): *Kants gesammelte Schriften*. Berlin: Royal Prussian Academy.
Kant, Immanuel (1980): *Critique of Pure Reason*. Norman Kemp Smith (Trans.). London: MacMillan
Kant, Immanuel (1987): *Critique of Judgement*. Werner Pluhar (Trans.). Indianapolis, Cambridge: Hackett.
Kant, Immanuel (2000): *Critique of the Power of Judgment*. Paul Guyer and Eric Matthews (Trans.). Cambridge: Cambridge University Press.
Kant, Immanuel (2007): *Critique of Pure Reason*. Paul Guyer and Allen W. Wood (Trans.). Cambridge: Cambridge University Press.
Kant, Immanuel (2012): *Lectures on Anthropology*. Allen W. Wood and Robert B. Louden (Eds.). Robert B. Clewis, R. B. Louden, G. Felicitas Munzel and Allen W. Wood (Trans.). Cambridge: Cambridge University Press.
Schiller, Friedrich (1982): *Letters on Aesthetic Education. In a Series of letters. English and German Facing*. Elisabeth M. Wilkinson and Leonard A. Willoughby (Eds.). Oxford: Clarendon Press.
Winnicott, Donald W. (2005): *Playing and Reality*. London: Routledge.

Lisa Schmalzried
Human Beauty, Attraction, and Disinterested Pleasure

Abstract: It is natural to describe experiences of human beauty as involving attraction. This attraction thesis presumably contracts Kant's thesis of disinterestedness. Therefore, I examine both theses and their compatibility. First, I will propose to analyze experiences of human beauty as experiences of amiability. Secondly, I will argue that amiability experiences are disinterested in a weak but not strong sense. My third point is that Kant defends strong disinterestedness. It follows from the assumption of the free play of our powers of cognition which is, for him, essential to explain the subjective-objective-hybridity of beauty judgments. Aesthetic dispositionalism provides another way to explain this hybridity, however. This explanation is not committed to the strong claim of disinterestedness. And it is compatible with the amiability thesis. So, one has no compelling reason to accept Kant's claim that all beauty experiences, including those of human beauty, need to be disinterested in a strong sense.

The thesis of disinterestedness is highly influential when it comes to the distinctive features of a beauty experience. According to this thesis, disinterestedness is one or even the characteristic feature of a beauty experience. This thesis can be traced back (inter alia) to the *Critique of the Power of Judgement*. Roughly sketched, Kant's idea is that we are pleased by an object's mere representation independently from its existence if we judge it as beautiful. Furthermore, our beauty experience does not give rise to an interest in the existence of the object. We only want to linger in the contemplation of the object's representation.

Kant elaborates the thesis of disinterestedness in §§ 1 to 5 while speaking about free beauty. In § 16, he introduces the difference between free and dependent beauty. Here, he also mentions the beauty of human beings for the first time. Human beauty is one of the paradigmatic examples of dependent beauty. Still, as I will argue below, Kant does not give up the thesis of disinterestedness concerning dependent beauty. This brings me to the topic of this paper: human beauty and disinterestedness. Should one agree with Kant that the experience of human beauty is also disinterested?

Doubts arise because it seems natural to connect human beauty with attractiveness. Just think about how we tend to react when meeting a beautiful person. Such a person does not just capture our attention; we feel drawn to her. The experience of human beauty seems to involve attraction. Let us call this the attraction thesis. But when I feel attracted to someone, I take a clear interest in the existence of this person. Her mere representation would not be enough.

So, Kant's thesis of disinterestedness and the thesis of attraction seem to conflict with each other. Should we follow Kant and accept that all beauty experiences have to be disinterested and that we are thus mistaken to describe our experience of human beauty as one involving attraction? Or does the thesis of attraction give us a reason to reject Kant's thesis of disinterestedness, at least concerning the experience of human beauty?

This paper proceeds in four steps to address these questions. In the first section, I will focus on the attraction thesis and elaborate on a modified version, the amiability thesis. I will show that Kant defends not only a weak claim but a strong claim of disinterestedness in the second section. Thirdly, I will argue that the amiability thesis is compatible with the weak but not with the strong claim of disinterestedness. Therefore, in the fourth section, I will examine whether one can and should defend the strong claim.

1 A Closer Look at the Attraction Thesis

Let us begin with the attraction thesis. According to this thesis, the experience of human beauty involves attraction. If we meet someone beautiful, we are typically pleased by seeing this person and feel drawn towards her. We want to get to know her and form a relationship with her. I assume this is a natural and obvious way to describe our experiences of human beauty. But not only how we typically react to human beauty supports the attraction thesis, but also our everyday language. We often do not differentiate between "human beauty" and "attractiveness" (Henss 1992, p. 253). For example, the writing assistant Grammarly suggests "attractiveness" as a synonym for "beauty." If we keep in mind that we judge someone as attractive only if we (or others) feel attracted to this person, equating "attractiveness" with "human "beauty" backs up the attraction thesis.

One might object that we can experience another human being as beautiful without feeling *sexually* attracted to her. Levinson (2011, pp. 197–199) reacts to this objection by distinguishing between judging and experiencing human beauty. Although we can judge another person as beautiful without feeling sexually attracted to her, we cannot non-sexually experience her beauty. This reply leads to two problems, however. First, it is unclear how one can judge another person as beautiful without experiencing her as beautiful. Levinson gives up what I consider a commonplace in aesthetics: beauty judgements are essentially experience-based (McMahon 2011, p. 53; Zangwill 2003, p. 68). We judge x as beautiful because and only if we experience x as beautiful. Secondly, Levinson must assume that we always experience human beauty in sexual terms, although there seem to be cases of non-sexual experiences of human beauty. I do not want to deny that we sometimes think that we non-sexually experienced someone as beautiful. Still, upon careful and honest self-reflection, we recognize that this experience had a sexual component. I doubt, however, that this is always the case. Sometimes, we experience someone as beautiful without feeling sexually attracted to this person. For example, as a heterosexual woman, I can experience another woman as beautiful, or as an adult, I can experience a child as beautiful.

But this concession does not mean we must abandon the attraction thesis. The objection rests on the mistake of equating attraction with sexual attraction. Although feeling sexually attracted is one way to feel attraction, it is not the only one. I have described an experience of attraction as an experience of being drawn towards someone. Attraction is more than mere pleasure; a desire or a wish comes into play. When feeling attracted towards someone, we wish to get to know this person and build or maintain a positive relationship with her, if possible. However, this relationship does not have to be sexual or romantic. There are other forms of positive close interpersonal relationships; just think of friendships. So, according to the attraction thesis, a wish for a relationship is part of an experience of human beauty. Still, it does not have to be a wish for a sexual or romantic relationship.

By saying that the experience of human beauty includes attraction, one is not committed to the stronger view that every experience of attraction is one of beauty in the case of human beings. To equate experiences of human beauty with experiences of attraction goes too far. Sometimes we feel attracted towards someone without wanting to call this person beautiful. But what makes an experience of attraction one of human beauty?

To answer this question, one might say that the threshold to call someone beautiful is much higher than the threshold to call someone attractive. Many people are (more or less) attractive, but few are truly beautiful. The intensity and duration of the pleasure and desire involved in the attraction experience might measure a person's attractiveness. So, one might suggest that an intense attraction experience qualifies as a beauty experience. But although the experience of human beauty is often intense, some beauty experiences are not intense in the just described sense. Furthermore, even some intense attraction experiences might not count as beauty experiences. So, there must be other differentiating features.

One might wonder whether the experience itself makes the difference or instead the features to which one responds in this experience. Whether one feels attracted to someone can depend on different aspects of the person in question. It can depend on sensual-perceptual characteristics, which determine how she looks, smells, or sounds, or on non-sensual-perceptual features like, for instance, her character traits or cognitive abilities. According to the sensory dependence thesis, beauty should depend (at least partly) on sensual-perceptual features (Schmalzried 2015; 2021, chap. 3.3). Consequently, only if one responds (in part) to sensual-perceptual features of a person's physical or expressive appearance, the resulting attraction experience might qualify as one of beauty.

The sensory dependence thesis is controversial, however. Especially when it comes to human beauty, there seems to be a good reason to reject it. In everyday life and the philosophical tradition, it is common to speak about inner beauty, referring to the beauty of a person's character, mind, or soul. But, as I argue elsewhere, the sensory dependence thesis should be defended regarding beauty (although not regarding all aesthetic properties) to differentiate beauty from other positive attributes (Schmalzried 2015; 2021, chap. 3.3). If so, one can analyze our way of speaking about "inner beauty" as a mere metaphor. In this article, let us accept the sensory dependence thesis. Is this thesis sufficient to distinguish experiences of attraction that qualify as beauty experiences from those that do not?

To anticipate the answer, accepting the sensory dependence thesis is still not enough. In the case of mere subjective experiences of attraction, when we reflect upon why we experience the person in question as attractive, we believe that we feel attracted to this person due to mere personal preferences or situational circumstances. At least if we reflect upon it, we do not think that others should react as we do to the person in question. We do not believe that the person's appearance generally merits such an experience. If we think about how we react when another person disagrees with us that the person in question is attractive, it also shows that we do not believe that she merits such an experience. Presumably, we would not be willing to quarrel with her. If our attraction experience is a mere subjective experience, we are content to say that we feel attracted to the person in question and if others do not feel the same, so may it be.

But besides these cases, some experiences of attraction are presumably universalizable. Here, we believe that others should also feel attracted because we think that we feel attraction not because of mere situational circumstances or personal preferences but rather because of preferences shared by all human beings under the right circumstances. So, these experiences are more complex than the purely subjective experiences of attraction: we feel pleasure, desire/wish to build and sustain a positive relationship with this person, and believe (at least upon reflection) that others should share this experience. Such experiences can be called experiences of amiability ("Liebenswürdigkeit") and not just mere experiences of attraction. The belief of universalizability thus marks the crucial difference between "normal" experiences of attraction and those which count as beauty experiences. In the case of beauty experiences, we not only experience a person as attractive but as *worthy of attraction*.

Including the belief of universalizability can capture an essential feature of beauty judgements in general. They claim universal validity and are, in this respect, (semantically) objective. At the same time, they are based on a subjective experience and are thus (epistemically) subjective (Schmalzried 2021, chap. II). I follow Kant (KU §8, §§ 32–33) and Hume (1985, pp. 230–231), who consider subjective-objective-hybridity one of the central features of beauty judgements. In § 4.3, I will come back to possible explanations of how this can be the case and whether we can also make sense of this hybridity when we analyze the experience of human beauty as one of amiability.

These elaborations show how one can incorporate two features often defended regarding beauty judgements, namely, their sensory dependence and their claim to universal validity, into the attraction thesis without giving up its main idea. Moreover, the experience of amiability involves pleasure and contains a conative component. But here, one might object that not all our experiences of human beauty include such a conative element. Sometimes we just want to contemplate a person's representation without wishing to get to know her or even form a relationship with her. We just want to look at her and take pleasure in her appearance. I must confess that I think that in most cases in which we see a person face to face (not just a picture, painting, or a tape of her) and see her as a person, our appetitive faculty is active. However, I cannot and do not want to rule out that some experiences of human beauty are mere contemplative experiences. How is this admission compatible with the analysis of the experience of human beauty as one of amiability?

To incorporate this idea, we must add another point: it might be possible that I experience someone as beautiful without any desire for a relationship. However, to count as a beauty experience, a belief in universalizability must come into play. Even if I do not experience a wish to get to know or to form or maintain a relationship with the person I experience as beautiful, I should believe that such a wish is a justified reaction to this person for others. So, even though I might not experience the entire attraction aspect of my beauty experience, I should indirectly experience it by thinking that others would justifiably feel attracted to the person in question.

This section has aimed to have a closer look at the attraction thesis. Although this thesis has some intuitive plausibility, it needs to be modified to count as a compelling analysis of the experience of human beauty. I have suggested analyzing the experience of human beauty as one of amiability: if we experience a person as beautiful, we are pleased by her appearance, desire/wish to build and sustain a positive relationship with her, and believe (at least upon reflection) that others should share this experience.

2 A Closer Look at Kant's Disinterestedness Thesis

Let us turn to the disinterestedness thesis. What does it mean to say that the aesthetic experience is disinterested? I do not want to answer this question in general but rather focus on Kant's account. In § 1 of the *Critique of the Power of Judgement*, Kant claims that beauty judgements are aesthetic. He thereby stresses that they are essentially experience-based—more precisely, pleasure-based.

The next question is what kind of experience the beauty experience is. According to Kant, it is an experience of disinterested pleasure: "The satisfaction that determines the judgement of taste is without any interest." (KU: 204) This characterization, in turn, leads to the question of what Kant means by "without any interest."

In § 2, Kant defines interest as "the satisfaction that we combine with the representation of the existence of an object." (KU: 204) This definition identifies interest with a certain kind of satisfaction. However, in the paragraph's heading, it sounds as if "without any interest" is an attribute of satisfaction and not itself a satisfaction (Zangwill 1992, p. 149). In his moral philosophical writings, Kant also does not equate interest with a certain kind of satisfaction but defines interest as a determining cause of the will. Interest is that "by which reason becomes practical, i.e. a cause that determines the will." (GMS: 459 fn., see also KpV: 79) To solve this potential tension between these two different definitions of interest, § 4 is helpful: "But to will something and to have satisfaction in its existence, i.e., to take an interest in it, are identical." (KU: 209) If one thus takes an interest in the existence of an object and then imagines that this object exists, one will be pleased (Fricke 1990, p. 16; Guyer 1997, p. 164). Therefore, Kant can identify an interest with a kind of satisfaction, but the more helpful definition is that an interest is a determining cause of the will.

Kant further distinguishes two kinds of interest: the interest of the senses and the interest of reason (MS: 212–213; GMS: 459–460 fn.). The interest of the senses rests on an inclination. Only when reason accepts an inclination, that is, makes it the determining cause of the will, does it transform it into an interest. The interest of the senses is always private because even if all human beings shared the same interest, this would be by mere chance. But human beings, as rational beings, also have a necessarily shared interest, namely, the pure interest of reason (GMS:

401 fn.). The interest of reason is based on the respect for the moral law, which is "self-wrought by a rational concept." (GMS: 401 fn.) Thereby, the interest of reason is the moral interest or, as Kant says: "All moral interest, so called, consists solely in respect for the law." (GMS: 401 fn.)

What does it mean that satisfaction in the beautiful is without any interest? First, satisfaction in the beautiful is not grounded in any interest in the object's existence. We are not pleased because we have taken an interest in the object's existence, wanted it to exist, and this wish has then been fulfilled. Put differently, the mere representation of the object evokes pleasure. Contra-factually formulated, it would also please if the object would not exist. Thus, it is free. In § 5, Kant states this most clearly by saying: "[...] for no interest, neither that of the senses nor that of reason, extorts approval." (KU: 2010) Let us call this thesis the weak claim of disinterestedness:

> **WCD:** An interest in the existence of an object does not ground the satisfaction in the beautiful.

But in § 5, Kant also points to a stronger thesis of disinterestedness when he writes: "All interest presupposes a need or produces one; [...]." (KU: 210) In a footnote to § 2, he also mentions this idea: "But the pure judgement of taste does not in itself even ground any interest." (KU: 205) These remarks suggest that Kant defends a stronger claim of disinterestedness:

> **SCD:** Neither does an interest in the existence of an object ground the satisfaction in the beautiful, nor does the satisfaction in the beautiful ground such an interest.

Kant's remarks about practical pleasure in *The Metaphysics of Morals* support this interpretation (MS: 212). Practical pleasure is either grounded in or grounds a desire. If one desires an object, one takes an interest in its existence. Thus, practical pleasure is interested (Fricke 1990, p. 16). Disinterested pleasure—Kant speaks of "contemplative pleasure" (MS: 212)—is neither grounded in nor does it ground an interest in the (continued) existence of the object.

To sum up the discussion so far, when Kant characterizes the satisfaction in the beautiful as disinterested, he focuses on the causes and effects of this kind of pleasure (Guyer 1978, p. 456; 1997, p. 152; Vandenabeele 2001, p. 706). He denies that any interest causes pleasure in the beautiful and that this pleasure gives rise to any interest. As interests are determining causes of the will, no connections to action exist. Therefore, it is all about the contemplation of the representation of the object.

3 Compatibility of the Amiability Thesis and the Disinterestedness Thesis

After modifying the attraction thesis into the amiability thesis and distinguishing between Kant's weak and strong disinterestedness thesis, the compatibility question arises again. Let us start with whether the amiability thesis is compatible with WCD. At first glance, the answer seems to be a clear no. One might say whether I feel attracted to someone depends on mere personal interest. But the experience of amiability contains, or upon reflection, gives rise to, a belief of universalizability. So far, of course, I have not explained how this can be. It could be the case that the belief of universalizability connected with the experience of amiability is ill-grounded. However, the fact that there are experiences of amiability at least gives a prima facie reason to think that mere personal interests do not ground these experiences.

Unlike the interest of the senses, all rational beings share the moral interest. This interest might ground the experience of amiability, one might consider. If so, the experience of amiability would have to be the expression that we are pleased that a good will exists. But if we saw that a person had a good will, we would have to react with respect. However, the experience of amiability is not the same kind of feeling as respect for the moral law. Furthermore, the experience of amiability is a reaction to a person's empirically accessible appearance. But by empirical observation, we can never know that a good will exists or that any action whose maxim is universalizable is done out of respect (GMS: 407). Hence one cannot consider the experience of amiability as an expression of the satisfaction of the moral interest.

One might concede to this and still wonder whether one does not see signs of a good will reflected in a person's outward appearance, which is why seeing this person satisfies a moral interest. When Kant speaks about the ideal of beauty, he claims that the aesthetic normal idea, the representation of the average human being, needs to be supplemented with "the visible expression of moral ideas, which inwardly govern human beings." (KU: 235) Put differently, one needs to see signs of good moral character in the gestures and facial expressions. Therefore, we take a great interest in the ideal of beauty (KU: 236). These remarks might illustrate how an appearance can satisfy the moral interest.

One might object that the pleasure in the ideal of beauty is not grounded in the satisfaction of a moral interest. The ideal is one of dependent beauty, and, as I will argue below, the pleasure still rests on the free play of our cognitive faculties. So, the ideal of beauty may later ground a moral interest but not rest on such. But even if we leave this point aside, I have not shown that expressive features that we can see as visible signs of moral character are the *only* relevant features to elicit an experience of amiability. It still could be possible to experience a human being as amiable whose appearance neither displays any signs of a moral nor an immoral character. So, it is implausible to explain the experience of amiability as the result of the satisfaction of the moral interest.

Furthermore, Kant starts a thought experiment in § 2: would a palace also please if it would not exist? Answering this question with yes suggests that the pleasure does not rest on an interest in its existence. The mere representation pleases independently of whether the palace exists or not. Now, if we think of an experience of amiability, we can think about whether we would have had the same experience even if the person in question would not exist. One might say that it is difficult to say whether this is the case, but fortunately (hyperrealist) paintings or animations of human beings might be an easy test case. I assume that, also in such cases, we could react with an experience of amiability. So, although we do not yet understand how this can be the case, it seems as if the experience of amiability can count as disinterested in a weak sense.

Let us turn to the second question: Can we also consider the experience of amiability to be disinterested in a strong sense (SCD)? This question is easier to answer. I have argued that the experience of amiability typically contains a desire to form or maintain a relationship with the person in question. This desire leads to an interest in the existence of the person. Otherwise, one could not be in a relationship with her. So, the experience of amiability can and does typically ground an interest in a person's existence. It is thus incompatible with SCD, according to which *no* experience of human beauty grounds such an interest.

The thesis of amiability is thus compatible with WCD but not with SCD. So, should one defend the thesis of amiability and give up SCD or vice versa? In the following section, I will explore why (according to Kant) one should accept SCD. If one finds good reasons for SCD, this brings the thesis of amiability into distress.

4 The Strong Claim of Disinterestedness Questioned

Kant writes towards the end of § 2: "Everyone must admit that a judgement about beauty in which there is mixed the least interest is very partial and not a pure judgement of taste." (KU: 205) This passage sounds as if he considered the thesis of disinterestedness to be valid and widely accepted, as if hardly anyone would seriously dispute it. Fricke (1990, p. 21) speculates that Kant may sum up a widespread opinion of his times. Kant is indeed not the first one to speak of aesthetic disinterestedness. The debate about aesthetic disinterestedness originates in 18th-

century Anglo-Saxon thought (Stolnitz 1961; Townsend 1987; Rind 2002b). But if one looks closer at Kant's predecessors, such as Shaftesbury, Hutcheson, or Hume, one sees that these authors only or mainly defend WCD (Schmalzried 2021, pp. 129–133). So, if Kant thinks that his claim of disinterestedness has intuitive plausibility because his predecessors accepted it, this will only support WCD.

His plausibility assessment in § 2 may indeed only refer to WCD because SCD is introduced later in the text, namely, in the footnote to § 2 (KU: 205 fn.) and in § 5 in the main text (KU: 210). And even if Kant also speaks about SCD, one has reason to challenge his assessment. For example, Guyer (1978, p. 449) and Crawford (1974, pp. 51–54) agree that WCD is intuitively plausible but deny that the same is true for SCD. And especially when one thinks about human beauty, one has reason to question SCD's immediate plausibility. At least a proponent of the amiability thesis would say that it begs the question of insisting on SCD's plausibility. So, further argument is needed to support SCD.

4.1 The Argument from Exclusion

As another look at the *Critique of the Power of Judgement* shows, Kant himself regards the thesis of disinterestedness as requiring justification: "We can find no better way of elucidating this proposition, however, which is of the utmost importance, than by contrasting to the pure disinterested satisfaction in the judgement of taste that which is combined with interest, especially if we can be certain that there are not more kinds of interest than those that are to be mentioned now." (KU: 205) Kant here suggests an argument for SCD (Crawford 1974, p. 42.): pleasure in the beautiful is different from pleasure in the agreeable and in the morally good. The pleasures in the agreeable and morally good exhaust all possibilities of how satisfaction and interest can relate to each other. Therefore, pleasure in the beautiful must be strongly disinterested. Otherwise, one could not distinguish between these three kinds of pleasure.

So, the first question is how pleasure in the agreeable and the good are interested. In § 3, Kant defines: "**The agreeable is that which pleases the senses in sensation.**" (KU: 205) As an interest is either an inclination accepted by reason or brought about by a concept of reason, reason needs to come into play. So, no interest grounds the satisfaction in the agreeable (Vandenabeele 2001, p. 708). But still, pleasure in the agreeable is interested insofar as it can establish an interest. Pleasure in the agreeable can become an inclination, which, in turn, can become an interest. Pleasure in the agreeable thus can, although it does not have to give rise to an interest.

Satisfaction in the good is interested in different ways depending on what kind of good it is. Pleasure in the morally good is the respect for the moral law. Respect for the moral law necessarily grounds an interest in the existence of the morally good. In the case of pleasure in the useful, pleasure precedes the interest: the pleasure of the senses can become an inclination, and the latter, in turn, can become an interest. As we have experienced something as pleasant, we may become interested in its existence. However, if we are interested in the existence of an object—either in itself or as a means to an end—this interest is why the existence of this object is pleasing. We are pleased with its existence because we wanted it to exist. Thus, pleasure in the useful can be the effect of a preexisting interest.

The decisive question is whether these ways of relating pleasure to an interest exhaust all possibilities. Let us begin with the question of how an interest might ground pleasure. Three options exist: pleasure might be based (1) on a private interest, (2) on a non-private, shared interest, or (3) on no interest at all. The first option describes the case of pleasure in the useful. The second might be the case of the morally good. However, respect for the moral law does not emerge from satisfaction of the moral interest. It is the other way around. So, pleasure in the beautiful might rest on a non-private aesthetic interest. Kant only distinguishes between the interest of the senses and that of reason, though, so he does not consider this possibility. So, pleasure in the beautiful must be disinterested as it is not grounded on an interest of the senses or of reason.

Let us now turn to the question of grounding an interest. Once again, three options exist: pleasure (1) optionally gives rise to an interest, (2) necessarily does so, or (3) does not ground one at all. The first option is taken by the agreeable and the second by the morally good. Therefore, the pleasure in the beautiful also needs to be disinterested in this sense.

However, there might be another level of differentiation. When Kant speaks about the interest evoked by pleasure in the agreeable, he says that it "exists a desire for objects of the same sort." (KU: 207) We thus desire certain kinds of objects to exist. We not only wish that a specific piece of chocolate exists, but that chocolate exists. Thought ahead, there also might be an interest in the existence of just *one specific object* (Allison 2001, p. 91; Guyer 1997, pp. 157–158). The interest connected with the beauty experience might be precisely such a specific object-bound interest. To support this claim, one can point out that one cannot entirely decode beauty in terms of object-related features. We cannot deduce judgements of beauty from concepts (KU: 215). Otherwise, they could not be essentially experience-based. If one accepts this distinction, the pleasure in the beautiful might differ from the agreeable and the good. However, pleasure in the beautiful can give rise to an interest, namely, an interest in the existence of a *particular* object. So, one could distinguish beauty from the good and the agreeable, even without SCD.

Apart from this, one does not need to speak about (dis-)interestedness of the respective experiences to differentiate beauty judgements from those about the agreeable and the good, as § 7 illustrates. Judgements about the agreeable are purely subjective judgements. They are like beauty judgements; both are essentially experience-based and made non-inferentially. They differ from each other in that only beauty judgements claim universal validity. In this respect, judgements of taste resemble moral judgements. They differ from the latter because judgements about the good are not essentially experience-based, as there are criteria for the correctness of moral judgements.

One may be concerned that Kant derives the claim of universal validity from the disinterestedness of the pleasure in the beautiful in § 6. The central distinguishing feature between agreeableness and beauty judgements may thus still depend on the claim of disinterestedness. But to derive the universal validity claim, Kant must only defend WCD (Guyer 1978, p. 454; 1997, pp. 149–150). Moreover, whether one must further justify the claim that beauty judgements claim universal validity is questionable. § 7 sounds like a basic assumption that cannot be justified further (Guyer 1997, p. 150). Rejecting the claim to the general validity of beauty judgements seems downright ridiculous (KU: 212).

So, the beautiful can be distinguished from the agreeable, the useful, and the morally good, even if one does not defend SCD. One can differentiate satisfaction in the beautiful from other kinds of interested satisfaction if the former can produce an interest in the existence of one specific object but not in the existence of certain types of objects. Furthermore, the distinctive features between judgements of taste and those about the agreeable and the good are that they are essentially experience-based, thus not based on any determinate concepts, and still claim universal validity.

4.2 The Argument from the Free Play

So far, I have not touched upon an important question: how does pleasure in the beautiful arise? This question leads to § 9. Here, Kant speaks of the central explanatory moment of his theory: the free play of the powers of cognition, which is the "key to the critique of taste" (KU: 216).

In the case of a judgement of cognition, our imagination provides an object's representation and our understanding the determinate concept under which the representation is brought. In the case of the free play of the cognitive powers, this normal functioning breaks down. The powers of cognition are in motion and are in a harmonious play without subsuming the representation under a determinate concept, thus, leading to a judgement of cognition. Pleasure in the beautiful is pleasure in this free play of the powers of cognition. And our judgement of taste is based thereon. The free play explains how we can feel pleasure in the beautiful without any interest being the ground for this pleasure. WCD thus follows from the free play of the powers of cognition.

Does SCD also follow from the free play? Guyer (1978, p. 456; 1997, pp. 160–161) denies this. Based on Kant's definition of pleasure in § 10, we can say that when one experiences a pleasure, one has an interest that the pleasure will continue. We thus also have an interest that the pleasure in the beautiful continues. Consequently, we are also interested in the continuance of the free play. For this, the representation of an object must continue to be present. Therefore, we are interested that the object continues to exist as the source of the representation. This interest is an interest in the existence of precisely this object. Kant would thus have to allow that the pleasure in the beautiful gives rise to an interest in the existence of a specific object.

Yet, another consideration contradicts Guyer's argument. If the contemplation of an object triggers the free play and one takes an interest that this play continues, one has an interest that the representation does not disappear. However, the representation can exist or persist independently of the object's existence. Relevant for the free play is only the representation of the object and not its existence. In that way, SCD also emerges from the free play of our cognitive powers.

These considerations are also essential to show that SCD applies to dependent beauty. Kant develops SCD in the first sections of the "Analytic of the Beautiful." As it becomes apparent in § 16, he only speaks about free beauty in these paragraphs. So, SCD might only hold concerning free but not dependent beauty. For the context of this paper, this worry is important because—as already mentioned in the introduction—human beauty is one of the paradigmatic examples of dependent beauty. So, I must address whether SCD also refers to dependent beauty.

Kant introduces the distinction between free and dependent beauty in § 16: "There are two kinds of beauty: free beauty (*pulchritudo vaga*) or merely adherent beauty (*pulchritudo adhaerens*). The first presupposes no concept of what the object ought to be; the second does presuppose such a concept and the perfection of the object in accordance with it." (KU: 229) As I have argued elsewhere, an internal or positive interpretation of dependent beauty is the most promising (Schmalzried 2014; 2021, pp. 252–259). Such an interpretation claims that the concept of an object and its perfection in accordance with this concept is necessary (although not sufficient) for a judgement of dependent beauty. So, one could judge an object as only dependently beautiful but not freely beautiful. Nevertheless—and this is the most crucial point for the present discussion—also the pleasure in the dependently beautiful rests on a free play.

I suggest that Kant's later remarks on aesthetic ideas help understand dependent beauty judgements better (for a similar idea, Stecker 1987, p. 93). At the beginning of § 51, he states that beauty is an expression of aesthetic ideas (KU: 320). An aesthetic idea is a "representation of the imagination that occasions much thinking without it being possible for any determinate thought, i.e., concept, to be adequate to it." (KU: 320) If something expresses an aesthetic idea, our understanding tries to find a concept adequate to the aesthetic idea's representation. Still, it must fail because no concept can ever be adequate. This failure, however, is incomplete because the concept partly matches the representation of the aesthetic idea. Due to this partial fit, our understanding can still hope to find a determinate concept that is entirely adequate to the intuition of the aesthetic idea. Therefore, the failure is also not frustrating. Furthermore, a playful element comes into play because through free association, again and again, new concepts come to one's mind, are tested, and fail, but the quest nonetheless remains stimulating. Suppose one does not claim that this 'search-and-fail game' or free play of association is fully conscious. In that case, this interpretation, which Guyer (2006, pp. 165–166) labels as multicognitive, is compatible with how § 9 describes the free play of our powers of cognition as self-reinforcing, animating, and not involving a single determinate concept.

§ 51 continues by saying: "[…] in beautiful art this idea must be occasioned by a concept of the object." (KU: 320) This addition helps better understand the difference between free and dependent beauty because, in § 48, Kant has described the beauty of art as dependent beauty (KU: 311). Thus, in the case of dependent beauty, the free play might not start without a concept of what the object is supposed to be. One needs a concept of the object to see something in it, which brings a determinate thought, that is, a concept, to one's mind. Our understanding then unsuccessfully, but not frustratingly, tries to put the intuition under this concept, and the free play of our powers of cognition begins.

To sum up, according to the argument from the free play, SCD is a consequence of the idea that the pleasure in the beautiful rests on the free play of our powers of cognition. As the pleasure in free and dependent beauty rests on the free play of our powers of cognition, SCD holds for free and dependent beauty and human beauty as a paradigmatic example of dependent beauty. But stepping outside Kant's theoretical framework, one can ask why one should accept his thesis that the pleasure in the beautiful rests on the free play. This brings me to the next section.

4.3 The Argument from the Aesthetic Deduction

As just said, the argument from the free play builds on the assumption that pleasure in the beautiful rests on the free play of our powers of cognition. Thus, defending SCD based on the argument from the free play, one must further argue that the free play must be the basis for our beauty experience. But is this the case?

Kant refers to the free play of our powers of cognition to explain how judgements of taste can be essentially experience-based and, at the same time, claim universal validity. The free play is thus a presupposition for the success of his aesthetic deduction. In § 38, Kant presents this deduction. The broad outline goes as follows: empirical knowledge should be possible to avoid skepticism. Universally communicable empirical knowledge, that is, empirical judgements that rightly claim to be universally valid, should exist. Empirical knowledge is only possible if understanding and imagination are active, and the power of judgement subsumes a representation under a concept. If the power of judgement functions differently with every human being, the subsumption would always proceed differently, and empirical knowledge would be in danger. In the case of a judgement of taste, the given representation is not subsumed under a definite concept, though our powers of cognition are still active. Understanding and imagination are in a harmonious play. But as we know from the case of empirical judgements, our power of judgement must function the same for all human beings. This explains how a judgement of taste can claim universal validity.

The main objection against Kant's deduction points to a dilemma. The dilemma is that the deduction either leads to an absurdity (first horn) or fails (second horn) (Meerbote 1982, pp. 81–83; Guyer 1997, pp. 284–288; Allison 2001, p. 187; Rind 2002a, p. 20, p. 25). The absurdity follows from the assumption that "the subjective condition of the use of our power of judgement" is "that subjective element that one can presuppose in all human beings (as requisite for possible cognitions in general)" (KU: 290). If one accepts this claim, our powers of cognition seemingly are in free play whenever we make or could make an empirical judgement. Hence, we should or could judge everything as beautiful, which seems absurd. One should give up the just-mentioned problematic assumption to avoid the dilemma's first horn: the free play thus does (potentially) not accompany each empirical judgement. But then, the aesthetic functioning of our power of judgement could be different from its "normal" functioning without endangering empirical knowledge. And then the deduction fails. One might object that it is implausible that our power of judgement always works in the same way for all human beings in the realm of empirical cognition but not in the aesthetic sphere. The problem, however, is that we cannot rule this out precisely because it is difficult to prove that two people always make the same aesthetic judgements under the same conditions.

I cannot discuss different attempts to save the deduction in this article. Instead, let us ask whether one can explain the subjective-objective-hybridity of beauty judgements without relying on the free play of our powers of cognition. I suggest that there is indeed such an alternative explanation. The foundation for this explanation is a specific form of aesthetic dispositionalism. The basic idea of aesthetic dispositionalism is the following: x is beautiful if x possesses the disposition to evoke a beauty experience under conditions C (Pettit 1983; Bender 1987, p. 38; Wiggins 1987; Zemach 1997, Carroll 1999, p. 191).

Aesthetic dispensationalism can easily explain how judgements of beauty can claim universal validity. A beauty judgement is true if the object in question possesses the relevant disposition. Otherwise, the judgement is false. Thus, like any realist position, dispositional realism can resort to the correspondence-theoretic explanation of the claim of universal validity.

At first, aesthetic dispositionalism also seems to explain why beauty judgements are experience-based easily. When we perceive something under the appropriate conditions, we have a beauty experience based on which we make a beauty judgement. However, Ginsborg (1998, pp. 459–462) and Pettit (1983, p. 25) object that aesthetic dispositionalism has problems explaining why beauty judgements are *essentially* experience-based. If I know that someone else has experienced an object x as beautiful under conditions C, I can learn from her that x is beautiful. I do not need to have experienced x as beautiful myself.

However, aesthetic dispositionalism is compatible with the thesis that beauty judgements are essentially experience-based under the following presupposition: knowing whether someone has satisfied conditions C is not only challenging but impossible. This is impossible if C defy complete critical decoding, although we might know that some states belong to C. If this is so, one is never justified in adopting the beauty judgement of another person because one can never know that she fulfils C. If so, a beauty judgement can only rest on one's own experience. But then our beauty experience must assure us to a sufficient degree that we ourselves have fulfilled C. Seen in this light, the claim to universalizability is a self-reflexive part of an experience of beauty. This self-reflexive moment of the experience of beauty assures us that we have perceived x under C. The experience itself provides the degree of certainty that entitles us to make a beauty judgement (for a similar thought, see Ginsborg 1998, pp. 463–465).

Of course, I have only given the broad outlines of a theory of human beauty based on aesthetic dispositionalism. Hopefully, it suffices to see that one can explain how a beauty judgement can be essentially experience-based and still claim universal validity without relying on the free play of our powers of cognition.[1] Is this enough to give this explanation preference over Kant's explanation?

I think that it is if we consider that this paper's focus lies on human beauty. Aesthetic dispositionalism can incorporate the idea that our beauty experience is an experience one of amiability and is not committed to SCD. As elaborated in § 1, it is natural to see a close connection between the experience of human beauty and attraction. Considering how both often go hand in hand, this connection does not seem to be merely coincidental. Moreover, based on Kant's theory, it is difficult to understand how one can have a beauty experience and be attracted to the person in question simultaneously because our appetitive faculty is inactive when we experience beauty. All this speaks against the assumption that the experience of human beauty is disinterested in a strong sense.

5 Conclusion

It is natural to describe our experience of human beauty as one involving attraction. This attraction thesis seemingly contradicts Kant's assumption that beauty experiences need to be disinterested, a belief widely held in the aesthetic debate. Therefore, this paper has taken it upon itself to shed more light on the connection and (in)compatibility between attraction and disinterestedness concerning human beauty.

In the first section, I have proposed that by analyzing the experience of human beauty as one of amiability, one can do justice to two ideas often defended concerning beauty judgements, namely, their sensory dependence and their subjective-objective-hybridity. In the second section, I have argued that Kant claims that no interest in an object's existence grounds satisfaction in the beautiful (WCD). He further claims that it also does not ground such an interest (SCD). The thesis of amiability turned out to be compatible with WCD but not with SCD in the third section. The experience of amiability appears to be not grounded on any interest. Still, as it typically contains a desire for a relationship, it gives rise to an interest in a person's existence. The fourth section has explained this by referring to aesthetic dispositionalism. In this section, I have also considered different arguments for SCD. It has turned out that SCD follows if one accepts that the

---

[1] A Kantian might object that Kant's deduction is more promising because it is ontologically parsimonious. However, it is disputed whether Kant indeed is an aesthetic anti-realist. Kulenkampff (1990) und Ameriks (2003, p. 318), for example, suggests that also Kant defends aesthetic dispositionalism. Ameriks argues that this secures the success of the aesthetic deduction, which he locates in § 22.

satisfaction in the beautiful rests on the free play of our powers of cognition. At least when it comes to human beauty, one has no reason to suppose, however, that the experience of human beauty needs to rest on the free play of our powers of cognition. Hence, contrary to Kant, I conclude that the experience of human beauty can give rise to an interest in a person's existence.

Abbreviations

All references to Kant's works are to Kant's *Gesammelte Schriften, Ausgabe der Preußischen Akademie der Wissenschaften* (Berlin: De Gruyter, 1902 ff.). For the translations used, see the bibliography.

The following abbreviations of individual works are used:

GMS Grundlegung zur Metaphystik der Sitten / *Groundwork of the Metaphysics of Morals*
KU   Kritik der Urteilskraft / *Critique of the Power of Judgment*
KpV Kritik der praktischen Vernunft / *Critique of Practical Reason*
MS   Die Metaphysik der Sitten / *Metaphysics of Morals*

Literature

Allison, Henry (2001): *Kant's Theory of Taste*. Cambridge: Cambridge University Press.
Ameriks, Karl (2003): *Interpreting Kant's Critiques*. Oxford: Clarendon Press.
Bender, John (1987): "Supervenience and the Justification of Aesthetic Judgements." In: *The Journal of Aesthetics and Art Criticism* 46. No. 1, pp. 31–40.
Carroll, Noël (1999): *Philosophy of Art: A Contemporary Introduction*. New York: Routledge.
Crawford, Donald (1974): *Kant's Aesthetic Theory*. Madison: The University of Wisconsin Press.
Fricke, Christel (1990): *Kants Theorie des reinen Geschmacksurteils*. Berlin: De Gruyter.
Ginsborg, Hannah (1998): "Kant on the Subjectivity of Taste." In: Parret, Hermann (Ed.): *Kants Ästhetik/Kant's Aesthetics/L'esthétique de Kant*. Berlin and New York: De Gruyter, pp. 448–465.
Guyer, Paul (1978): "Disinterestedness and Desire in Kant's Aesthetics." In: *The Journal of Aesthetics and Art Criticism* 36. No. 4, pp. 449–460.
Guyer, Paul (1997): *Kant and the Claims of Taste*. Cambridge: Cambridge University Press.
Guyer, Paul (2006): "The Harmony of the Faculties Revisited." In: Kukla, Rebecca (Ed.): *Aesthetics and Cognition in Kant's Critical Philosophy*. Cambridge: Cambridge University Press, pp. 162–193.
Henss, Ronald (1992): "*Spieglein, Spieglein an der Wand ...*"—*Geschlecht, Alter und physische Attraktivität*. Weinheim: Psychologie Verlags Union.
Hume, David (1985): "Of the Standard of Taste." In: Miller, Eugene (Ed.): *Essays: Moral, Political, and Literary*. Indianapolis: Liberty Fund, pp. 226–249.
Kant, Immanuel (2000): *Critique of the Power of Judgement*. Paul Guyer (Ed.). Cambridge: Cambridge University Press.
Kant, Immanuel (2001): *Groundwork on the Metaphysics of Morals*. Mary Gregor and Jens Timmermann (Eds.). Cambridge: Cambridge University Press.

Kant, Immanuel (2009): *Die Metaphysik der Sitten.* Frankfurt am Main: Suhrkamp.
Kant, Immanuel (2015): *Critique of Practical Reason.* Mary Gregor (Ed.). Cambridge: Cambridge University Press.
Kulenkampff, Jens (1990): "The Objectivity of Taste: Hume and Kant." In: *Noûs* 24. No. 1, pp. 93–110.
Levinson, Jerrold (2011): "Beauty is Not One: The Irreducible Variety of Visual Beauty." In: Schellekens, Elisabeth and Goldie, Peter (Eds.): *The Aesthetic Mind: Philosophy and Psychology.* Oxford: Oxford University Press, pp. 190–207.
McMahon, Jennifer (2011): "Critical Aesthetic Realism." In: *Journal of Aesthetic Education* 45. No. 2, pp. 49–69.
Meerbote, Ralf (1982): "Reflection on Beauty." In: Cohen, Ted and Guyer, Paul (Eds.): *Essays in Kant's Aesthetics.* Chicago and London: University of Chicago Press, pp. 55–86.
Pettit, Philip (1983): "The Possibility of Aesthetic Realism." In: Schaper, Eva (Ed.): *Pleasure, Preference and Value: Studies in Philosophical Aesthetics.* Cambridge: Cambridge University Press, pp. 17–38.
Rind, Miles (2002a): "Can Kant's Deduction of Judgements of Taste be Saved?" In: *Archiv für Geschichte der Philosophie* 84. No. 1, pp. 20–45.
Rind, Miles (2002b): "The Concept of Disinterestedness in Eighteenth-Century British Aesthetics." In: *Journal of the History of Philosophy* 40. No. 1, pp. 67–87.
Schmalzried, Lisa (2014): "Kant on Human Beauty." In: *Proceedings of the European Society of Aesthetics* 6, pp. 328–343.
Schmalzried, Lisa (2015): "Beauty and the Sensory-Dependence-Thesis." In: *Proceedings of the European Society for Aesthetics* 7, pp. 439–463.
Schmalzried, Lisa (2021): *Menschliche Schönheit.* Münster: mentis.
Stecker, Robert (1987): "Free Beauty, Dependent Beauty, and Art." In: *Journal of Aesthetic Education* 21. No. 1, pp. 89–99.
Stolnitz, Jerome (1961): "On the Origins of 'Aesthetic Disinterestedness.'" In: *The Journal of Aesthetics and Art Criticism* 20. No. 2, pp. 131–143.
Townsend, Dabney (1987): "From Shaftesbury to Kant: The Development of the Concept of Aesthetic Experience." In: *Journal of the History of Ideas* 48. No. 2, pp. 287–305.
Vandenabeele, Bart (2001): "On the Notion of "Disinterestedness": Kant, Lyotard, and Schopenhauer." In: *Journal of the History of Ideas* 62. No. 4, pp. 705–720.
Wiggins, David (1987): "A Sensible Subjectivism." In: Wiggins, David: *Needs, Values, Truth: Essays in the Philosophy of Value.* Oxford: Oxford University Press, pp. 185–211.
Zangwill, Nick (1992): "Unkantian Notions of Disinterest." In: *British Journal of Aesthetics* 32. No. 2, pp. 149–152.
Zangwill, Nick (2003): "Aesthetic Realism 1." In: Levinson, Jerrold (Ed.): *The Oxford Handbook of Aesthetics.* Oxford: Oxford University Press, pp. 763–793.
Zemach, Eddy (1997): *Real Beauty.* Pennsylvania: The Pennsylvania State University Press.

(c) **Disinterest Critics**

Dominic McIver Lopes
Pleasure, Desire, and Beauty

Abstract: Pleasure is standardly conceived as a state that motivates. This chapter considers three accounts of disinterested pleasure as motivating. On one, it motivates strictly internal states because it is non-conceptual. On a second, it motivates strictly internal states because the link between motivating internal states and world-oriented acts has been inhibited. On the third, it motivates only contemplative acts. All three accounts are coherent. However, none of the three accounts of disinterested pleasure is an account of aesthetic pleasure, where aesthetic pleasure serves either to demarcate aesthetic values or to explain why facts about aesthetic value are reason-giving. The conclusion is that we have no reason to appeal to disinterested pleasure in aesthetics.

We (mostly) want what we like, and we (mostly) like what we want. Philosophers working on pleasure posit a close link between pleasure and motivation. Yet some philosophers working in aesthetics characterize aesthetic pleasure as disinterested. Whether or not the characterization conflicts with the posit obviously depends on how each is interpreted. Moreover, how the characterization is interpreted should reflect the role of pleasure in accounts of aesthetic value. This paper articulates three interpretations where the characterization and the posit are consistent. In the spirit of a volume bringing together Kantian and contemporary perspectives, two echo Kant and one brings in philosophical reflections on affective science. Since none of the three does a good job of shedding light on aesthetic value, we have no right to hold that aesthetic pleasure is disinterested.

1 Aesthetic Value and Pleasure

Pushing back on Jerome Stolnitz' (1961) tale of the origins of aesthetic disinterest, Miles Rind decries any use of "disinterest" that is "neither its ordinary one nor any well-specified technical sense, but which rather waltzes about indeterminately" (2002, p. 85). Two errors lead to waltzing. First, its being hard to pin down stems partly from carelessness about the noun it modifies. We have disinterested taste,

Acknowledgments: My thanks to Murat Aydede, Jonathan Ichikawa, Alex King, an anonymous referee, and the audience at the 2021 meeting of the Western Canadian Philosophical Association.

https://doi.org/10.1515/9783110727685-011

disinterested judgements, disinterested attention, disinterested experience, disinterested appreciation, disinterested contemplation, and a disinterested attitude. Stolnitz elides them, and a modifier as promiscuous as this is game for nominalization—as when Susan Sontag describes disinterestedness as anything that is "detached, restful, contemplative, emotionally free, beyond indignation and approval" (1966, p. 27). Second, disinterest waltzes when cut free of a well-bounded explanatory task. Rind documents how early modern philosophers did not expect their comments on disinterest to do any significant explanatory work. Shaftesbury, for example, hardly meant to shed much light on beauty or taste when he compared the love of god to the love of beauty, as disinterested in the ordinary sense, indifferent to narrow self-interest (Rind 2002, pp. 73–74; Kovach 1974; Shelley 2020; see also Levinson 1995 and Riggle 2016). Therefore, chastened by Rind's admonition against waltzing, the way to proceed is by defending a well-specified technical conception of a disinterested phenomenon as one that does some heavy lifting in explaining what needs explaining. With this in mind, theories of aesthetic pleasure model it as disinterested and thereby promise to shed light on aesthetic value (for other approaches see Parsons and Carlson 2008, Van der Berg 2019).

Philosophical work on aesthetic value largely assumes consensus on a number of points, five of which are relevant here.

First, aesthetic values are such features of items as their being elegant, glorious, richly textured, serene, and cheerful (Sibley 1959, Zangwill 1995, De Clercq 2002, Lopes 2018, Chapter 2). Euler's identity ($e^{i\pi} + 1 = 0$) is elegant, this sunset is glorious, walks around barrio La Boca in Buenos Aires are richly textured, Hariprasad Chaurasia's performance of a composition for the *bansuri* is serene, and the exhaust of the first-generation Mazda MX-5 emits a cheerful growl. Nothing is aesthetically good (equivalently, beautiful) unless it is aesthetically good (that is, beautiful) in some specific way. Being elegant stands to being beautiful in the relation of determinate to determinable (Lopes 2018, pp. 128–129).

Second, an item always has a given aesthetic value because it has various, other, non-aesthetic features. The "because" is non-causal and invokes metaphysical explanation or grounding (Sibley 1965, Benovsky 2012, Lopes 2018, Chapter 10). The sunset is glorious because the pink is saturated to the brink of redness, Chaurasia's performance is serene by dint of the *bansuri*'s timbre and Chaurasia's control of microtones, and barrio walks are richly textured in virtue of its color palette and its geometry of acute angles. We tune the exhaust to a cheerful growl only by endowing it with certain non-aesthetic features, we preserve its cheerful growl only by ensuring it continues to have those features, and we change its aesthetic value only by changing its sound.

Third, aesthetic values are not confined to art—they are to be found in nature, ideas and intellectual structures, and designed artifacts too. Just about any kind of item can bear aesthetic value, and there is no kind such that what it is to be a member of that kind fixes what it is to be aesthetically good (Thomson 2008). In particular, aesthetic value is not identical to artistic value, the value that items have qua works of art. The sunset and the Mazda MX-5 are not works of art. Some values that items have qua works of art are not aesthetic (Lopes 2014). Work on aesthetic value must not bias towards art, especially fine art from Euro cultures.[1]

Fourth, as the second point of consensus implies, philosophers nowadays accept aesthetic realism, the claim that there are aesthetic value facts (cf. Todd 2004). It is a fact that Euler's identity is elegant, and it is a fact that Chaurasia's performance is serene. Cutting across the consensus, there are debates about whether or not aesthetic value facts are response-constituted (for references see Lopes 2018, pp. 182 and 196). Facts about us are facts nonetheless.

Fifth, aesthetic value facts are normative aesthetic reasons. Some definitions help to render the concept of an aesthetic reason.

Normative aesthetic reasons are not aesthetic evaluations. Evaluations are states of mind that attribute values, and aesthetic evaluations attribute aesthetic values:

> a state is an aesthetic evaluation = the state is a mental representation of some item as having some aesthetic value.

Not all mental representations are beliefs. I believe that Euler's identity is elegant, I hear the cheerful growl of the exhaust note, and I thrill to the glory of the sunset. Aesthetic evaluations are packaged variously as beliefs, perceptual experiences, and affective responses. Some have truth conditions, and some have accuracy conditions. Some also have satisfaction conditions: I want one day to take a richly textured ramble around barrio La Boca. Aesthetic value facts are facts represented by true, accurate, or satisfied aesthetic evaluations.

Accordingly, normative aesthetic reasons merit or lend weight to aesthetic evaluations. The fact that Euler's identity is elegant lends weight to the proposition that I should judge it elegant, the fact that the exhaust note emits a cheerful growl merits my hearing its cheeriness, and the fact that the sunset is glorious lends weight to the proposition that I should thrill to its glory. Failing to judge, hear, or feel these things is failing to think as I have normative aesthetic reason to think.

At the same time, normative aesthetic reasons are practical reasons, facts that lend weight to what an agent should do. Equivalently, they merit the agent's acting. The fact that Chaurasia's performance is serene is reason for me to queue it up on

---

[1] "Euro" denotes Europe and its descendant cultures.

my playlist when the pandemic anxiety grows too intense. That is, it lends weight to the proposition that I should queue it up. Failing to do so is failing to do what I have normative aesthetic reason to do. By the same token, the fact that walks around the barrio are richly textured merits my visiting Buenos Aires once the pandemic is over. Failing to do so is failing to do what I have normative aesthetic reason to do.

In sum, aesthetic values are determinates of beauty that are grounded in other features of items (not only art works) and that figure in normative aesthetic reasons. These five points of consensus set the stage for crafting theories of aesthetic value. Assuming that theories answer questions, a theory of aesthetic value might address one or both of two questions.

One is a demarcation question: what makes some values specifically aesthetic values? Being elegant and glorious are aesthetic values of Euler's identity and the sunset. A flan's yumminess, the cleverness of a distinction, the speed of the gazelle, Màiri's courage, Ravi's record-breaking run, and the umbrella's sturdy construction are not aesthetic values. What do they lack that we find in all and only aesthetic values?

Another question concerns the normativity of aesthetic value. Suppose we know what demarcates aesthetic values from other values. Knowing that leaves it mysterious why aesthetic value facts are reasons that lend weight to normative claims about what we should think or do. Why do the facts that Euler's identity is elegant and the sunset is glorious favor that anyone should respond to them in certain ways? Why do the serenity of Chaurasia's performance and the rich texture of walks around the barrio merit queuing up the former and arranging a trip to the latter?

Having surveyed the common ground and raised the questions that call upon a theory of aesthetic value for an answer, we are ready to bring in pleasure to help supply the answer. For centuries, philosophers have tied aesthetic value to pleasure. Plato wrote in the *Greater Hippias* that "the beautiful is that which is pleasing through hearing and sight" (298a). Francis Hutcheson took it as axiomatic that "the ideas of beauty and harmony, like other sensible Ideas, are necessarily pleasant to us, as well as immediately so" (1738, §14). For Bernard Bolzano, "the beautiful must be an object the contemplation of which causes pleasure in all people whose cognitive faculties are sufficiently developed" (2023 [1843], §11). Mary Mothersill voices the contemporary consensus that "what we take to be beautiful pleases us" (1984, p. 342). Recall Rind's admonition, though. Thoughts such as these must be put to work.

Here is a true a biconditional.

> For any item, x, any value, V, and any agent, A, necessarily, x is V iff x's being V merits A's taking pleasure in x's being V.

Over on the righthand side, read "pleasure" broadly. Pleasure is not always sensual or sensory—to mark this, some prefer to talk of "finally valuable experiences." Even then, finally valuable experiences need not be perceptions or perceptual imaginings. The beauty of Euler's identity is not within the ken of the five senses or their imaginative counterparts. Moreover, the biconditional represents value facts as normative reasons. Meriting A's taking pleasure is equivalent to lending weight to the proposition that A should take pleasure.

Note that the biconditional is true for any positive value, V. Aaron's flan is yummy just when it merits our pleasure. Fatema's distinction is clever just when it merits our pleasure. The gazelle is fleet just when it merits our pleasure. Màiri is courageous just when it merits our pleasure. Ravi's breaking the world record is an achievement just when it merits our pleasure. This is a sturdy umbrella just when it merits our pleasure. In general, an item is good in any way just when it merits our pleasure. By itself, the biconditional tells us little about aesthetic value.

Let aesthetic empiricism be a manner of crafting a theory of aesthetic value that rejigs the biconditional as a constitutive account (Lopes 2021b). In other words, aesthetic empiricism conjoins the biconditional with a constitutive claim. This is exactly how to think of what has long been the default theory of aesthetic value, namely, aesthetic hedonism (Shelley 2011, Watkins and Shelley 2012). For aesthetic values, V,

> aesthetic hedonism: (1) x is V iff x's being V merits A's taking pleasure in x's being V, and (2) x is V because x merits A's taking pleasure in x.

The "because" signals metaphysical explanation, not causal explanation. Clause (2) says that what makes it the case that x is V is that x has some other features that ground its meriting pleasure. The rough sketch provides a template for more specific variants of aesthetic hedonism (for overviews see Lopes 2018, Chapter 3, Shelley 2019, Van der Berg 2020).

Flip the direction of explanation and the result is a primitivist version of aesthetic empiricism. For aesthetic values, V,

> empiricist aesthetic primitivism: (1) x is V iff x's being V merits A's taking pleasure in x's being V, and (2) x merits A's taking pleasure in x because x is V.

What makes it the case that x merits pleasure is that x is aesthetically good in some way. Empiricist aesthetic primitivism assigns aesthetic value a role as explanans rather than explanandum. The value terminates the explanations (e.g., Johnston 2002, Shelley 2011, Gorodeisky and Marcus 2018, De Clercq 2019, Gorodeisky 2021).

Setting aside that they are mutually incompatible, can we take it that either aesthetic hedonism or empiricist aesthetic primitivism is true? How well do they point to answers to the demarcation or normative questions?

Neither fully demarcates aesthetic values. On the upside, both demarcate aesthetic values from some other values. After all, what makes Fatema's distinction clever and Màiri courageous is not that they merit our pleasure, and their cleverness and courage are not simply the properties that explain the pleasure they merit. On the downside, neither demarcates aesthetic values from other hedonic values (Eaton 1973). Warm baths are good just when they merit pleasure. Plausibly, their goodness is explained by or explains their meriting pleasure. Yet their goodness is not an aesthetic value. Playing kudoda is good just when it merits pleasure, and its ludic value is explained by or explains its meriting pleasure; yet its ludic value is not an aesthetic value. Presumably, fully demarcating aesthetic value requires us to locate the distinctively aesthetic pleasures.

Turn to the normative question—why do aesthetic value facts lend weight to what one should do or think? Here are three options. One is to reduce aesthetic normativity to hedonic normativity. The fact that Chaurasia's performance is serene gives me reason to act and think in just the same way as a game of kudoda's being intensely exciting gives me reason to act and think. We always have reason to get pleasure. Another option eschews hedonic normativity entirely. Some have argued that we always have reason to act autonomously and that aesthetic value facts are reasons to act autonomously (see Lopes 2019 on Bhattacharyya 2011 [1930] and Lopes 2021a on the third *Critique*). Those not hot on either option might tie distinctively aesthetic reasons to distinctively aesthetic pleasures.

If it does any work at all, and thereby avoids waltzing, then an appeal to disinterested pleasure answers the demarcation or normative question by means of a theory of aesthetic value. Modifying aesthetic hedonism, for aesthetic values, V,

> aesthetic hedonism*: (1) x is V iff x's being V merits A's taking disinterested pleasure in x's being V, and (2) x is V because x merits A's taking disinterested pleasure in x.

Modifying empiricist primitivism, for aesthetic values, V,

> empiricist aesthetic primitivism*: (1) x is V iff x's being V merits A's taking disinterested pleasure in x's being V, and (2) x merits A's taking disinterested pleasure in x because x is V.

Being precise about the explanatory work to be performed by appealing to disinterested pleasure brackets some logically independent claims. Disinterested pleasure need not be universal, it need not be culturally invariant, it need not be taken in an item in the absence of information about the item's context or history of making, and it need not be taken in response to only some elements of an item (Levinson 1995). What remains is to propose accounts of disinterested pleasure that can be plugged into theories of aesthetic value that answer the demarcation or normative questions.

2 Pleasures and Motives

If accounts of disinterested pleasure are accounts of a species of pleasure, then it makes sense to develop them with an eye to philosophical work on pleasure. Indeed, it is imperative to confront that work in as much as it appears to be in tension with approaches to disinterested pleasure in aesthetics. James Shelley characterizes Kant's approach, which has shaped all subsequent thinking: disinterested pleasure "does not issue in a motive to do anything in particular" (2020, §1.2). Nick Zangwill updates the jargon: "disinterested pleasure has a desire-free 'causal-functional' role" (1992, p. 152). Yet philosophers posit an essential tie between pleasures and motives. The tension is not a bad thing, if addressing it is a way to home in on a viable conception of disinterested pleasure.

Most work on pleasure focusses on theories of sensory pleasure, but we can generalize (for an overview and references, see Aydede 2018; in psychology the classic source is Melzack and Casey 1968). On all theories, pleasures represent what is sensed or otherwise experienced. There is the taste of matcha ice cream or the experience of being praised for a job well done. Added to the representational component is the pleasantness of the state. Traditionally, pleasantness was a distinctive felt quality. However, it is not obvious how felt qualities motivate, and no felt quality seems to be shared among and distinctive to all pleasures, which run from yummy matcha ice cream to esteem-building pats on the back. Contemporary theories therefore drop appeals to a distinctive felt quality and supplement the representational component with a conative state instead.

For present purposes, we need not decide whether the conative state is constitutive of pleasure or whether it is an essential corollary to it instead. Let us simply unpack the claim that pleasures necessarily motivate. Murat Aydede explains that,

> when I find the taste of the watermelon pleasant, I am undergoing a taste sensation registering certain physical features of the piece in my mouth, but at the same time the sensation is being affectively or hedonically "toned," making the object of the sensation (this piece of watermelon in my mouth) affectively, thus motivationally, salient to me (Aydede 2018, pp. 254–255).

The experience, as he goes on to say, "seems to have a certain kind of motivational tug or pull. We experience this pull as a kind of motivational bias, or even a premotoric *oomph*—some kind of felt urge" (Aydede 2018, p. 257).

A motive is any state of mind that explains an agent's act or thought. Arjun lets fly an arrow. To explain his act, we cite features of his mental state: he is representing the world as being a certain way, and he has an idea of what the world will be like as a result of his act, if it is successful. The elements might be a belief and a desire: he believes that there is a rabbit on the ridge, and he desires that he dine on *coniglio alla cacciatora*. Attributing the belief and desire to him retrospectively explains his behavior. Prospectively, attributing the belief–desire pair equips us to predict what he will do.

Motives explain but do not justify, except indirectly; normative reasons justify. The fact that there is a rabbit on the ridge is a normative reason for Arjun to let fly. When all goes well, his motive represents his normative reason: he correctly believes that there is a rabbit on the ridge. Accordingly, what explains his act represents the reason he has to act. Yet his belief is only part of his motive: what about the conative component? When all goes well, it also represents a normative reason. *Coniglio alla cacciatora* is nutritious, it is easy to prepare, it is delicious: these are all normative reasons for Arjun to desire that he dine on the dish. His letting fly is not justified without some reason of this kind.

The fact that the dish is delicious is reason for Arjun to want to prepare it. In general, the fact that a state of affairs is a source of pleasure is a reason to desire that the state of affairs obtain, and hence to bring it about. Having normative reason to desire that p does not entail desiring that p, but if someone has a normative reason to desire that p and their desiring that p would explain what they do, then that is mighty good (defeasible) cause to attribute the desire to them. If Arjun loves *coniglio alla cacciatora* and he bags the rabbit, then we can explain his bagging the rabbit as motivated by his wanting to enjoy the dish, absent defeating information.

Now the sun has set, and Arjun has dug into his rabbit stew. It tastes good. A state of pleasure inherently motivates being in that state of pleasure, hence performing any acts that maintain the state. The pleasure of eating *coniglio alla cacciatora* entails wanting that the pleasure persist. Pleasures motivate in an attractor mode and also in perpetuator mode.

So far, motives have been described as beliefs and desires, states with propositional contents. When all goes well, their contents are the reasons the agent has to think or act. However, many types of mental states have propositional contents and play the broad functional roles definitive of representational and conative states. A psychologically realistic picture of motives is an ecumenical one. Aydede proposes a functional theory of pleasure on which pleasure can be implemented psychologically via many state types. A pleasure is any type of state that provides: motivational bias ("more-of-this" or "less-of-that"), motor bias or action-preparedness, epistemic bias or appraisals of incoming information, preference bias, and categorized input for reasoning and decision-making (Aydede 2018, p. 258; see also Aydede and Fulkerson 2018). The types of states that play the functional role might be—or might be glossed as—evaluations or imperatives (e.g., Klein 2007, Bain 2013). Equally, they might not be.

Notice how, on the face of it, positing a necessary tie between pleasures and motives conflicts with the characterization of some pleasures as disinterested, or disengaged from desire. In managing this conflict, it would not be cricket to treat the posit as bedrock, trumping the characterization. If they are inconsistent, the characterization might triumph, provided that the appeal to disinterested pleasure does sterling explanatory work. Appearances aside, they might be consistent.

3 Kantian Compatibilism

A Kantian characterization of disinterested pleasure is consistent with positing an essential tie between pleasures and motives. This section transposes into contemporary terms a tenable reading of the Kantian characterization (Guyer 1978; Zuckert 2007, Chapter 6). No warranty is offered that the reading accurately represents Kant—see Part I of this volume for alternative readings. With the tenable reading on the table, we can ask whether disinterested pleasure demarcates aesthetic value or explains the normativity of aesthetic reasons. The news will not be good.

In Kant's system, disinterested pleasure is one of three types of pleasure, and it fits his general view of pleasure. Pleasures are not distinctive felt qualities, for Kant. Rather, a pleasure is a state that represents another representational state of the subject so as to motivate remaining in that very state (e.g., KU: 220; see Zuckert 2007, pp. 232–248). Let us say it provides an "internal motive." Pleasure in matcha ice cream represents a sensation of the ice cream's flavor and texture so as to internally motivate the sensation to continue. In alignment with the contemporary picture, pleasures combine representational and conative components.

The three types of pleasure vary with respect to both components. Sensory pleasures represent sensory responses, but their power to motivate extends beyond internal motives. Having tasted matcha ice cream, I am now pulled toward Konbiniya on Robson Street, where I can source the good stuff. The pleasure motivates future activity. To do so, it must reliably guide that activity by means of a determinate concept of matcha ice cream yumminess: given the concept, I initiate a chain of action that leads me to Konbiniya and that terminates in creamy-matcha sensory pleasure. As Rachel Zuckert explains, the pleasure "must not simply concern this object and my liking of it, but describe a reproducible state of affairs" (2007, p. 260). Let us use "desire" in a technical way, to name any conative state that motivates through concept application (KU: 220). Sensory pleasures implicate desires.

The same goes for practical pleasures—pleasures in the mental representations of goodness of ends or the goodness of means to ends. Friendship is good and thoughts of its goodness please. During the early days of the coronavirus pandemic, many took pleasure in seeing how well Zoom worked to connect friends and colleagues. Practical pleasures motivate activities such as making friends and using Zoom. The general pattern is one where an agent judges a state of affairs to be good, feels pleasure in so judging it, acts so as to bring it into being, and then feels pleasure at having done so (Zuckert 2007, pp. 255–257). The pleasure implicates desires that conceptualize the good states of affairs.

By contrast, disinterested pleasures do not implicate desires, because they are non-conceptual. A mental state with a given content is weakly non-conceptual just in case the subject can be in the state, with that content, without having the concepts needed to specify the content (e.g., Evans 1982, Bermudez 1995, Peacocke 2001, Hanna 2005, Roskies 2008). You might experience a particular shade of red —that one there—without having an ability to recognize the very same shade again. The state is not in fact a product of conceptual processing. By contrast, let a mental state with a given content be strongly non-conceptual just when the subject cannot be in the same state as long as they do exercise the concepts needed to specify the content. The experience of red is not like that, for it is the same state when you do recognize Pantone "Pepperoni Red." A disinterested pleasure is strongly non-conceptual because concept application would render it interested. Since desires are conceptual, it implicates no desires. It only motivates what all pleasures motivate, namely, staying in the same state. It provides what we might call a "strictly internal motive."

The strongly non-conceptual character of disinterested pleasure follows from Kant's story of its origins. Disinterested pleasures represent experiences of something like worldly form or pattern to which no concept is applied. No concept is applied because the pleasure is, or issues from, the harmonious free play of imagination and understanding (Guyer 2017 vs. Ginsborg 1997, pp. 348–350, and Ginsborg 2017). When you see an item as a rose, imagination supplies a structured sense impression, understanding supplies a concept, and judgement subsumes the sense impression under the rose concept. Stable equilibrium is achieved, and the play of imagination and understanding halts. But when imagination and understanding are in harmonious free play, you see an item, imagination structures sense impressions, and understanding delivers concepts, but no stable equilibrium is achieved. Rather, you are confronted with how the item is suitable for both imagination and understanding to keep on operating in free or dynamic equilibrium, both "enlivened through mutual agreement" (KU: 219). The state never halts with concept application (see Guyer 2006 for three models of the phenomenon).

Kant does say why the harmonious free play of imagination and understanding is a pleasure, but grant that it is. For now, what matters is its distinctive motivational character. Disinterested pleasure motivates as does any pleasure, internally, by motivating the continuation of the very same experience. Unlike sensory and practical pleasure, though, it is a strictly internal motive, because it is strongly non-conceptual, all external motives are desires, and desire is conceptual. As Zuckert puts it, a pleasure that is or issues from the harmonious free play of imagination and understanding does not represent "a single sensible property or combination thereof that could be correlated with pleasure," and "if we cannot specify what kind of object will cause us pleasure in the beautiful, nor claim, reliably, that such pleasure causally follows upon sensations [...] then our will can hardly be subsequently determined by such a judgement" (2007, p. 263).

As we can now see, the supposition that there are disinterested pleasures is consistent with positing an essential link between pleasures and motives. In the case of disinterested pleasures, the motives are strictly internal. Grant that there are disinterested pleasures, whether they are or issue from a harmonious free play of imagination and understanding or whether they are brought about in some other way. The question is whether identifying aesthetic pleasures with disinterested pleasures demarcates aesthetic value or explains the normativity of aesthetic reasons.

On demarcation, the key is that the Kantian story takes disinterested pleasures to provide motives that are strongly non-conceptual, hence strictly internal, given that desires are conceptual. The proposal is that all and only aesthetic values figure in motives that are strictly internal and strongly non-conceptual. So, are all aesthetic motives strictly internal and strongly non-conceptual? Are only aesthetic motives strongly non-conceptual, and hence strictly internal?

Some non-aesthetic motives are strongly non-conceptual. Miranda Fricker argues that one form of epistemic injustice is hermeneutical injustice, which can include an unjust distribution of conceptual resources (2007, Chapter 7). Her lead example is the concept of sexual harassment. The concept is recent, but sexual harassment is ancient. In the 1950s, women might have thought of what they experienced as "unwanted flirting," which underplayed what was happening while making its victims feel priggish, thereby subverting their power to resist it, compounding the injustice. The experience of being harassed was unpleasant back then. Moreover, the unpleasantness was not a strictly internal motive, for women sometimes attempted defensive countermeasures, albeit ones that were not maximally effective, and not what they would have done to parry actual cases of unwanted flirting. We should attribute their practical reactions to non-conceptually wanting to avoid sexual harassment, not to conceptually desiring to avoid unwanted flirting. What is more, the unpleasantness was strongly non-conceptual, not merely weakly non-conceptual. After all, a special unpleasantness stemmed from having the experience and lacking the concept. Those who nowadays have the concept and experience the harassment find it unpleasant, but they do not find it unpleasant in the same way as women did when some of the unpleasantness stemmed from not being able to bring the experience to heel, conceptually. Putting the point another way, we can be hedonically motivated to acquire new or better concepts. Therefore, unless the experience of our mothers and grandmothers was disinterested or unless hermeneutical injustice is an aesthetic badness, strongly non-conceptual (dis)pleasures need not be strictly internal motives, and acts need not be motivated by concept-involving desires.

Moreover, some aesthetic motives are not strongly non-conceptual if some aesthetic activities are best explained by attributing to agents pleasures whose contents include aesthetic value concepts. On the Kantian view, disinterested pleasure provides a strictly internal motive because we cannot correlate the pleasure with "a single sensible property or combination thereof;" we can have no bead on "what kind of object will cause us pleasure" that guides our actions. Not intending to take issue with Kant, Kevin Melchionne writes that,

> Without the ability to recognize my preferences and their sources, the pursuit of aesthetic satisfaction would be no more than a fishing expedition. Cultivation would become guesswork. [...] We would bounce more or less erratically from one experience to the next, without any hope of organizing our cultural consumption for greater satisfaction (Melchionne 2010, p. 132).

Such is the life in pursuit of disinterested pleasure. Melchionne objects that "a vital aesthetic life is functionally dependent upon self-knowledge: our choices as cultural participants or consumers are underwritten by beliefs about our responses to works of art" (2010, p. 132). We reliably evaluate the cheerful growl of the Mazda, the serenity of some of Chaurasia's performances, the elegance of Euler's identity, and the glory of sunsets. Were that not the case, they could not even serve as examples of the varieties of beauty. Were that not the case, we would not dial them up into our lives, as we evidently do. Indeed, a theory of aesthetic value is not much good that cannot explain the vast infrastructure that we have built to serve up beauties to suit our personal tastes or the tastes of the moment—museums, concert halls, and restaurants, movie and book reviews, music playlists, type foundries, clothing stores, and the design departments of Mazda and Apple. In these activities, we often let pleasure be our guide. Hence, the activities are best explained by attributing to us pleasures whose contents include aesthetic value concepts.

True, the Kantian might stick to their guns. Since the pleasures that guide us in these activities are not disinterested, the motives are not genuinely aesthetic. Presumably, a genuinely aesthetic motive is not simply an aesthetic evaluation, a state that represents an aesthetic value, because genuinely aesthetic motives exclude those aesthetic evaluations that represent aesthetic values conceptually. However, if this is the Kantian position, it fails to demarcate aesthetic values. Aesthetic values are not identical to the values that figure only in motives that are strictly internal and strongly non-conceptual.

Setting aside these worries about demarcation and the strong non-conceptuality of aesthetic pleasure, turn to the normative question. Why should anyone thrill to glory of the sunset? According to a hedonic theory of aesthetic normativity, the fact that the sunset is glorious is an aesthetic reason because it is pleasing, and anyone always has reason to take pleasure wherever it is to be found. However, the claim that aesthetic pleasures are disinterested plays no role in this answer to the normative question. The answer requires only that aesthetic values be generic hedonic values.

Zuckert (2007) and Lopes (2021a) propose alternative, more Kantian answers to the normative question that do draw on some of the specifics of Kant's picture of aesthetic pleasure. According to Zuckert, (1) aesthetic pleasure is awareness of formal purposiveness, so (2) aesthetic pleasure is awareness of the harmonious free play of imagination and understanding. Moreover, (3) the harmonious free play of imagination and understanding provides for conceptual amelioration, and (4) anyone always has reason to pursue conceptual amelioration. Therefore, (5) the fact that an item is beautiful is reason to take pleasure in it. Aesthetic normativity is cognitive normativity. Lopes infers from (1) and (2) that (3*) aesthetic pleasure is autonomous in the sense that it is self-legislated. Moreover, (4*) anyone always has reason to judge autonomously. Therefore, (5) the fact that an item is beautiful is reason to take pleasure in it. Aesthetic normativity is sourced in the normativity of autonomy.

The trouble is that neither proposal explains the normativity of aesthetic reasons by appeal to disinterested pleasure. Explanation is non-monotonic, so that from the fact that A explains C and the fact that A implies B it does not follow that B has any part in explaining C. For example, suppose that Rachel's students like her because she is wise, and suppose that her being wise implies that she is a good reader. It does not follow that she is liked because she is a good reader. What explains (5) is the origins of aesthetic pleasure in awareness of formal purposiveness and the harmonious free play of imagination and understanding, plus either (3) and (4) or (3*) and (4*). Given the assumption that only conceptualized desires motivate acts, it does indeed follow that aesthetic pleasure is disinterested. However, since explanation is non-monotonic, it does not follow that disinterested pleasure explains (5). The reason why the fact that an item is beautiful is reason to take pleasure in it is that the pleasure is or originates in awareness of formal purposiveness and the harmonious free play of imagination and understanding, not that it is disinterested. Disinterested pleasure is a fifth wheel in the explanation of (5).

An independent case can be made that some aesthetic evaluations are affective and have weakly non-conceptual content (Mitchell 2020). Nevertheless, the Kantian characterization of disinterested pleasures as strongly non-conceptual, providing strictly internal motives, fails to demarcate aesthetic value or explain its normativity.

4 Disinterest as Dissociation

§ 3 will satisfy nobody. On one hand, despite the warning that the tenable reading is tentative, Kantians might protest its contemporary idiom and problematic or cite details of the text or Kant's philosophical project to dispute the tenable reading. On the other hand, those not dedicated to doing aesthetics through Kant will wonder whether the Kantian apparatus and the characterization of aesthetic pleasure as strongly non-conceptual simply obscure the core insight, namely, that aesthetic pleasures provide strictly internal motives. As it happens, we do not need Kant to explore the insight; instead, we might approach disinterested pleasure in a more empirical spirit, as a positive counterpart of pain asymbolia. Although modeling disinterested pleasure on pain asymbolia will fail to explain what needs explaining, the failure will be instructive.

Inasmuch as hedonic states are realized in relatively discrete neural anatomies, components of the pain system can dissociate. Mindfulness practices have been shown to dissociate the representation of a pain stimulus from the motivating feeling of pain (Perlman et al. 2010, Gard et al. 2012, Thompson 2021). However, the question to ask here is whether the representation of a pain stimulus and a feeling of pain together dissociate from the motivation.

Some lesions to the insular cortex produce pain asymbolia, a strange deficit where people seem to experience pains that do not motivate behavior (Berthier, Starkstein, and Leiguarda 1988, Bain 2014, Klein 2015). Colin Klein translates and quotes from the first case report in 1928:

> The patient displays a striking behaviour in the presence of pain. She reacts either not at all or insufficiently to being pricked, struck with hard objects, and pinched. She never pulls her

arm back energetically or with strength. She never turns the torso away or withdraws with the body as a whole. She never attempts to avoid the investigator.

Yet she is not insensible to pain:

> Pricked on the right palm, the patient smiles joyfully, winces a little, and then says, "Oh, pain, that hurts." She laughs, and reaches the hand further toward the investigator and turns it to expose all sides.... The patient's expression is one of complacency (in Klein 2015, pp. 493–494).

The condition is rare, but some general observations are in order. Avoidance behaviors are absent: asymbolics do not guard against sometimes serious injury, they deliberately injure themselves, they feel no anxiety about bodily harm, and their facial expressions signaling pain are dampened. The indifference extends to threats of injury too. Yet they report feeling pain, and their testimony should be taken at face value because they used to feel pain in the normal way, their nociceptive systems remain in working order, and they grasp the concept of pain.

Whether or not pain asymbolia compromises the positing of an essential link between hedonic states and motives depends on how the data are interpreted. Suppose that Panos has pain asymbolia and his hand is being pricked. Here are two hypotheses consistent with the posit:

1. Panos has a feeling that represents body damage but is not unpleasant and does not motivate;
2. Panos has a feeling that represents body damage and is unpleasant and motivating, but an independent deficit inhibits his acting.

As David Bain puts it, what happens in (1) is like a security system that detects an intruder but raises no alarm, and what happens in (2) is like a security alarm that sounds though no one responds (2014, p. 306). Klein (2015) makes a case for (2). What Panos lacks is a capacity to care about his bodily integrity, and that kind of care is an enabling condition on pain's motivating power. The power of a hedonic state to motivate is like the disposition of a match to burn, which actually burns only when enabled by the presence of oxygen. Bain (2014) agrees that Panos lacks a capacity to care about his bodily integrity but makes a case for (1). In brief, pains are unpleasant and motivate only because they are felt evaluations of bodily damage as bad, but Panos cannot evaluate the damage to his hand as bad because he lacks the capacity to care about his bodily integrity.

For present purposes, the task is not to adjudicate reasons to prefer (1) or (2); the task is to weigh the prospects of characterizing disinterested pleasure on the model of (1) or (2). Suppose that Bella is feeling disinterested pleasure in a glorious sunset. Obviously, (1) very poorly models her condition, because it construes her as not feeling genuine pleasure. Taking (2) as a model, we might suppose that Bella's feeling, which represents the sunset's beauty, is pleasant and motivating, though it does not actually motivate, because a care condition that would enable it to motivate goes unmet. The trick is to identify the care condition.

To work the trick, we can exploit the structural parallel between Panos and Bella. In the case of pain asymbolia, the care deficit is just what explains observed behavior. We infer that Panos does not care about his bodily integrity because that would explain why he takes no particular steps to position himself to avoid injury, though he feels pain when injured. With respect to Bella, the care condition is the condition whose non-satisfaction would explain why she takes no particular steps to position herself to make sure that she sees or keeps seeing the glorious sunset, though its sight pleases her. When a matcha ice cream cart rolls up, blocking her pleasing view of the sunset, the pleasure is motivating her to move a bench over, but she nevertheless stays put. Disinterested pleasure is as strange as pain asymbolia.

What condition, going unmet, would explain her behavior? Obviously, the condition is self-oriented and practical, as its going unmet inhibits behaviors of Bella's. Perhaps the counterpart of caring about one's bodily integrity is caring about the integrity of one's will. Bella's belief that she will continue to see the sunset if she moves combines with her pleasure in the sunset's glory to motivate her to move, but she does not care about her capacity as an agent—about her capacity to act as she is motivated. Not caring that her will be done, she does not act. Call this the "care characterization."

Needless to say, Panos and Bella differ in important ways. Bella's behavior is not a consequence of a horrible brain injury. Her condition is common; his is rare. More importantly, her not meeting a care condition is no great misfortune. It would be too bad if her not meeting the same care condition stymied her pursuit of sensory pleasure and the other goods of life—family, friendship, career, and adventure. So, the fact that an item is beautiful must be normative reason for Bella to respond to it as she does, with the care condition offline. In other words, the care characterization must do some work in explaining the normativity of aesthetic reasons or in demarcating them from other reasons.

Why does the fact that the sunset is glorious lend weight to the proposition that Bella should have a pleasure that provides a motive to switch benches while taking the care condition offline? According to a hedonic theory of aesthetic normativity, aesthetic reasons are reasons to take pleasure, and we always have reason to take pleasure. Perhaps there is a class of pleasures that are available only because they do not lead to action. However, why think that such "tranquil" pleasures must tend to motivate Bella to switch benches? The claim must be that some pleasures can be obtained only by having their tendency to motivate quashed by disabling the care condition. The proposal would be that aesthetic reasons are reasons to take this special kind of pleasure, and we always have reason to take pleasure. The phenomenon is logically possible, but one might wonder how well it demarcates aesthetic values.

The care characterization of disinterested pleasure is weaker than the Kantian one: it does not imply that aesthetic pleasures cannot be predicted. Bella knows well how to repeat the pleasure she gets from the sunset. Rather, the care characterization implies that we cannot predict, in light of her disinterested pleasure, what she will do next. The trouble is that this result conflicts with the fact, noted above, that we have built up a vast and effective infrastructure to distribute aesthetic goods—museums, concert halls, and restaurants, movie and book reviews, music playlists, type foundries, clothing stores, and the design departments of Mazda and Apple. Infrastructures such as these work only because we do routinely position ourselves to access what they have to offer. You can predict, based on my pleasure in the serenity of Chaurasia's performance, that I have taken steps to place it on my playlist. Why? The pleasures that motivate me are ones that get me into gear as an agent.

One might reply on behalf of the care characterization that the activities described in the previous paragraph are not motivated by pleasures at all. Other, non-hedonic desires explain their occurrence. Your correct prediction that I have taken steps to add Chaurasia's performance to my playlist does not imply that I have done so out of pleasure. Fair enough, that is exactly what the care characterization requires. Given that implication together with the proposal that aesthetic values figure only in strictly internal motives, it follows that my non-hedonic motive for playlisting the Chaurasia cannot represent its aesthetic values. That is a large bullet to bite.

What about the claim that only aesthetic pleasures are disinterested in the sense that the care condition goes unmet? Are there no states of mind that are pleasurable and motivating but where no act is motivated because we switch off our agentive default? Is stopping to smell the roses strictly aesthetic? What rules out cases where one is on holiday as an agent, so that a pleasure in the truth of an idea, which would normally motivate acting on the idea, leads to no act, or so that pleasure in the goodness of an end, which would normally motivate adopting means to achieve the end, leaves one quiet? Provided that all goes well in these cases too, some non-aesthetic pleasures are disinterested.

So revisionary is the care characterization that it requires exceptionally strong reasons. Without them, it would be rash to maintain that aesthetic pleasure is disinterested, given the care characterization.

5 Pleasure in Contemplating

As much as they differ, §§ 3 and 4 are united in characterizing disinterested pleasures as those that provide strictly internal motives. According to the Kantian characterization, the motives are strictly internal because they are strongly non-conceptual, and only conceptually-laden desires motivate action. According to the care characterization, the motives are strictly internal because a condition needed for them to cause action is not met, taking them offline. The former comes with a heavy-duty systematic backstory, whereas the latter takes its cue from neuropathology. Perhaps it is a matter of taste which is easier or harder to accept. Can we reject both as viable characterizations of disinterested pleasure? What if disinterested pleasure provides motives that are not strictly internal? What if it instead provides motives for a specific type of act?

Having attributed to Kant the view that disinterested pleasure "does not issue in a motive to do anything in particular," Shelley further identifies that view with Kant's description of the pleasure as "merely contemplative" (Shelley 2020, §1.2, KU: 209). For Kant, contemplation is not an act, but, relaxing the point, one might regard contemplation as an activity. On a Kant Lite characterization, disinterested pleasures are those that provide motives to perform acts of contemplation—they are not strictly internal after all. Mohan Matthen (2017a, 2017b) offers such a characterization as "a plausible take on what Kant meant by 'disinterested pleasure'" that brackets other Kantian commitments (2017b, p. 105).

Matthen distinguishes between two pleasure systems. A phylogenetically ancient system yields relief pleasures, which come with restoration of physiological equilibrium. Examples are sneezing, scratching an itch, and quenching thirst. Pleasures such as these are not motivating; they are not impulses to perform a specific act. By contrast, the more recent system generates facilitating pleasures, which motivate continued engagement in the very activities that give rise to them. Take a ping pong volley. Keeping the ball in play causes pleasure that motivates continuing to keep the ball in play, which causes pleasure, which... Unlike relief pleasures, facilitating pleasures are forward-looking impulses to act.

The motivating power of facilitating pleasure drives the performance of acts that consume energy and demand attentive mental and bodily coordination. To keep the volley going, you must keep your eye on the ball and your opponent's whereabouts while positioning yourself to make well-executed returns, all the while planning what to do if the ball goes wild. The pleasure of keeping the volley going facilitates the exercise of a competence, a "coordinated group of mental and bodily 'preparations' that encourage, ease, and optimize" a performance (Matthen 2017a, p. 8).

Some competences develop spontaneously—for example, a toddler's learning their mother tongue—but most competences are learned through repeated, effortful trying. Learning of this kind is costly and difficult, but facilitating pleasure incentivizes learning by immediately rewarding the learner's efforts. In this way, it "enables productive agency" (Matthen 2017a, p. 13).

Competence in contemplating requires learning that is costly and difficult. Just contrast the aesthetic life of an infant with that of an adult. Learning to contemplate is incentivized by pleasure. According to Matthen, aesthetic pleasure is facilitating pleasure that is taken in the activity of contemplating an item and that provides a motive to engage in that very activity. Yet the pleasure is disinterested:

> immediate sensuous pleasure arises from the quiet tones and brightening ornamentation of Adhithi Ravichandran's morning raga. Listening to the raga gives me aesthetic pleasure; pleasure derived from other activities relative to it is not aesthetic. The pleasure that comes from pride in my expertise, or my zeal in offering a technical analysis of the music, is different and additional. [...] the pleasure of art is disinterested because all other pleasure taken in the raga is beside the point. (Matthen 2017b, p. 104)

In short, disinterested pleasure is what motivates and facilitates only acts of contemplation. The claim is not that it never coincides with other motives. It sometimes does. Wanting to be distracted from pandemic anxiety, I listen to the morning raga, and also take disinterested pleasure in the listening, which motivates continued (and future) listening. The claim is that disinterested pleasure does not motivate any but acts of contemplation.

Pleasures, like anything else, can be typed any which way. Characterizing some pleasures as the ones that motivate contemplation is neither objectionable nor virtuous per se. The question is whether the Lite Kantian characterization earns its keep. One advantage of the characterization is that it does not ask us to bite such big bullets. To begin with, aesthetic life is not a fishing expedition. On the contrary, disinterested pleasure facilitates learning trajectories. In addition, Bella's disinterested pleasure does not leave her immobilized on the bench when her view of the sunset is blocked. On the contrary, Matthen makes clear that contemplation comprises that "coordinated group of mental and bodily 'preparations' that encourage, ease, and optimize" it (Matthen 2017a, p. 8). Contemplating the rich texture of walks around the barrio means walking around the barrio. The characterization is already ahead in the game. So, does it answer the normative or demarcation questions?

The demarcation question concerns aesthetic value. In §§ 3 and 4, we assumed that aesthetic values uniquely figure in strictly internal motives. Now we ask whether aesthetic values uniquely figure in hedonic motives to contemplate, and only to contemplate (see also Sinnerbrink 2017, pp. 54–57).

Moved by the serenity of Chaurasia's performance and the brightening ornamentation of Ravichandran's, I create a playlist. My exercise of skill in making the playlist is a product of years of learning boosted by facilitating pleasure, and making the playlist is pleasing. I end up making playlists all night long. Throughout, I attend only to the aesthetic values of the works I consider for my compilation. Yet I never listen to any music. The pleasure in question is not disinterested, because disinterested pleasure only motivates contemplation, and surely there is no contemplating going on. Therefore, some pleasures that represent and are felt in response to aesthetic values are not disinterested.

Iris Murdoch collected stones. She chose them not as geological specimens, as personal mementos, or even as small beauties. She chose each one just for being itself, with its mundane and unremarkable features. One of her characters speaks for her:

> The wet stones were almost black. The dry stones were an absolute grey in which even the brightest sunshine could kindle no hint of any other colour. Anne picked up a stone. They were so similar, yet so dissimilar, like counters in a game played by some god. The shapes, very like, were never exactly the same. Each one, if carefully examined, revealed some tiny significant individuating mark, a shallow depression or chipped end, a short almost invisible line. (Murdoch 1980, p. 110)

In opposition to the existentialists, Murdoch could not regard "the contingent overabundance of the world" as nauseating or horrifying (Murdoch 1953, p. 59). She would pick up her stones and contemplate them with pleasure, just for whatever boring and ordinary properties they happened to have. Therefore, some pleasures that motivate acts of contemplation are not aesthetic evaluations.

An appeal to disinterested pleasure need not earn its keep by demarcating aesthetic from other values. Might Matthen's account answer the normative question? That question asks what makes it the case that the fact that walks around the barrio are richly textured lends weight to the proposition that anyone should go there for a walk. True, if anyone has reason to get pleasure, then anyone has reason to get disinterested pleasure. However, having reason to get pleasure is already enough to answer the normative question. What does the appeal to disinterested pleasure add? Maybe the thought is that we need to appeal to a special pleasure to explain why we have normative reason to perform a special act, contemplation. However, that thought is the one that spawned the demarcation question, and we have just seen that the account of disinterested pleasure fails to demarcate aesthetic pleasures.

Matthen's theory of facilitating pleasure arguably provides just the resources we need to make sense of aesthetic pleasure, which includes but is not limited to pleasure in contemplation (Lopes 2018, pp. 155–163). That task it performs perfectly well, with no need for the additional claim that facilitating aesthetic pleasure is disinterested.

Perhaps those who will not waltz are condemned to plod. Stepping through the details is the only way to expose the incoherencies to which tradition has inured us. Are there, as Arnold Berleant once hoped, advantages to a theory that obediently conforms to tradition (1994, p. 146)? Disinterested pleasure has long had its discontents (e.g., Bourdieu 1984, esp. pp. 485–502; Derrida 1987, pp. 45–48; Nehamas 2007). Historians have made out its ideological role in cementing the social position of Euro fine art in the eighteenth and nineteenth centuries (esp. Abrams 1985, Shiner 2001; see also Wolterstorff 2015). However, an error theory is not enough. If the incoherencies have been masked by false pictures of aesthetic activity, then plodding through the arguments is also the best way to depict aesthetic life in all its richness.

Abbreviations

All references to Kant's works are to Kant's Gesammelte Schriften, Ausgabe der Preußischen Akademie der Wissenschaften (Berlin: De Gruyter, 1902ff.). Translations are from The Cambridge Edition of the Works of Immanuel Kant.

The following abbreviation is used:

KU   Kritik der Urteilskraft / Critique of the Power of Judgment

Literature

Abrams, Meyer H. (1985): "Art-as-Such: The Sociology of Modern Aesthetics." In: *Bulletin of the American Academy of Arts and Sciences* 38. No. 6, pp. 8–33.
Aydede, Murat (2018): "A Contemporary Account of Sensory Pleasure." In: Shapiro, Lisa (Ed.): *Pleasure: A History*. Oxford: Oxford University Press, pp. 239–266.
Aydede, Murat (2023): "Pain and Pleasure." In: Scarantino, Andrea (Ed.): *Routledge Handbook of Emotion Theory*. London: Routledge.
Aydede, Murat and Fulkerson, Matthew (2018): "Reasons and Theories of Sensory Affect." In: Bain, David, Brady, Michael, and Corns, Jennifer (Eds.): *Philosophy of Pain: Unpleasantness, Emotion, and Deviance*. London: Routledge, pp. 27–59.
Bain, David (2013): "What Makes Pains Unpleasant." In: *Philosophical Studies* 166. No. 1, pp. 69–89.
Bain, David (2014): "Pains That Don't Hurt." In: *Australasian Journal of Philosophy* 92. No. 2, pp. 305–320.
Benovsky, Jiri (2012): "Aesthetic Supervenience vs Aesthetic Grounding." In: *Estetika: The European Journal of Aesthetics* 49. No. 2, pp. 166–178.

Berleant, Arnold (1994): "Beyond Disinterestedness." In: *British Journal of Aesthetics* 34. No. 3, pp. 242–254.

Bermúdez, José Luis (1995): "Nonconceptual Content: From Perceptual Experience to Subpersonal Computational States." In: *Mind and Language* 10. No. 4, pp. 333–369.

Berthier, Marcelo, Starkstein, Sergio, and Leiguarda, Ramon (1988): "Asymbolia for Pain: A Sensory-Limbic Disconnection Syndrome." In: *Annals of Neurology* 24. No. 1, pp. 41–49.

Bhattacharyya, Krishna C. (1930, 2011): "The Concept of Rasa." In: Bhushan, Nalini and Garfield, Jay L. (Eds.): *Indian Philosophy in English: From Renaissance to Independence.* Oxford: Oxford University Press, pp. 195–206.

Bolzano, Bernard (1843, 2023): "On the Concept of the Beautiful." In: Lopes, Dominic McIver (Ed.): *Essays on Beauty and the Arts.* Adam Bresnahan (Trans.). Boston: Hackett, pp. 35–80.

Bourdieu, Pierre (1984): *Distinction: A Social Critique of the Judgement of Taste.* Richard Nice (Trans.). Cambridge: Harvard University Press.

De Clercq, Rafaël (2002): "The Concept of an Aesthetic Property." In: *Journal of Aesthetics and Art Criticism* 60. No. 2, pp. 167–176.

De Clercq, Rafaël (2019): "Aesthetic Pleasure Explained." In: *Journal of Aesthetics and Art Criticism* 77. No. 2, pp. 121–132.

Derrida, Jacques (1987): *The Truth in Painting.* Geoff Bennington and Ian McLeod (Trans.). Chicago: University of Chicago Press.

Eaton, Marcia Muelder (1973): "Pleasure and Pain." In: *Journal of Aesthetics and Art Criticism* 31. No. 4, pp. 481–485.

Evans, Gareth (1982): *The Varieties of Reference.* Oxford: Oxford University Press.

Fricker, Miranda (2007): *Epistemic Injustice: Power and the Ethics of Knowing.* Oxford: Oxford University Press.

Gard, Tim, Hölzel, Britta K., Sack, Alexander T., Hempel, Hannes, Lazar, Sara W., Vaitl, Dieter, and Ott, Ulrich (2012): "Pain Attenuation Through Mindfulness Is Associated with Decreased Cognitive Control and Increased Sensory Processing in the Brain." In: *Cerebral Cortex* 22. No. 11, pp. 2692–2702.

Ginsborg, Hannah (1997): "Kant on Aesthetic and Biological Purposiveness." In: Reath, Andrews, Herman, Barbara, and Korsgaard, Christine (Eds.): *Reclaiming the History of Ethics: Essays for John Rawls.* Cambridge: Cambridge University Press, pp. 329–360.

Ginsborg, Hannah (2017): "In Defence of the One-Act View: Reply to Guyer." In: *British Journal of Aesthetics* 57. No. 4, pp. 421–435.

Gorodeisky, Keren (2021): "On Liking Aesthetic Value." In: *Philosophy and Phenomenological Research* 102. No. 2, pp. 261–280.

Gorodeisky, Keren and Marcus, Eric (2018): "Aesthetic Rationality." In: *Journal of Philosophy* 15. No. 3, pp. 113–140.

Guyer, Paul (1978): "Disinterestedness and Desire in Kant's Aesthetics." In: *Journal of Aesthetics and Art Criticism* 36. No. 4, pp. 449–460.

Guyer, Paul (2006): "The Harmony of the Faculties Revisited." In: Kukla, Rebecca (Ed.): *Aesthetics and Cognition in Kant's Critical Philosophy.* Cambridge: Cambridge University Press, pp. 162–193.

Guyer, Paul (2017): "One Act or Two? Hannah Ginsborg on Aesthetic Judgement." In: *British Journal of Aesthetics* 57. No. 4, pp. 407–419.

Hanna, Robert (2005): "Kant and Nonconceptual Content." In: *European Journal of Philosophy* 13. No. 2, pp. 247–290.

Hutcheson, Francis (1738): *An Inquiry into the Original of Our Ideas of Beauty and Virtue.* 4th ed. London.
Johnston, Mark (2001): "The Authority of Affect." In: *Philosophy and Phenomenological Research* 63. No. 1, pp. 181–214.
Kant, Immanuel (1790, 2000): *Critique of the Power of Judgment.* Paul Guyer and Eric Matthews (Trans.). Cambridge: Cambridge University Press.
Klein, Colin (2007): "An Imperative Theory of Pain." In: *Journal of Philosophy* 104. No. 10, pp. 517–532.
Klein, Colin (2015): "What Pain Asymbolia Really Shows." In: *Mind* 124. No. 494, pp. 493–516.
Kovach, Francis J. (1974): "Aesthetic Disinterestedness in Premodern Thought." In: *Southwestern Journal of Philosophy* 5. No. 1, pp. 59–68.
Levinson, Jerrold (1995): "Pleasure and the Value of Works of Art." In: *British Journal of Aesthetics* 32. No. 4, pp. 295–306.
Lopes, Dominic McIver (2014): *Beyond Art.* Oxford: Oxford University Press.
Lopes, Dominic McIver (2018): *Being for Beauty: Aesthetic Agency and Value.* Oxford: Oxford University Press.
Lopes, Dominic McIver (2019): "Feeling for Freedom: K. C. Bhattacharyya on Rasa." In: *British Journal of Aesthetics* 59. No. 4, pp. 465–477.
Lopes, Dominic McIver (2021a): "Beyond the Pleasure Principle: A Kantian Aesthetics of Autonomy." In: *Estetika: The European Journal of Aesthetics* 58. No. 1, pp. 1–18.
Lopes, Dominic McIver (2021b): "Two Dogmas of Aesthetic Empiricism." In: *Metaphilosophy* 52. No. 5, pp. 583–592.
Matthen, Mohan (2017a): "The Pleasure of Art." In: *Australasian Philosophical Review* 1. No. 1, pp. 6–28.
Matthen, Mohan (2017b): "Constructing Aesthetic Value: Responses to My Commentators." In: *Australasian Philosophical Review* 1. No. 1, pp. 100–111.
Melchionne, Kevin (2010): "On the Old Saw 'I Know Nothing about Art but I Know What I Like.'" In: *Journal of Aesthetics and Art Criticism* 68. No. 2, pp. 131–141.
Melzack, Ronald and Casey, Kenneth L. (1968): "Sensory, Motivational, and Central Control Determinants of Pain: A New Conceptual Model." In: Kenshalo, Dan R. (Ed.): *The Skin Senses.* Springfield: C. C. Thomas, pp. 423–439.
Mitchell, Jonathan (2020): "On the Non-Conceptual Content of Affective-Evaluative Experience." In: *Synthese* 197. No. 7, pp. 3087–3111.
Mothersill, Mary (1984): *Beauty Restored.* Oxford: Oxford University Press.
Murdoch, Iris (1953): *Sartre: Romantic Rationalist.* London: Penguin.
Murdoch, Iris (1980): *Nuns and Soldiers.* London: Penguin.
Nehamas, Alexander (2007): *Only a Promise of Happiness: The Place of Beauty in a World of Art.* Princeton: Princeton University Press.
Parsons, Glenn and Carlson, Allen (2008): *Functional Beauty.* Oxford: Oxford University Press.
Peacocke, Christopher (2001): "Does Perception Have a Nonconceptual Content?." In: *Journal of Philosophy* 98. No. 5, pp. 239–264.
Perlman, David M., Salomons, Tim V., Davidson, Richard J., and Lutz, Antoine (2010): "Differential Effects on Pain Intensity and Unpleasantness of Two Meditation Practices." In: *Emotion* 10. No. 1, pp. 65–71.
Plato (2014): *Greater Hippias.* Harold North Fowler (Trans.). Cambridge: Harvard University Press.

Riggle, Nick (2016): "On the Interest in Beauty and Disinterest." In: *Philosophers' Imprint* 16. No. 9, pp. 1–14.
Rind, Miles (2002): "The Concept of Disinterestedness in Eighteenth-Century British Aesthetics." In: *Journal of the History of Philosophy* 40. No. 1, pp. 67–87.
Roskies, Adina (2008): "A New Argument for Nonconceptual Content." In: *Philosophy and Phenomenological Research* 76. No. 3, pp. 633–659.
Shelley, James (2011): "Hume and the Value of the Beautiful." In: *British Journal of Aesthetics* 51. No. 2, pp. 213–222.
Shelley, James (2019): "The Default Theory of Aesthetic Value." In: *British Journal of Aesthetics* 59. No. 1, pp. 1–12.
Shelley, James (2020): "The Concept of the Aesthetic." In: Zalta, Edward N. (Ed.): *Stanford Encyclopedia of Philosophy*. https://plato.stanford.edu/archives/win2020/entries/aesthetic-concept, last accessed on Jan. 29, 2023.
Shiner, Larry (2001): *The Invention of Art: A Cultural History*. Chicago: University of Chicago Press.
Sibley, Frank (1959): "Aesthetic Concepts." In: *Philosophical Review* 68. No. 4, pp. 421–450.
Sibley, Frank (1965): "Aesthetic and Nonaesthetic." In: *Philosophical Review* 74. No. 2, pp. 135–159.
Sinnerbrink, Robert (2017): "Pleasure, Art, Culture: Remarks on Mohan Matthen's 'The Pleasure of Art.'" In: *Australasian Philosophical Review* 1. No. 1, pp. 50–60.
Sontag, Susan (1966): *Against Interpretation*. New York: Farrar, Straus, and Giroux.
Stolnitz, Jerome (1961): "On the Origins of 'Aesthetic Disinterestedness.'" In: *Journal of Aesthetics and Art Criticism* 20. No. 2, pp. 131–143.
Thompson, Evan (2021): "Conceptualizing Cognition in Buddhist Philosophy and Cognitive Science." In: *Proceedings and Addresses of the American Philosophical Association* 95, pp. 61–82.
Thomson, Judith Jarvis (2008): *Normativity*. Chicago: Open Court.
Todd, Cain Samuel (2004): "Quasi-Realism, Acquaintance, and the Normative Claims of Aesthetic Judgement." In: *British Journal of Aesthetics* 44. No. 3, pp. 277–296.
Van der Berg, Servaas (2019): "The Motivational Structure of Appreciation." In: *Philosophical Quarterly* 69. No. 276, pp. 445–466.
Van der Berg, Servaas (2020): "Aesthetic Hedonism and Its Critics." In: *Philosophy Compass* 15. No. 1, pp. 1–15.
Watkins, Michael and Shelley, James (2012): "Response-Dependence about Aesthetic Value." In: *Pacific Philosophical Quarterly* 93. No. 3, pp. 338–352.
Wolterstorff, Nicholas (2015): *Art Rethought: The Social Practices of Art*. Oxford: Oxford University Press.
Zangwill, Nick (1992): "Unkantian Notions of Disinterest." In: *British Journal of Aesthetics* 32. No. 2, pp. 149–152.
Zangwill, Nick (1995): "The Beautiful, the Dainty, and the Dumpy." In: *British Journal of Aesthetics* 35. No. 4, pp. 317–329.
Zuckert, Rachel (2007): *Kant on Beauty and Biology: An Interpretation of the Critique of Judgment*. Cambridge: Cambridge University Press.

James Shelley
Beyond Hedonism about Aesthetic Value

Abstract: In its simplest form, hedonism about aesthetic value, the standard account of aesthetic normativity, holds that an object's aesthetic value is the value it possesses in virtue of its capacity to provide aesthetic pleasure. I argue that hedonism cannot be true because it cannot reconcile itself with our concern to make true aesthetic judgments. Then I argue for an alternative account of aesthetic normativity that is not only consistent with that concern but the very expression of it. The argument for the alternative account largely consists of arguments against two theses associated with Kant: *subjectivism*, which holds that the ascription of aesthetic value to an object depends on the sentiments of the subject making the ascription and not on the subject's recognition of a property residing in the object, and *disinterestedness*, which holds that the ascription of beauty to an object neither depends on nor results in the subject's having a motive to act in regard to the object.

In its simplest form, hedonism about aesthetic value, the standard account of aesthetic normativity, holds that an object's aesthetic value is the value it possesses in virtue of its capacity to provide aesthetic pleasure. In § 1 of this paper, I argue that hedonism about aesthetic value is false. In §§ 2 through 4, I argue for an alternative account of aesthetic normativity. My argument for this alternative consists largely in arguments against two theses associated with Kant: *subjectivism*, which holds that the ascription of aesthetic value to an object depends on the sentiments of the subject making the ascription and not on the subject's recognition of a property residing in the object (Ginsborg 2015, p. 27), and *disinterestedness*, which holds that the ascription of beauty to an object neither depends on nor results in the subject's having a motive to act in regard to the object (Ginsborg 2019, par. 18). Though these theses are associated with Kant, I make no claim that Kant asserts either. Doing that would require that I interpret Kant on these matters, which I have no intention of doing. Unless I somehow act against my own intentions, therefore, it can be no objection against my refutations of subjectivism and disinterestedness that they rest on misunderstandings of Kant.

1 Against Hedonism

To my knowledge, the standard version of hedonism about aesthetic value received its first articulation in Monroe Beardsley's essay "The Aesthetic Point of View" (Beardsley 1970). There, Beardsley reports having been captivated by the Martian novels of Edgar Rice Burroughs as a child only to be repelled by them as an adult. Beardsley mentions this because he takes the possibility of aesthetic overvaluation, as exemplified by his youthful infatuation with the Martian novels, to be inconsistent with the account of aesthetic value he would otherwise endorse. According to that account:

> The aesthetic value of an object is the value it possesses in virtue of its capacity to provide aesthetic gratification. (Beardsley 1970, p. 45)

Suppose this account to be true. In that case, the young Beardsley could aesthetically undervalue a novel by taking less gratification from it than it has the capacity to provide. But neither he nor anyone else could aesthetically overvalue a novel since overvaluing it would require taking more gratification from it than it has the capacity to provide. To escape this difficulty, Beardsley emends the account so as to hold:

> The aesthetic value of an object is the value it possesses in virtue of its capacity to provide aesthetic gratification *when correctly and completely experienced.* (Beardsley 1970, p. 49, emphasis in original)

For the sake of convenience, let us refer to the original part of Beardsley's account as *the hedonic thesis*, since it proposes to reduce aesthetic value to the more basic value of gratification, and to the newly appended part as *the epistemic qualification*, since it enlists an epistemic notion to specify the capacity relevant to a thing's aesthetic value. The epistemic qualification purports to allow the hedonist to explain the possibility of both undervaluation and overvaluation and to do so in an intuitively symmetrical way: to undervalue is to take lesser gratification than the object is capable of providing when completely and correctly experienced; to overvalue is to take greater gratification than the object is capable of providing when completely and correctly experienced. Suppose we allow that the addition of the epistemic qualification solves the problem of explaining the possibility of overvaluation (hereafter, *the possibility problem*). It will not follow that it solves the problem lurking behind that problem, that is, the problem of explaining the undesirability of overvaluation (hereafter, *the undesirability problem*). For what needs explaining is not merely how our encounters with aesthetic objects may result in undervaluation and overvaluation but also why we are concerned that they result in neither. We take ourselves to have reason to value aesthetically valuable objects accurately, that is, in accordance with the values we take them to have independently of our finding them valuable. In this respect aesthetic engagements with things are not unlike moral engagements with people. But whereas our concern for accurate valuing in moral life is easily explained, our concern for accurate valuing in aesthetic life is not, as Richard Miller has insightfully observed:

> Someone engaged in moral judgment is rationally concerned to arrive at an objectively valid judgment. *Of course*, this concern is rational: if her judgment is false, she may wrong someone in relying on it [...]. Similarly, people engaged in enjoying art in the ways that lead to aesthetic judgment are concerned that their judgments be right. They question their own judgments, and are frustrated and humbled when they decide that their judgments were misguided. This seems a rational concern for rightness, too. But why is it, if the goal is the aesthetic one of enjoyment rather than the moral one of avoiding wrongdoing? (Miller 1998, p. 49)

The hedonic thesis, which Miller—like most everyone else—endorses, affords a ready explanation why we should avoid undervaluing. If our goal in engaging with artworks is the aesthetic one of enjoyment, then we have reason not to undervalue artworks since to undervalue them is to fail to take the enjoyment it is our aesthetic goal to take. But if that is the reason we should avoid undervaluing, then not only does the hedonic thesis not afford a ready explanation why we should also avoid overvaluing, it affords a ready explanation why we should pursue it. If our goal in engaging with artworks is the aesthetic one of enjoyment, then we have reason to overvalue artworks, since to fail to overvalue them is to fail to take the enjoyment it is our aesthetic goal to take. With respect to our concern not to overvalue, then, the hedonist seems not merely to get things wrong, but to get things backwards.

The explanation of aesthetic value that the hedonist asserts when she first asserts the hedonic thesis seems plausible. There is no denying that pleasure is valuable, nor that good works afford it, nor that good works are valuable in virtue of their affording it. Nor is there any obvious alternative. So, we sign on. Then the possibility problem arises: the value works have in virtue of their affording pleasure cannot be overvalued whereas aesthetic value can. So, the hedonist appends the epistemic qualification, which solves the possibility problem, and so we stay signed on, not realizing that the theory of aesthetic value to which we are signed on has been undone by the measure adopted to preserve it. The addition of the epistemic qualification solves the possibility problem only by converting the hedonic thesis from a theory of aesthetic value, according to which works have aesthetic value in virtue of the value of the pleasure they afford, to a hedonic theory of aesthetic evaluation, according to which works *are found to* have aesthetic value in virtue of the value of the pleasure they afford. For only if pleasure plays the role of indicating value, as it does in the qualified thesis, rather than that of making valuable, as it does in the unqualified thesis, can pleasure be the false indication of value in cases of overvaluation and undervaluation that a solution to the possibility problem demands. But if pleasure is the false indication of value when we inaccurately value and the true indication of value when we accurately value, then it is not also that which makes valuable when we accurately value. The undesirability problem is the problem you have when you try to get pleasure to function simultaneously as value-maker in your theory of value and as value-indicator in your theory of evaluation. When you try to do that and your theory of evaluation tells you that you have found some work too valuable, your theory of value will tell you that you have reason to find it that way, since it is more valuable when you do.

Miller wonders why we are concerned to make true aesthetic judgments given that our goal in engaging with artworks is the aesthetic one of enjoyment. I cannot see how our aesthetic goal in engaging with artworks could be one of enjoyment given our concern to make true aesthetic judgments. I therefore take myself to agree with Kant when he says that it is "foolish to be scrupulous with regard to the means for providing ourselves with it [enjoyment]" when enjoyment is all that is at stake (KU: 208).[1] For him, it is the agreeable, as opposed to the beautiful, that is valuable in virtue of the enjoyment it provides. Indeed, one way of drawing the distinction between the agreeable and the beautiful is to say that whereas you can find a thing more beautiful than it is, you cannot find a thing more agreeable than it is. You cannot find a thing more agreeable than it is because the value of an agreeable thing is just the value of the mental state by which you find it to be agreeable. That is why, with regard to the agreeable, it is "folly to dispute the judgment of another [...] as if it were logically opposed to our own" (KU: 212). You can find a thing more beautiful than it is because the value of a beautiful thing is not the value of the mental state by which you find it beautiful. This is what allows us to speak of beauty "as if it were a property of things" and allows the judgment that a thing is beautiful to "make a rightful claim to the assent of everyone" (KU: 212–213). Hence the failure of hedonism, at bottom, is the failure to observe a distinction between two orders of value on which Kant rightly insisted. To assert the hedonic thesis is to assert of the value of the beautiful the explanation of the value of the agreeable. To append the epistemic qualification is to attempt to atone for that mistake by getting the agreeable to mimic the objective behavior of the beautiful.

---

[1] Though Kant makes this point specifically to criticize a hedonic theory of moral value, he does so in wider context of providing a theory of aesthetic value, and the point holds true in the wider context.

To assert the epistemically qualified hedonist thesis is to assert the confusion—agreeableness objectified—whose expression is the undesirability problem.

Instead of first assuming some version of hedonism and then attempting to reconcile it, against its grain, with our concern that aesthetic judgments be true, suppose we begin with our concern that aesthetic judgments be true and allow it to point us toward a theory of aesthetic normativity worth holding. Miller provides a suggestion how to proceed. Recall that he thinks that our concern for the truth of moral judgments is easily explained. Recall also that he observes a similarity between our concern for the truth of moral judgments and our concern for the truth of aesthetic judgments—a similarity expressed in the way we question our own judgments in either case, and in the way we are frustrated and humbled, in either case, to discover that we have gotten things wrong. Miller treats this similarity as accidental, as something to be explained away rather than explained, because he regards our moral and aesthetic aims—the aims of avoiding wrongdoing and of pursuing enjoyment—as wholly disparate. But we are not operating under the hedonic assumption that enjoyment is our aesthetic aim. Nor need we be detained by the worry that our aesthetic aim cannot be the specifically moral one of not wronging others. The features of moral value that explain our concern to judge it truthfully are that it prescribes that we do certain things, that we take ourselves to have reason to do what it prescribes, and that doing as it prescribes requires judging truthfully what it prescribes. A theory that plausibly ascribed these same features to aesthetic value would explain our concern to make true aesthetic judgments.

Some will dismiss the very idea of such a theory. Some will find the notion of prescriptive aesthetic value as confused as I have found the notion of objective agreeableness. If aesthetic value were prescriptive—so goes the objection—then the judgment that a thing has aesthetic value would issue in a motive to do what it is that we regard aesthetic value as prescribing, just as the judgment that an action has moral value issues in a motive to perform that action. But the judgment that a thing has aesthetic value issues in no motive to do anything. To insist otherwise is to deny the disinterestedness thesis, a thesis without which we cannot explain difference between moral and aesthetic judgment.

Do we need the disinterestedness thesis to explain the difference between moral and aesthetic value? I do not see why. Instead of distinguishing between judgments of moral and aesthetic value according to whether they motivate, we might distinguish between them according to what or how they motivate. Or, putting the point in Kantian terms, instead of distinguishing between pleasure in the good and pleasure in the beautiful by holding the former alone to stand in a relation to the faculty of desire, we might distinguish between them by holding each to stand in its own distinctive relation to that faculty.[2] This alternative has advantages. One is that it allows us to preserve the explanation just given as to why we are concerned that our judgments of aesthetic value be true. Another is that at least some judgments of aesthetic value certainly *seem* to issue in motives. Suppose, modifying an example from Hannah Ginsborg, that someone judges, based on what she reads in a travel guidebook, that the Dada Hari mosque is beautiful (Ginsborg 2015, p. 25).[3] It certainly seems that her judgment would issue in a motive to visit the mosque.

2 Against Subjectivism

It might reasonably be objected that I have been too quick. For one thing, in assuming that someone might judge an object to be beautiful merely on the basis of reading that it is, I have contradicted subjectivism, a thesis for which a strong case can be made.

Subjectivism, as defined above, holds that judging an object to be beautiful (or to be aesthetically valuable, more generally) depends on the sentiments of the person making the judgment and not on that person's recognition of a property residing in the object. I take Hannah Ginsborg to be subjectivism's ablest defender. To her objectivist opponents, John McDowell and David Wiggins, she makes three concessions. She concedes, first, that it is no argument against their brand of objectivism that we judge beauty by pleasure since there is no reason why pleasure may not designate an objective feature in the object. She concedes, second, that it is no argument against their brand of objectivism that there are no rules by which we judge beauty, since there is no reason to think there are rules by which we judge color, which all sides agree to be objective. And she concedes, third and most importantly, that the phenomena favor objectivism. She concedes, that is, that aesthetic experience presents beauty as if it resided in objects independent of aesthetic experience, just as color experience presents color as if it resided in objects independent of color experience (Ginsborg 2015, p. 25). In making this final concession, she assumes the burden of proof. She acknowledges that the considerations she marshals in favor of her subjectivism must be such that the objectivist cannot ex-

---

[2] Kant recognizes only two ways of standing in relation to the faculty of desire: the way in which the agreeable stands (KU: 205–207) and the way in which the good stands (KU: 207–209). I am arguing for a third way.

[3] Ginsborg produces this example to show, contrary to the assumption that I am making, that one could *not* judge the mosque to be beautiful on the basis of what one reads. I consider Ginsborg's example at length below.

plain them with equal plausibility. Otherwise, we should take aesthetic experience at face value and side with the objectivist.

What are the considerations that Ginsborg marshals in favor of subjectivism, the considerations that purport to show that aesthetic experience is not as it seems? Ginsborg contends that were aesthetic experience as it seems—were beauty independent of experience in the sense McDowell and Wiggins take it to be[4]—then we could claim that things are beautiful without having experienced them for ourselves, which we cannot (Ginsborg 2015, p. 26). To spell this out, Ginsborg produces the guidebook example I appropriate above. In Ginsborg's version, the guidebook describes the Dada Hari mosque as both reddish-gray and beautiful. If the mosque's beauty were objective in the way its color is, Ginsborg argues, a reader who has never seen the mosque could claim that it is beautiful just as she can claim that it is reddish-gray. But she cannot. She can claim that the mosque *is said* to be beautiful, and she can claim that the mosque *is supposed* to be beautiful. But she cannot claim that the mosque *is* beautiful because part of what she conveys when she makes this claim is that she has experienced it for herself. This leads Ginsborg to conclude that

> [the] ascription [of beauty] to an object in any particular case depends on the sentiments of the particular human being making the ascription. [Moreover] the subjectivity of beauty is a matter, not only of its relation to human sensibility in general, but also to its relation to the sensibility of each particular individual who makes a judgment of beauty. (Ginsborg 2015, 27)

Ginsborg's argument for subjectivism, as I understand it, has something like this basic form:
1. S cannot claim that O is beautiful unless she has experienced O for herself.
2. Therefore, S cannot judge that O is beautiful—that is, she cannot ascribe beauty to O—unless she has experienced O for herself.
3. Therefore, beauty is subjective.

Though I think there is more than one thing wrong with this argument, I wish to confine attention for now to the second premise. According to it, Ginsborg's guide-

---

[4] McDowell and Wiggins understand beauty to be independent of experience in roughly the sense that reddish-grayness is. According to them, I can judge the Dada Hari mosque to be beautiful without experiencing it to be beautiful just as I can judge the Dada Hari mosque to be reddish-gray without experiencing it to be reddish-gray. The objectivism of McDowell and Wiggins, however, is less than robust. Both understood beauty and reddish-grayness to be anthropocentric in the sense that we cannot say what it is for the mosque to be either beautiful or reddish-gray without appeal to human sensibility. See McDowell 1998a and 1998b and Wiggins 1987.

book reader cannot judge that the Dada Hari mosque is beautiful by reading that it is beautiful in a guidebook. But surely the reader can come to have a motive—that is, she can come to regard herself as having a reason—to visit the mosque by reading in the guidebook that it is beautiful. My question is how this is possible. How can the reader come to have a motive to visit the mosque without judging that the mosque is beautiful? Ginsborg addresses this question, but what she says is inadequate. She has us suppose that "the guidebook had been written by a group of highly respected experts on Indian architecture, and that they had all agreed on the beauty of the Dada Hari Mosque." She has us suppose, further, that "[a reader of the guidebook] had visited all the buildings described in the guidebook except for the Dada Hari mosque, and that [she] agreed with the experts' judgment on each one of them" (Ginsborg 2015, 26). In such a case, Ginsborg maintains:

> [The guidebook reader] would now have reason to trust the taste of the guidebook writers. But [she] would still be in no position to claim that the Dada Hari mosque is beautiful. [Her] justified confidence in the experts' taste might improve [her] position in other ways. It might allow [her], for example, to predict that if [she] were to see the mosque, [she] too would find it beautiful. And it might, accordingly, provide [her] with a reason for going to see the Dada Hari mosque. But it would not allow [her] to follow the experts in asserting the beauty of the mosque. If asked, say, why [she] planned to visit the mosque, [she] could not reply "Because it is beautiful." The most [she] would be able to say in explanation of her desire to visit the mosque is that it is said to be beautiful or that it is supposed to be beautiful. By contrast, it would be absurd if [she] were to confine [herself], in talk of the mosque's color, to the claim that it is supposed to be reddish-grey. For the testimony of even a single reliable witness makes it possible for [her] to assert—albeit subject to possible correction—that the mosque *is* reddish-grey. (Ginsborg 2015, 26–27, emphasis in original)

Ginsborg here argues that the guidebook reader's motive for visiting the mosque cannot be that it is beautiful. If that were her motive, then, when asked why she is planning to see the mosque, she would be able to say (and presumably would say) "Because it is beautiful." Since she would not be able to say this (and so does not say it), it cannot be her motive. That much is clear. Less clear is Ginsborg's positive view of what the reader's motive is. Early in the passage, she suggests that it is the reader's prediction that she will find the mosque beautiful if she visits it. Later, however, she seems to suggest that it is what the reader says when asked for her reason, namely, that the mosque is said or supposed to be beautiful.

One problem with the first suggestion—that the reader's motive is her prediction that she will find the mosque beautiful—is that when asked why she is planning to visit the mosque, she does not say "Because I predict I will find it beautiful." She says "Because it is said to be beautiful" or "Because it is supposed to be beautiful." It is, of course, possible—and I shall have more to say about this later—that when asked for her motive, the reader says one thing when she means another. But Ginsborg cannot acknowledge this possibility without undermining her argument against the objectivist, who may then claim that when the reader says she is going to visit the mosque because it is supposed or said to be beautiful, she means that she is going because it is beautiful. A second and more serious problem is that the reader's prediction that she will find the mosque beautiful is not, by itself, a motive to visit the mosque. For suppose, altering the example, that the guidebook reader recognizes the guidebook authors to be experts not merely about Indian architecture but also about her own psychology. Suppose further that the authors assert that although the mosque is not beautiful the reader will find that it is. Under such circumstances, the reader will predict that she will find the mosque beautiful, but she will not, I think, take herself to have reason to visit it. (Unless, that is, she cares only about how the mosque makes her feel, in which case she cares for the agreeable and not the beautiful.) She will take herself to have reason to visit the mosque only if she predicts, not only that she will find the mosque beautiful, but that she will not be mistaken in finding it that way. She will take herself to have reason to visit the mosque, in other words, only if she judges that it is beautiful.

What, then, of Ginsborg's second suggestion—that the reader's motive for planning to visit the mosque is that it is said or supposed to be beautiful? There is good reason to think that this suggestion represents Ginsborg's considered view. Not only is it what Ginsborg has her reader say when she is asked for her reason, it is, as Ginsborg puts it, "the most [the reader] would be able to say" (Ginsborg 2015, 26). But notice that the most the reader would be able to say when asked for her motive for visiting the mosque is less than a motive for visiting the mosque. For suppose, altering the example, that the reader does not believe the mosque is as it is said or supposed to be. Then, although she will still believe that the mosque is said or supposed to be beautiful, she will not take herself to have any reason to visit it. She will take herself to have reason to visit the mosque only if she believes that it is as it is said or supposed to be. She will take herself to have a reason to visit the mosque, in other words, only if she judges that it is beautiful.

I therefore think that the reader will not regard herself as having a reason to visit the mosque if all she does is judge that it is supposed or said to be beautiful or predicts that she will find it beautiful. She must judge that it is beautiful. But if she can judge that it is beautiful on the authority of the guidebook, what prevents her from claiming that it is beautiful on the same authority?

The answer is nothing. Imagine an unscrupulous guidebook reader who, having never visited the Dada Hari mosque and wishing to suggest that she is a well-traveled connoisseur of fine architecture, says "The Dada Hari mosque is beautiful." What has she claimed if not that the Dada Hari mosque is beautiful? I grant that in claiming that the mosque is beautiful, she has violated a conversational norm. I grant that in claiming that the mosque is beautiful, she has suggested, falsely, that she has visited the mosque. But since nothing prevents her from violating a conversational norm or from suggesting falsely, nothing prevents her from claiming that the mosque is beautiful.

Or, to take a different kind of case, imagine a scrupulous guidebook reader who, when asked why she is planning to visit the mosque, says "Because it is supposed to be beautiful." What is she claiming when she says this? One possibility is that she is claiming simply that the mosque is supposed to be beautiful. Another possibility is that she is claiming, albeit in a qualified way, that the mosque is beautiful. Which of the possibilities obtains turns on questions under debate in the philosophy of language.[5] But whichever possibility obtains, this much is clear: the reader is claiming whatever she is claiming in order to communicate *that the mosque is beautiful*. Were she not communicating that the mosque is beautiful, she would not be giving a reason for visiting the mosque, which is what has been requested of her.

I therefore think that Ginsborg misrepresents the disanalogy between beauty and color. There is no disanalogy at the level of judgment. The reader can judge on the basis of testimony that the Dada Hari mosque is beautiful just as she can judge on the basis of testimony that the Dada Hari mosque is reddish-gray. Nor is there any disanalogy at the level of communication. The reader can communicate her judgment, made on the basis of testimony, that the Dada Hari mosque is beautiful, just as she can communicate her judgment, made on the basis of testimony, that the Dada Hari mosque is reddish-gray. There is, however, a disanalogy at *the level of conversational norm*. The reader cannot say "The Dada Hari is beautiful" without suggesting she has seen it, whereas she can say "The Dada Hari is reddish-gray" without suggesting that she has seen it. We have established that this disanalogy does not point to the subjectivity of judgments of beauty. To what then, it might be wondered, does it point?

I think there are probably many good ways of answering this question consistent with the objectivity of judgments of beauty. Here, I can at most gesture toward the answer I favor. When you say "O is beautiful," you suggest more than that you have experienced O for yourself. You suggest that in experiencing O for yourself, you have found O beautiful and therefore have what it takes to find O beautiful. What it takes to find O beautiful depends on the kind of thing O is, but it includes qualities it is good to have and correspondingly bad not to have. Often, it includes virtues—honesty, moral judgment, intelligence, bravery even—whose presence or absence in your character go in to making you the person you are. This explains

---

5 I am indebted here to a conversation with Tim Sundell.

why when you say "O is beautiful" you stake yourself in a way you do not when you say "O is supposed to be beautiful." I am not claiming that in saying "O is beautiful" people generally aim at suggesting good things about themselves, though some people sometimes clearly have this aim. (Think, for example, of the unscrupulous guidebook reader discussed above). I am claiming that there is a difference between the speech-act you perform in saying "O is beautiful" and the speech-act you perform in saying "O is supposed to be beautiful." I am claiming that there is a difference in the kind of commitment you make to O's being beautiful in each case, a difference underwritten by the difference in the way you risk yourself in the one case but not in the other. And I am claiming that there is no corresponding difference between the way you risk yourself when you judge first-hand that a thing is reddish-gray and the way you risk yourself when you judge on the basis of testimony that it is reddish-gray, and so no corresponding need to mark this difference in talk about colors.

I conclude that Ginsborg's argument for subjectivism fails. Both of its premises are false: you do not need to experience O for yourself in order to *claim* that O is beautiful, nor do you do need to experience O for yourself in order to *judge* that O is beautiful. If Ginsborg's argument for subjectivism is the best on offer, we had better take aesthetic experience at face value. We had better hold beauty to reside in objects independent of any particular subject's experience of it. We had better be objectivists.

3 Against Disinterestedness

Let us return to Ginsborg's guidebook reader. She reads that the Dada Hari mosque is beautiful. She judges, on the basis of what she reads, that the mosque is beautiful. She finds, in making that judgment by testimony, that she has a reason to visit the mosque. What is the relation between her judging by testimony that the mosque is beautiful and her finding that she has a reason to visit it? Here is a proposal: what the reader judges when she judges by testimony that the mosque is beautiful is that the mosque is such as to give her—and others—a reason to judge it to have just the beauty it has, where judging it to have just the beauty it has is something she can do only by judging on the basis of her own experience, in other words, by judging it aesthetically, that is, by experiencing it to be beautiful in some particular way that it is.[6] If that is right, the reader's testimonial judgment of beauty moti-

---

6 See Shelley 2022 for an account of what it is to experience an object to be beautiful and hence what it is to aesthetically judge an object to be beautiful.

vates an aesthetic judgment of beauty, since she cannot make the former without regarding herself as having a reason to make the latter.

Suppose the guidebook reader now acts on the reason she judges herself and others to have in making her judgment by testimony. She visits the mosque and judges aesthetically that it has the particular beauty that it has. It seems that there must be some overlap in content or implication between the aesthetic judgment she now makes and the judgment by testimony she previously made. Otherwise, it would be impossible for her aesthetic judgment to confirm or disconfirm her testimonial judgment. Otherwise, the two judgments, testimonial and aesthetic, would not both be judgments of beauty. If the reader's prior testimonial judgment holds the mosque to be such as to rationalize some particular aesthetic judgment of beauty, then the aesthetic judgment of beauty she now makes must also hold the mosque to be such as to rationalize some particular aesthetic judgment of beauty. Both judgments refer to the same particular aesthetic judgment of beauty by predicating of the mosque that it is such that it ought to be the object of that particular aesthetic judgment. If the reader's judgment by testimony that the mosque is beautiful motivates an aesthetic judgment that the mosque is beautiful, then the reader's aesthetic judgment that the mosque is beautiful motivates itself.

This claim—the claim that aesthetic judgments of beauty are self-motivating—will remind some of Ginsborg's claim that aesthetic judgments of beauty are self-referential. But to identify them would be a mistake. As I understand Ginsborg's self-referentiality claim, the reader's aesthetic judgment that the mosque is beautiful is not about the mosque but about itself, and what it says about itself is that it is the judgment that anyone in the same objective circumstances ought to make (Ginsborg 2015, Chapter 2). According to the self-motivation claim I am asserting, the reader's aesthetic judgment that the mosque is beautiful is not about itself but about the mosque, and what it says about the mosque is that it is such that it ought to be the object of that very aesthetic judgment regardless of objective circumstances. So, my claim differs from Ginsborg's with respect both to object and normative scope. We may put this latter difference by saying that whereas Ginsborg takes the judgment that the mosque is beautiful to be normative in the conditional way that all judgments are, that is, to be the judgment that everyone ought to make on condition that they are in the same objective circumstances as the subject, I take the judgment to be normative in the unconditional way that only judgments of aesthetic value are, that is, to be the judgment that everyone ought to make no matter their objective circumstances.[7]

---

[7] The claim that judgments of beauty are unconditionally normative in this sense is not the claim that they are overriding. It is a claim about normative scope and not about normative strength. I

This difference in normative scope matters. The claim that judgments of aesthetic value are normative in a special, unconditional way is required to explain not only how aesthetic judgments of beauty can confirm or disconfirm testimonial judgments of beauty, but also why, as Kant puts it, aesthetic judgments of beauty "strengthen[.] and reproduce[.]" themselves—why, that is, "we linger over the consideration of the beautiful" (KU: 222). For suppose that aesthetic judgments of beauty are normative merely in the conditional way all judgments are. Then it would seem that the guidebook reader has no more motive to linger over the consideration of the mosque's beauty than she has to linger over the consideration of its reddish-grayness. If, however, judgments of beauty are normative in the unconditional way I am suggesting, then the motive the reader has to alter her circumstances when she judges by testimony that the mosque is beautiful is the motive she has to remain in her circumstances when she judges aesthetically that the mosque is beautiful. That something is beautiful is a reason to consider it, whether considering it means taking up its consideration or lingering over it.[8]

Now, the reader's judgment by testimony, being a logical judgment, is not based on pleasure, and so not based on disinterested pleasure. From this, however, it does not follow that the reader's judgment by testimony is not accompanied by pleasure. Perhaps interested pleasure accompanies her judgment by testimony in something like the way Kant takes interested pleasure to accompany judgments of the good. After all, her testimonial judgment results in willed activity—her visit to the mosque, in this case—and Kant holds that all judgments resulting in willed activity necessarily involve interested pleasure (MS: 399). But whether or not interested pleasure accompanies the reader's testimonial judgment, it seems that that judgment must be practical rather than contemplative. This follows from the fact that the reader cannot judge by testimony that a thing is beautiful without at the same time regarding herself (and others) as having a reason to aesthetically judge it to have the beauty it has.

Hence the disinterestedness thesis, interpreted simply as the thesis that ascriptions of beauty do not motivate, is false, at least with respect to those ascriptions of beauty that are based on testimony. Such ascriptions are essentially motivating. But perhaps it will be replied that this result is uninteresting. Perhaps it will be replied that the disinterestedness thesis has never been thought to apply to judgments of beauty by testimony, but only to aesthetic judgments of beauty. I think there is something to this reply. Consider Ginsborg. It is not surprising that she

---

follow Katalin Makkai (Makkai 2010) and Richard Moran (Moran 2012) in asserting aesthetic judgments of beauty to be unconditionally normative in this way.

8 This does not imply that judgments of beauty based on testimony motivate aesthetic judgments of beauty to the degree that aesthetic judgments of beauty motivate themselves.

does not take up the question whether judgments of beauty based on testimony are motivating given her conviction that none exist. And I suspect that what is true of Ginsborg may be true of many other interpreters of Kant and of Kant himself. When they say that judgments of beauty do not result in desires or motives or reasons to act, they have in mind merely aesthetic judgments of beauty.

So, suppose we restrict the scope of the disinterestedness thesis such that it applies only to aesthetic judgments of beauty. The question remains whether, once we have acknowledged that there are judgments of beauty based on testimony and that they are motivating, we might still maintain that aesthetic judgments of beauty are not motivating. How might we picture this? In making her judgment based on testimony that the mosque is beautiful the guidebook reader takes herself to have reason to do something, namely, to make an aesthetic judgment that the mosque has the beauty it has. In making her aesthetic judgment, it might be held, the reader does not take herself to have reason to do anything, including making the aesthetic judgment she is making. She simply finds herself in a naturally self-perpetuating state of pleasure, and, having no reason to depart from that state, persists in it. Hence the judgment by testimony, because it gives the reader a motive to act, is practical, and any pleasure that accompanies it is interested. In contrast, the aesthetic judgment, because it gives the reader no motive to act, is contemplative and the pleasure that does accompany it is disinterested.

What, if anything, is wrong with this picture? What is wrong is that it makes it difficult to see how the reader's aesthetic judgment might confirm (or disconfirm) her testimonial judgment. For it must be possible for the reader, in aesthetically judging the mosque to be beautiful, to confirm that it was worth her trouble to visit the mosque in order to experience the mosque's beauty for herself, that is, to make the very aesthetic judgement she is making. But this just means that it must be possible for the reader, in aesthetically judging the mosque to have the beauty it has, to confirm that she has the reason to visit the mosque she judged herself to have when she judged by testimony that the mosque is beautiful. But, of course, she cannot judge herself to have this reason when she aesthetically judges the mosque if she does not judge herself to have any reason to do anything with respect to the mosque, including making the judgment about it she is making. In sum, if the reader's testimonial judgment of beauty motivates an aesthetic judgment of beauty, and if her aesthetic judgment of beauty can confirm her testimonial judgment of beauty, it seems that her aesthetic judgment of beauty must also motivate an aesthetic judgment of beauty. Indeed, it seems that her testimonial judgment and her aesthetic judgment must motivate the same aesthetic judgment. If the testimonial judgment motivates the aesthetic judgment, the aesthetic judgment motivates itself.

If this is right, we have reason to think that the disinterestedness thesis is in trouble even when restricted to aesthetic judgments of beauty. Of course, there is something the thesis gets right. When you make an aesthetic judgment of beauty, you are in a self-maintaining state. The question is whether this state maintains itself because you have no interest in leaving it or because you have an interest in staying in it. The question is whether aesthetic judgments of beauty are distinctive because they stand in no relation to the faculty of desire or distinctive because of the distinctive relation in which they stand to it.

I have been arguing throughout this paper for the latter. In § 1, I argued that our speaking of beauty as if it were property of objects precludes aesthetic judgments of beauty from issuing in hedonic motives. The arguments of § 2 abet the arguments of § 1, establishing that our speaking of beauty as if it were a property of objects owes to its being is a property of objects. The objectivity of aesthetic judgments of beauty makes them motivationally like judgments of goodness and motivationally unlike aesthetic judgments of agreeability. In the present section, I have been arguing that aesthetic judgments of beauty are self-motivating. In this respect they are motivationally like aesthetic judgments of agreeability and motivationally unlike judgments of goodness. When you aesthetically judge something to be beautiful or agreeable, you necessarily judge it to be such as to give you reason to make the very judgment you are making,[9] but when you judge something to be good, you necessarily judge it to be such as to give you reason to do something beyond making the judgment you are making. It is because aesthetic judgments of beauty are objective yet self-motivating that they stand in a distinctive relation to the faculty of desire. Pleasure in the beautiful strengthens and reproduces itself not because it is pleasure but because of what it discloses about its object, namely, its beauty.[10]

4 Beyond Hedonism

What, then, is it to say that the Dada Hari mosque is beautiful? It is to say, first, that the mosque possesses an objective property, one residing in the mosque independently of the sentiments of any particular subject. And it is to say, second, that that property consists in the mosque's being some particular way such that we have reason, independent of our circumstances, to experience it as being that way.

---

9 Aesthetic judgments of agreeability are not unconditionally normative because they are not universal.
10 Keren Gorodeisky's compelling reading of Kant on testimony and subjectivism suggests that the positions I have defended here are not as distant from Kant's as might seem. See Gorodeisky 2010.

If we generalize this second point, we arrive at the following account of aesthetic value:

> The aesthetic value of an object consists in its being some particular way such that we have unconditional reason to experience it as being that way.

This is the account toward which we have been working since we rejected hedonism in § 1. We rejected hedonism then because it cannot reconcile itself with our concern to make true aesthetic judgments. Either it enjoins that we aesthetically overvalue whenever possible, or it converts itself from an account of aesthetic value into an account of aesthetic evaluation, or it attempts, incoherently, to do both at once. The present account is not merely consistent with our concern to make true aesthetic judgments but expressive of it. Aesthetically valuable objects, it tells us, just are those we have unconditional reason to aesthetically judge as having just the aesthetic value they have.

Some will dismiss this account on the grounds that it does not attempt to explain why things having aesthetic value are valuable, something an account of aesthetic value must do. Some will hold that hedonism, whatever its failings, at least does that. I certainly have not meant to deny that for everything that has aesthetic value, there is something that explains why it has it. But I am happy to deny that it belongs to philosophy to tell us what it is. "What makes the Dada Hari mosque beautiful?" is a perfectly good question. Its answer, if the present account is right, is whatever makes the mosque such that we have unconditional reason to experience it as being such. If you want to know what that is, philosophy cannot help you. Nothing but your own experience can.[11]

Abbreviations

All references to Kant's works are to Kant's Gesammelte Schriften, Ausgabe der Preußischen Akademie der Wissenschaften (Berlin: De Gruyter, 1902 ff.). Translations are from The Cambridge Edition of the Works of Immanuel Kant.

The following abbreviations of individual works are used:

KU Kritik der Urteilskraft / Critique of the Power Judgment
MS Die Metaphysik der Sitten / Metaphysics of Morals

---

[11] For criticism on versions of this paper, I thank audiences at the Auburn Philosophical Society, the Conference on Disinterested Pleasure hosted by the University of Siegen, and the Workshop on Experience, Pleasure and Values hosted by New York University in Florence.

Literature

Beardsley, Monroe (1970): "The Aesthetic Point of View." In: *Metaphilosophy* 1. No. 1, pp. 39–58.
Ginsborg, Hannah (2015): *The Normativity of Nature: Essays on Kant's Critique of Judgment*. Oxford: Oxford University Press.
Ginsborg, Hannah (2019): "Kant's Aesthetics and Teleology." In: Zalta, Edward N. (Ed.): *The Stanford Encyclopedia of Philosophy*. https://plato.stanford.edu/archives/win2019/entries/kant-aesthetics, last accessed on Jan. 29, 2023.
Gorodeisky, Keren (2010): "A New Look at Kant's View of Aesthetic Testimony." In: *British Journal of Aesthetics* 50. No. 1, pp. 53–70.
Kant, Immanuel (1996): *The Metaphysics of Morals*. Mary Gregor (Trans.). Cambridge: Cambridge University Press.
Kant, Immanuel (2000): *Critique of the Power of Judgment*. Paul Guyer and Eric Matthews (Trans.). Cambridge: Cambridge University Press.
Makkai, Katalin (2010): "Kant on Recognizing Beauty." In: *European Journal of Philosophy* 18. No. 3, pp. 385–413.
McDowell, John (1998a): "Aesthetic Value, Objectivity, and the Fabric of the World." In: McDowell, John: *Mind, Value, and Reality*. Cambridge: Harvard University Press, pp. 112–130.
McDowell, John (1998b): "Values and Secondary Qualities." In: McDowell, John: *Mind, Value, and Reality*. Cambridge: Harvard University Press, pp. 131–150.
Miller, Richard (1998): "Three Versions of Objectivity: Aesthetic, Moral, and Scientific." In: Levinson, Jerrold (Ed.): *Aesthetics and Ethics: Essays at the Intersection*. Cambridge: Cambridge University Press, pp. 26–58.
Moran, Richard (2012): "Kant, Proust, and the Appeal of Beauty." In: *Critical Inquiry* 38. No. 2, pp. 298–329.
Shelley, James (2022): "Intelligible Beauty." In: *Aristotelian Society Supplemental Volume* 96. No. 1, pp. 147–164.
Wiggins, David (1987): "A Sensible Subjectivism?" In: Wiggins, David: *Needs, Values, Truth: Essays in the Philosophy of Value*. Oxford: Blackwell, pp. 118–214.

Author Index

Abacı, Uygar   15
Abramović, Marina   176f.
Abrams, Meyer H.   253
Adelung, Johann Christoph   187
Adorno, Theodor W.   172f.
Alberti, Leon Battista   17
Allison, Henry E.   18, 38, 41, 43, 48, 69, 92, 184, 186–188, 221, 225
Ameriks, Karl   48, 227
André, Carl   198
Anscombe, Gertrude E. M.   126, 149
Arendt, Hannah   128
Aydede, Murat   239–241

Bach, Johann Sebastian   93
Bain, David   241, 246f.
Baumgarten, Alexander Gottlieb   20–22, 87, 89
Baz, Avner   189
Beardsley, Monroe   135f., 258
Beiser, Frederick   12
Bell, David   192
Bender, John   226
Benovsky, Jiri   234
Berger, Larissa   4f., 15–18, 31, 33, 42, 47
Berleant, Arnold   184, 253
Bermúdez, José Luis   242
Berthier, Marcelo   246
Bhattacharyya, Krishna C.   238
Bolzano, Bernard   236
Bouhours, Dominique   122
Bourdieu, Pierre   72, 253
Brewer, Talbot   139
Brodskij, Iosif   123
Budd, Malcolm   68
Bullough, Edward   109
Burke, Edmund   53, 87

Cage, John   197, 199f.
Camp, Elisabeth   169, 178
Carlson, Allen   234
Caro, Anthony   197
Carroll, Noël   226
Carter, Elliott   197

Casey, Kenneth L.   239
Castiglione, Baldassarre   119, 125
Cavell, Stanley   161, 170
Cavedon-Taylor, Dan   137
Chardin, Jean Siméon   197f., 200
Châtelet, Albert   200
Chignell, Andrew   37
Cole, Michaela   144
Costello, Diarmuid   116–118, 121
Crawford, Donald W.   32, 41, 43, 47–49, 220
Croce, Benedetto   12
Crowther, Paul   2, 32, 46

Dahlstrom, Daniel O.   21, 28
D'Angelo, Paolo   119, 122
Danto, Arthur   116f.
David, Jacques-Louis   197f.
De Clercq, Rafaël   234, 238
Derrida, Jacques   115, 253
Dickie, George   2, 70, 110, 135–137
Diderot, Denis   198
Du Bos, Jean-Baptiste   22–24
Dunn, Nicholas   148

Eagleton, Terry   72
Eaton, Anne   141
Eaton, Marcia Muelder   238
Edgley, Roy   152
Eldridge, Richard   167, 174
Elster, Jon   124–126
Evans, Gareth   152, 242

Fan, Dahan   94, 100
Feijoo, Benito Jerónimo   122
Felski, Rita   155
Ferrara, Alessandro   128
Ford, Anton   150
Fricke, Christel   32, 38, 46, 191, 216f., 219
Fricker, Miranda   243
Fried, Michael   183, 185, 197–200, 203f.

Gadamer, Hans-Georg   108
Gard, Tim   246

Garroni, Emilio   106–108, 112 f., 128
Gaut, Berys   178
Gendler, Tamar Szabó   178
Ginsborg, Hannah   12, 41, 59, 226, 242, 257, 262–270
Gorodeisky, Keren   2, 4 f., 7, 39 f., 141, 143, 146, 148, 161, 238, 271
Gould, Carol S.   167, 176 f., 179
Gracián, Baldassare   122
Greuze, Jean-Baptiste   197
Grimm, Jacob and Wilhelm   48, 187
Grundler, Alexandra   153, 158 f.
Guyer, Paul   4, 6, 11, 13, 16, 18, 20, 32 f., 35, 38 f., 50–52, 59, 61 f., 65, 67, 69, 74, 78, 83, 88, 112 f., 118, 184, 186–189, 191, 216 f., 220–225, 241–243

Hampl, Patricia   155
Hampshire, Stuart   160 f.
Hande Tuna, Emine   118
Hanna, Robert   242
Heidegger, Martin   170
Henss, Ronald   212
Hilgers, Thomas   5, 7, 38, 167–174, 176–179
Hirschhorn, Thomas   127
Hohenegger, Hansmichael   107
Höwing, Thomas   92
Hughes, Fiona   6 f., 18, 188 f., 192–194, 204–206, 208 f.
Hume, David   13, 17, 24, 68, 73, 83, 109, 178, 215, 220
Husserl, Edmund   33
Hutcheson, Francis   11, 13, 17, 26, 220, 236

Jeffers, Oliver   135, 163
Johnston, Mark   238
Judd, Donald   198

Kafka, Franz   174
Kandinsky, Wassily   93
Kästner, Erich   93
Kemal, Salim   65
Kern, Andrea   51
Klein, Colin   241, 246 f.
Korsmeyer, Carolyn   137, 141, 145
Kovach, Francis J.   238
Kristeller, Paul Oskar   11

Kulenkampff, Jens   51, 227
Kuspit, Donald   33

Leibniz, Gottfried Wilhelm   122 f.
Leiguarda, Ramon   246
Leopardi, Giacomo   123 f.
Levinson, Jerrold   212 f., 234, 239
LeWitt, Sol   198
Longuenesse, Beatrice   32
Lopes, Dominic McIver   5–7, 234 f., 237 f., 245, 252
Lorand, Ruth   114

Makkai, Katalin   269
Makkreel, Rudolf   32
Malabou, Catherine   113, 127 f.
Malick, Terrence   174
Marcus, Eric   141, 238
Marivaux, Pierre Carlet de Chamblain de   122
Markosian, Ned   80
Matherne, Samantha   167, 169–171, 173
Matisse, Henry   155
Matthen, Mohan   250–252
Matthews, Eric   59, 62, 78, 187
Matthews, Patricia M.   32, 35
McCloskey, Mary   40, 74
McDowell, John   262 f.
McMahon, Jennifer A.   18, 212
Meerbote, Ralf   32, 39, 225
Melchionne, Kevin   244
Melzack, Ronald   239
Mendelssohn, Moses   4, 6, 11 f., 16, 20–28
Meredith, James Creed   59, 62–66, 70–72, 74–76, 78 f., 81, 84
Merleau-Ponty, Maurice   33
Merritt, Melissa   150
Miller, Richard   199, 259–261
Mitchell, Jonathan   246
Mitchell, Joni   155 f.
Monet, Claude   41, 44
Moran, Richard   150, 152, 160, 162, 269
Mothersill, Mary   236
Murdoch, Iris   252

Nanay, Bence   6, 109–113, 124
Nehamas, Alexander   3, 17, 253
Noë, Alva   112 f.

Parsons, Glenn 234
Peacocke, Christopher 242
Perlman, David M. 246
Perry, Imani 154
Pettit, Philip 226
Plato 236
Pluhar, Werner 186 f., 189, 194, 204, 208
Pollok, Anne 22, 26
Pound, Ezra 123
Poussin, Nicolas 197
Proust, Marcel 137, 157-159

Rauschenberg, Robert 197
Rembrandt 197
Riefenstahl, Leni 179
Riggle, Nick 1 f., 4, 40, 135–140, 143, 145, 149, 151–153, 157 f., 162 f., 234
Rilke, Rainer Maria 137
Rind, Miles 1 f., 88, 137, 220, 225, 233 f., 236
Robinson, Jenefer 25
Roskies, Adina 242

Schiller, Friedrich 193, 208
Schmalzried, Lisa 5, 7, 48, 167 f., 172, 175, 214 f., 220, 223
Schönecker, Dieter 52, 54
Scruton, Roger 69
Shaftesbury, Anthony Ashley Cooper, third earl of 11 f., 26 f., 220, 234
Shelley, James 1, 5, 7, 137, 140, 234, 237–239, 250, 267
Shiner, Larry 253
Sibley, Frank 61, 234
Sinnerbrink, Robert 251
Smith, Roland David 197
Smith, Tony 198
Smith, Zadie 155 f., 162
Sontag, Susan 234
Starkstein, Sergio 246

Stecker, Robert 224
Steinberg, Leo 118
Stolnitz, Jerome 11, 136, 220, 233 f.

Taylor, Charles 160
Thompson, Evan 246
Thomson, Judith Jarvis 235
Thuillier, Jacques 200
Todd, Cain Samuel 235
Townsend, Dabney 73, 220
Tugendhat, Ernst 170

Vaccarino Bremner, Sabina 128
Van der Berg, Servaas 234, 237
Vandenabeele, Bart 87, 89, 217, 220
Velotti, Stefano 6, 116, 122, 125

Walton, Kendall 116, 143
Watkins, Michael 237
Weil, Eric 112 f.
Wenzel, Christian Helmut 4, 6, 32, 51, 88–90, 94
Wiggins, David 226, 262 f.
Williams, Jessica 70
Williams, John 137, 143, 156, 158
Winnicott, Donald W. 183, 185, 196, 200–204
Wittgenstein, Ludwig 69, 175
Wolff, Christian 21
Wollheim, Richard 12
Wolterstorff, Nicholas 253
Wood, Peter 154

Zammito, John 38
Zangwill, Nick 5 f., 32, 60, 63 f., 70–73, 75, 77, 83, 87, 92, 212, 216, 234, 239
Zemach, Eddy 226
Zuckert, Rachel 18, 35, 38, 46, 69 f., 84, 241–243, 245

Subject Index

absorption   183, 185, 197–201, 203
action   3, 6, 22, 27f., 35, 43–45, 47, 71, 112–114, 117, 123–125, 142–144, 146f., 149, 160, 177, 198, 200, 204, 206–208, 217f., 241, 244, 248, 250, 261
adherent beauty -> dependent beauty, adherent beauty (*anhängende Schönheit*)
aesthetic attitude -> disinterested attitude, aesthetic attitude
aesthetic deduction   225, 227
aesthetic differentiation   108
aesthetic dispositionalism   211, 226f.
aesthetic empiricism -> primitivist version of aesthetic empiricism, empiricist primitivism
aesthetic experience   3, 11f., 18–20, 28, 31, 69, 72, 105f., 108–112, 114, 124–127, 135–141, 143–145, 149, 151, 154f., 157, 159, 163, 167f., 175, 198, 216, 262f., 267
aesthetic feeling   61, 67
aesthetic idea   18, 108, 116, 118–122, 126, 193, 224
aesthetic judgment (of beauty)   1, 6f., 11, 13, 41, 52, 71, 89–91, 96, 100, 105, 107–109, 112, 116f., 128, 146, 184–194, 199f., 203–209, 225, 257, 259–261, 268–272
aesthetic normativity   238, 245, 248, 257, 261
aesthetic properties   63, 83, 214
aesthetic realism   83, 235
aesthetic reasons   235f., 238, 241, 243, 245, 248f.
aesthetic testimony -> testimony
aesthetic value -> value
agreeable, agreeableness, pleasure in the agreeable   17f., 28, 31, 36–38, 40f., 43, 45f., 48f., 54, 60, 65, 71f., 75–77, 83, 87f., 92, 94, 97f., 101, 108, 140, 142, 145–147, 186, 220–222, 260–262, 265, 271
amiability   211f., 214f., 218–220, 227
appearance   4, 11, 13, 18, 28, 64, 72, 118, 168, 214f., 218f., 241
approbation (*Billigung*)   22, 26–28
argument from exclusion, elimination argument   48f., 220

art, artwork, fine art   3, 6, 11f., 14, 17–20, 22–26, 28, 41, 48, 63, 69, 93–96, 105f., 113f., 116–127, 141, 167–179, 185, 194–200, 205, 209, 224, 234–236, 244, 251, 253, 259f.
asymbolia   6, 246–248
attention   2, 4, 6, 23, 70, 89, 91, 110f., 136, 145f., 172, 174, 179, 195, 199f., 202, 211, 234, 263
attraction
– a. thesis 211–213, 215, 218, 227
– sexual a., sexually attracted 212f.
attractiveness   7, 211–213

canary wine   60, 77
care characterization   6, 248–250
charm (*Reiz*)   23–25, 93, 101, 146
cognition   13, 20f., 26f., 34, 68, 108, 111f., 123, 189, 204, 208, 225
– c. in general 46f., 112f., 121, 126, 189, 192
– faculties of c., powers of c. 41f., 46, 88, 90, 107, 211, 222–228
– judgment of c. 222
– sensory c. 220
color   17f., 24, 36, 63, 124, 149, 234, 262–264, 266f.
common sense (*Gemeinsinn*) -> *sensus communis*, common sense (*Gemeinsinn*)
communication   172f., 175f., 266
compatibilism   241
composition (musical)   17, 24, 234
contemplation, contemplative   1f., 4, 6, 14, 38–40, 51, 64, 79, 93f., 105, 145f., 154, 159, 177, 183, 185f., 190, 194, 198, 200–204, 211, 215, 217, 223, 233f., 236, 250–252, 269f.
control   105f., 124, 126–129, 201, 234

demarcation, demarcation question   7, 76, 236, 238f., 243, 245, 251f.
dependent beauty, adherent beauty (*anhängende Schönheit*)   6, 105f., 114–116, 118, 141, 186, 193, 211, 218, 223f.
desire   3–6, 15, 22–24, 26–28, 31f., 35, 37f., 43–46, 48, 52, 59, 62–65, 67, 71f., 74–83,

88, 92f., 97, 105, 124, 136, 138–145, 150–163, 186, 213–215, 217, 219, 221, 227, 233, 239–244, 246, 249f., 264, 270
- faculty of desire 2, 4f., 32, 35–39, 42, 44, 49, 52, 61–63, 65, 139f., 144f., 147, 159, 261, 271
determination by interests 183, 185, 187f., 191f., 194f., 199, 203, 207–209
determining ground of aesthetic judgment -> principle of determination (*Bestimmungsgrund*) of the judgment of taste, determining ground of aesthetic judgment
didacticism 12
disegno 17
disinterested attitude, aesthetic attitude 2, 5, 7, 110, 168–170, 172f., 177f., 234
disinterest thesis -> thesis of disinterestedness (TD), disinterest thesis, disinterestedness thesis
drawing (*Zeichnung*) 17, 24, 93

elimination argument -> argument from exclusion, elimination argument
emotion (*Rührung*) 20, 22–25
entertainment 122f., 172f., 175f.
evaluation 160, 206–208, 235, 241, 245–247, 252, 259f., 272
evil 177–179
exemplarity, exemplary 89, 113, 115, 120, 126f., 188, 200, 208
existence, existence of the object 2, 4, 11–16, 19, 21f., 26f., 35–45, 47, 51f., 54, 61–64, 83, 92–95, 97, 99, 101, 105, 114f., 186f., 194, 196, 204f., 211f., 216f., 219, 221–223, 227f.

facilitating pleasure (vs. relief pleasure) -> pleasure
felt fact of beauty 52, 54
film 25, 117, 125, 170–172, 174f., 179
fine art -> art, artwork, fine art
form of purposiveness, formal purposiveness -> purposiveness, purposive
form of the representation -> representation
free beauty 6, 105f., 114–118, 211, 223f.
free play (of the faculties / of the powers of cognition) 5f., 12, 14, 16–19, 31f., 40–44, 48–50, 68, 78, 88, 94, 99–101, 112f., 121,

126, 147f., 172, 175, 179, 183f., 188–190, 192, 194, 196, 205, 211, 218, 222–228, 242f., 245f.

genius 19, 118–120, 126
good
- aesthetically g. 234f., 237
- interest in the g. 36, 42, 46, 193, 207
- good will -> will
- morally g. 37, 47, 93, 97, 101, 142, 220–222
- pleasure in the g., satisfaction in the g. 36–38, 42, 47, 49, 76, 83, 88, 92f., 101, 108, 140, 145, 220f., 261
grounding 50, 91, 153, 204, 221, 234

harmony 17, 20, 42, 50, 113, 122, 188, 205f., 236
heautonomy 114
hedonism, hedonist theory about aesthetic value 7, 237f., 257f., 260f., 271f.
human beauty 7, 168, 193, 211–215, 219f., 223f., 226–228
humanity 94, 96, 99, 101, 193

ideal of beauty 193, 218
image, images 4, 11f., 19, 25, 28, 64
imagination 11–14, 16–19, 23, 27f., 41, 46, 50, 68f., 88, 90, 97–102, 111–113, 120f., 126, 140, 147, 188–190, 192f., 222, 224f., 242f., 245f.
infinite judgment 107f.
interest
- definition of i. 32, 35f., 49, 216
- empirical i. 18f., 83, 94
- intellectual i. 6, 12, 19, 83, 87, 92, 94–96, 101
- of the senses 98f., 101, 216, 218, 221
- of reason 216f., 221
interruption 25, 183, 185, 200–204

judgment of taste 2, 6, 11, 13, 16f., 19, 31, 39f., 48f., 51, 53, 59f., 64–76, 78, 82, 87–95, 102, 107f., 114f., 117f., 186, 193, 216f., 219f., 222f., 225

linger, lingering 3, 43–45, 48, 79, 146, 211, 269
logical functions for judging 87, 89f., 91f., 102

matter of the representation -> representation
meanings (*Bedeutungen*)   106, 112f., 116, 120
melody   17, 95
meta-perspective (of an artwork)   167, 170, 172f., 175f., 179
modality   15, 98, 107
Moment, der / Moment, das   87, 90
moments (of the Analytic of the Beautiful, of the judgment of taste)   6, 51, 87–89, 187
momentum   87, 90
moralism   12
morality   66f., 72, 94–96, 176, 178, 192f., 204
motives   5f., 239–241, 243–247, 249–251, 262, 270f.
myth
– of inactivity 2, 135, 146
– of the absent self 2, 7, 135f., 149

nature
– and genius 119–121
– vs. art 94–96, 116–118
negotiation   6f., 142, 183–185, 188f., 191f., 194, 196, 200–203, 206–209
non-conceptuality, non-conceptual   5, 38f., 49, 108, 233, 242–246, 250
non-sense (*Unsinn*)   120
normativity   12, 59, 70–74, 77–79, 82f., 236, 238, 241, 243, 245f., 248
– of aesthetic judgment / judgments of taste 59, 71–74, 78, 82
– of aesthetic reasons 241, 243, 245, 248
– of aesthetic value 236
– of autonomy 245

object (*Gegenstand*)   2, 4, 11–24, 26f., 32, 35–49, 51, 53, 59, 61–66, 70, 73, 76–78, 81, 89–94, 96f., 99–102, 105, 109–111, 113–118, 121, 124, 126, 135f., 140–151, 153, 155, 158f., 161, 173–175, 186, 189, 192–194, 196, 199, 202–206, 211, 216f., 221–224, 226f., 236, 239, 242–244, 246, 257–259, 262f., 267f., 271f.
objectivism (about aesthetic value)   262f.
open-minded thinking   207f.
orientation   185, 189, 191, 203–206, 209
overvaluation   258–260

pain asymbolia -> asymbolia
perfection, perfectionist   12, 20–22, 24, 28, 93, 101, 122, 193, 223
perspective   7, 98, 100f., 109, 118, 127, 141, 145, 168–178, 187, 190, 192, 199, 203, 206, 233
phenomenological meaning of the thesis of disinterestedness   32, 50–54
phenomenological model of pleasure -> pleasure
play
– play (Winicott) 183, 185, 200–203
– p. and games 184, 190, 192
– p. of the faculties -> free play (of the faculties / of the powers of cognition)
playful, playfulness   6f., 183, 185, 188, 190–192, 194, 196, 200–209, 224
– playful orientation 203, 206
pleasure
– aesthetic p. 13, 15f., 18, 59–61, 63f., 67–73, 78–83, 100, 142, 145, 147f., 187, 191f., 194–196, 204, 233f., 238, 243, 245f., 249, 251–253, 257
– definition of p. 32–35, 223
– facilitating p. (vs. relief p.) 250–253
– phenomenological model of p. 33f.
– practical p. 38, 217, 242f.
poetry   14, 174
practical   3–5, 38, 43f., 49, 55, 107f., 123, 140f., 145–147, 167–172, 176–178, 192f., 208, 216f., 228, 235, 242–244, 248, 269f.
pragmatism, pragmatist   12, 169
predicate   11f., 14–16, 150
presentational work   169f., 172f., 177f.
primitivist version of aesthetic empiricism, empiricist primitivism   237f.
principle of determination (*Bestimmungsgrund*) of the judgment of taste, determining ground of aesthetic judgment   6, 105–108, 112, 114, 117–119
private   3, 78, 80, 109, 140, 175, 216, 221
propaganda   172f., 176
purposiveness, purposive   31, 46–48, 54, 88, 91, 96–102, 112, 118–121, 126, 146, 148, 192, 204, 208, 245f.
– subjective p. 46, 88, 97f., 101, 120f.

- p. without a purpose / an end, formal p., form of p. 31, 46–48, 50, 88, 112, 120, 146, 148, 204, 245 f.
- and counter-p. 98–100, 102

quality   15, 34–36, 51 f., 87, 89–91, 97 f., 101 f., 107, 109, 187, 239
quantity   15, 87, 89, 97 f., 107

realism -> aesthetic realism
reason (*Vernunft*)   28, 38, 47, 52, 81, 98–102, 111, 113, 117, 127 f., 140, 192 f., 204, 208, 216 f., 220 f.
representation   2, 4, 11–17, 19–25, 27 f., 32–48, 50 f., 54, 61–65, 70, 77, 81, 83, 90–94, 98 f., 101 f., 105, 109, 114 f., 120, 126, 141 f., 144, 146, 150, 189, 205, 211 f., 215–219, 222–225, 235, 242, 246
- form of the r. 32, 45–48, 50
- matter of the r. 32, 45–47, 54
rules   68, 110, 115, 118–120, 122 f., 177, 184, 188, 190–194, 204, 206 f., 262

satisfaction (*Wohlgefallen*)   2, 4, 13 f., 16, 19, 26 f., 31, 35 f., 39, 47–49, 51, 53, 59, 63 f., 66, 71 f., 75–78, 81, 87–102, 107, 109, 125, 136, 138 f., 141, 143, 147, 150–152, 154–161, 163, 194, 201, 216–222, 227 f., 235, 244, 248
self   2, 4, 7, 19, 78–80, 135–141, 144 f., 148–153, 155, 157, 160–163, 168, 171, 200
self-consciousness   4, 7, 135–139, 147–157, 159, 162 f., 171
selfhood   7, 168, 171, 173, 175 f.
sensation (*Empfindung*)   18, 26, 32 f., 36 f., 39, 41, 45–50, 54, 66, 76 f., 92, 109, 220, 239, 241, 243
sense (*Sinn*), making sense   105 f., 111–113, 120, 124, 126–128, 174, 185, 203–205
sensory dependence thesis   214
sensus communis, common sense (*Gemeinsinn*)   88 f., 187
sentiment   11, 20, 22–26, 73, 155, 178, 257, 262 f., 271
- mixed sentiment 11, 20, 22, 25 f.
sexual attraction -> attraction
space and time   18
spirit (*Geist*)   18, 117, 122 f.

spontaneity   125 f.
subjective-objective-hybridity (of beauty judgments)   211, 215, 226 f.
subjectivism (about aesthetic value)   257, 262 f., 267, 271
sublime, sublimity   6, 11, 53, 87, 96–102, 108, 145, 156, 176, 187
supersensible substratum   105 f., 119

testimony   7, 60, 247, 264, 266–271
thesis of disinterestedness (TD), disinterest thesis, disinterestedness thesis   1–3, 5–7, 31 f., 39–42, 45–54, 67, 139, 211 f., 216–220, 261, 269–271
- negative vs. positive thesis of disinterestedness (TD+ / TD-, disinterest+ / disinterest-) 4, 6, 40–42, 93, 101, 139 f., 145 f.
- weak vs. strong thesis / claim of disinterestedness (WCD vs. SCD) 5, 7, 212, 217–225, 227
time -> space and time
tragedy   11, 22–24, 174
- paradox of t. 11, 22–24
transcendental philosophy   53, 88, 92, 127
transitional object   202 f.

universality, universal validity   3 f., 16 f., 19, 49, 53, 60, 65, 67 f., 70 f., 73, 78 f., 88 f., 91 f., 101 f., 109, 199, 205, 222, 225–227
universal voice   70, 73, 94, 187, 207

value   7, 15, 17, 19, 34, 106, 126, 136, 138, 140, 143, 151–154, 156–163, 175, 179, 196, 233–239, 241, 243–246, 249, 251 f., 257–262, 268 f., 272
- aesthetic v. 7, 196, 233–239, 241, 243–246, 249, 251 f., 257–262, 268 f., 272

will   4 f., 32, 37–39, 42, 47, 54, 126, 139 f., 147, 216–218, 243, 248
- good w. 218
world   5, 19, 26, 37, 68 f., 79 f., 83, 111–113, 123, 138, 144 f., 150–152, 154, 160 f., 167–171, 174, 176–178, 183–185, 191–193, 197–206, 237, 240, 252
- withdrawal from w. 185, 203 f.
- world-view 173, 176, 179

www.ingramcontent.com/pod-product-compliance
Lightning Source LLC
Chambersburg PA
CBHW020223170426
43201CB00007B/303